S0-AAG-815

The Culture of Sewing

Dress, Body, Culture

Series Editor **Joanne B. Eicher,** *Regents' Professor, University of Minnesota*

Advisory Board:

Ruth Barnes, *Ashmolean Museum, University of Oxford*
Helen Callaway, *CCCRW, University of Oxford*
James Hall, *University of Illinois at Chicago*
Beatrice Medicine, *California State University, Northridge*
Ted Polhemus, *Curator, "Street Style" Exhibition, Victoria & Albert Museum*
Griselda Pollock, *University of Leeds*
Valerie Steele, *The Museum at the Fashion Institute of Technology*
Lou Taylor, *University of Brighton*
John Wright, *University of Minnesota*

Books in this provocative series seek to articulate the connections between culture and dress which is defined here in its broadest possible sense as any modification or supplement to the body. Interdisciplinary in approach, the series highlights the dialogue between identity and dress, cosmetics, coiffure, and body alterations as manifested in practices as varied as plastic surgery, tattooing, and ritual scarification. The series aims, in particular, to analyze the meaning of dress in relation to popular culture and gender issues and will include works grounded in anthropology, sociology, history, art history, literature, and folklore.

ISSN: 1360-466X

Previously published titles in the Series

Helen Bradley Foster, *"New Raiments of Self": African American Clothing in the Antebellum South*
Claudine Griggs, *S/he: Changing Sex and Changing Clothes*
Michaele Thurgood Haynes, *Dressing Up Debutantes: Pageantry and Glitz in Texas*
Anne Brydon and Sandra Niesson, *Consuming Fashion: Adorning the Transnational Body*
Dani Cavallaro and Alexandra Warwick, *Fashioning the Frame: Boundaries, Dress and the Body*
Judith Perani and Norma H. Wolff, *Cloth, Dress and Art Patronage in Africa*
Linda B. Arthur, *Religion, Dress and the Body*
Paul Jobling, *Fashion Spreads: Word and Image in Fashion Photography*
Fadwa El-Guindi, *Veil: Modesty, Privacy and Resistance*
Thomas S. Abler, *Hinterland Warriors and Military Dress: European Empires and Exotic Uniforms*
Linda Welters, *Folk Dress in Europe and Anatolia: Beliefs about Protection and Fertility*
Kim K.P. Johnson and Sharron J. Lennon, *Appearance and Power*

DRESS, BODY, CULTURE

The Culture of Sewing

Gender, Consumption and Home Dressmaking

Edited by

Barbara Burman

Oxford • New York

HOUSTON PUBLIC LIBRARY

R01206 77806

First published in 1999 by
Berg
Editorial offices:
150 Cowley Road, Oxford, OX4 1JJ, UK
70 Washington Square South, New York, NY 10012, USA

© Barbara Burman 1999

All rights reserved.
No part of this publication may be reproduced in any form
or by any means without the written permission of Berg.

Berg is an imprint of Oxford International Publishers Ltd.

Library of Congress Cataloging-in-Publication Data
A catalogue record for this book is available from the Library of Congress.

British Library Cataloguing-in-Publication Data
A catalogue record for this book is available from the British Library.

ISBN   1 85973 203 8 (Cloth)
       1 85973 208 9 (Paper)

Typeset by JS Typesetting, Wellingborough, Northants.
Printed in the United Kingdom by Biddles Ltd, Guildford and King's Lynn.

To 14.12.1981 with love

Contents

Contents

Contents

Acknowledgements

History is the work of many hands and I am very grateful to the following people whose contributions have helped to shape this book.

It began with the hospitable and remarkable women who supported and participated in my oral history project on home dressmaking in 1995: Maureen Rose, Beryl Malcolm and Ida Ledger, Margaret Bernard, Evelyn Cozens, Muriel Davies, Elsie Della-Gana, Constance Etches, Olive Finch, Hilary Gardner, Paula Imbert, Irene Mainwaring, Jo Peterson, Victoria Randall, Peggy Richter, Hilda Saltmarsh, Mary Sellick, Deidre Stewart and Nesta Tovey. David Lea of the Wessex Film and Sound Archive was ever helpful and open-handed.

Thanks are also due to all those who gave papers or came as delegates to the *Home Dressmaking Reassessed* conference held at Winchester in 1996. Their work and enthusiasm underpinned the next stages and eventual compilation of this book. That conference was dependent too on the generous support given by Alison Carter, John Gillett, Martin Gregory, Alistair Penfold and Sue Veck. Lorna Poole and Tony Wheeler of the John Lewis Partnership also very kindly gave their valuable time and help.

Very special thanks are due to the contributing authors, whose work has formed the book you hold in your hand. Throughout its preparation they have been impeccably patient and co-operative; despite impossibly busy lives and different time zones, their commitment held it all together. It is very much their book. Tragically, Janet Arnold died just as she was completing her chapter; I extend a special tribute to her and the unique contribution to dress history she made through her scholarship and many publications.

Joanne Eicher and Kathryn Earle and the team at Berg have been marvelous. I thank them for their support and composure.

My thanks are also due to colleagues at Winchester School of Art in the University of Southampton, for their help and encouragement. Dr. Judy Attfield and Dr. Lesley Miller I must mention in particular and I am grateful too for the opportunity to develop ideas and share enthusiams with the students on the M.A. History of Textiles and Dress.

Acknowledgements

I thank family for supporting and tolerating me throughout this project. I celebrate three of them who helped in, and from, the past: Ada Gray [1875–1950], my maternal grandmother whose little sewing and darning samplers, made when she was eight years old, survive to inform and animate this project; my two all-time favourite Edwardians: my mother Constance, born in 1908, a fine and indefatigable dressmaker, needleworker and teacher, who inspired and supported this book but died just before it was completed and my late father Reginald, born in 1905, who took so much pride in her and in all good handiwork.

And in the here and now, I thank Briony, Charlie and Catherine, diplomats all three, for their tolerance and understanding, Theo for living so calmly with this project from its inception and coping with a pre-occupied mother and finally Tom, who makes everything seem possible, for his unstinting practical and moral support.

Barbara Burman

Notes on Contributors

Janet Arnold F.S.A. was one of Britain's leading dress historians. She did pioneering work on the cut and construction of clothes from the sixteenth to the early part of the twentieth century. From 1978 until her death in 1998 she held a Research Fellowship at Royal Holloway and Bedford New College, University of London. She lectured extensively in Britain and America. Her numerous publications include the *Patterns of Fashion* series and *Queen Elizabeth's Wardrobe Unlock'd*.

Christopher Breward is Reader in Historical and Cultural Studies at The London College of Fashion, The London Institute. He completed his postgraduate training on the Victoria & Albert Museum/Royal College of Art programme in the History of Design in 1998. His publications include *The Culture of Fashion* (1995) and *The Hidden Consumer* (1999). He sits on the editorial board of the journal *Fashion Theory* and is currently researching the relationship between fashion and urban life in London since the late eighteenth century.

Mary M. Brooks F.I.I.C., M.A., Dip.Tex.Cons., D.M.S. She is Head of Studies and Research at the Textile Conservation Centre, Winchester School of Art in the Faculty of Arts, University of Southampton. She undertook an internship at the Abbegg-Stiftung in Switzerland and worked in museums in the US and the UK. She was closely involved in the establishment of the UK Institute of Conservation Textile Section and is an active member of the ICON Conservation Committee Textile Working Group. She was editor of IIC *Studies in Conservation* from 1994–1996 and was joint winner of the first international Keck Award for Promoting Public Awareness of Conservation in 1994. Her research interests include the ethics of conservation, man-made materials, degraded silks and seventeenth century English embroidery.

Margaret M. Bubolz is Professor Emeritus of Human Ecology at Michigan State University. She recently wrote a history of the College of Human Ecology for its centennial year. She has over fifty years of professional experience in Home Economics, including several years of teaching home sewing to adolescents and women. Current research interests include the history of home economics, changes in the family and the family as source of human and social capital.

Cheryl Buckley is a Reader in the Department of Historical and Critical Studies at the University of Northumbria at Newcastle. Her research focuses on theories of design and gender, fashion and ceramics.

Barbara Burman teaches at Winchester School of Art in the Faculty of Arts, University of Southampton where she is Director of the Centre for the History of Textiles and Dress. Her publications and principal research interests focus on the production and consumption of fashion, dress and textiles of the nineteenth and twentieth centuries. She is currently Chair of the Design History Society.

Julie A. Campbell is the editor of *Virginia Cavalcade*, a magazine of history and culture published by the Library of Virginia in Richmond, Virginia, USA. She is the author of articles and book reviews in the *Journal of Arizona History, Clothing and Textiles Research Journal, Bloomsbury Review, Arizona Daily Star* and is principal author of *Studies in Arizona History* (1998). She was formerly associate editor of publications at the Arizona Historical Society from 1987 to 1994.

Joy Spanabel Emery, author of *Stage Costume Techniques*, is Professor and Acting Chair of the Theatre Department at the University of Rhode Island where she is the resident costume designer and curator of The Betty Williams Pattern Collection and Director of the Commercial Pattern Archive. She is president-elect of the Costume Society of America, Vice-President for Communications for the US Institute for Theatre Technology and a Fellow of the Institute and member of the College of Fellows, The New England Theatre Conference. She served as consultant to the Fashion Institute of Technology 1998 exhibition 'Dreams on Paper: Home Sewing in America'.

Nancy Page Fernandez teaches in the History Department at California State University, Northridge. Her research analyzes the impact of paper patterns, dressmakers' drafting systems and the sewing machine on household sewing to understand the role of unwaged work in the industrialization of women's dress fashion in America.

Andrew Godley is Lecturer in Economics at the University of Reading. He has recently published a number of articles on the United Kingdom clothing industry. His principal research interests are in Jewish social and economic mobility in the UK and the US.

Fiona Hackney teaches at Camberwell College of Arts, The London Institute and has lectured widely and participated in conferences in Britain and abroad. She is currently completing a Ph.D. at Goldsmiths College, University of London, on British magazines for women in the 1920s and 1930s. She has published on design and gender, most recently in *A Woman's Place: Women, Domesticity and Private Life* (1998), edited by Anabelle Despard.

Sally I. Helvenston is an Associate Professor at Michigan State University where she teaches courses in dress and textile history, material culture and apparel design. Her research interests include nineteenth century women's history and dress history. Recent projects include 'Home saint or parlor ornament? The dialectic between fashion and function in women's dress of the nineteenth century' and 'Tracing the history of the apparel and textile discipline 1840–1940.'

Eileen Margerum received her doctoral degree from Tufts University. She teaches advertising practice and history at Salem State College in Salem, Massachusetts. She has written on imagery in American print advertising and is now working on a biography of Palmer Cox, writer–illustrator of children's books.

Nicholas Oddy lectures in design history in the Department of Historical and Critical Studies at Glasgow School of Art. His main areas of research are in factory-made domestic goods in the late nineteenth and early twentieth centuries, particularly the cycle industry. He is on the steering committee of the International Conference of Cycling History and was editor of the *Proceedings* of the Eighth Conference (1998). His recently published work includes an essay on cycle design in *The Gendered Object* (1996). He also acts as a consultant to Phillips auction houses for cycles and other 'collectors items'.

Alexandra Palmer is the Nora E. Vaughan Fashion Costume Curator at the Royal Ontario Museum, Toronto, Canada. She is currently working on a social and cultural history of the couture trade in Toronto in the twentieth century.

Tim Putnam is Professor of Material Culture at the University of Plymouth. His research interests are consumption and the processes of design and making, with special reference to mechanical engineering and household arrangements. He co-edited *Household Choices* (1990) with Charles Newton and *The Industrial Heritage* (1992) with Judith Alfrey.

Helen Reynolds is a graduate of the M.A. History of Textiles and Dress at Winchester School of Art and is currently doing a Ph.D. on women's needle trade education at the London College of Fashion, The London Institute. Author of *Couture or Trade: A Pictorial History of the London College of Fashion* (1997) and 'The Utility Garment: its design and effect on the mass market 1942–45,' in *Utility Reassessed: The Role of Ethics in the Practice of Design*, ed. Judy Attfield, Manchester University Press, 1999

Sherry Schofield-Tomschin is an Assistant Professor of Clothing and Textiles at Virginia Polytechnic Institute and State University. She received her Ph.D. from Iowa State University in 1997. Her current research focuses on the effect of textile handcrafts in individual lives, particularly the aging.

Carol Tulloch teaches at the Royal College of Art and Middlesex University. Her publications include '"Out of Many, One People?": The Relativity of Dress, Race and Ethnicity to Jamaica 1880–1907' in *Fashion Theory* and 'Homeknitting: Culture and Counter-culture, 1953–1963' in *One-Off*. Her forthcoming book is *'The Birth of Cool: The Culture of Dress in the Black Diaspora'*.

Kathryn E. Wilson took her Ph.D. in Folklore and Folklife from the University of Pennsylvania. Her research there examined issues of gender, race and embodiment in the nineteenth century city. Current interests include the gender politics of dance in contemporary Latino communities. She works as Public Programming Coordinator at the Balch Institute for Ethnic Studies in Philadelphia, planning public events and exhibitions and directing outreach projects with local ethnic communities.

Introduction

Barbara Burman

At auction in 1998 at Sotheby's in London, Geri Halliwell sold clothing and memorabilia from her glamorous life in the Spice Girls band. She divested herself of her Ginger Spice persona, in eighty-nine lots, full of style idiosyncrasies of her own invention. The sale featured several dazzling outfits made at home by her equally inventive sister, including the skin-tight Union Jack mini-dress she had worn for the 1997 Brit Awards. This was created by stitching a canvas flag to a lace corset. It sold to the Hard Rock Hotel in Los Angeles for more than £41,000, so it looks as if it's heading for the status of a pop icon. In this case, the sewing machine on the kitchen table seems to have been a girl's best friend.

This book is the first of its kind to explore the history of home dressmaking. It is a collective effort and it demonstrates cultural and historical dimensions of its subject through a variety of case and period studies and approaches. It draws together into one volume several disparate threads of what is in effect a long and heterogeneous story. The chapters focus predominantly on the period from the middle of the nineteenth century to the present day, covering Britain and the USA. And here we meet the first of several considerations for the historian: home dressmaking over the last one hundred and fifty years presents us with a 'subject' no more or less readily defined than sex or cooking or childrearing or any other productive and consuming activity which took place in the same homes during the same period. Like the histories of sex and cooking and childrearing, the making of clothes at home has a history which enfolds a rich spectrum of cultural, social and economic practices. It touches most obviously on gender and consumption, but within these lie the further intricacies of fashion, age, class and, perhaps more subtly, identity and the presentation of self.

In recognition of this array of issues and meanings, the authors have not attempted the impossible task of being comprehensive. Nor is any particular methodology prioritized. Rather, using a variety of working methods, the book launches a suggestive and open-ended project. Like much work accomplished by women, home dressmaking is largely anonymous. Certainly it has left little official trace. By new enquiry and evaluation and through the enlistment of previously neglected sources, the authors have sought to recover and clarify its historical significance and open up possibilities for further research.

The purpose of the next few pages is to provide a context for the chapters which follow. The introduction ends by describing the place of the individual chapters within the book's overall structure. But, first, how the book was born forms part of its story. It stems from collective effort so it has as many academic and personal origins as it has authors but a conference held in 1996 at Winchester School of Art in Hampshire, England was a defining moment in several senses. 'Home Dressmaking Reassessed' was the first short conference staged by the School's then newly formed Centre for the History of Textiles and Dress. The Centre's purpose is to undertake and disseminate research, with particular interest in dress and textiles of the industrial age. Its short conferences aim to identify and explore topics of potential import-ance hitherto overlooked or marginalized in academic work and invited interdisciplinary speakers are encouraged to take their projects forward together. Home dressmaking was chosen because it was a particularly commonplace activity yet largely neglected in academic research. Whilst it had surfaced in published work as the topic of short essays or fragments in books or as postgraduate research (e.g. Beetham 1996; Burman 1994; Bradley Foster 1997; Elinor et al. 1987; Fernandez 1987; Fine and Leopold 1993; Levitt 1988; Walsh 1979; Williams 1996/97; Wilson and Taylor 1989) it had never been the subject of an extended publication. The conference in turn was preceded by an oral history project of the same name supported by the Wessex Film and Sound Archive in which I recorded the sewing life histories of eighteen retired working women. These stories, spanning the last eighty years, revealed many starting points for further enquiry, notably the variety of ways in which sewing skills were acquired including considerable ambivalence towards the school curriculum and teaching methods, the opportunities identified for expression of individual creativity, the variety of motivations and influences at play in the practice, the perceived relationship between homesewn and ready-made garments and changes in the retailing of home dressmakers' supplies and aids. These life stories reinforced a picture of home dressmaking as an important nexus in the wider social and economic patterns of production and consumption of clothing. From these stories the conference grew and then the book. But the voices of the original oral history project participants have been a consistent guide in the task of assembling the book. They have been a reminder of Raphael Samuel's advice that historians should heed the sources of what he called 'unofficial knowledge' and to remember that:

history is not the prerogative of the historian, nor even as postmodernism contends, a historian's 'invention'. It is, rather, a social form of knowledge; the work, in any given instance, of a thousand different hands. If this is true, the point of address in any discussion of historiography should not be the work of the individual scholar, nor yet rival schools of interpretation, but rather the ensemble of activities and practices in which ideas of history are embedded or a dialectic of past-present relations is rehearsed. (Samuel 1996: 8)

Some historians have regarded clothing as peripheral to historical enquiry, as too ephemeral or too everyday to warrant attention. Daniel Roche bluntly ascribed this to the 'indifference of historians to the real world of objects without high aesthetic value'. (Roche 1994: 502) Others have seen clothing largely in terms of fashion, requiring the chronicling of changes in style and form. This approach tends to overlook home dressmaking, although its role in the dissemination of designer styles has been noted. (Craik 1994:15) In recent years our understanding of clothing and fashion's cultural, social and economic significance has deepened. (Breward 1995; Brewer and Porter 1993; Craik 1994; Lipovetsky 1994; Perrot 1994; Roche 1994; Styles 1994; Wilson 1985) More inclusive and integrated approaches to dress history are needed to contextualize it within wider studies of consumption and production. (Fine and Leopold 1993) The ordinariness and domesticity of home dressmaking would seem to have contributed to its invisibility and the lack of analytical purchase on the part of historians in related fields. A recent text on popular magazines dismissed a paper-pattern manufacturer's monthly home dressmaking magazine of the 1920s (*Weldon's Ladies' Journal*) as 'mindless' because it prioritized patterns over editorial, despite the fact that it was a bestseller with a circulation figure of 442,631 a month. The purposes it served for all those readers are not considered. (Reed 1997:141) The authors of this book share the belief that the common and everyday character of their subject is precisely what makes it significant. Collectively they are claiming a proper place for it within our understanding of the material culture, and consumer culture, of the modern age.

In what terms can we frame the purpose of this book? The innumerable women of all social backgrounds who have been sewing clothes in their homes for generations collectively defy the simplistic and pervasive idea that *the* Industrial Revolution and the factories, mills, offices and shifting divisions of labour and capital which followed in its wake transformed the previously productive home into a haven of leisured consumption. Home dressmaking as an historical practice defies simple or exclusive polarization into either an act of production or an act of consumption, in much the same way as the 1950s rise of DIY. Within the context of dress history in particular, a closer look at home dressmaking offers an opportunity to develop our understanding of some of the important variables present in the age of mass production and mass consumption. Dress history has extended its frame of reference in recent years but it has yet to come up with a coherent model for identifying and explaining these. The studies in this book correspond with the task suggested by Fine and Leopold in *The World of Consumption*, their critique of narrowly consumerist- centred approaches to these issues. Their argument for rethinking the dynamics and effects of the Industrial Revolution readily extends to the period covered in this book: 'The transformation in the mode of work, in the mode of organisation of society more broadly (institutional, regional, rural and urban, etc.), in the family – all have to be considered in locating and structuring the role of the changing mode of consumption, with the latter both as a cause and effect, and as impediment and stimulus to the birth of modern capitalism'. (Fine and Leopold 1993: 137) Taken together, the chapters in this book explore changing modes and experiences in relation to the production and consumption of clothing.

The organization of the book and its boundaries are necessarily synthetic, in a positive sense. Firstly, the majority of the chapters explore home dressmaking in the age of the domestic sewing machine. Of course, the 1850s to the present day is an ample enough period and field of enquiry for any book, but in this case it reflects the fact that less is known about the production of clothes at home in the pre-sewing machine period. This is an understandable gap created by the various trends and preferences of scholarly activity in the past and the resources and discourses available at any time. Whilst home dressmaking and the cultural and economic values attached to it were undoubtedly redefined to an extent by the invention of the machine and its subsequent mass availability, nevertheless the home production of clothing has a much longer history, a history which awaits another book. It should be emphasized that this book suggests that the impact of the new machine on established domestic sewing practices was complex and still not fully researched.

Secondly, the British and North American scope of the book provides a coherent though large framework for the period but it excludes as much possible material as it includes. For example, making clothes at home in other industrialized societies or in small-scale societies round the world is another story and appears in a varied literature elsewhere.[1] The coherence here lies in the sequence of innovation and shifts in production and consumption in the two areas. However, even in terms of the early production of the domestic sewing machine alone, corporate efforts were made on an international scale. The argument that fashion became increasingly democratized during the period also requires lateral as well as more specific studies. Nevertheless, the

British-American axis of this book addresses the development of these and other complementary issues. The book also shows some of the different practices between the two areas.

Thirdly, the book highlights, though not exclusively, the unwaged making of clothing at home. Many readers who sew will recognize this as a common-sense category and at the same time acknowledge that unwaged needlework in the home was not necessarily differentiated in this way in terms of value or status. Women have sewed curtains, knitted jumpers, embroidered household linen, made dresses, darned and redarned, turned collars, mended and remodelled all manner of things for themselves and for their families, all within a range of domestic tasks deemed part of the household economy. Equally, women with enough will and hours in the day to do so have often used their needle skills purely for pleasure in the making of utilitarian and non-utilitarian items or in making a range of goods for sale for charity or as gifts. Many of the same women have reapplied the same variety of skills to sew for a network of neighbours or workmates for money, or taken in sewing as waged piece-work on a regular basis. In emphasizing the unwaged making of clothes, inevitably there is some artificial silence on all the other related domestic activities which use the needle. Our focus derives from the fact that the majority of the authors in this book are dress and design historians who are seeking to explore the history of the production and consumption of clothing from an angle thus far overlooked.

Fourthly, men have not featured explicitly in the book, but they are there as recipients of clothing produced at home by their wives or as onlookers or as the purchasers of the family sewing machine. Not surprisingly they tend to figure outside the home, named as manufacturers or as magazine publishers, working within a commercial framework, or as unnamed workers in the mills and factories associated with supplies for the home dressmaker. But this may be an unfair picture. Britain's 'Adult Learner of the Year' in 1998 was an ex-miner who put himself through several courses, took up embroidery and now teaches dressmaking. More research is needed to provide an account of men who have sewn at home.

There was a very common response from women and men who asked about the subject of this book during its preparation – they offered vivid reminiscences of themselves or a close relative sewing clothes and at the same time speculated whether home dressmaking was in decline. This chimes with two issues we encounter in this book: the special resonance and potency that home dressmaking appears to have in individual memory and life stories and the general sense in which its shifts in importance seem to elude precise measurement. To trace wider shifts in the popularity, prominence and function of home dressmaking, we have to turn to other sources. Here we encounter some of the more intractable parts of our subject. We have little opportunity to explore what is most probably a close relationship historically between the availability, quality and relative prices of ready-made clothes and the place of clothes made in the home. This potentially very revealing study is barely possible at this stage in our knowledge. The ready-made clothing industry, which we might expect to be more visible to the historian than the making of clothes at home, and 'perhaps the single most important industry in the economic history of the western world [. . .] has not yet yielded to a comprehensive academic investigation of its development . . .' (Godley 1997: 3) Historians are working in Britain and the USA with 'the legacy of a poorly recorded industrial development with few company archives to supplement the paltry official statistics.' In this respect and others, the persistent question about an apparent decline in home dressmaking over our period gets inconsistent answers.

For example, it has been said that during the 1920s in Britain home dressmaking was becoming 'widespread'. This is explained reasonably enough by the fact 'styles were simpler, home-made garments could look more professional, and home dressmakers were aided by the wider availability of simple technology: very cheap paper patterns, and the [. . .] sewing machine [. . .]' (Wilson and Taylor 1989: 95) This sense of an *increase* at this time in home dressmaking is borne out by the profusion of popular magazines devoted to it wholly or in part. Nevertheless, some research on consumer expenditure in Britain between 1920 and 1938 suggested a *decline*. It also pointed to a fly in the ointment for anyone approaching the problem by asking by how much the amounts of cloth consumed by home dressmakers rose or fell. The authors found there could be no precise disaggregation of those dress piece goods going to the clothing trade and those to individual consumers. Nevertheless they noted that 'it is generally acknowledged that the extent of home dressmaking diminished during this period'. The estimated expenditure on materials bought for home dressmaking (including knitting) and its decrease, as percentages of overall expenditure on all clothing (including footwear), were put at 8 per cent and less than 6 per cent in 1924 and 1938 respectively. Small as these figures sound, the actual value of materials bought for home dressmaking were still 'roughly' £20 million in 1924, £17 million in 1935 and £15 million in 1938. We are reminded by the authors of the uncertainty of these figures. (Stone and Rowe 1966: 6–7) This is representative of the tantalizing but slippery material we have to hand when we try to assess home dressmaking as a facet of general domestic expenditure.

To return to the sense of *increase*: we can guess, though not verify, that this may derive in part from more women amongst the new suburban classes taking up home dressmaking at the same time as the cheaper end of the factory ready-mades came within more working class budgets. These better-off women may have used home dressmaking as a means of varying and enriching wardrobes which were already reasonably well stocked. Their entry into the market for supplies may have coincided with sharper competition and splash on the part of retailers and magazines, leaving us with plenty of evidence of their products. This would echo the fact that the middle class grew in numbers and income in Britain from the mid-nineteenth century onwards. Equally, the apparent *decline* in home dressmaking expenditure may mask a lowering of prices by home dressmaking suppliers as they sought to compete in the high street with increasingly successful ready-made clothing. This difficulty in finding clear evidence to backup commonsense observations about the popularity of home dressmaking between the wars is typical of the subject. It is cited here as an illustration of a general difficulty. It points to the need for considerable further research if anyone wants a precise picture of home dressmaking today.

Two quotations from women who contributed to a survey designed to document consumer practices in clothing serve to remind us of how home dressmakers do not dance to the same tune as the 'ideal' consumer. As any home dressmaker knows, their activity doesn't necessarily show up on conventional sales graphs. They may use inherited sewing machines for generations and commonly they make up clothes in dress materials they've hoarded for years. 'I had an old Singer machine, circa 1893, which I inherited from my grandmother when I was 17 (in 1939). This was an old treadle [. . .] On this I made clothes for my mother, her sisters and myself and my sister – including her trousseau – until about 1947.' And, 'I have three dress lengths packed away waiting for me to find a pattern I like.' (Mass-Observation 1988) A glance at the high street, in Britain today at least, may show retrenchment on the part of both small and large retailers catering for home dressmakers but in the end we may have to accept that whilst broad trends may be described, such as sales of sewing machines or paper-patterns, other evidence suggests that the work and habits of home dressmakers is multifaceted and susceptible to so many variables that they remain outside precise measurement and are best understood in richer terms than mere numbers. 'I used to go to the material sales and buy lengths [. . .] and think, well, I can make that up into something and it could be two or three years before I'd make it up but I'd love it [. . .] I'm a terrible hoarder [. . .] there's something about bolts of material and the colours [. . .] if one was driven by budget, then there are other ways of dressing [. . .]' (Burman 1995: Interview with P.I.)

There has been a correlation between the clothing women made at home and what was available in the ready-made market. Women's ready-made clothing was slower than menswear to arrive at reliable standards and we would be wrong to assume that the price alone of ready-mades drove women to sew clothing at home. There is enough evidence of complaints about poor standards of materials, make, fit and style in manufactured clothing in the UK and USA to suggest that women also sewed at home to guarantee themselves better and longer-lasting garments. This is likely to have been a significant motive for home dressmakers throughout the second half of the nineteenth century and the first half of the twentieth. For those on low wages this created dilemmas. A study of New York working girls found many necessary but false economies in their purchasing of cheap ready-made garments. Very low wages, combined with a lack of savings on which to draw to invest in high-quality, longer-lasting goods, drove them to buy shoddy clothes, such as 'waists' (blouses), which needed frequent replacement. They had neither the time nor energy needed to break this cycle by making better or cheaper clothing at home. A typical young unmarried shop worker was exhausted by very long hours of demanding work followed by further time in rented accommodation, without family support, in doing the personal laundry work necessary to maintain the required level of appearance for her work. (Clark and Wyatt 1911) This cycle of clothing poverty was common amongst lower-paid women and especially problematic for those in office or shop work for whom a smart and clean appearance was a necessity of employment.

Happily, even if our larger picture of the economics of home dressmaking is somewhat blurred, then social history offers other sources to help us interpret it. Changes in women's employment and in their role within the family make an important context for this. For example, over the twentieth century we see working-class women losing ground as the central managing agent for the family: '[S]kilful budgeting was less important as the amount of a family's disposable income grew; in an increasingly consumerist society, being economical and making something out of nothing was less important than the ability to buy.' (Roberts 1994:136) The increase during the latter part of this century in the take-up of waged work by married women has an impact on our subject. 'It may well be that at some point during the post-war years the wages women could command crossed a certain threshold leading them to conclude that their domestic duties were an uneconomic use of their time.' (Lewis 1984: 218) As a result of this shift, we would expect to see home dressmaking functioning more as a leisure pursuit or as a necessity left increasingly to those who cannot enter the ready-made clothing market, for example those with non-standard body shape or disability. Some home dressmaking may be done as an antidote to ready-made fashions, by individuals who wish to stay outside or ahead of the trends. Some is done to create special garments for one-off occasions, such as weddings and formal dances.

The history of making clothes at home has few official custodians or celebrants in the museum world. Museum collections of dress and textiles, and the exhibitions drawn from them, tend to prioritize designers or developments in style or decoration; makers, processes, downmarket goods or consumption issues are less easy to evidence. But recent exceptions have been important. For example, the Museum at the Fashion Institute of Technology in New York staged the exhibition 'Dreams on Paper, Home Sewing in America' in 1997 and within the 'Forties Fashion and the New Look' exhibition of the same year at the Imperial War Museum in London there were many home sewn items, celebrated in terms of ingenuity and patriotism. (McDowell 1997) Museum display and interpretation of dress and textiles may be changing as a result of recent academic studies in museology and a generally increased interest in how museums and heritage sites relate to their audiences. One of the few museum-based general interest texts in this field gives coverage to home dressmaking. (Tarrant 1994)

The software and hardware of sewing clothes at home, the paper pattern and the sewing machine, are at extremes of ephemerality and durability. The fragile patterns have largely evaded museum collection, partly because they are used to death or hoarded, but also, one suspects, because they are perceived as very low on the hierarchy of material culture. This is changing. For example, Joy Emery's development of the electronic commercial pattern archive at the University of Rhode Island demonstrates what can be done once their historical importance is recognized. By contrast, sewing machines must be amongst the most enduring of all consumer durables. Museums have frequently interpreted them as 'engineering' or 'science', or emphasized them as evidence of male entrepreneurial invention and thus they have been happily collected and conserved in large numbers, usually devoid of reference to their significance in female use and the domestic environment. So too the story of private collectors who are often motivated by a greater interest in the machine than the sewing it performed or social role it played. By contrast, in the home, sewing machines often evoke vivid personal memories.

The increase in feminist women's history writing on both sides of the Atlantic particularly since the 1970s has greatly advantaged dress history in general and the subject of this book in particular. One key example of this has been the scholarship addressing the formalization of gender differences and the education and socialization of girls. This has shown the teaching of sewing embedded very early in education. (Craig 1945, Dyhouse 1981, East and Thompson 1984, Turnbull 1987) Rozsika Parker (1984) wrote an expanded and seminal history of needlework in which it is depicted as both an education in femininity and a means of resistance to it. Whilst her book omitted dressmaking, nevertheless much of its argument about the art/craft divide, the association of femininity with domestic practices and the capacity for needle skills to be used subversively still suggests new means of examining historical dimensions of dressmaking as women's practice. This echoes the established need for feminist history to build 'a new conceptual framework to make women's economic activity comprehensible.' (Alexander 1994: 4) Where oral history has been used to map structures of sexual difference and subjectivities, we can get even closer to the 'sewing machine on the kitchen table'. 'Listening to, or reading, women's own descriptions of their growing up places women's subjectivity, their own sense of themselves, at the centre of historical change.' (Alexander 1994: 206) In Alexander's work on the 1920s and 1930s, the focus on first jobs and changing appearance let home dressmaking be traced as both a useful economy and a despised 'making do', part of a mixed clothing strategy employed in the process of growing up, establishing sexual difference and self-esteem. The collection of oral and written autobiography to throw more light on working-class history has also revealed material on home dressmaking, appearances and 'making do'. (Thompson 1981, Burnett 1994)

Needlework was dramatized on the agenda of British social reformers by Thomas Hood's famous 'Song of the Shirt' in 1843. The hopelessness of the exploited seamstress, and sweated labour in the needle trades in general, was underscored by the allusion in the poem that by her endless labour she sewed her own shroud as well as the shirt. 'With fingers weary and worn, With eyelids heavy and red, A woman sat, in unwomanly rags, plying her needle and thread – Stitch! Stitch! Stitch! In poverty, hunger, and dirt, And still with a voice of dolorous pitch, Would that its tone could reach the Rich! – She sang this 'Song of the Shirt!' Concerns of this kind have continued to be voiced about the homeworker and other clothing trade workers ever since. (Thompson and Yeo 1973; Newton 1974; Walkley 1981; Rogers 1997) Just over a hundred years later in 1947 a popular song recorded by Betty Hutton made much the same point, except the sewing machine had replaced the hand-held needle: 'Oh the sewing machine, the sewing machine – a girl's best friend. If I didn't have my sewing machine I'd come to no good end, But I'm bobbin' the bobbin and pedal the pedal and wheel the wheel by day So by night I feel so weary that I never get out to play.' The act of sewing and the sewing machine itself have been both a livelihood and a wearisome burden. This book turns its focus on women who sewed at home for their own unwaged purposes, but the spectre of the sweated trades is never very far away and in many instances we know that women borrowed sewing skills developed in waged work for their own domestic uses and equally that many women at home after marriage sewed for pin money or wages alongside sewing for their families. When the long arm of the sewing machine manufacturers reached every community in efforts to extend the new-found market, their ingenious credit systems were a mixed blessing for hard-pressed families and working women. (Coffin 1994) Making clothes at home does not belong neatly in the public or the private sphere, it traverses both.

In the same years that manufacturers were developing the new domestic sewing machine Karl Marx was living in London writing *Capital*. In this work he defined the industrial sewing machine as a 'decisively revolutionary machine'. But when he wrote that the 'hour of the machine had struck', he understood it as a curse and not a blessing. In his view the sewing machine favoured the tendency towards centralized factory production. He argued that the shift from small to large-scale mechanized industry was catastrophic for various sectors of the labour force, deskilling and impoverishing craftsmen, depressing wages and driving production of machine-made goods to untenable levels. 'The fearful increase in death from starvation during the last ten years in London runs parallel with the extension of machine sewing.' (Marx 1990: 601) However, whilst Marx witnessed what he defined as the transformative effects of mechanized sewing, he also saw sewing in a more immediate, domestic context, as part of the poverty and insecurity of his own home life in London. The 'rags and tatters of his wife's sewing basket' reportedly lay on the table alongside his manuscripts and books, amongst an ill assorted jumble which included their children's toys and broken crockery. 'A seller of second-hand goods would be ashamed to give away such a remarkable collection of odds and ends.' (McLellan 1981: 35)

The reported details of this mid-nineteenth century household, as in so many others throughout the period, suggest a central and visible position for the sewing basket, albeit in a 'remarkable' way. In this case it lay on the table with the manuscripts, coequal evidence of the work of the household. The making, repair and alteration of clothing in the home was a transformative activity crucial to keeping up appearances and to sustaining all the possibilities inherent in the notion of respectability. It was an activity equally as unforgiving in its own way as the mechanized sewing in the factory system. Respectable clothing underpinned employability and creditworthiness. It was visible evidence of care and expenditure, demonstrating commitment to notions of physical cleanliness and moral hygiene. It provided for the public face of the family and allowed entry into public and civic events, church going and church-related events, outings, journeys and holidays. Evidence from the early part of the twentieth century gives a vivid illustration of the labour and engagement invested in clothing:

I've had a dress made out of dusters. The man next door to us when I was a girl worked for a coal dealer and they used to get bags of clean dusters for polishing their brasses. He used to bring dusters home, spotted muslin and three or four all alike. My mother has made me dresses out of them. I can remember one in particular when we walked to the park with it when Queen Mary was crowned [1911] and we all had to walk. There were no buses [. . .] and we had to walk. I had this cream dress with a blue sash on, made out of three dusters. I have taken things off my own back and made my children things. Necessity is the mother of invention. (Roberts 1994: 139–40. Oral testimony by Mrs. M.I.P., b. 1898.)

We cannot assume that home dressmaking always brought pleasure in either its making or its wearing. Home dressmaking has often been associated with a poorly fitted or eccentric appearance. The crime novelist P. D. James astutely captured the earnest, slightly off-centre look achieved by some home dressmakers: 'Miss Sparshott was a skilled dressmaker, an assiduous attender at [. . .] evening classes. Her clothes were beautifully made but so dateless that they were never actually in fashion; straight skirts in grey or black which were exercises in how to sew a pleat or insert a zip fastener; blouses with mannish collars and cuffs in insipid pastel shades on which she distributed without discretion her collection of costume jewellery [. . .]' (James 1981: 9)

Accounts of childhood are full of instances of the special discomfort which home dressmaking can cause. For example, H. G. Wells, writing of his early life in his parent's 'needy shabby' house-cum-shop in Bromley in the 1870s, recollected his mother's harsh life of drudgery bluntly, though often fused with tenderness. Despite her apprenticeship as a dressmaker in the 1830s and subsequent employment as a ladies' maid, with her 'poor dear hands [. . .] enlarged and distorted by scrubbing and damp', she darned 'with immense stitches. In addition she made all our clothes until such age as, under the pressure of our schoolfellows' derision, we rebelled against something rather naive in the cut. Also she made loose covers for the chairs and sofa out of cheap chintz or cretonne. She made them as she cooked and as she made our clothes, with courage rather than skill [. . .]'

H.G. Wells' account of his mother Sarah Neal echoes many other recollections of life on the verges of poverty. He describes her unremitting battle against dirt, domestic confusion and social slippage. For Sarah Neal and all those other women in this position, home dressmaking was part of a wider and necessary strategy to 'keep up appearances'.

My mother's instinct for appearances was very strong. Whatever the realities of our situation, she was resolved that to the very last moment we should keep up the appearance of being comfortable members of that upper-servant tenant class to which her imagination had been moulded. She believed that it was a secret to all the world that she had no servant and did all the household drudgery herself. I was enjoined never to answer questions about that [. . .] Nor was I to take my coat off carelessly, because my underclothing was never quite up to the promise of my exterior garments. It was never ragged but it abounded in compromises. (Wells 1934: 72–3)

For boys there has been a further clothing code or protocol. Clothes made at home by mothers are for little boys. As bigger boys grew towards manhood, one of many steps they have taken away from their mother's sphere of practical influence has been in the consumption of ready-made and tailor-made clothing. At this stage of life has come the deep, old divide between male tailoring and female dressmaking. For whilst waged and sweated female hand- or machine-workers have made much mass produced clothing for men, they have been invisible to the consumer and there has been little tradition for female tailors in shops. Thus a part of achieving adult masculinity has normally involved relinquishing direct contact with the female maker of clothing. Like other partings of the way and rites of passage, it has many possible significances for the individuals. The nineteenth century novelist Mrs Gaskell created the suffering unmarried mother Ruth as a dressmaker. Ruth sits sewing summer trousers at home for her young son

[S]he sighed to think that the days were over when her deeds of skill could give him pleasure. Now, his delight was in acting himself [. . .] this week, when she had been devoting every spare hour to the simple tailoring which she performed for her boy (she had always made every article he wore, and felt almost jealous of the employment), he had come to her with a wistful look, and asked when he might begin to have clothes made by a man?' (Gaskell 1985: 317)

Limited channels remained open however, and still remain so, to women who wish to make clothes for the men in their lives. There has been a long tradition for fiancées, sisters and mothers to make or decorate items of clothing which are peripheral to a man's main wardrobe, for example love tokens and gifts in the nineteenth century commonly included embroidered waistcoats or slippers and today items such as dressing gowns or knitted jumpers might play a similar role. In clothing as in other practical matters of everyday life, the mother of an unmarried adult son might also stand in for a wife with her needle. An English eighteenth century diary recorded such an instance. 'I am happy to have (John) here. Mended up slightly some shirts and nightcaps, all his things much out of repair. God knows he will find it a great and an expensive difficulty to renew them.' (Vickery 1994: 283)

This book has been divided into three parts and the chapters run broadly in chronological sequence within each one. The book's title deliberately draws attention to the all-important topic of gender. Gender runs its thread inextricably through the entire book, posing a variety of questions in each chapter. Such centrality makes it superfluous to give it a separate part in the book. Part 1 focuses on class and identity and explores how home dressmaking has been both represented *to* women and *by* women. Chris Breward and Fiona Hackney show how the rhetoric and images of popular British magazines represented home dressmaking over two different historical periods. They demonstrate how particular identities in femininity and modernity for women of different social classes came to be constructed and nuanced in the magazines and debate how through home dressmaking these were in turn related to shifting notions of fashion. Barbara Burman's period study of the Edwardian years in England shows how home dressmaking was widespread and examines ways in which it was used by women to negotiate the demands of class and employment. Women as makers of clothes have also chosen their own forms through which to represent themselves and Carol Tulloch demonstrates the interplay between making clothes, individual design and creativity and the continuity of Jamaican cultural practices. This has a resonance with Cheryl Buckley's study of Betty Foster and Mary Skelton, two working class women from the north of England, whose dressmaking histories reveal important issues of collective and individual identity and through which Buckley debates practices of feminist history. Sherry Schofield-Tomschin charts shifts documented over this century as various academic and commercial studies have sought to measure women's reasons for sewing clothes at home.

Part 2 brings six chapters together to examine how the making of clothes at home has interacted with the wider development of production and consumption over the last one hundred and fifty years. Julie Campbell traces the work of nineteenth century US Indian Army wives; using the evidence of diaries and letters she details the progress of their dressmaking work and tastes, in a demanding way of life outside the normal domestic context and beyond the reach of the burgeoning new urban fashion centres. Surviving personal documents are also examined by Kathryn Wilson but in the more settled circumstances in nineteenth century Philadelphia where she explores how the work of home dressmakers both adopted and contested increasingly centralized frameworks of commercial fashion. Manufacturers of sewing machines saw great sales potential in the traditions of making clothes in the home, but the domestic market was unfamiliar and ill-defined compared to the commercial market. Nancy Page Fernandez's study shows how nineteenth-century American manufacturers reached for new domestic consumers by promoting their machines through narratives and images which sought to foreground familiar aspects of femininity and class and distance their products from anxiety over change and industrialization. The creation of new consumers for sewing machines takes a different direction in Eileen Margerum's case study of Singer's sustained post-war advertising campaign to reach American teenage girls. By contrast a museum collection of clothes from one twentieth century English family is examined by Mary Brooks and reveals evidence of the role played by home dressmaking in the practice of consumer choice and taste. Alexandra Palmer's study of Toronto in the 1950s evaluates the hierarchic range of clothing options open to fashion-conscious women outside the conventional retail stores.

The third part of the book turns to the varied ways in which the skills and practices of home dressmaking have been disseminated and it seeks to draw facets of economic and cultural history together by making new correlations between the domestic and large-scale technological and commercial projects. Janet Arnold's case study of an early nineteenth-century book of dressmaker's patterns documents their production and dissemination in a period which pre-dates the invention of the sewing machine and the large scale production and distribution of paper patterns and reveals how the author-designer was concerned to overcome practical difficulties to see her work to fruition. Joy Emery maps the later commercial and technological development of the paper pattern and its significance for the dissemination of specific skills and the promotion of styles. Andrew Godley argues, in the case of Britain, that the female waged home-workers, a crucial component in the workforce of the nineteenth-century British clothing industry, led the growth in demand for domestic machines. Tim Putnam argues for the sewing machine as representative of a series of decisive changes in methods of mass production and traces both the vulnerability and inventiveness of the pioneer producers and the new questions raised by the subsequent shifts in consumer experience as the machine entered the home. Nicholas Oddy examines the role of design and aesthetics in the acceptance of the domestic sewing machine in the nineteenth-century parlour. The last two chapters concentrate on different aspects of dissemination through education and promotion. Margaret Bubolz and Sally Helvenston take the long view of American home economics to chart the cultural debates and questions which have surrounded the formal teaching of sewing to young women. Famously the British Government's Second World War interventions into the manufacture and consumption of civilian clothing included promotion of the 'Make-do and Mend' philosophy. Helen Reynolds examines the inception and impact of this unprecedented official focus on home sewing.

Note

1. The following are examples of publications which include reference to the history of clothing made at home and related activities in societies outside the scope of this book: R. Barnes and J. B. Eicher, eds, (1992), *Dress and Gender; Making and Meaning in Cultural Context,* Oxford: Berg; Bayly, C.A. (1986), 'The origins of swadeshi (home industry): cloth and Indian society, 1700–1930', in Arjun Appadurai, ed., *The Social Life of Things: Commodities in Cultural Perspective,* Cambridge: Cambridge University Press; J. B. Eicher, ed, (1995), *Dress and Ethnicity,* Oxford: Berg; J. Schneider (1987), 'The Anthropology of Cloth', *Annual Review of Anthropology,* Vol. 16; A. B. Weiner and J. Schneider, eds, (1989), *Cloth and Human Experience,* Washington D.C.: Smithsonian Institution.

References

Alexander, S. (1994), 'Women's Work in Nineteenth-century London: a Study of the Years 1820–1860s', in *Becoming a Woman and other essays in 19th and 20th century feminist history,* London: Virago, first published in J. Mitchell and A. Oakley, eds, (1976), *The Rights and Wrongs of Women,* London: Penguin.

—— (1994) 'Becoming a Woman in London in the 1920's and '30's', in *Becoming a Woman and other essays in 19th and 20th century feminist history,* London: Virago, first published in G.S. Jones and D. Feldman, eds, (1989), *Metropolis: London, Histories and Representations since 1800,* London: Routledge.

Beetham, M. (1996), *A Magazine of her Own? Domesticity and Desire in the Woman's Magazine, 1800–1914,* London: Routledge.

Bradley Foster, H. (1997), *'New Raiments of Self': African American Clothing in the Antebellum South,* Oxford: Berg.

Breward, C. (1995), *The Culture of Fashion, A New History of Fashionable Dress,* Manchester: Manchester University Press.

Brewer, J. and Porter, R., eds. (1993), *Consumption and the World of Goods,* London: Routledge.

Burman, B. (1994), 'Home Sewing and "Fashions for All", 1908–1937' in *Costume,* No. 28.

—— (1995), Interview with P. I. in *Home dressmaking Reassessed,* Oral History Project, Wessex Film and Sound Archive, Hampshire Record Office, Sussex Street, Winchester, Hampshire.

Burnett, J., ed, (1994), *Destiny Obscure: Autobiographies of Childhood, Education and Family from the 1820's to the 1920's,* London: Routledge, first published by Allen Lane, 1982.

Clark, S. A. and Wyatt, E. (1911), *Making Both Ends Meet: The Income and Outlay of New York Working Girls,* New York: Macmillan.

Coffin, J. G. (1994), 'Credit, Consumption and Images of Women's Desires: Selling the Sewing Machine in Late Nineteenth-century France' in *French Historical Studies* 18, No. 3, Spring.

Craig, H. T. (1945), *The History of Home Economics*, New York: Practical Home Economics.

Craik, J. (1994), *The Face of Fashion*, London: Routledge.

Dyhouse, C. (1981), *Girls Growing Up in Late Victorian and Edwardian England*, London: Routledge.

East, M. and Thompson, J., eds, (1984), *Definitive Themes in Home Economics and their Impact on Families, 1909–1984*, Washington, D.C.: American Home Economics Association.

Elinor, G. et al., eds, (1987), *Women and Craft*, London: Virago.

Fine, B. and Leopold, E. (1993), *The World of Consumption*, London: Routledge.

Fernandez, N. P. (1987), *'If a Woman Had Taste . . .' Home Sewing and the Making of Fashion, 1850–1910*, Ph.D. thesis, Irvine: University of California.

Gaskell, E. (1985), *Ruth*, Oxford: Oxford University Press (first published 1853).

Godley, A. (1997), 'The Development of the Clothing Industry: Technology and Fashion', *Textile History*, 28, No. 1, Spring (Special Issue on the History of the Ready-Made Clothing Industry).

James, P. D. (1981), *An Unsuitable Job for a Woman*. London: Sphere (first published 1972).

Lewis, J. (1984), *Women in England 1870–1950: Sexual Divisions and Social Change*, London: Harvester Wheatsheaf.

Levitt, S. (1988), 'Clothing Production and the Sewing Machine', *The Textile Society Magazine*, Vol. 9, Spring.

Lipovetsky, G. (1994), *The Empire of Fashion: Dressing Modern Democracy*, Princeton: Princeton University Press.

Mass-Observation Archive (University of Sussex): replies to Spring 1988 Directive, T1277 and W1505 respectively. Reproduced with permission of Curtis Brown Ltd, London. Copyright the Trustees of the Mass-Observation Archive at the University of Sussex.

Marx, K. (1990), *Capital: A Critique of Political Economy*, Volume 1, London: Penguin Classics edition. First published in English in 1867.

McDowell, C. (1997), *Forties Fashion and the New Look*, London: Bloomsbury.

McLellan D., ed., (1981), *Karl Marx: Interviews and Recollections*, London: Macmillan. (contemporary report quoted in Peter Stallybrass [1998], 'Marx's Coat' in *Border Fetishism: Material Objects in Unstable Spaces,* ed. Patricia Spyer, London: Routledge.)

Newton, S.M. (1974), *Health, Art and Reason: Dress Reformers of the 19th Century*, London: John Murray.

Parker, R. (1984), *The Subversive Stitch: Embroidery and the Making of the Feminine*, London: The Women's Press.

Perrot, P. (1994), *Fashioning the Bourgeoisie: A history of clothing in the nineteenth century*, Princeton: Princeton University Press.

Reed, D. (1997), *The Popular Magazine in Britain and the United States 1880–1960*, London: The British Library.

Roberts, E. (1994), 'Women and the Domestic Economy 1890–1970', in *Time, Family and Community. Perspectives on Family and Community History*, ed. Michael Drake, Oxford: Open University/Blackwell.

Roche, D. (1994), *The Culture of Clothing: Dress and Fashion in the Ancien Regime*, Cambridge: Cambridge University Press, originally published in French as *La Culture des apparences* by Librairie Artheme Fayard, 1989.

Rogers, H. (1997), '"The Good Are Not Always Powerful, Nor the Powerful Always Good": The Politics of Women's Needlework in Mid-Victorian London', *Victorian Studies*, Vol. 40, No. 4, Summer.

Samuel, R. (1996), *Theatres of Memory Volume 1: Past and Present in Contemporary Culture*, London: Verso.

Stone, R. and Rowe, D.A. (1966), *The Measurement of Consumers' Expenditure and Behaviour in the United Kingdom 1920–1938*, Vol. II, Cambridge: Cambridge University Press.

Styles, J. (1994) 'Clothing the north of England, 1660–1800', *Textile History* 25.

Tarrant, N. (1994), *The Development of Costume*, London: National Museums of Scotland, Edinburgh/Routledge.

Thompson, T. (1981), *Edwardian Childhoods*, London: Routledge.

Thompson, E. P. and Yeo, E., eds, (1973), *The Unknown Mayhew: Selections from the Morning Chronicle 1849–50*, London: Penguin.

Turnbull, A. (1987), 'Learning Her Womanly Work: the Elementary School Curriculum 1870–1914' in Felicity Hunt, (ed.), *Lessons for Life: The Schooling of Girls and Women 1850-1950*, Oxford: Blackwell.

Vickery, A. (1994), 'Women and the World of Goods: a Lancashire consumer and her possessions, 1751–81', in eds. John Brewer and Roy Porter, *Consumption and the World of Goods*, London: Routledge.

Walkley, C. (1981), *The Ghost in the Looking Glass: the Victorian Seamstress*, London: Peter Owen.

Walsh, M. (1979), 'The Democratization of Fashion: The Emergence of the Women's Dress Pattern Industry', *Journal of American History*, 66, September.

Wells, H.G. (1934), *Experiment in Autobiography*, Volume 1, London: Gollancz and Cresset.

Williams, B. (1996/97), *On the Dating of Tissue Paper Patterns*, Cutters' Research Journal, VIII, 3: 1–10 (Reprint of two 1990 articles.)

Wilson, E. (1985), *Adorned in Dreams: Fashion and Modernity*, London: Virago.

—— and Taylor, L. (1989), *Through the Looking Glass: A History of Dress from 1860 to the Present Day*, London: BBC Books.

Part 1

Home Dressmaking, Class and Identity

1

Patterns of Respectability: Publishing, Home Sewing and the Dynamics of Class and Gender 1870–1914

Christopher Breward

Edwin Pugh, a writer of the 'cockney school' of literary social realism, more used to describing the brash and greasy exterior fug of London street markets and music halls, provided a highly suggestive evocation of humble interior space as a point of contrast in his 1896 novel *The Man of Straw*.

> The amber sunshine poured in through the muslin curtains, drenching the room with light. It was a little room, plainly but nattily furnished. Everything in it was faded and touched with age; it was a clear, bright, honourable age, however, and not unlovely. A bowl of flowers stood on a table against the crisp white curtain; other flowers ranged in pots, crowded the window sill. There was a sewing machine in a corner – idle for the day was Sunday, and a great straw work-basket overflowing with reels of gay coloured silks and cottons, thimbles, scissors, tape and thread. A fire burned in the grate; a kettle hissed and sputtered on the coals. The table was spread for breakfast. A plump tabby cat had mounted a wide snug chair; and, with extended forepaws on the white cloth, was nosing the milk jug doubtfully. Over the fire sat a young girl, reading . . . The sunshine touched her lovingly, glinting her loose brown hair, blanching the whiteness of the tiny fist supporting her cheek, touching her smooth brow, glancing off to kiss her eyelids. She was clad in a grey stuff gown with a cunning frill of lace inserted at the neck, dimly visible through the golden brown tangle of her curls. A magic tangle for the callow heart of man to be enmeshed in. (Pugh 1896)

It is a description useful in its careful notation of several features which conform to the construct of the home dressmaker familiar from the pages of contemporary women's magazines, and more recent examinations of the manner in which historical gendered identities have been prescribed and controlled. His shabby-genteel heroine inhabits a socially precarious sphere made comfortable through the warmth of the sun and her skill as homemaker. Struggling against the ever-present threat of poverty, her purity and goodness are evidenced largely through the textiles and fittings she has placed in the room; the crisp whiteness of the curtains and the overflowing work-basket attest to her industry and selflessness. Her body, though, is delineated with rather less attention paid to the proprieties of domesticity. Glowing in the morning light her figure assumes connotations more usually associated with the public guile of the *femme fatale*, an alluring lace collar 'cunningly' attached to her dress, her hair entangling the affections of the author like the threads spilling from the direction of the sewing machine corner. Imposing itself between the cosy order of furnishings and flowerpots and the more ambiguous, corporeal attractions of gown, complexion and coiffure is an unspecified text. I would like to suggest that the text in this case is possessed of transformative powers, forming an imaginative link between both the irreproachable comfort and cleanliness of the setting and the more chaotic desires contained in the body of the reader/subject. Pugh doesn't tell us the title of her volume but I would hazard that it's a home dressmaking journal, a woman's magazine, instructing on the intricacies of curtain hanging and the modification of unfashionable necklines whilst encouraging escape through Worth syndicated plates and lyrical portrayals of society events.

This tension, between necessity and aspiration, becomes immediately apparent when focus is shifted from descriptions of feminized domestic activity, in which dressmaking plays a central role, to the pages of those magazines which promoted both the suitable and the illusory to late nineteenth-century female readers. In the light of current reappraisals of the separate spheres debate, how far can graphic and literary communications published with the stated aim of educating and aiding women in their sewing and other social and economically sanctioned practices be taken as representing the status of needlework and dressmaking in popular constructions of femininity, or the role of women in household and familial structures? Since the publication of Davidoff and Hall's important investigation of the manner in which early to mid Victorian middle-class women were assigned domestic responsibilities and attributes connected to the private sphere of home in opposition to the public world of work, successive historians of gender have attempted to establish in more detail how the material culture of private and public spheres both underpinned and contested such social prescriptions.

(Davidoff and Hall 1987; Sparke 1996) The relationship between authorial voice and reader intentions implicit in print culture such as the women's magazine plays an obvious role in such debates. (Beetham 1996; Breward 1994; White 1970) Furthermore, is there a fundamental problem in using such printed ephemera as anything but evidence of the ways in which female consumers attempted to escape such restrictive models anyway? In attempting to suggest responses to these questions I aim to present a limited case study of late Victorian magazine material to underline the notion that journalistic meanings were not fixed or simply didactic. I propose that dressmaker's paper patterns, editorials and plates carried a variety of messages besides the straightforward aid to home-making that dress history might have claimed for them.

Assumptions about the coherence or textual integrity of women's journals from the 1870's onwards are immediately undermined by the processes of basic content analysis. (Berridge 1986) The evidence of plates alone across the broad range of available titles, from those society papers serving the aristocracy to domestic magazines for the lower middle-class, appears to promote an undifferentiated ideal of high Parisian fashion, regardless of the economic position of the relevant readerships. Where an editorial acknowledgment of the social status of a specific audience might be expected, a superficial first reading suggests an equal coverage of the exclusive and expensive. With a closer textual analysis, target audiences emerge through the inclusion or exclusion of articles espousing home dressmaking and household budgeting, or critical discussions of material excess. The fissure thus seems to lie between image and word, the promotion of an ideal and the acceptance of a more prosaic reality.

Elite journals engaged with high fashion in an unselfconscious manner, reporting aristocratic style without apology. They structured a social framework that reflected subtle and complex shifts in fashionably correct behaviour that must have succeeded in alienating those less wealthy readers unaccustomed to the codings of couture.[1] The society journal *The Season* dictated that:

> The character of the leading toilettes of the present season may be divided into two distinct classes. One style which is greatly patronized by the aristocracy, fits closely to the figure at the front and sides, and is only supported by a small tournure; whilst the other is chiefly remarkable for its rich drapery and capricious arrangement. Let us hope that each will retain its place without detriment to the other, for charming and youthful as slim figures may look in these veritable 'fitting like a glove' costumes, the second style is equally becoming for stouter and less classical figures. (*The Season*, October 1887: 1)

As the text continued it placed emphasis on the aristocratic style, described as worn by the Austrian Court. The second, more democratic style, implicitly easier to construct at home, did not merit further analysis, and even within the paragraph quoted lies a subtext suggesting that aristocratic dressing, in its bespoke tightness was more elegant and classical than the stouter appearance of popular modes and figures. Confusion between the promotion of, and indulgence in, fashionable ideals, and an acceptance of a restricted budget or limited social experience, were more heightened in the middle quality journals. A greater availability of information regarding fashionable dress, its acquisition and manufacture, might well have been provided for the middle-class woman by the publication of cheaper, less exclusive titles, but the resulting blurring of lines between social divisions and appearance, inevitably led to a sense of insecurity regarding appropriate dress. A letter to the solidly bourgeois *The English Woman's Domestic Magazine* expressed the uneasiness presumably felt by many readers at the increasing awareness of fashion trends discernible amongst servants and trades people, similarly empowered by a growing access to patterns, fashion plates, needle and thread:

> My income is small, but I have to keep up a good appearance, and am therefore obliged to keep two servants, a cook and a housemaid. My cook I have had for nearly two years, and I have got on very well with her until the last few months. By degrees she has been getting gayer and gayer in her dress of late, and last Sunday when she started off for church, she wore a black silk made exactly like a new one I had had sent home in the beginning of winter, and a new bonnet which I am certain I saw in Madame Louise's window in Regent Street marked 25s. She looked as if she had stepped out of a fashion plate, all but her boots and gloves . . . I feel certain that if I remonstrate with her she will leave, do you not think I may as well discharge her at once? (*The English Woman's Domestic Magazine*, February 1876: 133)

It is not only the fact that mistress and servant are indistinguishable that offended, but the blatant similarity between everyday appearance and the extraordinary conventions of the fashion plate. The low- to middle-brow fashion paper *Myra's Journal of Dress and Fashion* avoided such problems by its straightforward editorial insistence that information relating to high fashion style should be widely available, and communicated in accessible forms so that it could be modified at home to suit all budgets. The inherent disparity between plates, text and the circumstances of the reader was diminished in *Myra's Journal of Dress and Fashion* by the honest practicality of editorial suggestions which emphasized their use as models to be manipulated, rather than supposed reflections of impossible grandeur. However, this ability to respond to all tastes simultaneously, occasionally led to reader dissatisfaction. An editorial regretted that:

I have been scolded for quoting Horace, and accused of extravagant tastes, and of being wealthy [. . .] If I may not talk of pretty things, if I may not go to the best houses for information, if I must go to Tottenham Court Road for bonnets and to The New Cut for furniture . . . I would willingly lay down a pen so fettered. But as another correspondent blames me for describing alpaca dresses and hopes space will not be taken up with print dresses, I am at a loss to please both . . . I will remark that everyone desirous of gaining information naturally seeks out the best authorities; and our readers would not thank us for a description of last years modes, at prices however moderate. The styles mentioned as imported from Paris by first class London drapers can be made in cheaper fabrics and simple trimmings . . . and the patterns we give in silk can be copied in less pretentious materials. (*Myra's Journal,* 1 May 1875)

From a brief survey of the voices adopted by a range of available women's journals, it becomes increasingly apparent that all engaged to some degree with an ideal of fashionability loosely based on elite Parisian models. Those magazines aimed at a wealthier readership pitched their contents at the level of reportage, responding to the very achievable desires of their intended audience. Any thrills experienced by those falling outside this catchment who may have stumbled across the Sandoz plates or Court Circulars were incidental and are not reflected back into the body of the text, though the evidence of over-fashionable servants suggests that such thrills were there to be taken.[2] Titles catering for the middle classes and below operated on two levels, offering both a dream of unattainable glamour that spoke to the deeper desires and imagination of the reader, with all the attendant problems of moral suitability and expense temporarily set aside and an opportunity to realise some of that glamour through economy, home-production and adaptation, in a framework cognisant of societal expectations and restrictions. In an analysis of the visual and literary dissemination of fashionable information from such sources it thus becomes important to consider these contradictions. It becomes necessary to evaluate the precise relevance of content to reader and publisher and the shifting relationships engendered between these two figures. (Anderson 1991:152)

In order to further test the extent to which a journal's market position and social profile might have informed the manner in which information was reported, and highlight the artificial and subjective nature of fashion copy itself, it may be useful to compare the issues of two competing journals published within the same week. The June 1883 issues of *Myra's Journal of Dress and Fashion* and *The Queen* were both available for sale on Britain's bookstalls and railway station kiosks by the third of the month at a price of 6d each. *Myra's Journal* was slightly better value with thirty-seven pages and an enclosed coloured fashion plate and paper dress pattern. *The Queen* offered only twenty-five pages and a coloured fashion plate, and although produced in a larger format, it was less profusely illustrated. Whilst the dangers of drawing conclusive evidence from such an isolated example are clear, a specific comparison may begin to reveal particular modes of address, suggesting the manner in which the journals acted as providers of information for the home sewer and the more casual browser.

Using the evidence of photographs, magazine articles and surviving clothing, dress historians have provided a picture of early 1880s fashionable style which stresses a schizophrenic adherence to two central styles. An emphasis on contrasting texture and applied decoration produced a highly-ornamented, complex silhouette, whilst at the same time the incorporation of tailoring techniques dictated an alternative and more severe outline that drew attention to the growing mass of the bustle. (Cunnington 1937: 325) However, illustrations and text in both publications both confirm and contradict such a prescriptive reading. Significantly the source of fashion information provides a point at which the journals diverge. *The Queen,* true to its role as a patriotic society journal fond of imperialist rhetoric, made little direct reference to Parisian fashion in its editorial reports, yet its descriptions of society dress, placed carefully under the heading 'London Fashions', bore close comparison both with the French plates and unapologetic reports on Paris fashion selected by *Myra's Journal. The Queen* correspondent noted that:

> White is much worn, and will be greatly made up for race and fete costumes. It is trimmed with either white or ecru lace with white, crushed strawberry, yellow or cherry ribbons. Some of the prettiest dresses are of soft white china silk, made with the plaited waterfall back, falling on to a broad pinked-out ruche; the skirt opens in front, and is turned back to show the petticoat of flounced lace interspersed with loops of baby ribbon; the bodice has a cascade of lace and ribbon down the front, sleeves reaching midway between elbow and wrist, with ruffles. (2 June 1883: 515)

It is significant that the language employed to describe new clothing across the range of late nineteenth-century fashion journals carefully constructed the total costume, as if from a pattern, whilst also providing a sensual evocation of the physical and visual sensations to be derived from the wearing and viewing of such a dress, the reading of which produces a pleasurable sense of fashionable 'inclusion' in itself. The emphasis on soft colour and intensive trimming was also outlined by the Comtesse de B. in an article titled 'Dress and Fashion from Paris' in *Myra's Journal.* But whilst *The Queen* presented its report as an objective representation of dress as worn in fashionable English gatherings, *Myra's Journal* retained and emphasized the glamour and prestige of French connections, encouraging its readers to sustain a fantasy of engagement with the spectacular world of elite luxury and conspicuous consumption. The comtesse suggested that:

> A very graceful stylish summer toilette is of pale chrysanthemum pink surah, and dark chrysanthemum voile, trimmed with ecru lawn. The skirt to the knees is of puffed and draped surah and is edged below with a wide surah pleating, the front covered with two fan pleatings of ecru lawn fastened at the knees by a large satin bow . . . a sash of pale pink ribbon outlines the basque and is fastened in front with a silver horse shoe buckle. (1 June 1883: 262)

A comparison of the two texts uncovers a seemingly similar ideal, layered, delicate and dreamlike as opposed to the rational, practical styles that surface in contemporary photography, particularly in images of the respectable and industrious middle classes. The rejection of inappropriate Gallic frippery that one might expect from a lower middle-class journal espousing the benefits of economical home provision is absent, at least in this stratum of *Myra's Journal,* implying that any search for an authentic and coherent dressmaking voice, imbued with the rhetoric of efficiency, is misconceived.

A further superficial similarity, undermined by specific appeals to a chosen audience, was doubly apparent in the presentation of the fashion plates. These were representations intended to embody the physical product of labour resulting from the adaptation of the free patterns which accompanied the journals, whilst also operating within their own framework as particular examples of a set graphic form or convention. Both plates originated from Paris and the respective proprietors drew attention to their source at the foot of the image: 'Myra's Paris Patterns and Models' (Figure 1.1) and 'Latest Paris Fashions Supplement to the Queen' (Figure 1.2). Essentially the models in both plates conform to the received signs of fashionability in 1883, which constituted a peaked bonnet, long tapered bodice, puffed sleeves, overskirt and bustle, short train and an emphasis on applied decoration. However, the styles presented by *Myra's Journal* are simpler, lacking the opulent layered characteristics of the *Queen* plate where the accompanying text was similarly weighted towards the luxurious:

> Shot silk in pink and lilac tints. Skirt striped with plaits of strawberry red satin, with which corresponds the ribbon loops and ends, that alternate with the rows of dusky lace on the shoulder cape. Bonnet in lattice straw or silk cord trimmed to correspond. Gauntlet gloves. Pattern of cape 1s 2d; overdress 3s 1d. (*The Queen,* 2 June 1883: 507)

Figure 1.1. Hand-coloured steel-engraved fashion plate presented with *Myra's Journal of Dress and Fashion*, 1 June 1883.

Whilst the description in *Myra's Journal* was less precise in terms of colour, it engaged to a greater extent with the vocabulary of dressmaking, emphasizing the journal's position both as a serious fashion paper, reflecting the concerns of a wider industry, and as an aid to home dress production. Furthermore, the editorial interpretation in the accompanying article, entitled

'Myra's Workroom', suggested a variety of possible materials presumably ranged according to taste or pocket. Nevertheless, an enjoyment of the tactile quality of textiles and the display effects of construction remain central to the meaning of the text and should not be read as incompatible with those more practical purposes:

> Our coloured plate illustrates one of the most stylish ways of making up a costume now in vogue. The skirt which is edged with a rich embroidery, is pleated under a pleated Molliere tunic; the curved and pointed bodice has a velvet plastron to match in colour with the embroidered edge; velvet parements are placed under the cuffs, but when embroidery to correspond is unobtainable, the plastron etc., can be made of this in place of the velvet. This style will be found useful for Indian silk embroidered skirts, for soft voiles, and stylish cambrics. (*Myra's Journal of Dress and Fashion*, 1 June 1883: 278)

Figure 1.2. Hand-coloured steel-engraved fashion plate presented with *The Queen*, 2 June 1883.

In conclusion, I hope to have indicated the possibilities opened up by a close analysis of journalistic aids to home sewing. Audiences appear to have been free to select or demand highly subjective definitions of fashionability, dependent as much on their particular social and economic circumstances as on the prescriptive dictates of Paris couture or London publishers. Such definitions might have meant anything from the purchase of a Worth dress, inspired by a description in *The Queen,* through to the adapting of a pattern presented with *Myra's Journal* in cheaper materials, to that dream of careless gentility snatched by our original reader during a quiet moment in the kitchen. As a final note, returning to the literary construction of reading and practice which introduced this chapter, I'd like to end with a quotation from Arnold Bennett who also captured the iconic allure of magazine imagery in a passage from his 1908 novel *The Old Wives Tale.* His description is pertinent in its evocation of the power of the reproduced image as a sign of imaginative escape. As a former editor of *Woman* during the 1890s, Bennett was in a privileged position to understand the multiple meanings that magazine content was able to generate in readers, who ultimately lay beyond the grasp of editorial control:

This print represented fifteen sisters, all of the same height and slimness of figure, all of the same age – about twenty five or so, and all with exactly the same haughty and bored beauty. That they were in truth sisters was clear from the facial resemblance between them; their demeanour indicated that they were princesses, offspring of some impossibly prolific King and Queen . . . the princesses moved in a landscape of marble steps and verandahs, with a bandstand and strange trees in the distance . . . The picture was drenched in mystery, and the strangest thing about it was that all these highnesses were apparently content with the most ridiculous and outmoded fashions . . . But Sophia perceived nothing uncanny in the picture, which bore the legend 'Newest summer fashions from Paris. Gratis supplement to Myra's Journal.' Sophia had never imagined anything more stylish, lovely and dashing than the raiment of the fifteen princesses. (Bennett 1908: 35–6)

Notes

1. For a more detailed explanation of the social profile, publication details and circulation figures of the periodicals cited in this chapter see: Breward 1992: 18–39 and Appendix; Jobling and Crowley 1996: 9–41; White 1970: 304–27.
2. For a discussion of the collaborations which took place between couture houses and fashion magazines and the broader context of fashion illustration see: Coleman 1990: 41; Ginsburg 1980: 11; Steele 1988: 111–30; Roskill 1970: 391–5; Reed 1997.

References

Anderson, P. (1991), *The Printed Image and the Transformation of Popular Culture 1790–1860*, Oxford: Clarendon Press.

Beetham, M. (1996), *A Magazine of her Own: Domesticity and Desire in the Woman's Magazine 1800–1914*, London: Routledge.

Bennett, A. (1908), *The Old Wives Tale*, London: Chapman & Hall. Reprinted London: Pan (1964).

Berridge, V. (1986), 'Content Analysis and Historical Research on Newspapers', in M. Harris and Lee, A., eds, *The Press in English Society from the Seventeenth to the Nineteenth Century*, Toronto: Farleigh Dickinson University Press.

Breward, C. (1992), *Images of Desire: The Construction of the Feminine Consumer in Women's Fashion Journals 1875–1890* (unpublished MA dissertation), London: Victoria & Albert Museum/Royal College of Art.

—— (1994), 'Femininity and Consumption; The Problem of the Late Nineteenth-Century Fashion Journal, *Journal of Design History* 7:2, pp 71–90.

Coleman, E. (1990), *The Opulent Era: Fashions of Worth, Doucet & Paquin*, London: Thames & Hudson.

Cunnington, C. W. (1937), *English Women's Clothing in the Nineteenth Century*, London: Faber.

Davidoff, L. and Hall, C. (1987), *Family Fortunes: Men and Women of the English Middle Class 1780–1850*, London: Hutchinson.

Ginsburg, M. (1980), *An Introduction to Fashion Illustration*, London: Victoria & Albert Museum.

Jobling, P. and Crowley, D. (1996), *Graphic Design: Reproduction & Representation since 1800*, Manchester: Manchester University Press.

Pugh, E. (1896), *The Man of Straw*, London: Heinemann.

Reed, D. (1997), *The Popular Magazine in Britain and the United States 1880–1960*, London: British Library Press.

Roskill, M. (1970), 'Early Impressionism and the Fashion Print' *The Burlington Magazine*, June 1970: 391–5.

Sparke, P. (1996), *As Long As It's Pink: The Sexual Politics of Taste*, London: Pandora.

Steele, V. (1988), *Paris Fashion: A Cultural History*, Oxford: Oxford University Press.

White, C. (1970), *Women's Magazines 1693–1968*, London: Michael Joseph.

2

Made at Home by Clever Fingers: Home Dressmaking in Edwardian England

Barbara Burman

I was busily at work on my dress yesterday evening (by the way, what a deal of work there is in a dress!) Diary entry 1905 (Thompson 1987: 72)

The Edwardian years in England have been described as 'the aftermath of the Victorian age, and the watershed of the modern age', a time when 'all the expansionist and imperialist features of the previous century were still displayed to excess and all the political tensions and economic frailties of the present century were becoming apparent.' (Beckett and Cherry 1987: 7) For women of all classes it was a time of new challenges and paradoxes. Nevertheless, despite the richness of the terrain, the reluctance of dress historians to engage with the full range of factors at work during these years has resulted in a literature top-heavy on the dress of the elite and leisured classes.[1]

Social class is a term full of slippage and pitfalls, past and present. It is also famously difficult to extract any absolute definitions about class-related practices, to which home dressmaking is no exception. Nevertheless, class was a term in use at this time and it serves here as a rudimentary framework for some of the formative distinctions which women perceived in the world around them. In claiming a place for the study of everyday clothing, this chapter suggests that dressmaking at home during this period,[2] though nuanced by class, was commonly held to be an economic and social necessity. The chapter concentrates on women of the working and middle classes. Whilst it is not a study of the huge number of waged homeworkers who sewed at home on work put out by factories and workshops, nevertheless historical realities frequently break down such tidy distinctions. The even larger number of girls and women employed in domestic service at this time escape the limited brief of this chapter, though they form an important element in home dressmaking; for example, those who served as nursery maids were often expected to make and maintain clothing for the young children in their charge.

Recent writing has explored the rise and significance of consumer culture. (Brewer and Porter 1994; Bronner 1989; Fine and Leopold 1993; McCracken 1990; Strasser et al. 1998) This has also been the context for an interest in retailing, particularly the department store, as a cultural and social history. (Lancaster 1995; Miller 1981) Within dress history there has been new work on the interrelationships between production and consumption which has mapped, for example, a more extensive history for ready-made clothing. (Lemire 1997) This chapter, however, argues that within this enlarged sense of the accessibility and significance of ready-made consumer goods, the making of clothes at home continued to form a central part of commonplace clothing strategies. Mechanized production of ready-made clothing increased and appears to have met, or created, new needs. 'The new ready-made clothes had at first met a demand from small tradesmen, office workers, etc. and their families but towards the end of the nineteenth century there was an acceleration in demand from the skilled and semi-skilled manual workers and their families. This was accompanied by a reduction in prices . . .' (Morris 1986: 39). Nevertheless this development did not enfranchise everyone, so to speak, as a consumer of ready-mades nor, by the start of this century, was it to dislodge for a generation or more to come the wide variety in clothing consumption practices which had for so long characterized most households. This chapter argues that the consumption and experience of everyday clothing during the Edwardian period was defined to a large extent by factors outside the ready-made market and in particular it points to how home dressmaking was sustained as an important aid for women negotiating wider social shifts and tensions in their lives.

In London a young, unmarried woman clerk (who did a certain amount of her own dressmaking) wrote in her diary in 1908: 'A procession of Hunger Marchers [. . .] joined us, each man brushing against me with his clothes as he passed.' (Thompson 1987: 132–3) Hunger and fear were not mere public spectacle, they were close at hand. In her own place of work, a grocer's, she noted in the same month 'the latest injustice has been putting Miss Williams on very difficult and worrying work, at a wage of 18/- in place of a man earning £2 per week. Trade is bad everywhere and the papers are full of distressful accounts. One wonders what the winter will bring. Dad is working late every night through a lessened staff. Feel very depressed and strange.' When read against these powerful, defining experiences, the consumption and purpose of clothing in everyday life acquires more precise significance.

It resonates with what one historian of the period called the 'immense and obvious divergences in standards of living' and 'innumerable common situations in which Edwardians were made to feel their precise station in life'. (Thompson 1992: 285)

This chapter deals briefly with three main issues. Firstly, home dressmaking was vital to the task, hard to define yet demanding, of 'keeping up appearances'. For example, for women of the skilled working and lower-middle classes, conformity, or at least a good approximation, to the dress codes of their peers in their own community was an essential means both of subscribing to respectability and claiming its entitlements, on which so much depended.[3] For better-off women this was also perceived as no less pressing than for those on the edge of poverty. The experience was familiar to earlier generations:

> Within recent history decent clothing has been a necessity for any woman or girl child who wants to enter the social world: it's her means of entry and there are rules that say so . . . The practice reveals [. . .] the way in which an external set of social rules might become a form by which a household operated. In its turn, this economic system of a household might provide a means to a child's understanding of herself. (Steedman 1986: 89)

Secondly, within these general considerations, women were also becoming subject to a variety of relatively new codes of dress and appearance generated by the workplace. Largely unwritten, but nevertheless coercive, these arose for significant numbers of women in new areas of 'clean' waged work outside the home, for example, clerks, typists, shop workers and elementary teachers who faced the challenge of sustaining appropriate appearances despite very low incomes. The Edwardian period is marked out by the degree to which home dressmaking had a crucial role to play in these circumstances.

Thirdly, during this period home dressmaking was defined by a general shift towards its commodification, as 'the commodity became and has remained the one subject of mass culture, the centrepiece of everyday life, the focal point of all representation, the dead centre of the modern world.' (Richards 1991: 1) Increasingly the activity of home dressmaking became entwined within complex processes in manufacturing, retailing and consumption which seemed to draw fashion and fashionable goods inexorably to the centre stage of modern life, processes which have attracted considerable academic attention in recent years. (Fine and Leopold 1993; Fraser 1981; Glennie 1995; Lipovetsky 1994; Miller 1981; Richards 1991; Wilson 1985) So, whilst home dressmaking by definition was a small-scale activity which continued to take place in homes of all descriptions during the Edwardian period, as it had done in the previous century, at the same time it was contested by large-scale commercial interests, colonized by 'the roaring worlds of production and consumption'. (Richards 1991:15)

Evidence about everyday domestic sewing is hard to come by in the context of urban poverty. With family life characterized by frequent bouts of unemployment, overcrowded housing and other deprivations, it might seem safe to assume that the purchase of materials or paper patterns was unlikely or sporadic. Certainly, without a sewing machine considerable hand labour was required to make even a child's garment, but observations made between 1909 and 1913 in a study of poor households in Lambeth in London suggest however that a significant amount of clothing was made for children from new cloth. It identified the 'vexed question' of over-use of cheap inflammable flannelette. (Pember Reeves 1913: 64) In general the report noted the 'clumsy clothes' of children (Pember Reeves 1913: 7) and the need for the men to be clothed and shod for waged work taking priority over women's clothing. The report cited one young mother as 'intolerably proud' of owning a large sewing machine; she made all her baby's clothes and most of her own, whilst they lived in 'one small and dismal room'. The sewing was fitted in between cooking, laundry, cleaning and carrying the household's clean and dirty water up and down two floors to the yard. (Pember Reeves 1913: 160–1) In Robert Robert's Salford sewing machines, 'drop heads if possible', were longed for luxuries, on a par with pianos, bicycles and gramophones. (Roberts 1990: 32) Observations made house by house in York for Rowntree's study of poverty included commentary on the benefits a sewing machine could have for the household. 'Mrs. X. has a sewing machine, and is clever at making or altering clothes; she gets many old clothes given to her.' (Rowntree 1913: 318)

In households of this kind evidence for the social role and economic contribution of home dressmaking is shadowy and difficult to gauge[4] although some general patterns emerge. It is clear that amongst the poorest unskilled working class, the provision and maintenance of family clothing was managed by women, 'the hidden matriarchy of the urban poor'. (Chinn 1988: 11) In this context, with 'nothing wasted under the vigilant eyes of an improvising wife' (Chinn 1988: 69) home dressmaking included extensive work to repair and remake clothing for basic needs as part of a fluid clothing survival strategy which included the pawn shop (Tebbut 1983), clothing clubs (Roberts 1977: 317), second-hand clothing and hand-me-downs. 'Clothes – always second-hand. Off the barrow down the market place. Penny left and ha'penny right we used to call them . . .' (Thompson 1981: 17) For women with skill but no resources to buy new materials, jumble sales were another source of serviceable clothing. A skilled Nottingham woman who took in occasional fine hosiery for finishing was described by her daughter. 'And mother made a point of going, she'd got a knowing eye and she would look them over. They came from better class people [. . .] she saw a grey flannel dressing gown [. . .] in good condition. She washed it, cut it, unpicked it, turned it inside out and pressed it and she made me the most wonderful frock I ever had for Sunday.' (Thompson 1981: 75) The richness of this sort of evidence emphasizes the value of written and oral autobiographies in their own right and also when more formal records are scarce.

Although it took place in the home with all its implied constraints, home dressmaking was not done within particularly consistent domestic parameters. Women who were able or keen seamstresses used their skills for a wide variety of purposes, defined by differing social and economic needs and motives, all subject to change as their personal circumstances changed. If they sewed solely for personal need it was common to combine this with making clothing as gifts for friends or relatives or for the more needy. In the following example, a mother with six out of her ten children surviving, working from her home as a dressmaker and married to an insurance agent, lived a lower-middle-class lifestyle. Her paid dressmaking occupied a significant proportion of her time. One of her daughters recalled their life in Lancashire: 'On the machine all the time, soon as one baby was born she's back on the machine again.' (Thompson 1981: 107–8) Yet despite the pressures of sewing to generate cash for the family budget, she found time to sew for her children, dressing them 'right' to maintain appearances '. . . she always kept us nicely dressed and no one knew we were poor.' This necessitated renovating old clothes as well as making new ones. Given an old coat, she unpicked it and 'made us a new coat, turned it, washed it and made a new coat out of it . . . I was always dressed right through making things do. She made us lovely white dresses to walk in. We always dressed nice then and on Sundays we had all our best clothes put on and put them away . . .'

This woman also made frocks as gifts for the children of poorer neighbours so they could take part in a Whit Walk. But clothing which was known to be home-made was an ambivalent sign. Whilst it spoke of respectable thrift or neighbourly generosity, it was also an unwelcome badge of poverty. The period is marked by frequent reference to everyday efforts to evade or disguise the visible effects of poverty. There was much private 'making do' with the needle, for example, the Nottingham woman cited above. 'She'd got a standard and she wasn't going to let anyone know that she fell below that standard.' (Thompson 1981: 74) Writing from first-hand experience in his 1906–7 novel, Robert Tressell depicted a painter and decorator's family moving into a street where they were thought by their white-collar neighbours to be a disgrace. Their son was 'the only tolerable one [. . .] he was always very well dressed; so well indeed as to occasion some surprise, until they found out that all the boy's clothes were home-made. Then their surprise was changed into a somewhat grudging admiration of the skill displayed, mingled with contempt for the poverty which made its exercise necessary.' (Tressell 1993: 77)

It is an important characteristic of clothing in this period that individuals within a wide diversity of class and income used private dressmakers for making, recycling or renovating garments. Dressmakers were common as local sole traders in their own homes as well as those who sought more exclusivity by renting rooms in shopping streets and they offered a vast range of quality and price; there was one to suit every pocket. The customers of a bricklayer's wife in London, who took in odd sewing and dressmaking jobs in 1910/11, paid her between 6d and 9d for plain blouses which took half a day to make. Her best customer was a fruiterer's wife. She 'showed the visitor an old skirt out of which she was making a child's coat and a pair of knickerbockers; she was to receive 1/- for each garment.' (Black 1915: 89) Despite the efforts of this 'admirable mother' of nine, the visitor noted how little it would take for the household to 'fall to pieces'.

In brief, the home production of clothing by women in financially and socially precarious working families met a wide variety of needs inside and outside the home. The maintenance of respectable appearances, making ends meet for a family and acts of charity were often interwoven. By skill, inventiveness and expediency such women created significant support networks for themselves, their kin and community. This way of using sewing skills no doubt fuelled middle-class criticism that the poverty was caused by the poor and that poor women didn't know how to plan or budget for their families. (Chinn 1988: 56) In practice, many acted decisively to meet clothing needs whenever available resources allowed. Where such women themselves were not in regular employment outside the home, their own consumption of clothes and shoes was often subordinated to the needs of the other employed members of the family and school age children. Clearly there were significant local differences in employment and consumption patterns, for example in textile areas many more women were in full-time or part-time waged employment than was the case elsewhere and this affected the time and cash available for making or buying clothing. Local studies provide insight into the range of options available. For example, Elizabeth Roberts concludes from her study of working-class standards of living in Barrow and Lancaster that a 'substantial part of the clothing and household linen and floor-covering used by the working classes of both towns was not bought in normal retail shops but was acquired in some more economical way.' (Roberts 1977: 317) In general, we see working-class women, by necessity, producing and consuming clothing largely outside the formal structures of large-scale manufacturing and retailing. 'What things the poor did own then, most made gallant use of.' (Roberts 1990: 41)

The equivocal reputation of ready-made clothing supplied another motive for the continuation of home dressmaking in Edwardian England. Although the production and consumption of ready-made clothing was already well established by the turn of the century (Chapman 1993; Sharpe 1995), the trade having grown in the nineteenth century from the production of uniforms, shirts and workwear to include cheap work suits for men, ready-made clothing for women in the Edwardian period was rarer and still often regarded as badly made and ill-fitting. The materials used were frequently of poor quality, unwashable for a variety of reasons and quick to fade and wear. There may have been multiple factors behind these uneven standards (Fine and Leopold 1993). To some extent the fragmented and sweated nature of clothing production was not in itself conducive to quality or value. Some insight into this was offered by an enquiry into married women's work begun in 1908: a woman home-worker sewed blouses by machine in her own home, receiving up to 2/9 a dozen. She could make the dozen in a day or day and a half. 'She was emphatic in her declaration that cheap work paid best because it could be done so rapidly. It is certainly true that some practised workers can run through their machines at an amazing speed, and with very little apparent attention.' (Black 1915: 69–70)

Middle-class women not undertaking regular waged work inside or outside the home had both the time to make clothes to express their own creativity and access to the leisure occasions on which to wear them. 'She was putting the finishing touches to a 'reform' dress [. . .] it was so classic, simple and graceful. Its hue was a soft shade of green – its trimmings a pointed yoke of white canvas, whereon was worked in orange and pale yellow silks the quaintest of Japanese designs.' (Thompson 1987: 103) But middle-class women were taking up paid work in greater numbers (Holcombe 1973) and evidence suggests that clothing could represent a time-consuming problem for them. A middle-class teacher described what had become, by the end of the nineteenth century, a common pattern of mixed expenditure and acquisition and therefore a very flexible, cost effective approach:

I have my clothes made at very good shops, *not* the most fashionable, and always of the best materials, as I think it is most economical in the end; but I spend very little on fripperies, such as beads and feathers. I generally have two new dresses a year. *I make my own blouses because the ready-made ones are too cheap and poor.* If I had time, I think I should enjoy making other things, but I have too much to do. I generally do my own mending, but sometimes lately I have had a woman in to do it. (Collet 1902: 76 italics supplied)

Here home dressmaking was regarded as a common-sense alternative to unsatisfactory ready-made garments. Her strategy, though based on a larger budget and different values, echoed the eclecticism seen in working-class clothing practice. The second-hand trade, though by more discreet means than street barrows, also served such women. For example, the genteel ladies' weekly newspaper *The Lady* carried large quantities of classified advertisements for new and nearly new clothing, suggesting that many readers stretched their budgets by buying and selling clothes in this market.

Popular fiction represents home dressmaking in an important though subtle role in better-off middle class Edwardian England. Tasks using the needle were shown as moments when women could talk together. Their sewing was depicted as soothing in times of crisis and as an occupation combining thrift, domesticity and sociability. Sometimes this appears emphasized by scenes in which men talk to sewing women; masculinity became more evident by its contrast to this embodiment of femininity, and vice versa. But the act of sewing can be seen in popular fiction to play out more than just unquestioned symbols of femininity. A closer look at the sewing in one fictional household gives us several pointers.

In a scene in a novel of 1910, a middle-class widowed mother sits in her London dining room sewing a white blouse for one of her grown daughters. (Smedley 1910) The blouse is needed urgently for the young woman's departure that evening on her first foreign holiday. Unexpectedly her maid (in this case of rather shabby gentility, this 'general' maid is the sole residential servant) shows an important male visitor into the room. Dismayed that the visitor has not been shown to the drawing room and flustered to be found dressmaking with her table 'littered with stuffs and paper patterns' she tries 'to sweep them up together' as she speaks. In this novel the widow has frugally but successfully brought up five children on a hundred pounds a year. Now they remain at home as unmarried and employed young adults with incomes of their own, through whose conversations and actions the author speculates about up-to-the-minute issues such as gender relations and employment for women. For example, another of the daughters enjoys her office job and gets a 'thrill of delight every morning' when she sits down at her 'nice clean typewriter'. This daughter has a busy social life with her peers outside the family home. She sews her own clothes for work and leisure wear 'dextrously', sitting by the fire with her mother. 'The few evenings that young lady spent at home [sewing clothes] were intervals behind the scenes, devoted to preparations for public conquest.'

In another novel by the same author the status-conscious wife of a securely employed house agent discusses domestic economies with him. '"There's the gardener," went on Mrs Maddox. "We needn't have him every week and I can *make down* my green cashmere into Jessica's and Catherine's best dresses for this winter; I can quite well *do up* my terracotta. Oh, there are lots of ways in which we can economise.'" (Smedley 1911, italics supplied) For his part, Mr Maddox anxiously contemplates cancellation of the subscription to his monthly 'review'.

These novels represent home dressmaking as a private but time-consuming 'behind the scenes' activity for women, a hidden but nevertheless vital means of creating, transforming and securing appropriate public images for the sake of the individual and their family. It takes place within a domestic space where it is shared, both in terms of skills and knowledge passed between family members and as a gift of time and resources from one family member to another, typically mother to child or sister to sister or brother.[5] Both thrift and creativity are emphasized, as is the opportunity to govern very closely the clothing of the younger daughters. References are made to the newer middle-class young women entrants to the world of waged work and the stories play off privacy and the minutiae of keeping up appearances in the changing outside world. They trace an appropriation of home dressmaking not as an unwelcome echo of the sweatshop but as an act of self-sufficiency and ingenuity.

There is much evidence to suggest a correlation between the new working woman and the shrewd development of the market in sewing machines, home dressmaking magazines and paper patterns. These women and girls were described by the *Englishwoman's Review* in October 1909 as 'the vast army [. . .] One meets them by the hundred, pouring into London between 8 and 9 in the morning – a spectacle which would have astonished our grand-mothers.' Whilst women remained constantly at about 30 per cent of the total workforce through this period, there was real growth in non-manual jobs for them within that overall percentage.[6] But these white-collar jobs tended to be at the lower end of the clerical hierarchy. 'The movement of women into non-manual occupations did not by any means involve a leap to middle-class status.' (Lewis 1984: 158) However, white-collar work produced new conditions for social mobility and social interchange which began to rearrange former established social classifications. Amongst shorthand typists of the period there was a mixture of social backgrounds but a gradual increase in the numbers of working-class entrants who 'did not take with them the values of the worker in manual labour, but of the class above them' (Davy 1986: 131) The nuances in dress involved in these perceived social shifts seem likely to have played a central role in dress consumption and dress codes within even reasonably small groups of workers. So too would workplace hierarchy, based on seniority or types of work. For these particular white-collar working women, clothing consumption in these contexts should be seen as rational, a purposeful act which served as a form of investment, part of a strategic construction of an image of competence, reliability and employability.

The move of women into office work had been gaining momentum from the 1870s. However, this shift in employment for women was often contested and dogged by unequal pay, and 'clean' jobs for women were frequently terminated by the marriage bar. In these circumstances, there was considerable pressure to conform to certain sorts of appearances. Employers assumed standards. For example, a woman who had dealt with 34,000 female applicants for posts as telephone operators noted that it was 'unnecessary to say that girls showing real uncleanliness of dress or habit never get beyond the first interview.' (Minter 1906: 192) A story published in *Fashions for All* home dressmaking magazine in April 1908 told how a secretary eventually married her boss. She first caught his eye by her neat attire. '" Miss. Gregory, I like the way you dress", he said, with a startling abruptness. "I've had girls here who got themselves up as if they were going to a party instead of to their work. Satin and lace and things don't belong to an office. I hope you won't let yourself get tempted into them."' The need to find ways and means to dress appropriately constituted a defining and significant task on a daily basis, a form of work in its own right.

Much of the white-collar worker's capacity to own and sustain appropriate workwear was dependent on her home base. It was still fairly unusual for girls and young women to live away from the parental home between leaving school and marriage. With an early school-leaving age and with marriage in the mid to late twenties, it was not uncommon for a decade in between to be spent living at home whilst in waged work. This extended period in the parental home and community also brought extra duties, such as helping with younger siblings, nursing the sick or helping needier neighbours. But whilst the girl or woman wage earner was also engaged in her community and home, and frequently relinquished control to her mother of substantial amounts of her wage, the pay-off was that the business of being properly clothed was much facilitated. Time taken for buying cloth and other items, making clothes, dealing with dressmakers, mending, recycling, renovating and laundry were done with the support of mothers or sisters, who brought a wider range of skills and the opportunity to share tasks and resources. Trading within an established network of family and friends seems to have been common. 'I'll tell you what Mother used to do, she had a friend that kept a shoe shop, and instead of Mother paying the money for our shoes, she used to do all the sewing. So we got our shoes that way. So she earned them before we wore them.' (Thompson 1981: 108)

Getting and maintaining clothing by ingenious manipulation of resources is confirmed for example in a study of the budgets of working girls and women. (Board of Trade 1911)[7] Though not the primary purpose of the report, it reveals a remarkable creativity in the task of coping with clothing. It indicates that home support was crucially important in strategies employed to keep 'alive and decent', that these were very varied and, not surprisingly, almost ceaseless. For example, it tracks the expenditure of a girl clerk who had her boots and shoes mended eight times in the year. Hat shapes and trimmings were purchased, suggesting millinery made at home. Dresses were sent to be dyed. Two pairs of stockings were sent to be refooted for a penny less than the cost of one new pair. Insertions were put into blouses, skirts were lengthened. Dress protectors were purchased to make garments last longer. A mackintosh, a major item, was bought second-hand. The report records gifts of cloth for making up, mothers sewing for daughters, mother managing all the laundry, girl workers taking up after-work dressmaking classes or sewing gifts for friends. The report would suggest these particular workers had escaped the cyclical expenditure trap of dependence on cheap but shoddy ready-mades. 'Everybody knows that good clothes, boots or furniture are really the cheapest in the end, although they cost more money at first; but the working classes can seldom or never afford to buy good things; they have to buy cheap rubbish which is dear at any price.' (Tressell 1993: 296) Home dressmaking, covering a variety of skills from cutting out to renovating, was clearly one important way in which decency was maintained and workplace standards of dress achieved on low and uncertain wages.

Yet despite widespread evidence of its everyday importance, home-dressmaking was within disputed territory. Against the wider background of tensions and frailties of the period there are vivid examples of paradoxes inherent in how sewing was perceived. For example, employers in the clothing trades had long been associated with the most exploitative practices. One investigator of the day wrote of the 'evil of underpayment', 'the dreadful spectre of unemployment' and the 'intolerable weight of human burdens'. (Meyer and Black 1909: 11–18) The much-visited Daily News Sweated Industries Exhibition of 1906 in London, seeking to raise public awareness and solve these long-standing problems by legislation on minimum wages, elicited responses of horror and pity by placing real workers in its exhibition, including women from the needle trades. (Beckett and Cherry 1987: 72) In this situation, needlework by women was denounced. By contrast the much larger Franco-British Exhibition of 1908 showed women's needlework, in the context of other craft exhibits, in its Palace of Women's Work with the intention of depicting the opportunities open to women craft workers. At this same event, Harmsworth's new and aggressively marketed home dressmaking magazine *Fashions for All – The Ladies' Journal of Practical Fashions* won a prize for its 'pretty, dainty stand' showing tissue paper mock-ups of its 'charming frocks and frills' which could be made up from its home dressmaker's paper patterns. (Burman 1994: 75–6) Needlework and home dressmaking were championed as profitable and fulfilling activities for women in the context of the 1908 exhibition.

Simultaneously, the desire for, and consumption of, fashionable clothing, itself frequently the product of sweated labour, was closely associated with women and femininity itself. 'When all is said and done, recollect that the personality of a woman is more or less bound up in her toilette.' (Pritchard 1902: 3) The period was marked by further development of consumerism and the spectacular displays put up by the retailers, alongside the increasingly sophisticated images in the mass-circulation fashion magazines of the period, gave fashion an unprecedented presence at this time. It has been said that fashion became 'essential to the world of modernity, the world of spectacle and mass-communication' and 'fashion is as much part of the dream world of capitalism as of its economy'. (Wilson 1985: 12–14) Interpretations of these wider phenomena vary but it is clear that the publishers, manufacturers and retailers involved in the home dressmaking market for magazines, sewing machines and paper patterns pressed the case for their goods, in large part, on the grounds they now offered quick and affordable access to fashionable appearance. The Edwardian years are marked by this commercial manœuvre; home dressmaking was pulled further into the marketplace, to be sold back to consumers as an emblem of modernity and style. Simultaneously, fashionable ready-made clothing competed for attention, offering instant style with all the pleasures of shopping. Despite criticism of their quality, factory and sweatshop goods were starting to compromise their home-made equivalents.

Although the Edwardian years were full of expanding opportunities for women, as they took them up, they were inevitably caught up in wider challenges and contradictions. Of particular impact on women and perceptions of their role was the idea that the British race was degenerating and the nation slipping from its former 'natural' supremacy. Degeneration was represented as a physical and moral as well as a political and economic process. Attempts to theorize solutions for regeneration and improvement often prioritized women's role as wives and mothers as central agents for change. '[T]he relationship between family and state was subtly changing [. . .] Child-rearing was becoming a national duty not just a moral one [. . .]' (Davin 1978: 13) Thus the education of girls and the proper place and duties of women were debated within powerful anxieties about the nation and its future. At the same time the campaigns for female suffrage dramatized women's issues and pushed them high up the public agenda. Some middle-class commentators were nervous about working girls breaking free from domestic influence and using their wages to taste other pleasures. 'The average working girl is intensely individualistic, very excitable, and pleasure-loving, and her sense of responsibility is little developed [. . .] To-day, at the most susceptible age of fourteen, they are sent out to factories as wage-earners, and become to a large extent independent of home control.' (Montagu 1904: 235) In this view, the acquisition and practice of domestic skills, including sewing, were argued for as a necessary constraint and social cement and a woman who didn't sew was potentially disruptive.

A closer look at how working-class and lower-middle-class girls in state schooling were expected to acquire the skills necessary for making clothes at home shows the period marked by emergence of an increasingly uncomfortable disjuncture between the schoolroom curriculum and everyday needs. The curriculum had been designed to develop the needle skills necessary for domestic service and motherhood. With needlework compulsory since the mid-nineteenth century, the curriculum looked anachronistic as it lagged behind technological developments. (Figure 2.1) Lengthy and finely handsewn

Figure 2.1. Sewing class of twenty-five girls and one sewing machine. London c. 1915. By permission of the Imperial War Museum.

seams continued to be promoted in the schoolroom long after the sewing machine rendered them redundant. Pattern cutting also continued to be taught long after cheap and attractively fashionable paper patterns were widely available. It has been argued that such was the strength of the older established ideologies of femininity, in their different moulds for working- and middle-class girls, that these conservative practices dominated educational thinking in spite of new everyday needs outside the classroom. (Dyhouse 1981, Turnbull 1987)

Whilst educationalists, reformers and others wrestled with the 'Woman Question', the manufacturers moved towards increasing commodification of the home dressmaker's needs. By the start of the century reliably sized and well-planned paper patterns were commonly available. Patterns existed for outerwear, underwear and nightwear, for morning, afternoon and evening frocks, skirts and blouses as separates for many occasions, clothes for sports and holidays, for children, adolescents and grown women. Unlike the home dressmakers of a generation or two before, their Edwardian counterparts could make clothes as stylishly as they wished from patterns designed to provide up-to-the-minute fashions promoted with clear seasonal differentiation and frequently with full directions for making-up. There was no shortage of advice to accompany them, particularly when new styles were introduced. The language often mixed promise and exhortation. There was much emphasis on the variety of choice available in the look of the finished article and on speed, simplicity and ease of construction. A downmarket weekly *The Girls' Friend*, 2 April 1910, was fairly blunt.

> The one-piece blouse with seams only at the under-arms is the blouse of the season, and this very simple design is made up in all materials from richest lace and satin to the most simple of washing goods. Do please just look at the dainty little blouse and the diagram of the simple pattern, and then if you do not feel capable of making it up you will never be able to make anything at all, for even to the utmost novice in the art of dressmaking there can be no difficulty.

The plentiful advice on making-up hints at journalism's recognition of the limited experience and skills the readers may have gained in the schoolroom. They exploited the lure of easy style and fitted it to the pockets and lifestyles of busy women. For women whose school needlework lessons seemed dull and unproductive, by comparison these paper patterns offered a seductive combination of economy and ready fashion. By the same token sewing machines were sold in a variety of models and prices to meet different needs. Most town centres had specialist and semi-specialist retailers offering machines on easy terms with plentiful after-sales instruction and support for their customers. (Figure 2.2) Drapers' shops stocked a wide choice of sundries and materials, larger drapers frequently meriting separate departments, for example, for silks and 'Manchester' goods. Cheaper materials could be had from smaller traders and market stalls.

Figure 2.2. Sewing machines for sale with free gifts in Hove, Sussex. *The Journal of Domestic Appliances, Sewing Machine and Cycle Gazette*, 1 August 1910. By permission of the British Library.

The market in publications for home dressmakers in these years successfully consolidated strategies initiated in the last two decades of the nineteenth century. The US company Butterick had a trading operation in Britain which proved a model for others. They quickly saw a trading advantage in directly linking their production of dressmakers' paper patterns to retail outlets and to a series of periodicals and seasonal catalogues, all of which utilized a large mail order supply business. Paper patterns were ideal items for mail order and also worked well as incentives for buying periodicals by being easily inserted as free gifts. In the early years of this century we see London-based companies continuing to develop their own variations on this basic model (Figure 2.3). Weldon's, for example, published a whole stable of long-lived periodicals, such as *Weldon's Illustrated Dressmaker* which ran from 1880–1935. Leach's followed a similar trend. The market was nuanced in its target consumers. In their own particular social hierarchy, *Fashions for All, Myra's*

Figure 2.3. A home dressmaking guide and five patterns came free with *Mother and Home* in February 1916. By permission of the British Library.

Journal, The Lady and *The Queen* were consonant with more expensive aspirations than *The Girl's Friend* or *Mother and Home,* for example, which addressed less advantaged readers. These magazines in total and the patterns associated with them suggest a considerable range of social difference in readerships. Like Butterick, *Fashions for All* launched a successful high profile shop for their paper patterns in London's West End in 1908, including a 'Cut-to-Measure' pattern service. (Dilnot 1925: 36) Most of the magazines invoked Paris with some frequency to emphasize that their finger was on the pulse of fashion. Despite lingering arguments in the trade press in the early years of the century about the intrinsic merit of advertising, it was mass advertising for mass circulation which fuelled these magazines. Circulation figures are notoriously unreliable at this time (Reed 1997: 129) but in a rare certified disclosure the monthly *Fashions for All* claimed over 191,000 per month. (Newspaper Press Directory 1909: 290) There were upwards of fifteen London-based magazines circulated nationally at any one time in which home dressmaking was predominant or an important feature.

It is likely that sales were helped by the magazines developing the specialist target group of adolescent girls. They offered features or specialist supplements for 'tomorrow's woman' with attractive pattern styles for this age group, pointing out to mothers the long-term benefits of feminizing teenage girls by getting them to sew and budget. They also highlighted the economies and advantages of home dressmaking in fitting or disguising awkward and fast-growing body shapes. The rhetoric here echoed the recognition and problematizing of adolescence evident in the new and copious literature on the subject. (Dyhouse 1981) This in turn often reflected the fears expressed in some quarters about the potential damage to traditional middle-class feminine attributes done by waged work, the vote and perceived acceleration in the pace of modern life. The home dressmaking magazines appeared to offer their readers some respite from such fears through a measure of practical control over important aspects of adolescent consumption. Some appeals were made to teachers to use the pictures and patterns to overcome resistance to sewing lessons. 'The children will talk, play – anything during needlework hour – rather than attend to their stitching. "Sewing is dull" they say, but they would not find it so if, instead of being set to sew endless seams, they were allowed to make simple little garments [. . .]' using a 'pretty picture' and 'an interesting pattern.' (*Fashions for All*, July 1909) At the same time this magazine seized the opportunity to stress the importance of its ready supply of new ideas for needlework teachers hoping to impress the school inspectors.

In conclusion, given the crowded and demanding lives of many Edwardian women, one incentive for home dressmaking seems likely to have been a shortfall in the quantity or dissatisfaction with the quality, style or price of ready-made clothing. Developments in waged work for women created new needs partly met by home dressmaking. Fashion was taking deeper root in popular culture. Commercial interests already established in the nineteenth century made vigorous efforts to link their home dressmaking products to the consumption of fashion. Aggressive marketing of stylish paper patterns and allied magazines of practical advice helped to give it a fashionable gloss.

The significance of home dressmaking in these various contexts could be more fully understood by seeing it within the wider repertoire of clothing acquisition and value, but it is difficult to correlate the practice with any firm trend in the consumption of clothing generally. We must look to economic historians for these broader studies. Although they are agreed that more work is necessary before trends can be ascertained, there is a useful guideline which says that consumption of clothing as a proportion of household expenditure remained fairly constant between 1880 and 1914. (Godley 1995: 52) However, there is no reliable picture of national trends in clothing consumption to tell us how households divided their expenditure between, for example, piece goods for home dressmaking and ready-to-wear garments. Nevertheless, evidence from other sources can be used to see how home dressmaking figured for individuals within their clothing strategies. As has been said in another context, 'working men and women doubtless continued to dream, to "think" and to use their goods with different accents'. (Agnew 1993: 31) Far from becoming marginalized by the mechanized mass production of ready-made clothing, home dressmaking can be said to have played a productive and crucial role in the economies and cultures of a wide range of households.

Notes

1. The following are examples of exceptions: Rolley (1990); Wilson and Taylor (1989: 43–73); Hall (1992: 138–53, 188–201).

2. Edward VII acceded to the throne in 1901 and died in 1910. In this chapter I extend the term 'Edwardian' from 1901 to the First World War. For broad introductions to the period, see Beckett and Cherry (1987) and Thompson (1992).

3. For insight into the experience of class, respectability and community, see the documented oral history in Thompson (1992), Thompson (1981), Roberts (1977, 1984); see also Chinn (1988), Davies (1992), Lewis (1984) and Ross (1985). Social class and the socialization of girls is explored in detail in Dyhouse (1981).

4. The anti-sweating campaign, the case for Trade Boards and minimum wages and concerns about the widespread social effects of urban poverty produced reports such as Lady Bell (1911), Meyer and Black (1909), Black (1915). They represent a rich source of information about working women's lives, though cast largely in terms of middle-class concerns. As a source for working-class dress history in particular they are useful but with some obvious limitations.

5. See parallels with Peter Corrigan, 'Gender and the Gift: the case of the family clothing economy' in S. Jackson and S. Moores, eds, *The Politics of Domestic Consumption: Critical Readings*. Prentice Hall/Harvester Wheatsheaf, London (1995).

6. For example, the census of 1901 noted that female clerks, to take just one group, had trebled in number since the previous census. Growth continued until in 1911 the census recorded 179,000 women clerks.

7. I am preparing for publication a study on this and similar reports of the period.

References

Agnew, J.-C., (1994), 'Coming up for air: consumer culture in historical perspective' in Brewer and Porter, eds, *Consumption and the World of Goods*, London: Routledge.

Anderson, G., ed., (1988), *The White-blouse Revolution: Female Office Workers since 1870*, Manchester: Manchester University Press.

Beckett, J. and Cherry, D. (1987), *The Edwardian Era*, London: Phaidon Press and Barbican Art Gallery.

Bell, Lady (1911), *At the Works: A Study of a Manufacturing Town,* London: Nelson Shilling Library.

Black, C., ed., (1915), *Married Women's Work, being the report of an enquiry undertaken by the Women's Industrial Council*, London: Bell.

Board of Trade (1911), *Accounts of Expenditure of Wage-earning Women and Girls*, London: HMSO.

Brewer, J. and Porter, R., eds, (1994) *Consumption and the World of Goods*, London: Routledge.

Bronner, S. (1989), *Consuming Visions: Accumulation and Display of Goods in America 1880–1920*, New York: Norton.

Burman, B. (1994), 'Home Sewing and '*Fashions for All'*, 1908–1937' in *Costume*, No. 28.

Chapman, S. (1993), 'The Innovating Entrepreneurs in the British Ready-made Clothing Industry' in *Textile History,* 24 (1) pp. 5–25.

Chinn, C. (1988), *They Worked All their Lives: Women of the Urban Poor in England, 1880–1939*, Manchester: Manchester University Press.

Collet, C. (1902), *Educated Working Women*, London: King.

Davies, A. (1992), *Leisure, Gender and Poverty: Working Class Culture in Salford and Manchester 1900–1939*, Buckingham: Open University Press.

Davin, A. (1978), 'Imperialism and Motherhood' in *History Workshop Journal*, No. 5, Spring.

Davy, T. (1986), "A Cissy Job for Men; a Nice Job for Girls': Women Shorthand Typists in London, 1900–39' in eds. L. Davidoff and B. Westover, *Our Work, Our Lives, Our Words: Women's History and Women's Work*, London: Macmillan.

Dilnot, G. (1925), *The Romance of the Amalgamated Press*, London: Amalgamated Press.

Dyhouse, C. (1981), *Girls Growing Up in Late Victorian and Edwardian England*, London: Routledge.

Fine, B. and Leopold, E. (1993), *The World of Consumption*, London: Routledge.

Fraser, W. (1981), *The Coming of the Mass Market, 1850–1914,* London: Hamish Hamilton.

Glennie, P. (1995), 'Consumption within Historical Studies' in D. Miller, ed., *Acknowledging Consumption: A Review of New Studies*, London: Routledge.

Godley, A. (1995), 'The Development of the UK Clothing Industry, 1850–1950: Output and Productivity Growth' in *Business History* Vol. 37, No. 4.

Hall, L. (1992), *Common Threads: A Parade of American Clothing*, London: Little, Brown and Company.

Holcombe, L. (1973), *Victorian Ladies at Work: Middle-Class Working Women in England and Wales 1850–1914*, London: Archon Books.

John, A., ed., (1986), *Unequal Opportunities: Women's Employment in England 1800–1918*, Oxford: Blackwell.

Keep, C. (1997), 'The Cultural Work of the Type-Writer Girl' in *Victorian Studies*, Vol. 40, No. 3.

Lancaster, B. (1995), *The Department Store, A Social History*, London: Leicester University Press.

Lemire, B. (1997), *Dress, Culture and Commerce: the English clothing trade before the factory, 1660–1800*, Basingstoke: Macmillan.

Lewis, J. (1984), *Women in England 1870–1950: Sexual Divisions and Social Change*, London: Harvester Wheatsheaf.

Lipovetsky, G. (1994), *The Empire of Fashion: Dressing Modern Democracy*, Princeton: Princeton University Press.

McCracken, G. (1990), *Culture and Consumption*, Bloomington: Indiana University Press.

Meyer, Mrs C. and Black, C. (1909), *Makers of Our Clothes: A Case for Trade Boards*, London: Duckworth.

Miller, M. (1981), *The Bon Marche, Bourgeois Culture and the Department Store, 1869–1920*, London: Allen and Unwin.

Minter, F. J. (1906), 'The Selection of Operators' in *The National Telephone Journal*, London: December.

Montagu, L. H. (1904), 'The Girl in the Background' in E.J. Urwick, (ed.), *Studies of Boy Life in our Cities*, London: Dent.

Morris, J. (1986), *Women Workers and the Sweated Trades: The Origins of Minimum Wage Legislation*, Aldershot: Gower.

Newspaper Press Directory (1909), London: Mitchell.

Pember Reeves, M. (1913), *Round About a Pound a Week*, London: Bell (republished 1979, London: Virago, with an introduction by Sally Alexander).

Pritchard, E. (1902), *The Cult of Chiffon*, London: Grant Richards.

Reed, D. (1997), *The Popular Magazine in Britain and the United States 1880–1960*, London: The British Library.

Richards, T. (1991), *The Commodity Culture of Victorian England: Advertising and Spectacle, 1851–1914*, London: Verso.

Roberts, E. (1977), 'Working Class Standards of Living in Barrow and Lancaster 1900–1914' in *Economic History Review*, Vol. XXX, No. 2.

—— (1984), *A Woman's Place, An Oral History of Working Class Women, 1890–1940*, Oxford: Blackwell.

Roberts, R. (1990), *The Classic Slum: Salford Life in the First Quarter of the Century*, London: Penguin.

Rolley, K. (1990), 'Fashion, Femininity and the Fight for the Vote', *Art History*, Vol. 13, No. 1.

Ross, E. (1985), '"Not the sort that would sit on the doorstep": Respectability in pre-World War I London neighbourhoods' in *Working Class History,* No. 27, Spring.

Rowntree, S. E. (1913), *Poverty: A Study of Town Life,* London: Nelson.

Sharpe, P. (1995), ' 'Cheapness and Economy': Manufacturing and Retailing Ready-made Clothing in London and Essex 1830–50' in *Textile History,* 26 (2), pp. 202–13.

Smedley, C. (1910), *Service, A Domestic Novel,* London: Chatto and Windus.

—— (1912), *Mothers and Fathers,* London: Chatto and Windus.

Steedman, C. (1986), *Landscape for a Good Woman: A Story of Two Lives,* London: Virago.

Strasser, S., McGovern, C. and Judt, M., eds (1998), *Getting and Spending: European and American Consumer Societies in the Twentieth Century,* Cambridge: Cambridge University Press.

Tebbut, M. (1983), *Making Ends Meet: Pawnbroking and Working Class Credit,* Leicester: Leicester University Press.

Thompson, P. (1992), *The Edwardians: The Remaking of British Society,* London: Routledge.

Thompson, T. (1981), *Edwardian Childhoods,* London: Routledge.

Thompson, T. ed., (1987), *Dear Girl: The Diaries and Letters of Two Working Women (1897–1917),* London: The Women's Press.

Tilly, L. A. and Scott, J. W. (1989), *Women, Work and Family,* London: Routledge.

Tressell, R. (1993), *The Ragged Trousered Philanthropists,* London: Flamingo. First published 1914.

Turnbull, A. (1987), 'Learning Her Womanly Work: the Elementary School Curriculum 1870–1914' in Felicity Hunt, (ed.), *Lessons for Life: The Schooling of Girls and Women 1850–1950,* Oxford: Blackwell.

Wilson, E. (1985), *Adorned in Dreams: Fashion and Modernity,* London: Virago.

—— and Taylor, L. (1989), *Through the Looking Glass: A History of Dress from 1860 to the Present Day,* London: BBC Books.

3

On the Margins: Theorizing the History and Significance of Making and Designing Clothes at Home

Cheryl Buckley

Making and designing clothes at home is a form of design practice common to many women. Throughout the twentieth century women have made clothes by hand, aided by a sewing machine finding space on the kitchen table, and squeezing sewing between other domestic responsibilities. The process of making and designing, the clothes themselves, and the ways in which they were worn, reveal aspects of women's identities. This chapter examines some of the methodological and theoretical questions which arise for design historians studying the ways in which working-class women made clothes for themselves, their families, and the local community in Britain between 1910 and 1960. It focuses on the life and design activities of Mary Skelton (neé Hunt) who lived in South Durham between 1897 and 1982 and Betty Foster (neé Halliday, born 1929) who has lived for most of her life in West Yorkshire.[1] Both women worked from home making and designing clothes: Betty Foster made clothes for herself and her family throughout her life, whereas Mary Skelton, who was trained by tailors and worked in her parents' small clothing workshop before marriage, made clothes for her family, but also for sale in her local village.

A number of familiar questions about women's relationship to design and to history resurface in this research, alongside some new ones. Most important is how can one write about the place and significance of this type of design within women's lives without merely replicating value systems that contribute to its marginalization? In this discussion of design, I am interested in the way that it functions as a process of material and visual representation and as an '*aide-mémoire*', a term used to highlight the way designed objects act as signifiers for memory. (Kirkham and Attfield 1996: 3) Linked to this is the question of my own motivations and role as I write about an activity which has special meaning for me as daughter and niece in a large family of women, several of whom made clothes at home.

Women's Histories: Identity, Place, Subjectivity

Arguably an account that addresses such questions requires a new way of speaking and a new position from which to speak, as a number of feminist writers have argued. (Alexander 1994; Braidotti 1994; hooks 1991; Massey 1994; Morris 1988; Roberts 1984, 1995; Steedman 1985)

> I am located in the margin. I make a definite distinction between that marginality which is imposed by oppressive structures and that marginality one chooses as site of resistance – as location of radical openness and possibility [. . .] We are transformed, individually, collectively, as we make radical creative space which affirms and sustains our subjectivity, which gives us a new location from which to articulate our sense of the world. (hooks 1991: 153)

Most of these writers have tried to conceptualize female subjectivity and the place of the female subject in historical writing within a contemporary theoretical context which is indifferent if not hostile to the notion of the subject. Indeed how to frame the subject and subjectivity and how to respond theoretically to the attack on these from post-modern theorists are questions which underlie this study. Feminists have been particularly interested in these questions because of their implications for feminist historical and critical studies. (Flax 1990; Moore 1988; Morris 1988) Although much can be said on the latter, it is surely significant that 'exactly at the moment when so many of us who have been silenced begin to demand the right to name ourselves, to act as subjects rather than objects of history, that just then the concept of subjecthood becomes problematic.' (Massey 1994: 215)

For this study, which deals with women who have been largely invisible in history, formulating some sort of theoretical position in relation to the subject is particularly important. Sally Alexander argues that subjectivity and sexual identity are 'constructed through a process of differentiation, division and splitting, and is best understood as a process which is in the making, is never finished or complete'. (1994: 107) Rosi Braidotti uses the terms 'figuration' or 'nomadic' to suggest the 'situated' nature of subjectivity: 'The subject is not an abstract entity, but rather a material embodied one [. . .] the embodied subject is neither an essence nor a biological destiny, but rather one's primary location in the world, *one's situation in reality.*' (Braidotti 1994: 238 italics supplied).

This history or account of working-class women who made clothes at home is shaped by the politics of my own 'location', my mother's and her family's.[2] Partly in response to this sense of personal involvement, but also because of the widely held perception that there is a crisis within feminism, the possibility of trying to speak more directly in a manner which connects with women outside academic discourse is very appealing.[3] As bell hooks said: 'I have been working to change the way I speak and write, to incorporate in the manner of telling *a sense of place*, of not just who I am in the present, but where I am coming from, *the multiple voices within me*'. (hooks 1991: 146, italics supplied)

A sense of place, of who 'I' am, and of how I interpret and represent the lives of others shapes this study of dressmaking, a significant cultural activity for countless women. Although women from across class boundaries made and designed things throughout their lives, this particular activity remains on the margins. This is compounded by the fact that the 'things' are clothes and they were made locally, mostly at home. The 'home' in which these clothes were made and designed was subject to change and its meaning was shaped and renegotiated over time, rather than remaining an idealized 'haven' in which essentialist notions of feminine identity were fixed. (Colomina 1992; Grosz 1995; Massey 1994; Spain 1992) For many women, it was a flexible space by necessity in which a kitchen or front room could double as a sewing space. Betty Foster, for example, used her sewing machine on a stool in the front room of her two up, two down terraced house after she was married. Various activities operated out of her home including a fish hawking business which she ran with her husband and his parents. This involved cleaning and gutting fish and dealing with invoices, orders and receipts.[4] She also made and designed most of her own clothes as well as her family's (my sister's and mine included) at home and she took on domestic and parenting responsibilities as well. Similarly the dressmaking workshop run from home by Mary Skelton's parents was a small-scale industrial enterprise, strictly organized with a labour hierarchy and labour divisions. From the same 'home', Mary's mother later ran a bakery as well as the dressmaking workshop due to changing family circumstances.[5] Clearly for both women 'home' was a more fragmented place than the frozen space of patriarchal mythology.

Different economically, the coalfields of South Durham before the Second World War, and the West Riding of Yorkshire after it, shared a sense of 'place' particularly for women. As Mowat argues, women suffered more than men during those economically difficult periods which dogged the coal industry after the Great War before enjoying some respite in the 1950s and 1960s. (Mowat 1987: 483–7) These mining areas were geographically isolated, largely rural but dominated by the huge industrial scars that were the spoil heaps. Dirt was endemic from the coal-fires, pit clothes, and the coal-processing and it was women who generally did battle to keep houses and children 'decently turned-out'. A strong sense of community dominated these mining villages, as large family networks and friends helped each other out. Substantial gardens and allotments produced vegetables to be sold and exchanged, often for other 'services' such as dressmaking. My father, in the large metal greenhouse inherited from his father and in his large garden, grew all manner of vegetables to feed his family and to sell locally or to give to the wider family. A sense of 'place' then is dominant in the lives of Betty Foster and Mary Skelton and it helped to form their relationship to dress-making. Dressmaking was often shared, done collaboratively, or exchanged for another essential commodity.

For feminist historians, the 'specificity', which emerges from such 'situated' or local knowledge, enables one to 'identify the gaps, the silences in histories – not only in the hope of restoring a fuller past, but to write a history which might begin from somewhere else'. (Alexander 1994: 234) Arguably home dressmaking, as one of these silences, could provide a key for those attempting to speak from somewhere else, and as bell hooks suggests, to speak in a different manner. To write a fuller account of home dressmaking requires a change in the nature and manner of the debate regarding what constitutes design, who is the designer, and how we understand the meaning and significance of design. The activities of the home dressmaker and the products which resulted do not correspond neatly to 'typical' design methods or archetypal objects. Also the designer's role is much more negotiated and divergent than the usual 'model' and the value and significance of the designs cannot be assessed using criteria which stress innovation, commercial success or viability and uniqueness.

Arguably dress and dressmaking are cultural sites where identity, place and memory figure prominently. As designed objects and as a design method, they are 'unspeakably meaningful', yet undervalued by historians. (Carlyle 1931) In talking to people about their lives, the significance of specific items of dress is readily apparent. Older women recalling their lives in the 1920s and 1930s, for example, although imprecise about some events, could readily describe those for which clothes held special significance, such as what they wore for particular dances, the colour shades of their going-away outfits, and how their husbands dressed when they first went out together. My mother still talks lovingly of the shop-bought red coat which was my father's first gift to her in early courtship. Memory is clearly one way of trying to glimpse individual subjectivity alongside more orthodox methods. 'Life histories, as they tell us something of what has been forgotten in cultural memory, always describe, or rehearse a history full of affective subjectivity. As with a poem, they may suggest the metonymic signs of femininity particular to a generation.' (Alexander 1994: 234)

Taking a more subjective view which draws on feelings and memories provides a way of thinking differently about the individual meaning of clothes and offers a justification for revaluing this particular design activity which is cross-generational, connecting mothers, daughters, aunts and sisters. As Juliet Ash has argued, 'clothes relate to our feelings more than perhaps any other designed artefacts, and thus require "subjective" as well as "objective" analysis.' (Ash 1996: 219) These generational ties which can be mapped out in the history of home dressmaking give an insight into the broader history of women's lives as well as the peculiarities of individual ones. Home dressmaking can provide a context for exploring family relationships, after all it is an activity in which women learn and teach each other skills which form their feminine identities.

Memories and written and oral accounts of individual life histories are methods which enable the particular meaning of dressmaking to be interpreted. Although few actual garments remain, family photographs can provide a useful prompt for remembering and reconsidering the significance of individual designs and the circumstances of their production and consumption. (Kirkham 1996: xiii–xiv) Although I interviewed my aunt, Betty Foster, and my mother, June Buckley, formally for this research, my knowledge and understanding of the role of dressmaking in their lives is cumulative and based on memory and it is difficult to separate the formal and informal parts of that knowledge.[6] Dressmaking has been an important activity throughout my family life and I have sharp memories of particular garments – their production and their consumption.[7] This personal involvement gives me a keen sense of responsibility about interpreting their particular dressmaking activities and in locating them as 'subjects' in history, albeit as 'nomadic', differentiated and incomplete ones.

Dressmaking in Women's Lives

My aunt, Betty Foster, was born in 1929, one of ten. Betty, and her sister June Buckley (my mother), went into domestic service after leaving school where they learned numerous 'traditional' female skills. Betty worked for the racehorse owner and distiller Johnny Walker at his house 'Merry Lodge' in Newmarket and my mother worked for the father of England cricketer Norman Yardley in the nearby mining village of Royston in Yorkshire. Neither were taught to cook, clean or sew by their mother, although both taught their own daughters.[8]

Betty learned to use a sewing machine when she was in domestic service as a parlour maid. The machine was normally reserved for use by the lady's maid, but Betty was allowed to use it to make up her first dress. This was machine- and hand-sewn, cut with a pattern from a piece of checked material sent by Granny Davenport, her paternal grandmother. After she returned from Newmarket in 1949–50 to work with my mother at Blakey's wallpaper shop in nearby South Elmsall at her father's instigation, Betty taught my mother to sew and knit.

Once married (Betty in 1954, and June in 1955), they divided the knitting and the sewing between them – generally Betty sewed children's clothes and June did the knitting, although Betty, who could cut her own patterns, would also cut out fabric for June to make up.[9] Betty learned to cut patterns through practice. She would take clothes apart to cut patterns from them and she would borrow friends' clothes and cut patterns from them turned inside out. She was particularly fond of pleats, and she inserted pleats of all types into her designs.[10] (Figure 3.1) Betty clearly *designed* clothes as well as *made* clothes. She not only designed the overall form (often adapted from one seen in the High Street), she carefully chose fabrics and colours, as well as selecting and combining specific design features for sleeves, necklines, waistlines, belts, yokes and pleats.[11] My mother, in contrast, had a more limited role. She selected and bought fabrics and colours, but she largely made up the clothes that Betty had designed and cut out, although there was always discussion between the two sisters as to the overall shape and design of each particular item. However, in knitting, June took on a more creative role by adapting and developing her own patterns and by combining stitches to her own designs. Between them, they supplemented their husbands' incomes – June married a miner and Betty married a market stallholder who sold tripe and twin sets![12]

After marriage, Betty had been given a Singer hand sewing machine by her husband's aunt which she used throughout the next decade making clothes for her own daughter, Alyson (born 1962) and for my sister Michelle and me, (born 1959 and 1956, respectively). Both my younger sister and I were dressed through childhood in mainly home-made clothes. It is important to emphasize that this was not always down to cost as neither family were particularly poor.[13] Rather it was due to the apparent shoddiness of much shop-bought clothing which were turned inside out before buying to check that the seams were well sewn.[14]

My mother taught her daughters to sew and knit and as a teenager I made all manner of clothes to be 'in fashion' and there are still instances when I'm prepared to get my sewing machine out (bought for my twenty-first birthday by my parents).[15] My mother dressed my sister and myself very smartly mainly in home-made clothes, but on passing my eleven-plus examination, which would take me to grammar school and beyond, my reward was not a satchel and books like my more serious-minded peers, but a brown trouser suit from C&A worn with an orange blouse.[16]

Mary Skelton (1897–1982) made clothes throughout her life: before marriage as paid work both outside the home and inside the home in her parents' clothing workshop and then after marriage from her own home for her husband, her three children Ronald, Rose and Gwenyth, and for local people. Mary Skelton's experiences are particularly interesting in the context of this discussion because she had formal training as a tailoress both in her parents' business and with tailors in Stockton and Middlesborough. Her life was characterized by hard work due mainly to changing family circumstances and because her husband was poorly paid. Her father, George Hunt, was an itinerant farm labourer from Cheshire who moved to Stockton to work in the engineering industry. Instead he learned tailoring skills, eventually running a small workshop from home with his wife, Elizabeth, making pinafores (he was known as the 'pinny man'), black stockings, pit socks, tablecloths and bloomers. As well as the clothing workshop, they also ran a bakery from adjacent buildings.

By the age of twelve, Mary Hunt was working in the family business, although still attending school:

> By 10 Mother got me my own button-holer and my own knitter, as well as a scaled down sewing machine. The 'finishing off' things were put on a big chair, and my heart would sink! First: I had to do all those dratted buttons and holes. A best pinafore took 2 on the yoke, 1 at the waist. For bloomers 1 at each knee, 2 on the swiss band, and 2 more at the back flap. I hated bloomers. (Skelton 1996: 11)

The system of production was small-scale and flexible.[17] Only Mary's mother, father and the 'top hand' made complete items and only her mother cut fabric, knowing exactly how much she could get out of yardage and how much profit would be made. Mary's father went out delivering clothes and collecting new orders and as a small child Mary had accompanied him on these trips around the south-west Durham coalfield, often being away for a week at a time. Mary recalls: 'Looking back I see I had a privileged lifestyle, though I had thought it mostly hard work. I never felt better than others at school, though I was much better dressed [. . .]' (Skelton 1996: 14)

In 1912, at the age of fifteen, Mary's life changed drastically. Following a business friend's defaulting on a loan for which Mary's father had acted as guarantor, the businesses had to be sold. George Hunt took a £5 single outward ticket to Canada to make his fortune. His wife, two daughters and a son had to look after themselves, although he sent a small amount of money each month to help out. With some determination and foresight, Elizabeth Hunt persuaded the tailors Coates and Sedgewick on Stockton High Street to take on Mary to gain her certificate of apprenticeship without the normal £25 premium. According to Mary:

> I felt exploited as I knew all of the trade and went straight onto bonus sewing but without the money. My day began at 8.30 am. A half hour midday for our sandwiches from home, and at 5 pm the employers gave us cups of tea and a jam and bread sandwich. We worked until 8.30 at night. By year two I got 1s 6d weekly. The third, up to a florin weekly. At the end of my time and the precious certificate I worked for them just long enough to become top hand at bodices, then to Hill Carters for more money. All of half a crown a week, and piece work. (Skelton 1996: 16)

Like many working-class women whom I've interviewed, Mary was prepared to move from job to job for better wages irrespective of the criticism which she attracted:

> Because money was tight at home, I did the very worst thing in the eyes of the Good Templars and the Salvation Army where I was a chorister. I started work for the Jews in Middlesborough! The flat rate of someone of my calibre was then 6s 0d weekly, but in no time at all I got to 'second' hand, and then 'top' hand again, and making 10s 0d plus bonus on top. The Jews were, in fact, the best employers I had. They provided us with tea for morning break, 45 minutes to have lunch [. . .] and more tea, and our working week finished at 9pm on Friday nights. (Skelton 1996: 16; Buckley 1990: 34–5)

With decent employment outside the home secured, Mary started making ladies' blouses 'at weekends, at night, between church, park walks and meals.' Mary and her mother aimed to undercut shop-made blouses:

> Slowly I gained customers by word of mouth, touting my goods around the back doors of the better off, or making up *my own pencil outlined designs* (italics supplied) with something just that bit different from the shops. Thus, between Mother and me we went in for custom made goods instead. I soon developed it into nightwear, chemises and other clothes [. . .] Days I acted as top hand at the Jewish workshop, four nights a week I worked on orders and we managed to live as decently as before, or nearly. (Skelton 1996: 17)

Mary Skelton married in 1915, aged eighteen. Her husband worked for the railway company in south-west Durham and the family lived in a railwayman's house at Hunwick Station just outside Bishop Auckland. When Mary married she gave up paid outside work, as was typical, but because of the low wages earned by railway workers, she continued to work from home making all her children's clothes and making clothes for local people. According to Gwenyth: 'Anything she had was kept for years, renovated, returned, and furbished up.'[18] She used an old Jones sewing machine and made her patterns using the Haslam system of home dressmaking which was a large kidney-shaped board which could be adjusted for different sizes and styles.[19] She was also adept at sketching designs from shops and then adapting elements from them to create an entirely new design for which she would produce a pattern. She never bought a paper pattern, although she copied designs of clothes from Pontings of London's catalogues to which her mother subscribed. This ability to cut patterns apparently just by 'the eye' was the result of years of first-hand knowledge of garment construction and design.

Rethinking the Evidence, Retelling the Story

Except for the notebook and her daughter's memories, there is little left to show for Mary Skelton's prolific activities as a designer, craftswoman and maker of clothes. There are a few family photographs which show Mary's designs including one of Mary with Rose and Gwenyth in Blackpool in 1939 (Figure 3.2). These photographs are the only record of her designs. Looking at them they appear to be 'nothing special' – just everyday clothes worn by working-class people between the wars – and yet they point to a significant part of this woman's life. Indeed the photographs and the accompanying narratives from Mary's diary and Gwenyth's testimony suggest the possibility of a different sort of history of fashion and clothing than that usually told. With interpretation, they can give us some idea of the hard work, the sense of value and pride, and the pleasure gained by women from designing, making, and wearing good clothes. In her notebook, Mary Skelton described the excitement of being a bridesmaid for her mother's sister, and the clothes that she wore: 'I was ever so proud, and mother made the dress in white silk, onto a square yoke. She also bought me real white buckskin shoes with pearl buttons. And she trimmed a white leghorn bonnet lined beneath the brim with pleated chiffon, the top trimmed with fabric forget-me-nots.' (Skelton 1996: 7)

Within my own family, there are more photographs which flesh out the record of what was made. There is a photograph of Betty Foster taken when

Figure 3.1. Betty Halliday at 'Merry Lodge', Newmarket, c. 1947, wearing a dress she designed and made herself. By kind permission of Betty and Wallace Foster.

she was in domestic service at Newmarket from c. 1947 wearing a dress which she designed and made in a green fabric with white spots, and pleats on a hip level yoke. (Figure 3.1) There are numerous photographs of my sister and I wearing clothes designed and cut by Betty and made up by my mother, June. One from 1957–58 (the year before my sister was born) on holiday at Cleethorpes, in which I am wearing a hand-sewn sleeveless dress in deep lemon, orange, pink and green made up by my mother from pieces cut by Betty, and my mother is wearing a homesewn navy and white gathered skirt. A 1962 photograph (Figure 3.3) shows my sister and I aged three and six with our mother and her friend Joan and her children on a 'club trip' to the Yorkshire coast.[20] My sister and I are wearing lemon and white crepe check homesewn dresses, again cut out by Betty. A 1964 photograph from a holiday at Mablethorpe's Golden Sands Caravan Park when we stayed in Betty's caravan, shows my sister and I wearing blue glazed cotton dresses which my mother made up from Betty's cut out pieces. We're also wearing my mother's hand-knitted cardigans in pale blue.

Figure 3.2. Mary Skelton at Blackpool on holiday c. 1939 with her daughters Rose and Gwenyth. By kind permission of Gwenyth Batey.

Histories which deal with artefacts and lives like these are fairly uncommon. They fall between the gaps of disciplines, or they are women's history, local history, anonymous history. To compound this, these subjects are difficult to research because sources are limited. Although latterly museum curators have begun to address the gaps in their collections, past conventions of museological practice reinforced a hierarchy within fashion by privileging the designs of named individuals, high profile boutiques, and garments which are culturally or technically innovative.[21] In addition there are few testimonies of working-class women who designed and worked at home for the family.[22] Clothes made by women for consumption in the home by their families or for consumption in their local communities had only limited value, both in terms of exchange value and aesthetic value. With regard to the latter they were rarely innovative, they were usually eclectic in design being copied from numerous sources and they were not normally unique. Indeed Betty Foster and my mother worked collaboratively, thereby rendering attribution difficult.

Figure 3.3. The 'club' trip to the Yorkshire coast, 1962. Left to right: Michelle Buckley, June Buckley, Cheryl Buckley, Sharon Kemp, Joan Kemp and Avril Kemp. Michelle and Cheryl are wearing dresses designed and cut by Betty Foster and made up by their mother. By kind permission of June and Derrick Buckley.

Furthermore they tended not to be made from sumptuous materials, and although they were often of excellent quality, they were recognizably hand-made. These designs did have special qualities which gave 'added value' for their wearer – they were exclusive in that the unique combination of design elements, materials and colour was distinctive to that one particular garment – however, in a period in which shop-bought clothes had a great deal of cachet, they were looked down upon as 'home-made'. With regard to exchange value, even when these type of clothes were made and sold as part of the local economy, they were part of the unofficial economy and not easily quantifiable.

Although feminists have problematized questions of history, value, power and identity in order to recover and explore aspects of women's social, cultural and political lives which remain unarticulated or have been under-stated, the women home dressmakers that form the focus of this study are barely remembered. Yet I would argue that such accounts can provide invaluable insights into aspects of British social, cultural and creative lives, and, in particular, changing feminine identities. The clothes which these women designed and made can hint at forgotten, individual subjectivities which belong not just to a specific generation, but also to a particular 'place'.[23] Mary Skelton's 'life history' as a home dressmaker provides an opportunity to identify some of the gaps to which Sally Alexander pointed. Both collective and individual memories, especially those focused on the family, play a crucial part in elucidating the importance of home dressmaking to Betty Foster and my mother. These memories are partly shared by me, although their feelings for each other – shaped by the hardships of their childhood and adolescence – permeate their life histories. Today Betty Foster recalls her designs for home-made clothes with great clarity: she remembers the fabrics, the colours, and the design details (especially pleats). With my mother, she shares the memory of their lives through the clothes that they made. Together they recounted for me their connected histories through an account of their burgeoning dressmaking and knitting prowess which saw them through domestic service, shop and factory work, courtship and marriage, children and family, only slowing down in recent years. With caveats, I think that there is a persuasive case for pursuing and exploring 'those inter-generational lineages of mostly oral and feminine identification and exchange' through the history of something so ordinary as home dressmaking. (Alexander 1994: 234)

In conclusion, studying marginalized creative activities such as home dressmaking, throws a number of theoretical themes into sharp relief for those interested in feminist design histories. In particular, it highlights the fact that the history of making clothes at home is not just about the technologies of production and the processes of consumption, rather it is about design as a mechanism for the material and visual representation of feminine identities. It raises certain questions about the different tools that feminists might use to write about those identities and the different places that they might speak from as historians in order to locate a renegotiated female subjectivity at the centre of the historical narrative rather than on its margins. For the women that I have spoken to for this study, making clothes marked out different stages of their lives, connecting feelings and memories with family and friends. It related intimately to the specific places and locations in which they lived, rather than just the chronological, temporal sequence of their lives. Dressmaking defined various stages in Mary Skelton's, Betty Foster's and my mother's lives and the meaning of this is inextricably tied to their 'personal landscapes', just as it also connects to mine. It is this interconnectedness which places a responsibility on us to construct historical accounts which address the gaps, the silences and the margins of our disciplines.

Notes

1. I came upon Mary Skelton's own story during oral history research on cultural identities in north-east England undertaken as part of a larger project in the Department of Historical and Critical Studies at the University of Northumbria. (See Buckley 1996) Betty Foster, a home dressmaker from the mid 1940s, is my mother's sister, and I was prompted to elicit her story as I became involved in research connected closely with my own personal history. My mother, June, is the third eldest of seven sisters and three brothers, Betty is second eldest. They were brought up in South Hiendley in the mining area of the West Riding of Yorkshire.

2. Pat Kirkham (1995) has written on a similar theme. I gratefully acknowledge her help and many useful suggestions for this chapter.

3. There has been a spate of recent newspaper articles covering the so-called 'crisis' in feminism, although as one writer pointed out, feminism has been described as being in crisis at numerous times throughout the century. However, as well as the classic post-feminist line, that feminism is now defunct as the quest for equality has been achieved, there are other more persuasive arguments that it is overly academic, detached from women's experiences, and too middle-class. Arguably there is still a need to write accessible and interesting accounts of women's history which connect with their lived experiences. For example, Linda Grant 'Black, white and shades of grey' and ensuing letters in *The Guardian*. (Tuesday 3 June 1997: 8)

4. The preparation of fish for hawking was mainly done in an adjacent shed, although inevitably these activities spilled over into the domestic spaces of the home. The house in question was on Highfield Road in Hemsworth, West Riding of Yorkshire. Interview with my aunt, Betty Foster and my mother, June Buckley, 29 May 1997.

5. Interview with Gwenyth Batey, 30 January 1996. Letter from Gwenyth Batey to Cheryl Buckley, 5 December 1992.

6. Mary Skelton and Betty Foster provide an interesting comparison in terms of their approach to dressmaking over a period spanning 1915 to 1965. Their lives and dressmaking skills and designs can be glimpsed from diaries, oral accounts and photographs. I first talked to Gwenyth Batey, Mary Skelton's youngest daughter, in 1992–93 after she had written me a ten page letter (interestingly Gwenyth is one year older than my mother). When we met, she showed me family photographs and a hand-written notebook in which her mother had kept recollections of her life, which Gwenyth subsequently transcribed for me. Interview with Gwenyth Batey, 30 January 1996. Letter from Gwenyth Batey to Cheryl Buckley, 5 December 1992. Mary Jane Skelton's recollections, transcribed by her daughter, Gwenyth Batey, February 1996. I also have a number of family photographs which Gwenyth and Rose allowed me to copy. I would like to record my thanks to Gwenyth for all her help and to Rose and Gwenyth for access to the photographs.

7. I have a strong bond with my aunt after spending considerable time with her as a child before her own daughter was born. Typically, when my daughter, Kate was born, she sent me a bolt of woollen 'tartan' fabric, which she had bought on

holiday in Scotland, for me to make up for Kate.

8. Interview with my aunt, Betty Foster, and my mother, June Buckley 29 May 1997. Apparently their mother was too busy looking after ten children to teach them much, although she did show them how to make peg rugs using waste pieces of fabric and old clothes.

9. Interview, 29 May 1997, Foster and Buckley. Both Betty and my mother recall only being bought new clothes every Whitsun. These were bought from shops or they were made up by a local dressmaker, Mrs Goodyear.

10. When I saw her on 22 August 1997 to look over family photographs for this article, she drew and described numerous types of pleats that she had inserted into garments.

11. Shopping for fabrics usually took place on Barnsley and Hemsworth markets. Foster and Buckley, 29 May 1997.

12. My mother and Betty bought twinsets from his stall on South Elmsall market.

13. My father, for example, was in work throughout his life until he retired from the mines in 1985. He was a faceworker and earned relatively good wages. My parents shared, relatively, in the increased prosperity of post-war Britain, buying a television and fridge in the early 1960s and a second-hand Morris Traveller in 1967. They never moved from their first house, which they rented from the National Coal Board and subsequently bought in the early 1980s. Betty and her husband, Wallace, were in business after marriage working with his parents hawking fish from a van around the nearby mining villages. They put down a deposit on a house in 1955, bought a Ford Prefect in 1956 and in 1957 bought a caravan. Foster and Buckley, 29 May 1997.

14. They shopped for clothes in nearby large villages such as Hemsworth and South Elmsall and at the Co-op in Barnsley. Foster and Buckley, 29 May 1997.

15. In my teens and early twenties I made many of my clothes including skirts, jackets, trousers, and I knitted cardigans and sweaters well into my thirties. I've largely given up now, although I still make curtains occasionally.

16. Living in a close-knit mining community and surrounded by a large family, clothes were an act of defiance for me in adolescence.

17. In Stoke-on-Trent, it was common to find small pottery businesses of this type operating from out-buildings at home. As Pat Kirkham suggests, this type of small clothing workshop was not typical in other parts of the North-East of England, although it is typical of those in the East End of London, then a major centre of the garment trade.

18. Letter from Gwenyth Batey to Cheryl Buckley, 5 December 1992.

19. The fashion collection held by Tyne and Wear Museum Service in Newcastle upon Tyne has a substantial set of Haslam pattern boards and books covering children's wear, lingerie, blouses, skirts and accessories. Apparently these were patented by 'Miss F.A. Haslam, Ord House, Berwick-upon-Tweed & North East', as the 'Haslam System of Dresscutting'.

20. The 'club trip' was the annual outing organized by Havercroft Workingmen's Club. Normally the whole village would be deserted on these days.

21. Museums such as The North of England Open Air Museum at Beamish, County Durham, and Tyne and Wear Museums in Newcastle-upon-Tyne, Gateshead and Sunderland have begun systematically to collect working-class clothing, and 'typical' High Street fashions over the last ten or fifteen years, however due to previous collecting policies there are huge gaps in their collections of this type of clothing which are also now harder to fill.

22. Roszika Parker (1984) deals with embroidery, some of which was done at home, although interestingly her book still focuses on the exceptional rather than the ordinary.

23. Sally Alexander (1994: 234) writes of the way that life histories can 'suggest' the femininity of a particular generation, however, in my view, particular garments or ways of home dressmaking which were intimately connected with (and sometimes marked out) the stages of individual lives, can function similarly.

References

Alexander, S. (1994), *Becoming a Woman and other essays in 19th and 20th century Feminist History*, London: Virago.

Ash, J. (1996), 'Memory and Objects' in Kirkham, P. and Attfield, J. (eds) *The Gendered Object*, Manchester: Manchester University Press.

Braidotti, R. (1994), *Nomadic Subjects. Embodiment and Sexual Difference in Contemporary Feminist Theory*, New York: Columbia University Press.

Buckley, C. (1990), *Potters and Paintresses. Women Designers in the Pottery Industry, 1870–1955*, London: Women's Press.

—— (1996), 'Modernity, Femininity, and Regional Identity: Women and Fashion in the North East of England, 1919–1940' in Faulkner, T.E., (ed.), *Northumbrian Panorama: History and Culture in the North East of England* , London: Octavian Press.

Carlyle, T. (1931), *Sartor Resartus*, London: Curwen Press, (first published in 1831) also quoted in Wilson, E. (1985), *Adorned in Dreams: Fashion and Modernity*, London: Virago.

Colomina, B. (1992), *Sexuality & Space*, New York: Princeton Architectural Press.

Flax, J. (1990), *Thinking Fragments: Psychoanalysis, Feminism & Postmodernism in the Contemporary West*, Berkeley and Los Angeles: University of California Press.

Grosz, E. (1995), *Space, Time and Perversion*, London: Routledge.

hooks, b. (1991), *Yearning: Race, Gender and Cultural Politics*, London: Turnaround.

Kirkham, P. (1995), 'The personal, the professional and the partner(ship): the husband/wife collaboration of Charles and Ray Eames' in Skeggs, B. (ed.) *Feminist Cultural Theory. Process and Production*, Manchester: Manchester University Press.

Kirkham, P. and Attfield, J., eds., (1996), *The Gendered Object*, Manchester: Manchester University Press.

Massey, D. (1994), *Space, Place and Gender*, London: Polity Press.

Moore, S. (1988), 'Getting a Bit of the Other: The Pimps of Postmodernism' in Chapman, R. and Rutherford, J., *Male Order: Unwrapping Masculinity*, London: Lawrence and Wishart.

Morris, M. (1988), *The Pirate's Fiancee: Feminism, Reading, Postmodernism*, London: Verso.

Mowat, C. L. (1987), *Britain between the Wars, 1918–1940*, London: Methuen.

Parker, R. (1984), *The Subversive Stitch*, London: The Women's Press.

Roberts, E. (1984), *A Woman's Place: An Oral History of Working-class Women, 1890–1940*, Oxford: Blackwell.

—— (1995), *Women and Families: An Oral History, 1940–1970,* Oxford: Blackwell.

Skelton, M. J. (1996), *Recollections transcribed by her daughter, Gwenyth Batey,* Notebook, author's own collection.

Spain, D. (1992), *Gendered Spaces*, Chapel Hill and London: University of North Carolina.

Steedman, C. (1986), *Landscape for a Good Woman: A Story of Two Lives*, London: Virago.

Woolf, V. (1945), *A Room of One's Own*, London: Penguin. First published in 1928.

4

Making Modern Women, Stitch by Stitch: Dressmaking and Women's Magazines in Britain 1919–39

Fiona Hackney

'The entire affair of the sewing lesson seemed to me infinitely ridiculous. I thought longingly of my Mother running up dresses on her little old sewing machine, but nobody mentioned sewing machines here; you were expected to learn to sew by hand. It was part of your education.' (Elias 1978: 382)

'I think the difference between home-made and shop-bought clothes was the quality, cut and the fit of it and, of course, the finish; the finish never suited us because as far as we were concerned shop bought clothes were second rate.' (Mansell, 1996)

These recollections of the experience and significance of sewing and dress-making – the first, an account of sewing lessons at an elementary school in New Cross, South London as part of a broadly middle-class education in the 1920s, and the second, recounting a working-class woman's preference for home-made rather than off-the-peg clothing – signal divergent, and I would suggest, class-related accounts of sewing and dressmaking during the 1920s and 1930s. By this I do not mean that every middle-class girl found sewing a torture, or that every working-class woman chose to make her own clothes, but rather that the differing social, cultural, institutional and economic contexts in which home dressmaking was experienced affected the meaning of the activity and its results. While Eileen Elias struggled against the strictures of sewing classes (without the aid of a machine), still an essential component of feminine education despite her school's assurance to educate girls for careers as worthy as those of their brothers, Flo Mansell was proud of skills acquired during her dressmaking apprenticeship, which enabled her to make better-quality clothes and to dress in a style she described as 'a cut above'. For Eileen Elias, sewing represented the prescriptions and limitations of an ideology of femininity, whereas Flo Mansell viewed dressmaking as both creative and liberating and her use of her skills on her own behalf could in itself be seen as an empowering act.

Notions of style, new feelings and moods, took on a particular resonance for women in the inter-war period; while changes in legislation signalled greater independence there was often little perceptible difference in the quality of women's lives. (Lewis 1984; Beddoe 1989; Bourke 1994) Research into the lives and conditions experienced by working-class women such as that undertaken by Margery Spring Rice (1981), and Leonora Eyles (1922) suggests that poverty, hardship and ill health remained commonplace. However, one significant area of change was in the introduction of new forms of mass entertainment: cinema, radio, advertisements and the new consumerism, much of which was aimed at women, and in which women's magazines and their representation of practices of dressmaking played a central role.

Throughout the period a perceptible tension existed between changing structures of publishing, the style and address of magazines, and the composition of audiences. The aim of this essay is to examine this tension through a range of representations and readings of modern femininity, notions of fashionableness and practices of dressmaking, focusing on the popular women's magazines *Home Chat* , *Woman's Weekly* and *Woman*. Because of their dependence on advertising and consequent foregrounding of consumption, the magazines' construction of the ideal 'modern woman' was necessarily middle-class; however, as contemporary readership surveys show, the majority of their readers (the bulk of the new female readership) were working- and lower middle-class.[1] A particular focus will be the transforming relationship between differentiated gender and class identities constructed within, through, and around an emerging culture of modern femininity in magazines calculated to appeal to a mass audience, and the resulting shifts and changes in the meaning and significance of dressmaking.

Modern Magazines and Modern Femininity

The 1920s was a boom period for magazine publishing in Britain. In January 1920 the *Bookman* observed, 'We are being flooded by new monthly and weekly magazines and story papers', (*The Bookman* 1920: 348) while Punch simply dubbed it 'the magazine age.' (*Punch* 1924: 122).[2] The ascendancy of a handful of massively capitalized publishing firms, principally the Amalgamated Press (A.P.), Newnes, D.C. Thomson, and in the 1930s Odhams, accompanied the production of a mass of diverse publications aimed at women, often with relatively low circulations.[3] Mary Grieve, the editor of *Woman*, accounts for this in terms of the social and economic composition of readerships:

> Prewar divisions of taste and income set a strict limit on the number of like- minded women it was possible to gather together. Habits of cooking and entertainment, uses of leisure, aesthetic preferences, standards of home-making, vocabulary and hygiene all had so many shades of acceptance that there was some excuse for the proliferation of magazines, now so uneconomic as well as redundant. (Grieve 1964: 90–1)

Given the diverse nature of the audience, new strategies had to be developed to target, consolidate and, where possible, extend markets. Magazines were tied to specialized readerships and 'the reader' increasingly became a focus of attention. Alfred Harmsworth (later Lord Northcliffe), the creator of the A.P., the most prolific and innovative group dominating magazine publishing, had been one of the first to recognize both the enormous potential of targeting a female readership and the importance of catering to 'feminine interest' as a means of uniting and holding that audience. (Dilnot 1925: 23) His solution was to create magazines which promoted a discourse of domestic and decorative femininity (combining a 'daintiness that appealed to every woman' with practical advice) to as wide an audience as possible using the organizational structures and technologies of modern mass publishing. (Dilnot 1925: 22–3) A.P. published some ninety titles altogether with a combined circulation of more than eight million copies per week by 1931.

Feminine interest remained predominant as advertisers recognized women as an important consumer group, and publishers were keen to point out the particular advantages of their medium, stressing their ability to attract and influence female readerships. (Eley 1932: 166–82; Emanuel 1934) However, new appeals were required to maintain the interest of advertisers and audiences alike. During the 1920s 'service' magazines addressed to the 'modern woman', such as *Good Housekeeping* and *Modern Woman* (founded in 1922 and 1925 respectively), established a discourse of modern femininity through consumption, employing a wider visual vocabulary of photofeatures, new techniques of layout and design, and an increasing amount of display advertisements. (White 1970: 96)[4] Assumptions about the gendered nature of perception and women's 'natural' response to the emotional appeal of visual imagery meant that, as modern advertising became increasingly associated with selling through innovations in visual style, the modern became conflated with the feminine to the extent that femininity became *the* marker of modern consumer culture. (Wood 1927; Herrick 1939: 175)[5]

By 1938 the industry was in crisis, extreme measures were called for and successful firms prospered through innovation.[6] After studying European and American examples, Odhams' director Elias (later Lord Southwood) determined that the key to commercial success was a magazine which proclaimed its modernity through visual drama. (Minney 1954: 279–4) The introduction of new printing technologies enabled the firm to use fine quality four-colour photogravure for large runs of magazines (White 1970: 116–7). The result was *Woman*, the leading title of a 'new wave' in women's publishing. When *Woman* first hit the magazine stands in June 1937 its full-colour, large-scale format revolutionized the women's magazine market in Britain. Colour became a key tool in the creation and direction of a new market of female consumers, and colour reproduction itself became a powerful signifier of modernity. (Craik 1994: 97–8)[7] The 'new weeklies' promoted a new form of modern femininity, one of style and appearance, and were considered a most effective arena in which to display the spectacle, and play out the dramas of modern consumption for the mass of female consumers.

Modern femininity served the double purpose of attracting readerships while reinforcing advertisers' confidence, yet, it was an uncomfortable amalgam of modern desires (for career, social freedom) and what the magazines considered to be essential feminine instincts for husband, home and family. As such, it could be seen as a form of what Alison Light (1991) has called 'conservative modernity', or the 'ambiguous' modernity of suburbia which connoted both the new and the traditional. (Oliver et al. 1994: 77–83) The elision of the modern with the traditional was a popular theme used in contemporary advertising discourse in order to make new commodities acceptable by embedding them in reassuringly familiar images, values or modes of address. (Ohmann 1996: 206–8) The result was that nineteenth ideals of domestic and decorative femininity were grafted on to an aspirational consumer discourse of the modern, with all the tensions and contradictions which this implied.

Publishing and Dressmakers' Paper Patterns

In Britain pattern making grew up as a reader-service feature of women's magazines. Despite their availability in shops and department stores, during the inter-war period paper patterns remained a central feature of women's magazines, and were considered essential in targeting the lucrative 'feminine' market.[8] In 1908 the A.P., which claimed *Home Chat* had been the first paper to give free dressmaking patterns to its readers, organized a special department for fashion papers. Organized by Mr Leslie Cook, new titles included *Fashions for All*, *Home Fashions*, *Children's Dress*, *Mabs Fashions* and the *Bestway Series*. Bestway was a large business which employed a staff of one hundred preparing patterns and had a factory and plant sited in Whitefriars Street, London, with a retail outlet which operated first in the West End, then from a large building in Oxford Street West. Bestway was an enormous success; up to 20 million patterns were circulated every year, 'originating some millions of styles and playing a significant role in dressing the British public'. (Dilnot 1925: 22–3, 36)

Although a business concern in its own right, Bestway was publisher-owned and to a large extent designs were a result of the company's intimate partnership with A.P. magazines. Editors played a crucial and, on occasion, creative role in deciding what was to be featured in their magazines. Mary Dilnot, who as a young sub-editor worked on *Woman's Weekly* in the later 1930s, recalled how

> Bestway was a service department to any magazine, but they were certainly very closely associated to *Women's Weekly* because we did so much on them. Bestway produced their own patterns and designs were featured in the magazine. Sometimes the editor would commission a special design, in which case a freelance would come up with a range of ideas. The editor would choose and Bestway would make up the pattern – a Miss Taft used to run the Bestway business. Usually we would feature Bestway patterns and our fashion editor Miss Baumar, who was a freelance, would do the drawings for the magazine. (Dilnot 1995)

Dilnot emphasized the interdependent nature of pattern selling and magazine publishing. It was assumed that in the readers' eyes the magazine had to 'pay for itself': an economic or useful pattern could justify buying 'a little treat to enjoy the fiction'. (Dilnot 1995) Clearly it was no coincidence that dress and knitting patterns regularly featured on the front covers of magazines such as *Woman's Weekly* (Figure 4.1) with bylines announcing the latest serial. The format and style of these magazines meant that they were closer in appearance to knitting or dressmaking patterns than upmarket fashion magazines such as *Vogue*. Work and pleasure, practicality and fantasy were thus neatly elided in the story/pattern paper. Similarly, on the fashion pages drawings provided reliable information about the position of seams or the inclusion of pleats, while the captions made suggestions about colours and materials, creating a fantasy atmosphere and mood in the text.

Figure 4.1. Cover, *Woman's Weekly*, 5 November 1932. Dressmaking and knitting patterns were an important incentive for purchasing this magazine which was one of the most successful of the period. The range of 'looks' which could be achieved by adapting the basic pattern shows how dress patterns combined the economic benefits of mass production with the desire for individuality and difference. By permission of IPC.

Reading, Looking and Making Meaning

In an essay on the significance of interpretations and reworkings of the New Look by working-class women in the 1950s, Angela Partington defines mass-market fashion as a medium through which women were encouraged (or trained) to adopt differing identities, learning the process of masquerade. In addition, by consuming 'improperly' (that is according to their own needs, unknown to designers or fashion editors) they actively articulated class difference. (Partington 1992: 156) With its emphasis on making, dressmaking allowed plenty of scope for reworking and reinterpretation, and women stressed this aspect of using patterns. (Mansell 1996) However if, as Partington suggests, the making of meaning depends on specific contexts of use and can alter in differing communities and according to different cultural codes – in this case, the overlapping communities and cultures of modern femininity, dressmaking, and class – it may not be necessary to change the look of an object in order to alter its significance.

Theoretical work on consumption and reception suggests that the ways in which women look at, read and use texts are highly complex. Masquerade implies an acting out of images of femininity which require an active gaze to decode, utilize and identify with them. It thus proposes a simultaneous combination of identification and objectification, enabling a space to open up which allows the woman to be engaged enough to identify, while maintaining a critical distance (Partington 1992:156–7). Meanwhile, research on reading has demonstrated a resistance to media representations of femininity among female readers of mass culture. Knowledge of genres and how they work, or the practice of reading 'against the grain', enables readers to perceive fiction as just that, related to yet distinct from their own lives (Frazer 1987: 407–25; Radway 1987). The active and critical gaze, enabling the simulation or rejection of femininity presupposes knowledge of and, therefore, confirms the existence of a feminine cultural code. Before considering these ideas in relation to evidence of how women used dressmaking patterns and fashion pages, I wish to consider a range of representations of modern femininity constructed in women's magazines.

Mabs: The 'Ideal Modern Type'

Foremost amongst the strategies developed to encourage reader identification were a range of new ideals of modern femininity associated with the excitements of the city, new values of youth, activity and convenience. From the 1920s representations of the 'sporting girl' or the 'bachelor girl' were addressed to younger, single working women whose numbers increased during the period. (Beddoe 1989) Simple, comfortable, unrestrictive clothes, such as easy-to-make tennis dresses or easy-to-care-for town clothes for business, suited the needs, incomes, lifestyles and aspirations of this audience. Magazines regularly featured articles on women tennis champions such as Suzanne Lenglen, whose energetic, athletic style of play and revolutionary costume (short skirts, soft shoes and headband) were highly influential on manners and dress. Tennis styles were recommended for wear on and off the court, and fashion pages placed great emphasis on the importance of physical freedom, comfort and mobility: 'All sports, nowadays, are taken so seriously that anything in the least calculated to hamper movement or to get in the way of playing a hard game is ruthlessly set aside in favour of free-fitting skirt and easy upper parts.' (*Home Chat* 3 May 1924: 228) Following editorial advice and employing paper patterns, cheaper materials and less sophisticated cuts and accessories, it was easy for readers to replicate the sports styles of Patou or Chanel and thereby access the look of modern fashionability.

In 1924 *Home Chat* ran a competition using innovative strategies to bind dressmaking to notions of the modern and the feminine, prescribed and legitimated by the magazine. The espoused aim was to discover 'the ideal modern type'. (*Home Chat* 3 May 1924: 227) Named the 'Mabs Girl', she was to be selected from readers' photographs of themselves wearing Mabs (an editorial creation) designs, and these were to be printed in *Home Chat* over a period of months. Not only an inventive piece of marketing, this strategy enabled the magazine to construct a range of approved images of modern femininity while simultaneously appearing to dissolve the boundary between editorial and reader, by *literally* representing readers in the text. Despite the search for an 'ideal modern type', criteria for qualification was inclusive rather than exclusive:

[T]he famous dress artist and designer [. . .] does not use a model. She puts her very charming clothes on a figure that is to her the ideal modern type – plump, but slim, big-eyed, neat-haired, neat ankled, and *not too ravishingly beautiful to be unbelievable* [. . .] there must be lots of *Mabs types* about. Some are fair and some dark, some fat and some thin, some old and some young, some flappers, some matrons, but they have *the Mabs look*. (*Home Chat* 3 May 1924: 227)

Mabs represented an achievable ideal which was calculated to appeal to any or all *Home Chat* readers irrespective of age, colouring, or size; employing knowledge and skills acquired from the magazine to construct their appearance (dress patterns, hairstyles, pose), they too could become, and indeed demonstrably were, the ideal modern type. The Mabs types were emblematic of a standardized, mass produced culture of femininity which simultaneously offered the reliability of sameness, and appeared to accommodate difference and individuality. Mabs fashions were democratizing (making fashion and fashionability available to more women), encouraging women to manage their *own* appearance, yet the process was carefully managed by the magazine in order to reinforce its role as arbiter of modern taste and style.

Usefully, the photographs provide first-hand evidence both of *Home Chat's* concept of modern femininity and, at least some, of their readers' interpretations of this. (Figure 4.2) Hair, when short, was waved, modest and well-groomed, suggesting a practical yet romantic style; a restrained but

Figure 4.2. Mabs Types, *Home Chat*, 5 July 1924. This page shows readers' photographs sent in response to a competition to find the 'ideal modern type', run by Mabs the magazine's fashion and dressmaking editor. Wearing dresses made from Mabs Patterns, their poses demonstrate that they were well versed in the codes of fashionable style and appearance. Author's collection.

confident femininity, reminiscent of the pictures of royalty and aristocracy which featured on the magazine's editorial pages. Mabs modern ideal, although including the image of the flapper, was by no means revolutionary. Rather it reworked and updated the concept of the Lady which, as Margaret Beetham has observed, simultaneously offered itself as an image of radical equality and a mark of hierarchy. (Beetham 1996: 207) Incidentally, the sensational treatment which the flapper received in the national press during the period was totally absent, supporting Billie Melman's assertion that women's magazines absorbed contemporary notions of modern femininity, depoliticized and dramaticized them. (Melman 1988: 112)[9]

The success of competitions such as this depended on the peculiar ability of photography to integrate a sense of the real with the ideal, a quality with which contemporary fashion photographers were well acquainted. (Everard 1934) The self-conscious poses and the far-away, dreamy looks evident in readers' photographs demonstrate that they too were well versed in the language of fashion photography and advertising which, like the format of the periodical itself, both rooted them in the here-and-now and promoted them towards a potentially different future. While such images helped fix notions of modern femininity, the choice of the photographic medium itself aligned the modern with the feminine in significant ways. Through high profile campaigns such as those featuring the Kodak girl, roll film and hand-held cameras, targeted at a domestic female market during the period, women were rapidly becoming associated with modern lifestyles, new freedoms, and a new style of femininity. (Taylor 1994) Hand-held cameras were often advertised in *Home Chat* (28 September 1929: iii) and the informality of the readers' photographs, many of which were taken in outdoor locations, indicates their use. In the spirit of the Modernist dictum, 'the medium is the message', the modernity of the Mabs type was significantly underscored and reinforced by the decision to use readers' photographs.

Selling the Page: The Drama of Visual Consumption

The autographed articles of Alison Settle, *Woman's* first fashion editor,[10] emphasized the virtues of achieving a smart and practical look, simultaneously chic and inexpensive, which enabled women to make the most of themselves and 'look their best'. (*Woman* June 1937: 1) Together with *Simplicity* patterns, Settle's advice was described as 'style news by one who really knows' and sold to readers as part of a complete package, termed the 'Fashion Service'. (*Woman* 12 June 1937: 62) Later Settle was replaced by Anne Edwards whose background was in advertising. (Grieve 1964: 104) Despite Settle's commitment to practical fashion for the ordinary woman, the change was indicative of a move away from the notions of 'good taste' espoused by a design elite, towards a mass market magazine dependent on high circulations and advertising revenue and, as a consequence, promoting a new set of values and feminine ideals.

Such concerns were elaborated in a new fashion feature called 'Diagram Dressmaking', which gave straightforward instructions and a basic 'key' pattern to make a range of simple garments. The process of dressmaking became increasingly simplified and standardized, presupposing a wider and less skilled audience. Advice on fine discriminations of taste was replaced by information on how to cheaply and easily create a fashionable product which, at the same time, could be tailored towards individual requirements. The pattern for the 'pencil petticoat', for instance, was designed to be adapted according to the wearer's exact measurements. (*Woman* 25 September 1937: 11) Diagrams and black and white photographs replaced idealized artists drawings. The approach was one of practical steps to sophisticated style and the mood evoked by the model's pose had more in common with Hollywood glamour than Paris couture. Photography proved particularly useful in this respect for, while it was thought to bring a new sense of realism to images, in fact it served to construct the new feminine ideals with more authority. (Everard 1934)

The use of simpler technologies of dressmaking culminated in the cut-out dress offers introduced in 1937 with an artificial satin nightie for 4s 11d. (Grieve 1964: 205) Readers were invited to send off for ready-cut pieces of fabric; full instructions were given in the magazine, while photographs depicted each stage of assembling the garment. The pattern and style were as simple as possible. All designing was undertaken in *Woman's* own fashion department, as was the grading and sizing, which enabled the magazine to manage the choice of colour, style, quality of material, cut and accessories, serving to reinforce its role as a style authority. Mary Grieve stressed the democratic and mutually beneficial nature of the scheme, which rather than emphasizing the exclusiveness of dress, formed a 'bond' and a 'shared sense of achievement' amongst readers, fostering a 'sense of success' and strengthening the relationship between readers and magazine. (Grieve 1964: 203–4) As with the A. P. pattern department, what started as a sideline to the paper's activities developed into a big business in its own right.

On the fashion page the named expert was completely replaced by a standardized package: the 'Simplicity Pattern Service' (including patterns and the *Simplicity Sewing Book*). Promoted as 'the smartest and easiest way to good dressing', (*Woman* 25 September 1937: 46) the Simplicity Pattern Service promised women a smart, up-to-date appearance which, at the same time, signified good taste. In much the same way, mass produced commodities such as vacuum cleaners, or gas cookers were sold as a mechanical maids, enabling the modern housewife to perform domestic work without any loss of status. By the 1930s a sewing machine was a familiar item in many working-class homes. (Wilson and Taylor 1989: 95)[11] This, in addition to inexpensive patterns (from 9d to 1s; the *Simplicity Sewing Book* cost 1s), simpler styles and easy-to-follow instructions meant that more women had the opportunity to achieve a smart and 'professional' look. Despite growing anxieties about the status of home-made garments, and the idea that home-made was inferior,[12] Simplicity worked hard to reinforce the economic benefits of dressmaking and represent it both as a pleasurable and creative activity:

> Ask any well-dressed woman how she manages it in these days of so very limited incomes and she'll answer 'patterns' and be proud of it. It's the best way of achieving the perfect fit to suit yourself in such an inexpensive way – it's such fun, too, running riot among the bales of this season's brightly coloured woollens! (*Woman* 25 September 1937: 46)

The Simplicity Service replaced the fashion expert with a standardized guide to style, while offering the potential for diversity and individual interpretation. As with Mabs, women were commodified and addressed in the language of advertising as identifiable types, however, they were also provided with information enabling them to make their *own* decisions about style, cut, finish and material, and the skills with which to realize their ideas.

Mary Grieve (1964: 106–7) considered that editorial educated readers in making judgements as consumers, providing them with 'a background of knowledge and discrimination'. An active, informed and critical reader appeared central to her perception of how magazines worked. In order to understand something of how women, primarily working-class women, used these magazines, their fashion pages and patterns, I turned to two sources: oral history with women magazine readers, and a series of interviews undertaken by Mass-Observation during the period.

'Though We Work In The Mill We Like Good Clothes': Readers And Dressmaking

In 1940, as part of a Mass-Observation project investigating women's dressmaking during the war, P. F. began to explore influences on dress. (Mass-Observation 1940b, 1940a)[13] She concluded that the 'visual' media made the greatest impact on people, 'what they see about them in the streets, and what they read in their daily paper or twopenny weekly'. (Mass-Observation 1940c: 8–9). Interestingly, while most respondents considered films and film stars to be the major influence on fashion, when asked what affected them personally, interviewees acknowledged the importance of observation, the press, and 'fashion books' which were seen to offer attainable images, relevant to individual circumstances and local conditions.[14] Women were most ready to acknowledge the effects of the mass media on fashion, and were also more aware than men of the influence of the press and magazines; *The Daily Mirror* and *Woman* were mentioned most frequently. (Mass-Observation 1940c: 8–9)[15]

The results confirmed editorial assumptions about the importance of personal address and visual appeal, and underlined the degree to which magazines were integrated into the fabric of everyday life. In addition, they demonstrated the degree of resistance to external influences which women, in particular, claimed.[16] For instance, one young woman commented:

> I always look at them [magazines]. I only have that book *Woman*. I think *Woman* is one of the best. Well, really I would dress to suit myself. I think if you go in for fashion just because someone else is wearing it you never get anywhere. (Mass-Observation 1940c: 10)

That dressing 'to suit oneself' was the second largest category of replies from women seems to contradict their ready acknowledgment of the press and fashion books as a source of influence. However, I would suggest that this response signified the importance of making active, informed and critical choices about appearance or, at the very least, acknowledged the importance of other factors, such as economic considerations. It certainly contradicts the stereotypical notion of women as impulsive consumers ruled by emotions rather than intellect. At the same time, it underlines the desire for an individual appearance at the very time when new forms of production, retailing and promotion were increasingly standardizing clothing. The comment suggests a degree of assertiveness and independence of mind similar to that which I encountered amongst magazine readers I interviewed. While enthusiastically recounting how they used and collected dress and knitting patterns, they were reluctant to represent themselves as passive receivers of magazine messages; the word 'influence', in particular, was loudly rejected. Madge, who lived with her mother in Chatham in Kent and worked in London as a civil servant, stressed that magazines provided ideas which she would try out if she felt they were attractive, and realistic:

You'd think, oh yes, there's a nice idea, I'll try that out if it was possible – if it was out of my reach, I'd say blow that! I didn't feel that I had to be really glamorous or whatever. I think there was always the feeling that you wanted to look attractive ... I always wanted to look presentable. The magazines gave me ideas. (Taylor 1994)

I would suggest that a strong element of negotiation was, and is, involved both in deciding what constituted being 'presentable' or looking 'attractive' and in the process of reading or using magazines and dressmaking patterns. Magazines and their patterns were clearly important in providing a model of appropriate appearance – suggesting 'ideas' – yet their use and inter-pretation must be considered within the context of a range of other factors, equally as important in determining decisions about dress and appearance.

A larger Mass-Observation survey conducted with working-class families in 1939 (Mass-Observation 1939a)[17] reveals the use of magazines and home dressmaking as part of a complex network of activities including (interviewers are identified by their initials): purchasing clothes through clubs (G.W. 5 April 1939); the co-operative stores (C.M. 25 April 1939); repairing clothes (C.M. 9 May 1939); and dedicated regimes of window shopping (C.M. 5 April 1939).[18] Most often, the determining factor was the desire to be well dressed despite a severely restricted budget; as one young woman said, 'Though we work in the mill, we like good clothes.' (C.M. 5 April 1939; C.M. 9 May 1939)[19] The purchases of a young married winder are indicative of the complex pattern of decisions, activities and priorities involved in the creation of an up-to-date appearance:

This year she had a summer coat made by a friend, which saved money; at the same time she got gloves, bag, hat, shoes; the whole costing £3 about [. . .] (she) is making herself two dresses for holidays, washable cotton and silk [. . .] This year (she) didn't look much at shop windows before buying clothes, as (had) fixed up material and style with friend who made it. Takes *Woman's Weekly*; it features dressmaking and fashion; she learnt dressmaking for two years at night school after leaving school [. . .] (C.M. 9 May 1939)

To occasionally employ a dressmaker (often a friend) seemed to be normal practice and still worked out cheaper than shop-bought, allowing a little extra for the all important accessories. (C.M. 5 April 1939)[20] Most bought coats and items demanding greater dressmaking skills. For many, their mothers made their clothes; if they did make something themselves it would be a simple summer dress or washing frock in an easily worked fabric such as cotton or celanese (a synthetic fabric widely advertised in women's magazines). Those who made their own clothes had generally undertaken an apprenticeship or attended night school, which gave free access to 'dress books' (fashion magazines). (C.M. 25 April 1939; G.W. 18 April 1939)[21]

The women who displayed the greatest enthusiasm for magazines tended to be those interested in being fashionable and up-to-date, confirming magazines as a source for obtaining the latest information on styles quickly, easily and cheaply. They were usually younger, in their twenties or thirties, working and either living with their parents or recently married, for instance, a weaver earning about £1 per week, is described as being 'interested in her clothes and in being up to date [. . .] likes to look at fashion books; exchanges them with other girls'. (C.M. 8 May 1939) Whilst 'Bargain patterns' and the value offered by magazine patterns were an incentive for many (C.M. 25 April 1939), Madge Taylor observed: 'Of course the shop patterns were only thruppence. The attraction of the ones in the magazines were that they were modern. It was an up-to-date thing, it guided you about what to buy and that sort of thing.' (Taylor 1994) Unsurprisingly, being single was an important determinant in maintaining enthusiasm for fashion and, 'living up to the moment'.[22]

Dressmaking skills could give younger women some degree of independence in deciding the clothes they made and wore at a time when mothers were most often in charge of the family budget (including clothes) even until children left home, which for girls usually meant marriage and could be well into their twenties or later. (Lewis 1984)[23] As such, dressmaking could be experienced as a liberating, even subversive, activity enabling young women to define their appearance and identity without regard, or in direct opposition, to their mothers' opinions – a right of passage in the process of becoming a woman. (Alexander 1994) Many women I spoke to recalled how their mothers had disapproved of their reading, it was considered a waste of time when there were more important household duties to be done. Romance and fashion magazines were viewed with particular suspicion because of the nature of the adult world into which they initiated girls. (Lowdell and Huff 1994; Ash 1994; Randle 1994) More pragmatically, dressmaking also filled a gap for girls in the retail market. The Lancashire retailer R. K. reported that there was a lack of ready-made clothing (both in terms of size and style) for growing girls between the ages of thirteen and seventeen, who were increasingly deciding for themselves what they would wear. (C.M. 29 March 1939)

The pleasure of having 'good things', 'new things', 'something nice', 'quality at an affordable price', was reiterated often. A thirty-two-year-old mother of two who made all her own and her children's clothes said, '[I]f one buys a reliable pattern and good material things look very nice [. . .] in new things you feel on top of the world.' (G.W. 18 April 1939) The acquisition of new clothes was special and usually coincided with a social event, a holiday or a wedding. (C.M. 29 March 1939)[24] The prevailing practice was to buy a 'complete rig-out' once a year and this, rather than seasonal standardization, determined consumption (C.M. 25 April 1939)[25] Quality meant cut, finish and fit in order to achieve that all-important 'smart' appearance. Flo Mansell explained her preference for home-made rather than ready-made clothes:

> I made dresses, skirts, jackets, coats, I made the lot. Before the War people either had them made or made them themselves, if they could. There wasn't really an awful lot of ready-made that was of any consequence, if you know what I mean. If you bought ready-made it would be shoddy, you know. I suppose we were snobbish in a sense really. Well, we wouldn't have known any different because we didn't have any money at home, it was only because we saw how the other half lived you tended to think that anything else wasn't good enough, so if we could do it then we did [. . .] we did look smart because of our ability, and everybody in the road that couldn't do the same as us used to think that we were a cut above, only because our clothes were just that little bit better. (Mansell 1996)

Possessing something of 'consequence', looking 'smart', appearing a 'cut above': Flo's knowledge and skills as a dressmaker enabled her to perform a transformation of style which she associated with social class. Flo refers to herself as snobbish, yet she clearly differentiated between the fantasy world of the fashion images and the reality of her own life.[26] While, underlining the importance attached to dress and appearance in defining identity during the period, I would argue that such transformations of style must be understood within the social context in which they took place. The clothes Flo made had meanings specific to her social environment, the road she lived in, the Saturday night dance she went to. As with regional variations in consumption, the uses and meanings made by the social individual were something over which the magazine had little control.

Lastly, it is important not to underestimate the time and effort dressmaking involved. Flo enjoyed the activity and spent most evenings sewing and dressmaking, however, for a growing number of women this proved undesirable, or even impossible.[27] Miss M., a weaver in her forties who lived with her eighty-year-old mother and did all the housework after work, told Mass-Observation that she hated sewing, even putting a button on, and always bought ready-made clothes. (G.W. 5 April 1939) A survey conducted on home sewing in the mid-1940s indicated that home dressmaking was becoming increasingly rare: although 96 per cent of the sample of women of all ages did some sort of sewing, only 27 per cent were 'creative sewers', doing dressmaking rather than simply darning, patching and repairs. (Research

Services Ltd. 1947)[28] That a slightly higher percentage of AB income group housewives, and C-class non-housewives sewed suggests that sewing continued to be associated with higher levels of income and a degree of free time.[29] However, my discussions with women gave the impression that their reluctance to sew was often linked to their perception of their mothers' lives and their wish to live differently themselves; they had better things to do than sew at home, particularly with the greater availability of popular leisure activities such as the cinema and dancing. (Lowdell and Huff 1994; Ash 1994; Randle 1994) Meanwhile, changes in factory production enabling an increase in good quality, inexpensive ready-made clothing were putting local dressmakers out of business. (Wilson and Taylor 1989: 92–3) The decline in dressmaking simultaneously marked a decline in those nineteenth century ideals of femininity associated with, and learnt through, activities such as hand-sewing which Eileen Elias found so tedious and frustrating. However, the reality for a growing number of 'modern women' was that they had neither the time, patience nor, in some cases, energy to make clothes when they had more important, if not always more pleasurable, things to do.

Conclusion

As Wilson and Taylor observed (1989: 95), for *Woman's* editor Mary Grieve, who regarded herself as a feminist and 'left of centre', there was no conflict between feminism and commercial women's magazines. She was not alone in this, the new consumerism was widely perceived as progressive and empowering, bringing a higher standard of living and new freedoms to a greater number of people. Achieving a fashionable, smart appearance using mass produced dress patterns and ideas from magazines signalled success both as a consumer and as a woman. In their promotion of a range of new ideals through fashion and dressmaking women's magazines could be seen to be contributing to a culture of modern femininity which offered women new ways of visualizing themselves, new fantasies and desires, and the knowledge and skills with which to realize them. At the same time, the effect of magazines as educators of tastes and values must be understood within specific contexts of use and meaning-making. Integrated into the fabric of readers' everyday lives they competed with other, equally important needs, desires and necessities. In addition, women's knowledge of the magazine genre and dressmaking skills enabled them to decode, resist, adapt, or recreate mass produced ideals. Even for those with little money, being up-to-date and looking smart was important. It signified a sense of belonging, and of participating in the new commercial cultures of fashion and modern femininity.

Notes

1. A small number of surveys of the press which included women's magazines were carried out during the period: London Research and Information Bureau, 1927; Repford Ltd., *Investigated Press Circulations*, 1931–32; the Institute of Practitioners in Advertising conducted a *Survey of Press Readership* in 1939.

2. In her history of women's magazines, Cynthia White (1970: 309–16) lists fifty five new titles published between 1920 and 1939, in addition to the thirty-two already in existence. Forty-five were relatively short-lived, folding before the end of the Second World War, while a further fifteen disappeared in the mid-1950s and early 1960s, a period of marked change as magazine publishing faced a new era of women's liberation and competition from other forms of mass media, specifically T.V.

3. Arthur O. Richardson, *Modern Advertising*, Vol. 1. (1930s). Richardson (director of the advertising agent Samson, Clark and Co.) gave 'estimated sales' for *Woman's Weekly* – 380,000; *Home Chat* – 224,000; for 1938 Cynthia White gives (circulation figures) *Woman's Weekly* – 498,000; *Home Chat* – 127,000; *Woman* – 750,000, compared with over 3,000,000 for *Woman* in the 1950s and 1960s.

4. Service magazines were aimed at middle- and lower middle-class consumers; their main function was to render the woman reader 'intimate personal service', information and advice, with a secondary emphasis on entertainment. Other titles included: *My Home* (1928), *Everywoman's* (1934), *Woman and Home* (1926), *Woman and Beauty* (1930), and *Wife and Home* (1929).

5. Throughout the 1930s aspirational depictions of the modern appeared increasingly in cheaper weeklies. The A.P. published a weekly title *Modern Weekly* which combined romantic serials and consumer advice. Throughout the 1930s weeklies such as *Home Chat* and *Woman's Weekly* allotted ever more pages to advertising and included promotions for named products in editorial features.

6. In 1938 there were 234 weekly 'general interest' periodicals published in Britain, with a recorded weekly circulation of 18,635,000, a decrease from 21 million in 1935 (Kalder and Silverman 1948: 86, 96). A Gallop Poll concluded that only 21 per cent of the public read magazines regularly: '[T]he reasons for this were unclear, but it has been suggested to be the result of competition from other forms of consumer spending with the growth of hire purchase, and the introduction of new commodified forms of leisure and entertainment.' (McAleer 1992: 66)

7. At this stage colour reproduction meant illustration rather than photography; although American fashion monthlies such as *Harper's Bazaar* and *Vogue* regularly used colour throughout the 1930s, colour photography was not used in Britain until the 1950s. (Grieve 1964: 196)

8. The promotion of ready-to-wear garments was confined to small advertisements towards the back of magazines. Although firms such as Corot regularly advertised in monthlies, I found no examples in weeklies, even the new colour weeklies, until the later 1930s. Working-class women I interviewed told me that mail-order clothes were too expensive, and the only reference which I found in the Mass-Observation Archive to a woman using mail-order advertisements was a teacher's wife who did

not save up for clothes but bought them from her husband's salary, suggesting greater affluence.

9. The Amalgamated Press owned the *Daily Mail*, and although I have come across an earlier article in *Home Chat* (22 February 1919: 225) which sensationalizes the flapper – 'What the Bishop Said to "Home Chat"' 'Plain words on the Terrors of Dope' – this was not general for the period.

10. Her qualifications included the posts of ex-editor and director of *Vogue*, member of the Council for Art and Industry and chairman of the Fashion Group of Great Britain.

11. Britain followed the American model. The American paper-pattern industry developed alongside the creation of networks of national department stores and retailers who saw the potential of home dressmaking due to the marketing of efficient sewing machines.

12. A defensive tone crept in, coupled with articles such as 'No more hand-made look about your dresses'. (*Woman* 1 January 1938: 28)

13. Mass-Observation was founded in 1937 by Tom Harrisson, Charles Madge and Humphrey Jennings with the intention of conducting a comprehensive investigation into British social life. One of the first investigations to be undertaken was a study of Bolton and Blackpool, known as the Worktown Study. In addition to a team of investigators, including artists and writers such as Naomi Mitchison, 'observers' were recruited among 'ordinary' people attracted to the idea of writing about their everyday lives and taking part in what M-O described as a 'democratic social science'. The papers of Mass-Observation are now available to researchers at the University of Sussex. Feare describes this group as a 'small Metropolitan sample of working-class people'. Reproduced with permission of Curtis Brown Ltd, London. Copyright the Trustees of the Mass-Observation Archive at the University of Sussex.

14. Both Mass-Observation interviewees and women readers I spoke to used the term 'books' in reference to magazines; it is generally associated with working-class readers. The results included 20 per cent films and film stars; 16 per cent the press; 4 per cent respectively royalty, fashion books and war; and 16 per cent didn't know. Women were described as 'nearly always' identifying the press and films, whereas men were more vague or didn't know. On the cultural practice of viewing and processes of identification see Stacey 1994; Thumin 1991.

15. When asked the question, 'How do you form your opinions about fashion?' 26 per cent of women and only 10 per cent of men cited the press; 13 per cent of women gave fashion books and 13 per cent gave shops (no men gave these); 24 per cent of women gave 'Myself' as opposed to 10 per cent of men. None gave films. Other papers included the *Daily Express, Daily Telegraph, Daily Herald, Daily Sketch* and certain Sunday papers. Other women's magazines mentioned were *Woman and Home, Woman's Weekly* and *Ladies Companion*.

16. Mass-Observation rather patronizingly described this as women's expression of, 'an almost exclusively female pride in her own originality and immunity from outside influence.' Significantly claims by the majority of male respondents to be influenced by what they call 'observation' rather than anything in the media is

not interpreted as pride in immunity from influence. On problems with Mass-Observation's methodology and issues of gender, see Stanley 1990 and 1995.

17. Two thousand part-time and twelve full-time observers were involved in making a study of clothes and fashion. The interviewees were working-class, mainly working as weavers and living in Bolton. Daughters regularly worked and sometimes mothers also.

18. Miss M., a forty-year-old weaver, buys her clothes through club cheques, a side-line of the insurance man for her Burial Club; the advantage is they can be bought before you have paid for them. (G.W. 5 April 1939) Interview with Mrs K., the family had shares in the Co-op clothing club and this supplied the daughter with most of her clothes. (C.M. 25 April 1939) Mrs J., described as 'keen on fashions and looks in shop windows. Likes *Woman's Own*. Likes looking in Manchester shops, but prefers to shop in Bolton. Looks around until she sees what she likes, no regular shop.' Often a mother and daughter would visit the shops together, comparing a week or two before they buy, for instance Mrs B. (C.M. 5 April 1939)

19. Expenditure on clothes would often come second to more essential items such as food, or competed with other luxuries such as holidays. Mrs B. (C.M. 5 April 1939) and her husband economized on their clothes 'for the sake of the children': 'Last year the family sacrificed their holiday in June, to buy clothes. But they got about a bit. They hope to have a holiday this year.'

20. (C.M. 5 April 1939) Mrs J., recently married, weaver: 'I had two (dresses) made for me, they cost 4 shillings material, 5 shillings for the making. If you buy them, they cost about 10 shillings and 11 pence.' In addition to shopping in department stories, Madge and her friend Joy both got clothes made-up for them. Madge remembered buying the material and getting dresses made-up in order to be in fashion, it was also 'cheaper that way', while Joy got things made-up because off-the-peg didn't fit her; although she didn't do dressmaking herself she had plenty of friends who did. (Taylor and Drewett-Browne 1994)

21. Mrs (name unknown), aged thirty-two. Her husband is a foreman earning £5 per week and she has two children, a girl of six and a boy of five-years-old: 'She can even do coats because her mother let her go to a suit and coat maker and there she picked up a lot.' (G.W. 18 April 1939) E. L., an eighteen-year old winder: 'When getting clothes, has a good look round the shops and a look at the fashion books in the library.' (C.M. 25 April 1939) An eighteen-year-old weaver, 'is keen on looking at shop windows. Doesn't look at dress books except when she goes to night school for dressmaking class.'

22. Older single women were also interested in clothes and their appearance. Miss N., forty-year-old weaver: 'She takes a keen interest in clothes, likes to see what are the new styles [. . .] Having a sister in the trade helps a lot [. . .] Also reads the Women's Page in the *Daily Mail* – alternatively the *Daily Telegraph*, which is a much better page and much more up to the moment.' (C.M. 4 April 1939)

23. Even when a girl had left home a mother's advice could be sought as an essential guide to taste and etiquette. Mrs J., 'It's different now I'm married. Up till then my mother got all my clothes.' (C.M. 5 April 1939) Flo Mansell: 'We used to make the

decisions but she used to say whether it was right for us or not [. . .] whether it suited us because otherwise when you're young you can easily fall into a trap where you wear something that is totally unsuitable for what you want it for.' (Mansell 1996)

24. The holiday period known as The Sermons (May and June) being the peak time in Lancashire. Kearsley said that the practice varied in different parts of the country and that in Lancashire it was more traditional than actual to buy clothes at Easter. The increase in sales in June applied to all kinds of clothes, including underclothes. (C.M. 29 March 1939)

25. For an example of what an outfit could consist of and cost, Miss E. L. (eighteen-years-old): swagger suit 23s, hat 3s 11d, gloves 1s 11d, blouse 4s 11d, shoes 10s 11d. (C.M. 25 April 1939) R. K., however, noted a growing tendency towards the seasonal standardization of designs which he attributed to the influence of fashion publications, citing the introduction of a fashion page in the *Bolton Evening News* as evidence; this could also be read as the elision of mass-media practices with patterns of regional or class consumption.

26. When looking through the pages of *Woman*, Flo dismissed the Alison Settle fashion spreads but identified with the later Simplicity patterns and advertisements saying 'we used to wear things just like that.' (Mansell 1996)

27. Flo Mansell sewed for her family, three sisters and friends. (Mansell 1996)

28. Sample of 4,034 women. This was true with only slight variations according to region, age and income group, however, may be partially attributed to shortages due to the War (including magazines and patterns).

29. Of the housewives interviewed, 98 per cent were home sewers. Non-housewives were aged between thirty-three and forty and were presumably single women. The majority of those who sewed (89 per cent) learnt at school before the age of fourteen, and 52 per cent used their own sewing machine. Of the women I interviewed, few sewed, although nearly all knitted.

References

Alexander, S. (1994), *Becoming a Woman and Other Essays in Nineteenth and Twentieth Century Feminist History*, London: Virago.

Ash, Kathleen (1994), Interview with the author, 13 June.

Beddoe, D. (1989), *Back To Home and Duty: Women Between the Wars 1918–1939*, London: Pandora.

Beetham, M. (1996), *A Magazine of Her Own? Domesticity and Desire in the Woman's Magazine 1800–1914*, London: Routledge.

Bill, K. (1993), 'Attitudes Toward Women's Trousers: Britain in the 1930s', *Journal of Design History*, Vol. 6, No. 1: 45–54.

The Bookman (1920), Vol. 50, No. 5, January.

Bourke, J. (1994), *Working-Class Cultures in Britain, 1890–1960*, London and New York: Routledge.

Braithwaite, B. and Barrel, J., (1995), *Women's Magazines: The First Three Hundred Years*, London: Peter Owen.

Craik, J. (1994), *The Face of Fashion,* London and New York: Routledge.

Cross, G. ed., (1990), *Worktowners at Blackpool: Mass-Observation and Popular Leisure in the 1930s*, London: Routledge.

Davidoff, L. (1973), *The Best Circles: Society Etiquette and the Season*, London: Croom Helm.

Dilnot, G. (1925), *The Romance of the Amalgamated Press*, London: A.P.

Dilnot, Mary (1995), Interview with the author, 2 February.

Eley, H. W. (1932), *Advertising Media*, London: Butterworth.

Elias, E. (1978), *On Sundays We Wore White*, London: W.H. Allen.

Emanuel, P. (1934), 'The Power of the Weekly Press', *Commercial Art*, Vol. 17, July–December: 82–7.

Everard, J. (1934), 'Advertising to Women by Photography', *Commercial Art*, Vol. 17, July–December: 1–7

Eyles, L. (1922), *The Woman in The Little House*, London: Grant Richards.

Frazer, E. (1987), 'Teenage Girls Reading "Jackie"', *Media, Culture and Society*, Vol. 9.

Gaines, J. and Herzog, C. (1990), *Fabrication. Costume and the Female Body*, London: Routledge.

Grieve, M. (1964), *Millions Made My Story*, London: Gollancz.

Herrick, G. (1939), 'America Sells the Page', *Art and Industry*, Vol. 26, January–June: 170–82.

Kalder, N. and Silverman, R. (1948), *A Statistical Analysis of Advertising Expenditure and of the Revenue of the Press*, Cambridge: Cambridge University Press.

Lewis, J. (1980), 'In Search of a Real Equality: Women Between the Wars' in Gloversmith, F. (ed.) *Class, Culture and Social Change. A New View of the 1930s*, Sussex and New Jersey: Harvester Press.

—— (1984), *Women in England, 1870–1950: Sexual Divisions and Social Change*, London and New York: Harvester Wheatsheaf.

Light, A. (1991), *Forever England: Femininity, Literature and Conservativism Between the Wars*, London, Routledge.

Lipovetsky, G. (1994), *The Empire of Fashion: Dressing Modern Democracy*, Princeton: Princeton University Press.

Lowdell, Lena and Huff, Lilian (1994) Interview with the author, 10 September.

Mansell, Flo (1996), Interview with the author, 14 January.

Mass-Observation Archive: Topic Collection. Personal Appearance and Clothes (1939a), Press Release on Fashion Group talk, 22 April.

—— (1939b) Box 1 File C, Various Interviews.

—— (1940a) Letter to M. S., 2D, 29 January.

—— (1940b) Letter to P. M., 2C, 2 February.

—— (1940c) Opinion Forming: Fashion, 2B, 16 May.

McAleer, J. (1992), *Popular Reading and Publishing in Britain 1914–50*, Oxford: Oxford Historical Monographs, Clarendon Press.

Melman, B. (1988), *Woman and the Popular Imagination in the Twenties: Flappers and Nymphs*, London: Macmillan.

Minney, R. J. (1954), *Viscount Southwood*, London: Odhams Press.

Nevanas, B. (1934), 'Making Fashion Drawings Look Fashionable', *Commercial Art*, Vol.16, January–June: 27–31.

Nicholls, N. (1934), 'The Sales-Stalk', *Commercial Art*, Vol.16, January-June: 181–4.

Ohmann, R. (1996), *Selling Culture: Magazines, Markets, and Class at the Turn of the Century*, London, New York: Verso.

Oliver, P., Davis, I., Bentley, I. (1994), *Dunroamin. The Suburban Semi and its Enemies*, London: Pimlico.

Partington, A. (1992), 'Popular Fashion and Working-Class Affluence', in Ash, J. and Wilson, E., (eds.), *Chic Thrills. A Fashion Reader*, London: Pandora Press.

Penrose, E. (1937), 'What I Expect of a Fashion Artist', *Art and Industry*, Vol. 23, July–December.

Punch (1924) 'A Guide to Short Story Writing', Vol. 167, July.

Radway, J. (1987), *Reading the Romance: Women, Patriarchy and Popular Literature*, London: Verso.

Randle, Avis (1994), Interview with the author, 30 June.

Spring Rice, M. (1981), *Working-Class Wives*, London: Virago.

Stacey, J. (1994), *Star Gazing: Hollywood Cinema and Female Spectatorship*, London: Routledge.

Stanley, L. (1990), 'The Archaeology of a 1930s Mass-Observation Project', *Department of Sociology Occasional Paper No. 27*, Manchester: University of Manchester.

—— (1995), 'Women have servants and men never eat: issues in reading gender in Mass-Observation's 1937 Day Diaries', *Women's History Review*, Vol. 4, No. 1: 85–102.

Taylor, J. (1994), 'Kodak and the "English" Market Between the Wars', *Journal of Design History,* Vol. 7. No. 1: Oxford: Oxford University Press: 29–42.

Taylor, Margaret (Madge) (1994), Interview with the author, 29 April.

—— and Drewett-Browne, Doreen Joy, (1994), Interview with the author, 24 April.

Thumin, J. (1991), *Celluloid Sisters: Women and Popular Cinema*, London: Macmillan.

White, C. (1970), *Women's Magazines 1633–1968*, London: Michael Joseph.

Wilson, E. and Taylor, L. (1989), *Through the Looking Glass. A History of Dress from 1860 to the Present Day*, London: BBC Books.

Wood, E. (1927), 'Some Problems of Advertising to Women', *Commercial Art*, 1927.

5

Home Sewing: Motivational Changes in the Twentieth Century

Sherry Schofield-Tomschin

Sewing has been a home activity for centuries, but with the introduction of the first practical sewing machine by Isaac Singer in 1853, sewing took on a new role in many American households. Home sewing became a player in American clothing production. Sewing became the weapon against the economy, rising labour costs, and the declining quality and fit of ready-to-wear clothing. In addition, sewing became a form of management concerned with the purchase, use, and care of clothing, and ultimately savings of money, time, and/or energy. (Creekmore 1963) Beyond utilitarian efforts, sewing allowed opportunities for originality and creativity. Home sewing served as a hobby or leisure activity (Robbins 1973), promoting relaxation and therapeutic effects for participants. (Schofield-Tomschin 1994) This chapter will chronicle the changing motivations for American home sewing during the twentieth century.

Although not its main purpose, it also addresses the changing interest of academics toward home sewing. By necessity, this chapter relies heavily upon surveys and material of a similar nature. Most of the surveys reported were completed for an academic audience, and, therefore, are considered to have information that is more generalizable to the American public. Of interest, is the number of master's dissertations that were concerned with home sewing motivations, and the direct correlation between the time that these were completed and the fluctuating interest of Americans toward home sewing. However, as the 1980s approached, and home sewing in America was generally in decline, information that was available had more of an industry or popular press focus, and therefore may not be as reliable. But this information, too, helps us to narrate the shifting motivations of American home sewing.

Economy

The economy has frequently been stated as a motivation for home sewing. In fact, fabric retailing is considered to be 'contracyclical' in nature, meaning it does well when other industries are in a recession. (Queenan 1988: 15) One of the first studies on record that attempted to report the reasons for making garments at home found economics to be a strong motivation. During 1925 and 1926, O'Brien and Campbell surveyed 1,697 women in rural and urban communities from thirty-two states. (1927) The lower cost of home-made garments was reported as the major reason for home sewing (90.2 per cent). When the respondents were subdivided by size of community and income, those in rural communities or with lower incomes more frequently sewed for the economic savings associated with home-sewn garments. However, as the size of the community and income levels increased, the economic motivation diminished. Better materials (62.0 per cent) and suiting individual needs (62.7 per cent) rated nearly as important as sewing for lower cost (73.7 per cent) for participants with higher income levels.

In 1948, *Business Week* reported an increase in both sewing machine and pattern sales, as well as an upsurge in enrolment in sewing classes, and indicated that home sewing popularity was surpassing pre-war levels. (Hofmann 1948) Reasons given for the home sewing increase included the high cost of ready-made clothing and women's reduced presence in the workforce. Ten years later, *Time* magazine reported that the home sewing boom was as strong as ever. It was estimated that approximately 20 per cent of all women's and female children's clothes were made at home, and that women sewed an average of four to six garments per year. ('Sew and Reap' 1958)

Although the economic hardships of the 1920s had diminished, economics was still found to be a major motivator for home sewing. Lutz (1958), Mitchell (1959) and York (1961) surveyed women in Illinois, Texas, and Oklahoma, respectively, on the sewing practices of women in their region. All three of the women theorized that creativity and/or personal enjoyment would surpass economics as the primary sewing motivation. Although in each study results varied by respondent's marital status, occupation, age, number of dependants, and size of the community, economics was found to be the leading motivator. However, consistent across all three studies was also the importance of sewing for creativity, originality, personal enjoyment, better fit, and better quality.

While the economy fuelled home sewing in the first half of the century, the changing economy had the reverse affect in the later half of the century. As more women entered the workforce and became involved outside of the home, the hours that could be devoted to household tasks, such as home sewing, decreased. In response to this phenomenon, Conklyn (1961) compared the relationships between the reasons why people sewed and their occupation, their spouse's occupation, and marital status. The five sewing motivations that Conklyn investigated were economics, aesthetics, use of leisure time, use of fabric on hand, and other. Economics was identified as the primary reason for home sewing by the single, the non-employed, and those married to spouses with blue-collar jobs. Single employed women more frequently sewed household items rather than apparel for economic savings, and non-employed women sewed more garments for economic reasons than the other groups. Aesthetics became the stronger motivation for employed women or those women whose spouses had white-collar jobs.

Chan (1976) theorized that sewing for creativity was used to compensate for characteristics perceived to be lacking in the job, and that the primary sewing motivation would no longer be economics. The fifty respondents in the study indicated that although creativity and economics were both important motivations, economics was a more dominant motivation. In addition, sewing for economics was significantly related to both the age of the respondent and to the number of children living at home; older women and women with a larger number of children at home had a higher score on sewing for economic reasons.

Economics seemed to have been the major motivation for home sewing in these studies. But even as early as 1960, Johnson reported that new developments were making it possible to buy ready-made garments more economically, and that home sewing for thrift was a thing of the past. Loker (1985) found that the cost of producing home-sewn garments was more expensive than ready-to-wear garments when shopping and construction time were included in the total cost. Courtless (1982) reported in a consumer expenditure survey that as spending for sewing increased, so did spending on ready-to-wear. In addition, consumer profiles completed between 1973 and 1990 (Blenkarn 1986; Hofmann 1990; Riley 1984; Robbins 1973; Sewing Market Update 1990), showed that home sewing was actually more popular with the middle- and upper-income households, suggesting that sewing for economics was losing its status as the primary home sewing motivation.

It appears that sewing for economic benefits was becoming a complex sewing motivation. Could there be a direct correlation between the age of home sewers and the motivation of sewing for economy? Chan (1976) noted a significant relationship between the age of her respondents and the motivation of economic savings. However, studies in the last quarter of the century did not support home sewing as financially economical. Was it possible that women, particularly older women who had life-long habits of prudence, perceived a need for thrift even though the actual economies of their household no longer made it a necessity?

Quality

If economics was questionable as the primary sewing motivation, then what was driving home sewing? The search for better quality was a motivation the surfaced in earlier research studies. As early as 1927 O'Brien and Campbell reported home sewing as an alternative to better quality, in terms of both better quality construction and better quality materials. Throughout the research, quality was identified as a subsidiary motivation for home sewing. Robbins (1973) identified the lack of quality found in store-purchased apparel items as a factor contributing to the increase of home-sewn garments during the 1970s. Similarly, Shannon (1980) reported that the lack of quality and availability of ready-to-wear items might have been the reason for heightened interest in home sewing. Increased quality in construction and materials was also identified as a motivation for home sewing in Conklyn (1961), Johnson (1960), and York's (1961) studies. A nationwide consumer survey (Conklyn 1981) reported that dissatisfaction with the quality of ready-to-wear apparel was a reason for their home sewing participation.

Kean and Levin (1989) identified clusters of home sewers using sewing orientations as identifiers. Their study identified better quality as a benefit of home sewing and went one step further, classifying members of the clusters as 'prosumers'. They identified a prosumer as one who jointly produces and consumes economic goods and services. Home sewers seem to be producing goods to obtain both the kind and quality of product desired. Similarly, Johnson, Littrell, and Reilly (1991) recognized dissatisfaction with the quality of ready-to-wear garments, in both construction and materials, as the primary reason why women sought home-based sewing services.

When Griffin and O'Neal (1992) conducted a study on the characteristics of fabric quality, home sewers were chosen as their subjects because the investigators assumed that home sewers were more quality conscious than was the average clothing buyer. Home sewers were also perceived as more likely to make decisions based on fabric quality. Although the study was designed to identify critical characteristics used in fabric evaluation, the study confirmed that fabric quality was the most important consideration when individuals purchased fabric for home-sewn items.

Studies have revealed that quality has consistently been a factor in home sewing in the twentieth century. (Blenkarn 1986; Conklyn 1961; Drohan

1987; Johnson 1960; Johnson, Littrell and Reilly 1991; Lutz 1958; O'Brien and Campbell 1927; York, 1961) Although quality was never determined to be the primary motivator in any of the studies mentioned, it is apparent that home sewers, possibly more than other consumers, find quality in both construction and materials an important consideration and motivation for home sewing.

Fit

Another motivation mentioned in earlier research, was the motivation of sewing for better fitting garments. York (1961) and Shannon (1980) both reported that fit was a motivation for home sewing participation in their studies. York reported that 47.5 per cent of her respondents were searching for better fit with home sewing. Better fit was also enumerated as a benefit of home sewing in Shannon's (1980) report on home sewing increases.

Although earlier studies on home sewing did not mention a correlation between age fit, a 1994 study by the present author found that there was a direct positive relationship between age and sewing for better fit. As the participants ages increased, so did their motivation of sewing for better fit. In 1990 over 12 per cent of the population was over the age of sixty-five (US Bureau of the Census). Was it possible that as America ages, older consumers are striving for better fitting clothes that ready-to-wear garments fail to provide? Woodson and Horridge (1990) compared the differences in body measurements of women sixty-five years of age and older to both commercial basic patterns and Voluntary Product Standards PS 42-70. These differences included prominent abdominal extensions, lowered bustlines, sloping shoulders, rounded backs, and increased horizontal measurements in the hips and waistline. Could it be that home-sewn apparel is an attempt to solve the problem of ready-to-wear garments that do not provide the fit necessary for the sixty-five and older segment of the population?

But better-fitting clothing also includes clothing for the physically limited or deformed. Reich and Shannon (1980) found the need to obtain a custom fit due to a health problem or body irregularity as a reason for home sewing. Their study involved a mailed questionnaire that enabled them to cluster types of health problems with needed clothing style features. Many clothing design features that physically limited people needed for ease in dressing were not available on ready-to-wear garments. Modified apparel, such as those with hook and loop tape fasteners, are available through mail-order catalogues, but are often more expensive and involve a longer time to acquire. Home sewing is often the answer for those with physical limitations who are trying to improve functionality and fashionability, which is sometimes lost when functionality becomes the focus of the garment.

Creativity

Sewing for better quality and better fit have fairly consistently been identified as home sewing motivations, but never as primary motivations. So, if the economic necessities and benefits of home sewing had diminished, and sewing for improved quality and fit were not primary motivations, then what was becoming the principal motivation for home sewing? In a discussion about the new directions in clothing construction, Johnson (1960) stressed the changing needs and living patterns of women who did home sewing. Johnson reported that a survey of home sewers revealed that 41 per cent sewed for creativity and relaxation, as a result of changing lifestyles, increased tensions and limited opportunities for self-expression, whereas only 33 per cent sewed for economy. Home sewing, with its modern sewing machine, well-styled patterns, and simplified construction techniques may have answered the need for self-expression and creativity. It was estimated that in 1971, 44 million females between the ages of twelve and sixty-five sewed. (Hull 1971) In 1974 the estimate was 50 million. (Conklyn 1974) Rather than stressing economics specifically, pattern and sewing companies stressed individuality and original fashions at a reduced price. (Hull 1971) The major reasons for sewing outlined by Fessler (1971) were: (1) to be creative, as sewing was a valid leisure activity; and (2) to cut retail expenditure.

Although Lutz (1958), Mitchell (1959), and York (1961) all attempted to verify creativity as the major benefit of home sewing, they were unsuccessful. Robbins' (1973) analyzed the fabric-retailing industry and suggested that one factor for the industry's rapid growth in the 1970s was that home sewing provided a creative outlet for better-educated homemakers. However, it wasn't until 1981 that a survey reported in 'Consumers Say' found that sewers were motivated more by personal satisfaction and creative expressions than by economic reasons. (Conklyn 1981) This was supported by Courtless (1985) in a study that reported the amount of time spent sewing by 365 women employed outside the home. Of the respondents, 40 per cent sewed as a leisure activity or hobby, giving them an opportunity to be creative. Courtless concluded that creativity was a stronger sewing motivation than economics.

Johnson, Littrell, and Reilly (1991) sought to identify the typical reasons individuals used independent, home-based, sewing services. Using telephone interviews and a mail survey, five groups of users were identified by the study: (1) comprehensive users; (2) custom garment and alteration users; (3) mending and alteration users; (4) alteration users; and (5) mending users. Of the five groups identified, the custom garment and alteration group, who were typically non-sewers, supported the use of home sewing because it allowed for greater creativity.

For many, it seemed that the product of the sewing process became the motivation. In an attempt to determine the motivations or satisfactions which individuals associated with leisure activities, such as home sewing, Hawes (1978) asked respondents to evaluate thirty-two satisfaction statements that applied to their three favourite pursuits. Of the female respondents, 42.6 per cent chose creative crafts or handicrafts, which included home sewing, as their most popular leisure activity. Of the satisfaction statements chosen to coincide with the activity, being creative received the highest personal satisfaction, followed by developing a skill, learning new things, peace of mind, and self-respect.

Leisure

Again, the emphasis in home sewing was shifting. Although creativity was considered a strong motivation for home sewing and a form of personal expression, home sewing also lead to a realization of self-worth and personal satisfaction. Participation in home sewing was a response to changing consumer attitudes. With the success of the industrial revolution much of the demand for tangible goods such as housing, food, and clothing had been satisfied. Maslow (1959) stated that once an economy is productive enough to satisfy most people's basic needs, people spend more time and money to satisfy their inner needs. Americans had come to expect four necessities: food, clothing, shelter, and leisure or recreation (Dunlop 1987). Leisure, defined by Hawes, Blackwell, and Talarzyk (1975), is time not obligated to work, work-related activities, life-maintenance activities, routine family duties and responsibilities, or routine social and civic responsibilities. Vandeventer (1993) identified satisfaction with one's own life and having one's personal needs fulfilled as a common consumer attitude of the 1990s.

Leisure or recreational activities can have a positive affect on those who use them. A benefit can include economic measures and improved conditions for/of an individual or group. (Driver 1992) Leisure can impact the physiological, psycho-physiological, economic, and social aspects of life. Although home sewing may not have the impact that some other forms of leisure may have, the handwork required can be a definite physiological benefit to many people. For those with a hand injury or arthritis, home sewing can be therapeutic. (Reinhardt 1992) Home sewing, classified as a manual-manipulative activity, was associated with the specific satisfactions of sense of achievement, being creative, and financial help. (Donald and Havighurst 1959)

The same handwork that can have physiological benefits can also promote psycho-physiological benefits, including reduced tension and anxiety, mental and physical relaxation, positive changes in mood, and enhanced outlook on life. (Driver 1992) Working with one's hands, according to Reinhardt (1992), may be the ultimate way to beat stress and tension. Handwork puts a person into a more relaxed state where there is more freedom for creativity. It is almost a form of hypnosis. Reinhardt stated that maximum benefits are realized if one spends 30 minutes to an hour each day on the activity. When sewing is viewed as a recreational experience, it can be an antidote to tensions, stresses and anxieties confronting individuals.

Mood is a prevalent and relevant by-product of leisure activities. (Hull 1990) Mood, which is used to denote a set of subjective feelings (i.e. pleasure, happiness, sadness), occurs as a consequence of leisure experiences. This induced mood can influence the behaviours and cognitions of persons long after they leave the leisure activity. Positive moods tend to promote feelings of control. In an interview with three home sewers, all interviewees mentioned the feeling of control over the end product as a direct benefit of home sewing. (Shaw 1986) This sense of control over daily events may determine the effect stress can have on the psychological and physical well-being of an individual, according to a Wellness Letter published by the University of California (Lutz 1992). Mood also impacts health. Stone et al. (1987) suggested that the immune system is strongest during times of positive moods. Positive moods, such as those associated with leisure activities, can have a positive effect on the immune system. (Hull 1990)

Previous studies on home sewing have included mood-related responses that included enjoyment, relaxation, and pleasure. O'Brien and Campbell (1927) had not included 'for enjoyment' as a possible choice on their questionnaire concerning reasons for home sewing, but commented on the numerous occasions 'for enjoyment' was included as an additional response. Johnson (1960) suggested that educators emphasized how home sewing as a hobby makes life pleasanter, easier, and more fruitful. Courtless (1985) analyzed the time employed women spent sewing. She found that although only 15 per cent recorded sewing in the seven-day study, 40 per cent mentioned sewing as an occasional hobby. Those who found sewing to be a leisure activity were motivated by the rewards of personal satisfaction and enjoyment. A survey that was reported in 'Consumers Say' (Conklyn 1981) found that when consumers were asked the question, 'Why do you sew?' the most often checked reply was: 'For pleasure.'

Hawes (1978) identified thirty-two satisfaction statements derived from leisure activities. In a nationwide survey of 1,000 households, respondents were asked to evaluate the importance of these satisfactions as it related to each of three of their favourite leisure activities. Among women, regardless of particular pursuits, the most important satisfactions selected were 'peace of mind', 'chance to learn about new things', and 'chance to get the most out of life while I can still enjoy it'. Among men, the most important satisfactions were 'peace of mind', 'chance to get the most out of life while I can still enjoy it', and 'adventure and excitement'.

When Hawes (1978) compared the different satisfaction statements to particular pursuits, the most popular female activity was creative crafts or handicrafts. This included home sewing, which was chosen by 42.6 per cent of the female respondents. The satisfaction associated the most with this activity was 'being creative'. The most popular male activity was gardening, lawn care, and landscaping, chosen by 13.9 per cent. The same satisfaction as with the females, 'being creative', was associated most with the creative crafts or handicrafts activity. The Hobby Industries of America (1990) found that 67 per cent of those surveyed participated in some form of home sewing, which was identified in their survey as 'needlecrafts'.

Blenkarn (1986) identified home sewers as those who defined home sewing as a household activity, as opposed to those who defined it as a leisure activity. Of the 107 home sewers in the study, 38.7 per cent considered sewing as a leisure activity, 38.7 per cent as a combination of leisure and housework, 13 per cent as something other than housework or leisure, and 9 per cent strictly as housework. Drohan (1987) conducted a similar study using adults enrolled in continuing education sewing classes. Drohan's results showed that 45.5 per cent considered sewing as a leisure activity, 30 per cent as a combination of leisure and housework, 20 per cent as something other than housework or leisure, and 3 per cent strictly as housework.

It appeared that more people perceived and participated in home sewing as a leisure activity. However, when Kean and Levin (1989) attempted to profile clusters of home sewers for the purpose of market segmentation by using sewing orientations as identifiers, the largest group, the Utilitarians, were significantly more concerned about economics and the practicality of sewing. Their 105 respondents clustered into five segments: Utilitarian (n=39), Practicals (n=16), Craft-oriented (n=24), Upscale (n=17), and Indifferent (n=9). The Indifferent and Practical also rated economic aspects highly. As a result of this study Kean and Levin suggested that fabric stores should be strongly oriented toward home sewing for economic reasons rather than for creative reasons.

New Motivations

The divergent responses throughout the century prompted me as it had prompted many graduate students before me, to conduct a study (Schofield-Tomschin 1994) to investigate the benefits and needs sought by home sewers. Grounded in the literature, the motivations of sewing for (1) economics; (2) better quality; (3) improved fit; (4) creativity; and (5) psychological/physiological benefits were considered to be the basis for my study and a guide in the formation of the survey instrument. In order to reach a larger number of home sewing respondents, I chose to implement a mailed survey that was designed to measure the extent to which individuals perceived their personal needs were being met through home sewing. A ten-page question-naire was developed, containing sub-scales for each of the five identified motivations, information on sewing practices, demographics, as well as space for additional comments. The sub-scales included statements of satisfaction, borrowed and/or adapted from previous research, that might be achieved when sewing for that particular motivation, determined by the use of Likert type scales. Using a stratified random sampling method, I distributed 665 survey instruments to individuals living in the states of Minnesota, North Dakota and South Dakota who subscribed to *Sew News*, an American-based home sewing publication.

I found significant differences (n=423) among the sewing motivations considered in the study, (Schofield-Tomschin 1994). Sewing for psychological-physiological reasons was ranked the most important sewing motivation. In fact, the five highest satisfactions, across all sub-scales, were, 'It gives me a sense of accomplishment', 'I feel that I am being creative,' 'A feeling of self-confidence', 'A feeling of independence and self reliance', and 'A chance to develop a skill'. The first and last three responses were from the psychological/physiological sub-scale, and the second response was from the creativity sub-scale. Respondents considered home sewing as very therapeutic. 'Very relaxing', 'A way to get away from my work, accomplish a lot of things, and gain insight', and 'A passion that I immerse myself in for enjoyment, and to learn from others of the same mind' are a few of the highest-ranking responses.

I did not find that the motivations of sewing for creativity and sewing for quality were significantly different motivations from each other for the respondents in the study (Schofield-Tomschin 1994). However, they were significantly more important than the motivations of sewing for economy and sewing for fit. The highest-scored satisfaction statement for creativity was 'I feel that I am being creative.' For quality, the respondents chose the satisfactions of 'I can get better quality for the money' and 'The clothes I make last longer than ready-to-wear.'

When considering the motivation of sewing for economics, over 50 per cent of the respondents said they would not quit sewing, even without economic savings available (Schofield-Tomschin 1994). In general, I found that sewing for economics was not as important a motivation as the other identified motivations, with the exception of sewing for fit. Sewing for fit was the least important motivation, and interestingly was positively correlated to the age of the respondent (r=.91). As the age of the respondent increased, so did the importance of sewing for fit. A correlation was also considered between age and sewing for economics. Although the economic benefits of sewing may have diminished, individuals' perceived needs may not have changed, particularly older individuals who may have sewn for economic necessity at one time. A Pearson Correlational Matrix resulted in only a moderate positive correlation of .69. According to my study, more people perceived and participated in home sewing as a leisure activity. Leisure activities promote more relaxed conditions, which in turn promote other benefits such as a general sense of well-being.

Many motivations converged over the course of the twentieth century to spur home sewing. Most noticeable was the economic motivation; home-sewn garments could be constructed at a reduced cost compared with ready-to-wear. In addition, better-quality goods and construction techniques could be incorporated. Similarly, for those who had fitting concerns, home sewing provided better fitting opportunities. However, as economic necessities diminished, home sewing became a venue for creativity and originality, and eventually a process for relaxation and alleviation of stress. Home sewing became therapeutic as sewers sought to find a counterbalance in their busy lives.

Acknowledgement

My thanks to Dr. Robyne Williams for her valuable insight and advice on my M.A. dissertation.

References

Blenkarn, D. L. (1986), *Home Sewing: Satisfaction with Sewing as a Household Production Activity*, M.A. dissertation, University of Alberta.

Chan, K. J. (1976), *The Relationship of Motivation for Sewing, Amount of Sewing Perceived Depersonalization of the Job, and Creativity*, M.A. dissertation, Oregon State University.

Conklyn, N. B. (1961), *Amount and Kinds of Home Sewing Done and the Reasons Given for Sewing by a Group of Homemakers*, M.A. dissertation, The Ohio State University.

—— (1974), 'Clothing, Textiles and Home Sewing,' *Consumer's Research Magazine*, 57 (10): 50–59.

—— (1981), 'Consumers Say They Sew for Pleasure,' *Homesewing Trade News*, 1, December: 14–16.

Courtless, J.C. (1982), 'Home Sewing Trends,' *Family Economics Review*, 4: 19–22.

—— (1985), 'Time Spent in Sewing by Employed Women,' *Family Economics Review*, 4: 1–3.

Creekmore, A. (1963), *Behaviours and Their Relationship to General Values and to the Striving for Basic Needs*, Ph.D. dissertation, Pennsylvania State University.

Donald, M. N. and Havighurst, R. J. (1959), 'The Meanings of Leisure,' *Social Forces*, 37: 355–60.

Driver, B. L. (1992), 'The Benefits of Leisure,' *Parks and Recreation*, December: 18–24, 75.

Drohan, A. (1987), *Motivations of Adults to Participate in Sewing Courses*, M.A. dissertation, University of Alberta.

Dunlop, R. (1987), 'The Fourth Necessity: Satisfying Our Inner Needs,' *American Legion Magazine*, 122, June: 20–21, 50–51.

Fessler, B. (1971), 'Education's Role in Home Sewing Industry,' *What's New in Home Economics*, 35 (4): 11–13.

Griffin, M. L. and O'Neal, G. S. (1992), 'Critical Characteristics of Fabric Quality,' *Home Economics Research Journal*, 21 (2): 73–9.

Guilford, J. P. (1965), 'Intellectual Factors in Productive Thinking' in S. Parnes and H. Harding, eds, *Productive Thinking in Education*, Washington, D.C.: National Education Association: 5–20.

Hawes, D. K. (1978), 'Satisfactions Derived from Leisure-time Pursuits: An Exploratory Nationwide Survey,' *Journal of Leisure Research*, 10 (4): 247–64.

——, Blackwell, R. D. and Talarzyk, W. W. (1975), 'Consumer Satisfactions from Leisure Time Pursuits,' *Advances in Consumer Research*, Chicago: Association for Consumer Research, 2: 817–36.

Heywood, L. A. (1978), 'Perceived Recreative Experience and the Relief of Tension,' *Journal of Leisure Research*, 10 (2): 86–97.

Hobby Industries of America (1990), 'Survey of Attitudes and Purchase Habits of Consumers of Craft/Hobby Products: A 1990 Profile of the American Consumer,' HIA Nationwide Consumer Study, Conducted by Market Facts, Inc., Hilliard, Ohio.

Hofmann, D. (1948), 'Home-sewing Booms Singer' in *Business Week*, 14 August: 75–80.

—— (1990), 'An Ancient Skill, Sewing, is Revived' in *New York Times*, 14 November: C1.

Hull, R. B. (1971), 'I Made it Myself!' (1971), *Forbes*, 107, 15 April: 43–4.

—— (1990), 'Mood as a Product of Leisure: Causes and Consequences,' *Journal of Leisure Research*, 22 (2): 99–111.

Johnson, D. (1960), 'A New Direction in Clothing Construction,' *Journal of Home Economics*, 52 (9): 752–3.

Johnson, J. S., Littrell, M. A. and Reilly, R. (1991), 'Consumers of Customized Sewing Services,' *Clothing and Textiles Research Journal*, 9 (2): 7–15.

Kean, R. C. and Levin, C. O. (1989), 'Orientations Toward Home Sewing,' *Clothing and Textiles Research Journal*, 8 (1): 28–34.

Loker, S. (1985), 'Ready-to-wear or Home-sewn Clothing,' *Fabrications* Winter: 3–4.

Lutz, R. M. (1958), 'Why Illinois Women Enroll in Adult Classes in Clothing,' *Journal of Home Economics*, 50 (2): 113.

—— (1992), 'Making Time for Yourself,' *Wellness Letter*, 9 (2): 7, University of California, Berkeley.

Maslow, A. H. (1959), 'Creativity in Self-actualizing People,' in H. Anderson ed., *Creativity and its Cultivation*, New York: Harper and Brothers: 83–95.

Mitchell, M. F. (1959), *A Study of Home Sewing Practices of a Group of 100 Women in Lubbock County, Texas,* M.A. dissertation, Texas Technology College.

O'Brien, R. and Campbell, M. (1927), 'Trends in Home Sewing,' Government Document #a1.38: 4. Miscellaneous publication, Washington, D.C.: U.S. Department of Agriculture.

Queenan, J. (1988), 'Pattern of Success: Hancock Does Well in Bad Times Too,' *Barron's*, 11 January: 15, 40.

Reich, N. and Shannon, E. (1980), 'Handicap: Common Physical Limitations and Clothing-related Needs,' *Home Economics Research Journal*, 8 (6): 437–44.

Reinhardt, C. (1992), 'Personal Pleasures,' *McCall's*, February: 18.

Riley, M. (1984), 'Sewing in a New Age,' *What's New in Home Economics*, November: 7.

Robbins, S.M. (1973), 'The Fabric Retailing Industry,' *Financial Analysts Journal*, May–June: 70–4, 92–101.

Schofield-Tomschin, S. (1994), *Perceived Needs and Benefits of Home Sewing: A Regional Study*, M.A. dissertation, North Dakota State University.

'Sew and Reap,' (1958), *Time*, November: 70–2.

'Sewing Market Update '90' (1990), Independent Consumer Research from the publishers of *Sew News*.

Shannon, M. J. (1980), 'Home Sewing Makes a Comeback as More Women Polish Up Long-dormant Skills,' *Wall Street Journal*, 10 April: 1.

Shaw, P. (1986), 'Relaxing With Crafts,' *Creative Ideas for Living*, May: 16, 18.

Stone, A. A., Cox, D. S., Valminarsdottir, H., Jandorf, L. and Neale, J.M. (1987), 'Evidence that Secretory IGA Antibody is Associated With Daily Mood,' *Journal of Personality and Social Psychology*, 52 (5): 988–93.

US Bureau of the Census (1990), *US Census*, Washington, DC: Government Printing Office.

Vandeventer, E. (1993), 'Demographics Drive Buying Trends' from *Textiles, Apparel and Home Furnishings Current Analysis: Standard and Poor's Industry Surveys*, 161 (11, Section 1, 18 March): T61–T65.

Woodson, E. M. and Horridge, P. E. (1990), 'Apparel Sizing as it Relates to Women Age Sixty-five Plus,' *Clothing and Textiles Research Journal*, 8 (4): 7–13.

York, M. D. (1961), *Practices and Opinions of a Select Group of Homemakers with Regard to Home Sewing*, M.A. dissertation, Oklahoma State University.

6

There's No Place Like Home: Home Dressmaking and Creativity in the Jamaican Community of the 1940s to the 1960s

Carol Tulloch

Introduction: The Famished Creative Spirit

The African-American author Alice Walker asks how and when did her mother 'feed her creative spirit'. (Walker 1984: 239) As co-provider, mother and wife, Walker's mother worked all day in the fields, made all her children's clothes, the sheets and the quilts for the beds, in addition to the 'traditional' duties expected of her. It was in what Walker terms, the 'ambitious gardens' which her mother cultivated around and in their 'shabby house', working on them before she left for her field work and in the spare time available on her return. Her 'hobby' was to draw admirers from miles around. Walker maintains that her mother's ingenuity in finding time and space to cultivate her creativity, to champion the creative spirit, saved her mother's sanity:

> I notice that it is only when my mother is working in her flowers that she is radiant, almost to the point of being invisible – except as Creator: hand and eye. She is involved in work her soul must have [. . .] being an artist has still been a daily part of her life. This ability to hold on, even in very simple ways, is work black women have done for a very long time. (Walker 1984: 241–2)

Walker's memorialization of her mother's need and ability to feed the creative spirit offers a personal anecdote of an individual as an example to consider other cases and, in turn, a group. Walker contextualizes this inquisition into the thirst of the creative spirit amongst African-American women and acknowledges Virginia Woolf's earlier discussion of the feminist creative discourse in her seminal work of 1929, *A Room of One's Own*. Both authors lament the loss to history of the material epitaphs borne out of the creative practices conducted by women. This has been attributed to either a lack of public recognition, or women's inability to fulfil their creative potential due to patriarchal control or social deprivation. (Walker 1984: 235–7) Debate on this issue is extensive. (hooks 1982; Nunn 1987; Darwent 1998) Walker recommends that 'we must fearlessly pull out of ourselves and look at and identify with our lives the living creativity some of our great-grandmothers were not allowed to know.' (Walker 1984: 237)

The focus of this essay is a consideration of how home dressmaking can feed the creative spirit of working-class Jamaican women who have lived in Jamaica and Britain.[1] If an Oxford English Dictionary definition of the word spirit is 'the vital animating essence of a person', then the creativity which emanates from an individual is not simply concerned with creating and making objects, but is simultaneously about maintaining and representing the individual, the self. This compound of creativity, the aesthetic-self and its impact on a collective identity, provides the structure for this work. Essentially, it is located in contextualizing the practice of home dressmaking and the finished garment within wider cultural issues. The limitation of this work's length has necessitated such a reductive outline and does not afford an extensive study into the practice of home dressmaking by a large number of Jamaican women.

By the early twentieth century, home dressmaking was a characteristic cultural and social feature of Jamaica.[2] It was practised by most racial and ethnic groups as a means of socialization amongst the middle class and a necessity for the working class. It was a compulsory subject within the education system for boys and girls up to the age of ten. Independent professional dressmakers were to be found in their thousands – the 1891 census lists 3,656 professional dressmakers based in Jamaica's capital, Kingston, and 18,966 throughout the island.[3] The paper will concentrate on the oral testimony and dressmaking history of Mrs Anella James,[4] an exponent of this cultural legacy. Anella was the second youngest of eleven children of a working-class family. Her story spans from 1936 to 1965, from the rural town of Slygoville in the parish of St Catherine, Jamaica, to Ilford, Essex, where Anella emigrated in 1961.

Although the case study of an individual 'cannot speak for the collective', (Chamberlain 1995: 95) it can, I argue, contribute to the overall identity of a culture and to a specific recreational practice such as home dressmaking.

The subjective study of Anella's interaction with home dressmaking allows concentration on the relativity of the practice to an individual's sense of aesthetic-self. A supplementary consideration is the consequential effect on, or interpretation of, the collective identity. To this end I want to expand on Mary Chamberlain's thesis that:

> Memory and the individual are indivisible [. . .] If we recognise that memory rather than being confined to, and by the individual, manifests elements of a shared consciousness and is part of the process of social production, then oral sources offer the potential for entering into a wider cultural milieu. In that sense, the individual voice may be representative of the collective voice and provide evidence of broader attitudes, values and patterns of behaviour.
>
> Several such voices may confirm cultural practices [. . .] What may appear to be an individual and fragmented account, is representative of the totality and it is the totality which provides, through affirmation or denial, meaning. (1995: 96)

Memory, then, is shaped by language and images, priorities and expectations which are in turn influenced by the collective as 'culturally and socially determined', therefore the individual and the collective memory affect one another. (Chamberlain 1995: 95–6)

I acknowledge the problems associated with the empirical resources of oral history, such as whether statements are true or false. Inexact dates and a propensity to expound other areas are among the 'peculiarities of oral history'. Nonetheless, 'oral sources tell us less about events as such than about their meaning, and their value lies in the areas of language, narrative and subjectivity.' (Chamberlain 1995: 95)[5] The photographs of Anella's home-produced designs have enabled me to arrive at different historical evidence and the associated meanings of her work. One of the advantages of oral history and memory is the insight they give into groups generally not catered for in history books, such as black women. Additionally, this intimate method, whether between interviewer and interviewee or from autobiography can extract not only facts but subliminal emotions and meaning, as Walker has demonstrated.

Making and Meaning

The act and energy of making and the associated meanings of the garment produced permeate this introduction to the home dressmaking culture of Jamaican women. In the early 1960s Paul Holbourne, a nineteen-year-old British Mod, experienced a cultural revelation and personal awakening, following the observation of the dress styles worn by West Indian immigrants.

We have to get all our clothes made because as soon as anything is in the shops it becomes too common. I once went to a West Indian club where everyone made their own clothes. It was fantastic, everyone was individual, everyone was showing themselves as they really wanted to be [. . .] They were just expressing themselves as everyone should be entitled to do, be it in homes or private clubs or in the streets. (Hamblett and Deverson 1964)

Within the context of this essay the making of clothes by an individual, as opposed to a ready-made garment, has a double-edged quality. The process applied to the making of clothes as an individualized and private action and that of the finished garment in the use of an individual's image, as a personalized, forceful agency, is imperative to the establishment of a collective identity. Add to this equation the maker producing their own designs and the formula becomes potently expressive. The questions, 'What went into the making?' and 'What does it mean?' add to our understanding of the subjectivity of home dressmaking and the creation of new clothes.

Andrew Harrison argues that making things is part of a constructive cultural activity and is a part of the fabric of a society. In this sense it is valid to consider the home-made garments worn by Jamaican women as 'objects of communication' and 'a vehicle for thought [. . .] such objects demand our understanding and interpretation, and in doing so demand at the same time [. . .] an understanding of the maker of them'. (Harrison 1978: 1) Anella calls the process of home dressmaking she practices, 'freehand dressmaking'. The very term 'freehand', in association with creativity and making, possesses an innate sense of liberation for the practitioner. The method rejects the use of paper dress patterns, thereby requiring the dressmaker to possess competence, skill and confidence in order to draw onto, or even cut directly into, the fabric. Anella does not lay much store by patterns as she feels they can lead one astray.[6] Her philosophy is, 'if you aim for what you want, you just get it [. . .] whatever you're sewing, it's inside of you.'

This is the nub of the system. Freehand dressmaking is the creation of individualized designs which may be inspired by a variety of sources, not predetermined by a bought paper pattern. These are produced as quick sketches or, according to Anella, 'from your knowledge'. In bypassing the use of paper patterns, this practice relates to certain definitions of so called 'high culture'. Harrison has applied the term 'free design' to the act of designing while making in fine art. He explains that 'free design' is possible through the build-up of extensive knowledge and skill in all areas of the subject; but only through practical exploration can this knowledge be developed and amplified. In order for it to be successful, free design relies on the competence of the maker, their extensive knowledge and a range of procedures and ideas. (Harrison 1978)

The freehand method of home dressmaking and the manipulation of designs to create something new challenges established rules of copyright. From Anella's experience, and that of other Jamaican women, the design and styling of clothes associated with this method consists of observing designs from a variety of sources – in a shop window, magazines or from films – as the basis for inspiration and adapting the design details to personal taste and body shape. The oral history of Mrs Gloria Bennett substantiates this. Gloria emigrated to Britain from Jamaica in 1959 and settled in Doncaster, South Yorkshire, where she has remained a well patronized dress-maker to the black female community.[7] She learnt the freehand method as a teenager by watching others at their work and making clothes for herself:

> You used to get your styles out of a magazine out in Jamaica and you used to see nice little styles in there and then I would just sit down and cut out a dress without using a pattern then, but now I use patterns because I think it is much easier than messing about, laying out the fabric, measuring from here to here, how far your darts should go. (Bennett 1991)

In Britain Anella had access to a wealth of inspiration – shop windows, magazines, television, mail-order catalogues – but in rural Slygoville of the 1940s and 1950s, she visited the cinema only once, and unlike Gloria, did not have access to magazines. Her main source of information on the changes in cultural tastes and values was the radio. Therefore Anella relied very much on her own ideas and observations of the city and its people when she visited Spanish Town and the capital of Jamaica, Kingston:

> If a person asks you to make them a nice dress, they would normally give you no idea what style, I would look at that person and think, this material would be nice in a lovely square neck, or this material would be nice in a lovely V-neck or off the shoulder style. (James 1996)

When Anella designs and makes clothes to match the character of a client, the process is not interrupted or corrupted. Because of the liberating nature of freehand dressmaking the procedure is one of synchronization between creative thought and creative action. Once the measurements have been taken there is little time delay between the desired design and the creative action of cutting it out in the actual fabric. There is no lengthy paper pattern manipulation to detain the process – it is nigh on automatic.[8] If a definition of design is 'the practice of organising various elements to produce a desired result' and design 'deals exclusively with organisation and arrangement of form',[9] in this instance then the process of making is not separated 'from decisions concerning the form being made'. (Lambert 1993: 45) Therefore I propose that Anella is best defined as a designer-maker.

The Wonder Years

Anella was taught sewing skills at school from the age of eight.[10] The process was slow and impractical, beginning with making bookmarkers. Once in the 'higher class' Anella made a doll's petticoat, followed by the accompanying dress. Her home was to be the more serious training ground. Anella's mother was also a dressmaker, whom she describes as 'a clever person' who just measured, cut, basted and sewed. Along with her sisters, they would practice on their mother's hand Singer sewing machine, 'I would use it to sew little skirts and things for myself.' In the late 1940s, due to her increased output of home-made and designed garments for herself and clients, Anella purchased her own Pinnock foot-operated sewing machine for about £30. As a tool and enhancement in the creative act of dressmaking, the sewing machine also signifies values invested in it by the individual. For Anella, her sewing machine is supreme.[11] Her recollections of her first sewing machine, the Pinnock purchased in Spanish Town, are full of detailed minutiae. The terms available for buying a sewing machine during the 1940s and 1950s were hire purchase or a percentage would be paid in advance and the remainder within thirty days and the machine would remain at the cash price. The Pinnock came with fourteen discs. Each one represented a particular stitch style – zig zag, straight stitch etc. To use a stitch, a disc would be placed into the top of the machine.

Conversations with Anella and Gloria, my mother and my grandmother,[12] indicate that during the period under consideration clothes made by a dressmaker had far more cachet than ready-made garments. I argue the attraction lay in the fact that the whole process alluded to glamour and social status: the personal attention and the creation of an individualized garment which fits the individual well – both of which avoided the social stigma of wearing something too common and ill-fitting. This distinction between the two clothing types available for working-class Jamaican women surfaces in the derisory nomenclature given to a range of ready-made clothes:

In the market place they used to sell ready-made or 'Wretch-e-dung' dresses hanging up [. . .] The reason why they were called 'Wretch-e-dung' you would find these things hung up, dresses overlapping one another [. . .] when somebody saw a dress they liked, they asked the market holder to '"Wretch-e-dung", fetch that one down.' Those dresses were cheaper than one from the dressmakers. If you went to the store to buy a piece of cloth to make a dress it would cost you more money to go and buy it and make it, but at the same time it was made-to-fit and to look stylish in. (James 1996)

Anella's clients in Jamaica and Britain included men and women of all age groups, who generally depended on her to produce the ideas. Anella was particularly proud of the fact that she was adept at catering for the older female age group:

> I used to sew for them, I knew exactly what they wanted. In those days old ladies didn't wear short sleeves they preferred three-quarter-length sleeves.
>
> They liked pockets because most of the old ladies used to smoke a pipe (white chalk pipes) [. . .] These were patch pockets, or sometimes I would give them a little style, something special when they were going to a wedding, a little inserted pocket, or flap pocket because they would take their pipes with them, women in their 60s and 70s, people even older. They liked their skirts full and nice. Plain and print [fabrics], no dark colours, pinks and blues. (James 1996)

'Print' during the 1940s and 1950s was the generic term for all floral designs. Generally customers would ask Anella to choose the fabric for them and the request for a print was a clear indication to Anella that a floral design was required. Another colloquial term was 'the Blue Dress'. As Anella explains, this was the equivalent of what is now described as casual wear: 'Some of the old ladies would ask for a "Blue Dress". Not that it was actually a "Blue Dress", but they asked for a dress to wear to market, everyday wear. It might be in gingham, chambray or "old iron blue", [that is] denim.' When thinking of a design for the older ladies, Anella had to also bear in mind that they generally did not like their necklines too high or too low, and the opening should be at the front, not the back, for ease of accessibility. The garments Anella designed and produced for her elderly clients were a concerted attempt to achieve an 'expression of function' and 'self-justifying aesthetic'. (Lambert 1993: 23–4) In essence she had pursued the solution of the combination of 'functional form with beauty'. (Lambert 1993: 4) This is partly attributable to Anella's sensitivity to the needs of the individual client.

By the 1950s Anella was a wife and the mother of six children. In order to make extra cash, she gave sewing lessons to girls in her home, in addition to producing and selling her own range of men's and children's clothing:

> I would buy a bale of cloth with all kinds of fabric [in it]. The amount of garments you could get out of it [. . .] could make a lot of money. From the bits and pieces I would make children's clothes, and use the good pieces to make things for men. I would sometimes have a length of khaki which could make a pair of trousers and

a shirt [. . .] I would cut out about a dozen, say, pink knickers, [. . .] I would just stitch them on the machine in a long line. I would buy a little decorative edging, elastic for the legs and waist. I would sell these to people at the weekends, for 6d and 4d, going to people's homes because I was looking after the children in the week. (James 1996)

This unusual relationship of men engaging a seamstress to make their clothes cannot be dealt with fully within this brief chapter. Her ability to make a good pair of trousers won over the confidence of the notoriously fashion-conscious black man in Jamaica and in Britain. (Tulloch 1992) Anella's skills were considered more than adequate to suppress the fear and stigma generally associated with 'home-made' clothes produced by a woman.[13] The matriarchal subtext of the social character of Jamaica may have some bearing on this.

Home-made Respectability

After 1945, Britain experienced the disconcerting status of full employment. All who wanted work had access to jobs, with thousands to spare. Britain's solution to this was to look to its colonies and invite British subjects to fill the plethora of blue-collar vacancies. The West Indians, responded slowly at first. On 21 June 1948 only 547 Jamaican men arrived on the SS *Empire Windrush*. In 1959 approximately 29,397 West Indians, including some 12,573 Jamaican men, women and children, had migrated. (Glass 1960: 3–7) The resounding effect of this phenomenon was recorded widely throughout the media at the time and up until the present day.[14] Photographs of smiling yet bewildered men, women and children arriving at Southampton docks or Waterloo station, all of whom were immaculately dressed in tailored suits or crisp dresses, appropriately accessorized, became documentary evidence of the 'Colour Problem'.[15] To a working-class woman from rural Jamaica such as Anella, who had previously only travelled a few miles to Kingston, this was an incredible adventure and opportunity, weighted by the ambivalence of fear and excitement and managed with courage and trepidation. For although Britain was a foreign land, to Anella and thousands of other West Indians, Britain was also viewed as 'Home' and the 'Mother Country'.

My reference to home stretches beyond the four walls of a house and a home, to incorporate geography and a sense of one's place in society. In the context of Anella's story, and consequently that of the other women who emigrated to Britain from the West Indies, 'home' is an ambiguous, contested site – torn between the physical and geographical definitions in Jamaica and

Britain. The construct of 'home' was a duplicitous layer of ambiguities based on their dual identity as Jamaicans and British subjects, who emigrated to Britain from their native homes, leaving their physical homes behind to establish new ones. The geographical and material home of Britain was both strange and familiar, it held positive and negative qualities, it offered protection and aggression, home was connection and disconnection. West Indians preferred the term 'migrant' to 'immigrant'; because, as British citizens, they were only flitting between one part of the Empire and another. (Glass 1960: 1) All of which, I argue, affected and reflected Anella's sense of identity and place as a black woman in Jamaica and Britain which was to find expression in part through the practice of freehand home dressmaking. Home, then, is not purely considered as the physical building which stands as a symbolic and symptomatic expression of the good mother and/or wife, rather what is primary here is 'the identity of the home dweller'. (Pile 1996: 55)

Dress and self-image acted as an accessible conduit to all of this. They enciphered their desires and values, to be *seen* by the British public as respectable, and also cultural, social and economic values – on a more prosaic level, simply coping. (Hall 1984: 2–9) 'When I was coming here I made a tight hobble dress, straight dress, there was a bolero attached to the front of the dress with hand embroidery on the front of the dress and around the hem, [hand embroidered by Anella]. It was mauve.' (James 1996) This kind of testimony is supported by Gloria who remembered vividly the dress style she composed for her entrance into Britain:

> It was aquamarine trimmed with black. The dress was narrowly gathered at the waist, with black dropped in the front, a sweetheart neck. Because, you know, you were travelling, you came dressed up, black gloves, black shoes and I think I even came in a bloody hat. Coming so posh you know, I came in a hat. I made that dress. (Bennett 1991)

Such evocative descriptions of sheath-like dresses shamelessly accentuating the female form, and their co-ordinated accessories, the *frisson* of decorative highlights and the universal hat, were amongst the material trappings of respectable femininity demanded by the global conservative social etiquette of the period. This was supported by high fashion and such taste-making publications as *Vogue* and *Queen*. In this instance, Anella's engagement with fashion was founded on three things: the ethnic values of her black community, a limited budget and, lastly, on the signification of 'a distance from the world of necessity and an ability to indulge in a level of luxury [and] the idea of fashion as display was integral to the pursuit of femininity.' (Sparke 1995: 44)

Anella emigrated to Britain, along with her husband, out of necessity, because of the crippling state of underemployment in Jamaica (Glass 1960; Pryce 1979: 10–13) and the desire to gain a better standard of living for themselves and their children. The negative reaction to the presence of the 'Coloured Guests' (Glass 1960:1) brought the feasibility and complexities of this move into sharp relief. The issues of acceptance and survival of black people since 1948 and ensuing racial debates have been widely documented. (Johnson 1985; Gilroy 1987) Freehand home dressmaking, with its associated subjective aesthetics, was a way of negotiating these realities. In this creative act Anella could attain the pleasures of display and sensuality. I suggest that what Anella expressed in the presentation of herself as well-dressed was an ingrained belief in the power of glamour. The Hollywood movie, more than any other medium, projects the power of glamour and throughout Anella's lifetime Hollywood has maintained that to be well-dressed, and to project glamour, is to wield a sexual power, albeit subversive. 'Movies clearly state that fashion and glamour are fundamental to a woman's definition – in her own eyes, [. . .] and in the eyes of society.' (Basinger 1993: 114) Anella's wholehearted engagement with the aesthetics of glamour, I believe, was to achieve a positive definition of her own self and as a representative of her community.

A photograph of Anella taken in the mid-1960s is an image entirely composed by her. (Figure 6. 1) The fully lined, gold lamé dress was styled with a 'boat neck to make it a little different'. Anella dyed the white gloves a mustard colour to match her dress. Her handbag and shoes were black, the latter suede. To crown her head, Anella wears a bandeau that she covered with velvet to match the lavish texture of the suede shoes. For me, the most pertinent design motif of the dress is the asymmetrical panel detail across the front of the dress, and positioned by a self-fabric corsage on the left of the waist. This styling detail certifies the 'difference' most strongly – but what is this difference? To return to Chamberlain:

> Appearances represent identity; they signal femininity. On a broader level, clothes are part of the iconography of womanhood. But they also indulge the imagination and the senses. Clothes represent a definition or statement of difference, independence and autonomy. They may also signal defiance and deception. 'I ent show poor' [. . .] Such definitions may be illusory, but dressing well places women in the centre, as creators of the illusion, [. . .] The signal may be subtle, but then the best deceptions are. (Chamberlain 1995: 106)

The difference being indicated by this generation of Jamaican women, encoded by the time and place of mid-1960s Britain, was not a conscious

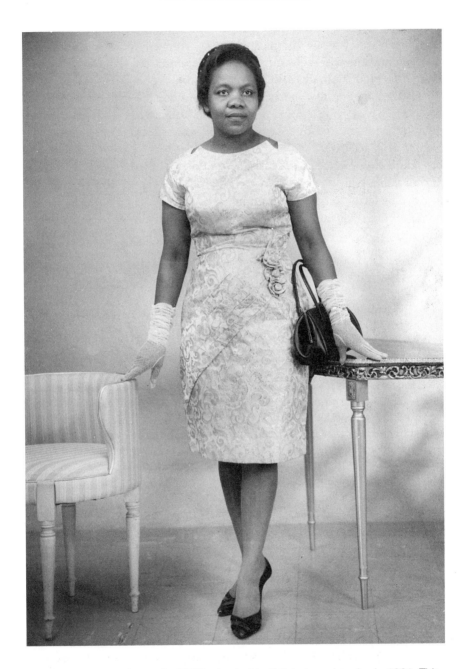

Figure 6.1. Anella James (b. 1930) migrated to Britain from Jamaica in 1961. This studio photograph was taken at Griffiths & Sons, East London in the mid 1960s. The dress was designed and produced by Anella through the 'freehand' method of dressmaking, originally for a wedding.

subversive action to flout the accepted values of British dress codes and fashions. It was, I propose, a means to integrate these codes with their own idiosyncratic inflections that advocated *their* cultural values, *their* 'colouredness'[16] *their* 'Jamaicanness'. What freehand home dressmaking had facilitated for Anella and her fellow Jamaican dressmakers was the subliminal emotions and meanings in being a Jamaican woman in Britain and the assertion of her own aesthetic-self and by extension a collective identity. Here in the oral history of Anella, freehand home dressmaking extends beyond Anella and her family, to produce goods for sale to her local community and to reach and to support a kinship based on a particular identity constructed and inspired by the peculiarities of a given place. The parameter of the home and home dressmaking is extended into wider significance and the aesthetic-self.

Notes

1. I concentrate on Jamaican women, as my research and the interviews conducted over the past ten years have been associated with the Jamaican community in Britain and Jamaica. There is of course evidence of issues raised in this essay applicable to women from other Caribbean Islands. See Bryan (1991) and Shepherd et al. (1995)

2. The dressmaking skills of Jamaican women were highly recommended in travel guides. British travel writer Bessie Pullen-Berry assured potential female visitors to the island that Jamaican dressmakers were 'excellent copyists and clever machinists who, provided they were given a good pattern, would turn out a well-made skirt for about 6s and a blouse for a little less, in 2 or 3 days'. (1903: 47)

3. Jamaica Gazette, Kingston 18 June 1891. The first store to offer a costumes and dresses made-to-order department was Alfred Pawsey & Co. in 1905. See Robertson (1987–88).

4. The paper will also make reference to other Jamaican women to counterbalance the oral history of Anella James.

5. Allessandro Portelli, 'The Peculiarities of Oral History', *History Workshop Journal*, No. 12, Autumn 1981. Quoted by Mary Chamberlain. (1996: 95)

6. In the mid-1970s Anella attended an evening class at Waltham Forest College, as she felt it was time to learn what she termed, 'the British Method of dressmaking'. It was also a way of interacting with other black and white women. She discovered that, fundamentally, the basic concepts and procedures were the same as the freehand method, apart from the ubiquitous paper pattern. The classes did not convert Anella to the use of paper dress patterns. Only for an extremely complex style will she draft her own pattern.

7. Mrs Gloria Bennett practised dressmaking as a supplementary income to her full-time work as a bus conductor. Her client base has decreased since the 1980s. Reasons for this are purely speculative. I suspect easier access to more reasonably-

priced clothing, the pervasive culture of 'designer clothing', desired by a younger Black British market, though this group continue to turn to Gloria for bridal wear, which, in the 1990s, is her main area of production.

8. It was a tradition in my family, and not unusual amongst other West Indian and some of the white working-class families I knew as a child, to have a new outfit for Christmas Day. For the special day of 1972 I purchased a new top, but had no 'bottom' to go with it. The actual chain of events is difficult to recall, but I do remember one minute, on Christmas Eve, my mum preparing the food for Christmas lunch, and the next she was laying out some cream fabric on the floor and cutting out a circular skirt for me. My mother used no pattern, neither did she draw an outline of the desired skirt onto the fabric. She just checked my waist measurement, and the length and the circumference of the hem that I wanted. I do remember a deal being struck that my mother would complete the body of the skirt if I sewed the hem. What is vivid in my memory is the apparent ease with which my mother dexterously executed the skirt amid the commotion of Christmas preparations: she cut out the skirt as if following an imaginary outline, then assembled the skirt, sewing the centre back seam, securing the zip and then waistband, passed the skirt to me to complete whilst she returned to the kitchen to complete the festive food preparations.

9. Norman Bel Geddes, *Horizons in Industrial Design*, 1934. Quoted by Susan Lambert. (1993: 45)

10. Anella's experimentation with the restyling of her clothes began at the age of six. She individualized the standard dress styles reserved for children, to the chagrin of her mother. Anella reduced the tent-like dress into a waisted silhouette by cutting and 'bad' hand sewing, so that she could look more like her older sisters.

11. My interview with Anella in January 1996 was conducted beside her industrial sewing machine, without any prompting from me.

12. Mrs Roslyn Agatha Simpson, my grandmother, emigrated to Britain from Jamaica in 1953. My mother emigrated to Britain from Jamaica in 1954.

13. Anella taught herself to make men's trousers by unpicking a pair in order to study how they were cut. In Britain this knowledge proved indispensable to West Indian men. She could reduce the voluminous 'Wind Breaker' trousers into the slimmer and cropped cigarette pant styles of the 1960s. This Jamaican nickname derived from the fact that due to the voluminous style of the trouser, the trousers filled up like a balloon when the wind blew.

14. The fiftieth anniversary, in 1998, of the arrival of the SS *Empire Windrush* attracted significant coverage in the popular media, which examined its continuing historical and cultural legacy.

15. *Picture Post*, June 1956.

16. I have used this term as indicative of the political thinking amongst the average West Indian at this time and for consideration of its relevance to the ethnicity and identity of this community. Many of this generation still use the term 'coloured' over 'black' in reference to themselves, because of the political connotations of the latter.

References

Basinger, Jeanine (1993), *A Woman's View: How Hollywood Spoke to Women, 1930–1960*, London: Chatto & Windus.

Bennett, Gloria (1991), Interview with the author, July.

Beverley, B. Dadzie, S. and Scafe, S. (1985), *The Heart of the Race: Black Women's Lives in Britain*, London: Virago.

Birmingham Feminist History Group, (1979), 'Feminism as Femininity in the Nineteen-fifties?' in *Feminist Review*, Vol. 3.

Bryan, R. (1991), *The Jamaican People 1880–1902: Race Class and Social Control*, London: MacMillan Education.

Buckley, C. (1998), 'On the Margins: Theorizing the History and Significance of Making and Designing Clothes at Home' in *Journal of Design History*, Vol. 11, No. 2.

Chamberlain, M. (1995), 'Gender & Memory: Oral History and Women's History' in Shepherd et al. (1995).

Darwent, C. (1998), 'The Woman Behind the Chairs' in the *Independent on Sunday*, 13 September.

Gilroy, P. (1987), *There Ain't no Black in the Union Jack: The Cultural Politics of Race and Nation*, London: Hutchinson.

Glass, R. (1960), *Newcomers: The West Indians in London*, London: Centre for Urban Studies and George Allen & Unwin.

Hall, S. (1984), 'Reconstruction Work' in *Ten 8*, No. 16.

Hamblett, C. and Deverson, J. (1964), *Generation X*, London: Library 33, Anthony Gibbs & Phillips Ltd.

Harrison, A. (1978), *Making and Thinking: A Study of Intelligent Activities*, Sussex: Harvester Press.

hooks, b. (1982), *Ain't I A Woman: Black Women and Feminism*, London: Pluto Press.

James, Anella (1996), Interview with the author, January.

Johnson, B. (1985), *I Think of My Mother: Notes on the Life and Times of Claudia Jones*, London: Karia.

Lambert, S. (1993), *Form Follows Function? Design in the 20th Century*, London: Victoria and Albert Museum.

Nunn, P. G. (1987), *Victorian Women Artists*, London: Women's Press.

Onyekachi, W. (1998), *Empire Windrush : Fifty Years of Writing About Black Britain*, London: Victor Gollancz.

Pile, S. (1996), *The Body and the City: Psychoanalysis, Space and Subjectivity*, London and New York: Routledge.

Pryce, K. (1979), *Endless Pressure*, Middlesex: Penguin.

Pullen-Berry, B. (1903), *Jamaica As It Is*, London: T. Fisher Unwin.

Robertson, G. (1987/1988), 'Advertisements for Clothes in Kingston 1897–1914' in *Jamaica Journal*, November 1987–January 1988.

Shepherd, V. Brereton, B. and Bailey, B., eds, (1995), *Engendering History: Caribbean Women in Historical Perspective*, London: James Currey; Kingston: Ian Randle.

Sparke, P. (1995), *As Long as it's Pink*, London: Pandora.

Tulloch, C. (1992), 'Rebel Without a Pause: Black Street Style and Black Designers' in Ash, J. and Wilson, E., eds, *Chic Thrills: A Fashion Reader*, London: Pandora.

—— (1997), *Fashioned in Black and White: Women's Dress in Jamaica, 1880–1907*, unpublished M.A. dissertation V&A/Royal College of Art.

Walker, A. (1984), *In Search of Our Mothers' Gardens: A Womanist Prose*, London: The Women's Press.

Woolf, V. (1977), *A Room of One's Own*, London: Grafton. First published in 1929.

Part 2

Home Dressmaking and Consumption

7

Wearily Moving Her Needle: Army Officers' Wives and Sewing in the Nineteenth-Century American West

Julie A. Campbell

When nineteen-year-old Ellen McGowan married James Harwood Biddle in 1862, her groom, an army officer, gave her $20 in gold as an incentive to sew a calico dress. Ellen was doubtless possessed of many accomplishments, but the mysteries of sewing eluded her. In fits and starts she cut fabric, wrestled with patterns and ripped out seams, but eventually Ellen Biddle had a handmade dress. Before long she easily turned another gift from her husband – a length of 'beautiful blue-and-white French organdie muslin' – into a lace-trimmed gown. (Biddle 1907: 38–9) Her husband had spent the $20 wisely, for Ellen Biddle had gained a useful skill that she valued and needed when they headed for military posts in the western United States. She and her comrades – the wives of officers in the Indian-fighting army from the 1850s through the 1890s – found themselves far from professional seamstresses, well-stocked dry-goods stores and up-to-date fashions. So they turned to needle and thread – and to their own labour and ingenuity.

Most of the women were from the East or the Midwest and had grown up in middle-class or upper-middle-class families, with all the education and privileges of such an upbringing. The US Army assigned their husbands to posts all across the West but made scant allowance for accompanying wives and children, classifying them all as camp followers, a term the army also applied to laundresses (who were military employees), the wives of enlisted men and prostitutes. Their journeys to the remote posts served as the women's introductions to frontier army life: bone-rattling, lengthy travel via horseback, steamship, wagon and train. They set up housekeeping in dwellings which might be one-room adobes, log cabins, or small brick houses – their husbands' ranks determined the quality of housing and higher-ranking officers could and did turn them out of their homes. The officers' wives also contended with the threat of Indian attacks, the danger their husbands faced in the line of duty, harsh climates, hit-or-miss medical care, providing a suitable education for their children and the huge expenses of living on the frontier and of moving every few months or years. (Stallard 1991)

They depended on the other officers' wives for companionship, finding a supportive, army-wide circle of women who shared common experiences and standards. Though they sometimes brought African-American or Irish women with them as servants or hired the wives of enlisted men as house-keepers, they could not and did not socialize with such women because they belonged to a lower social class. (Stallard 1991) When Julia Kirkham Davis and her infant son arrived at Camp McDowell, Arizona,[1] in 1869, '[T]he officers crowded round with amazement to see the newcomers, the lady,' she remembered. 'Of course we two women, my nurse and I, were the greatest curiosities. There was already one other lady in the camp, and now the female society would be doubled.' (Schreier 1988: 191–2) The 'other lady' was the one other officer's wife; Davis did not count as 'society' her nurse and the many laundresses who probably lived at McDowell. The nineteenth-century army was nothing if not socially stratified, and the women's clothing styles also reflected the divisions of status.

The women brought to their new homes carpets, furniture, kitchen gear and, of course, their wardrobes. The journey to remote military posts often proved hazardous to belongings: steamboats sank, wagon-laden bridges collapsed and prairie fires blazed. Trunks full of clothing might sit out in the rain for days, resulting in mildew which ruined garments beyond repair. (Fougera 1940; Custer 1885, 1890) The women did not necessarily miss the individual garments (and friends always helped out with loans or gifts of clothing), but they did long for 'the thousand and one accessories of a woman's wardrobe', wrote Martha Summerhayes, whose own wardrobe burned up along with the steamship carrying it to Fort Yuma, Arizona, as well as 'the accumulation of years, the comfortable things which money could not buy, especially at that distance'. (Summerhayes 1908: 148)

As Summerhayes and her comrades soon learned, money could buy precious little in the way of ready-made clothes, patterns and fabric on the frontier. They made purchases from mail-order catalogues and asked friends and relatives to send things, but such methods cost time and money. A new army wife at Fort Bayard, New Mexico, in the early 1870s discovered that mail-order clothes often required complicated alterations. (Boyd 1894)

Summerhayes (1908) ordered garments to replace the ones burned on the boat, but it took two months for the package to reach her in Arizona. From San Francisco, before moving to her new post in Arizona, Frances Boyd (1894) ordered clothes from New York, which failed to arrive before she left. An officer en route from California to Arizona collected the box and delivered it to Boyd – fourteen months later. On another occasion, Boyd paid over $22 in express charges for a $20 hat, which turned out to be a frothy bonnet rather than the modest hat she had ordered. The charges for stagecoach delivery often cost more than ready-made clothes or than fabric and a dressmaker's fee.

Army women also turned to sources close at hand, the military sutlers and local merchants. As the only purveyors of goods in remote areas, suppliers charged accordingly and, if they carried clothes at all, they offered mostly men's articles and carried only the plainest dresses for women. As Lydia Lane packed up her family for their 1867 trip from Fort Union, New Mexico, to the East, she sighed at the thought of buying the necessary clothing from 'the smiling members of Ketchem & Cheatam'. (Lane 1893: 153) The officers' wives prized infrequent assignments to military posts near such established towns as Prescott, Arizona, and Santa Fe, New Mexico, for those communities boasted well-stocked millineries, dry-goods stores and dressmakers. (Carriker and Carriker 1975) In 1869, Alice Blackwood Baldwin was happy to find the millinery and dressmaker's shop in Hays City, Kansas – even though it was next door to a saloon, which abutted a butcher's shop with a pigpen behind it. (Carriker and Carriker 1975) Saving money was a constant concern, as officers' pay was modest. Given such circumstances of time, money and distance, officers' wives began to sew and repair their clothing themselves, as well as garments for their children, husbands and servants.

If the women already knew how to sew, as did Ellen Biddle, they had won half the battle. However, many of them had patronized dressmakers back home before they encountered frontier life and all they knew of sewing was fancywork such as embroidery and needlepoint. Elizabeth Bacon Custer fell into this category. Her husband was George Armstrong Custer, famed for his youthful heroism in the Civil War and, in the late 1860s and the 1870s, as a notorious Indian fighter and leader of the Seventh Cavalry. (Figure 7.1) On one journey through Texas, Elizabeth lost the bodice of her riding habit. She borrowed a jacket from her husband as a substitute[2] while she spent several weeks ripping, copying, basting and stitching the replacement. (Custer 1889)

On her next project, a dress, Custer accidentally cut the fabric so that the design ran one way on the bodice but another on the skirt, a mistake which spurred her husband to tease her mercilessly. Elizabeth wrote her parents

Figure 7.1. Left to right: Eliza Brown Denison, Elizabeth Bacon Custer and George Armstrong Custer. The Custers and their servant posed for this photograph on 12 April 1865, three days after the end of the Civil War. Elizabeth Custer is wearing her military-style riding habit. Courtesy of the Little Bighorn Battlefield National Monument, Crow Agency, Montana, USA.

back in Michigan, 'I remember how you both wanted me to learn [to sew] when I was at home, and I almost wished I had, when I found it took me such ages to do what ought to have been short work.' (Custer 1889: 88) Elizabeth Custer thought her home-made gowns 'looked pretty botchy' (Custer 1890: 257) until she developed her skills with a needle. Other women knew how to sew but were unable to adjust patterns and fit garments properly. Martha Summerhayes's home-made dresses turned out to be cool, comfortable, and 'something like a bag', she reported. (Summerhayes 1908: 199)

Most of the women probably did their sewing by hand. In 1865 Margaret Carrington and other women took their sewing chairs from Fort Leavenworth, Kansas, to their new post in Wyoming and George Custer arranged Elizabeth's sewing chair and workbasket next to his desk so that he could read to her while she stitched. Sewing machines were rare on the frontier, although they were slowly becoming available and affordable back home. In 1865 *Demorest's Illustrated Monthly and Mme Demorest's Mirror of Fashions* magazine offered a $55 Wheeler & Wilson sewing machine as a premium with the purchase of thirty-five subscriptions at $3 each, enabling neighbouring women to form a kind of collective and share the expensive labour-saving equipment. (*Demorest's* 1865) At Fort Ellis, Montana, in 1879, Frances Roe counted herself lucky to possess a machine. (Roe 1909) In 1869 Lydia Lane paid $40 for one, then turned a nice profit at her moving sale when another army wife bought it for $100. (Lane 1893) In 1868 Frances Boyd's husband generously spent a month's pay on a machine that turned out to be beyond repair (Boyd 1893), and in 1874 Martha Summerhayes happily inherited a sewing machine that came with her new quarters at Fort D. A. Russell, Wyoming. (Summerhayes 1908)

To obtain patterns and fashion news, the women pored over magazines. The publications featured black-and-white and colour illustrations of dresses and other garments; written descriptions of trims, fabrics and colours; and small patterns which women traced and enlarged. In 1866 Margaret Carrington read *Frank Leslie's Illustrated Weekly* and *Demorest's* (Carrington and Carrington 1890), while Elizabeth Burt in 1868 preferred *Godey's Lady's Book.* (Mattes 1960) Elizabeth Custer, however, pledged her loyalty to *Harper's Bazar* and its fold-out patterns.[3] One of her husband's soldiers joked of the patterns' intricate appearance that 'no better map of our marches could be found'. (Custer 1890: 257) In April 1862, *Godey's* published an article on Madame Demorest's 'Science of Dress-Cutting' (407): 'a system which is founded absolutely on scientific principles [. . .] and enables any lady possessing a model to make her own dresses perfectly'. (*Godey's* 1862: 407) Army women also turned to pattern books, as did Emily McCorkle FitzGerald in 1876 when her mother mailed them to her in Sitka, Alaska. (Laufe 1962)

Appetites whetted by a tempting gown in *Godey's* or *Demorest's*, the women headed to the sutlers' stores on the military posts in search of fabric. Simple calico,[4] which Indian women bought, was plentiful there, but the stores lacked the wools, silks and fine cottons which the army women preferred and to which they were accustomed. Reflecting their status as officers' wives from comfortable backgrounds, they generally used calico only for furniture covers and curtains. The association with the Indians bothered Margaret Carrington, who disparaged the 'red squaw cloth' and Alice Baldwin, who thought it fit only 'for the squaws'. (Carrington and Carrington 1890: 97; Carriker and Carriker 1975: 72) As lowly as the women thought it was, calico was expensive, sometimes $1 a yard, a sum which Elizabeth Burt refused to pay for her servant's dress. (Mattes 1960) In 1875 Emily

FitzGerald found the Sitka price of 15 cents per yard too dear, so she asked her mother to send two or three lots of calico, nine to ten yards each, for garments for her servant. (Laufe 1962) Although FitzGerald possessed an extravagant length of black cashmere, which she had probably brought to Alaska from the East, most army women of all ranks made do with the material at hand, such as the wife of the baker at Fort C. F. Smith, Montana, who made dresses for her daughters from flour sacks. (Mattes 1960) Such simple, inexpensive fabrics as 'linsey-woolsey, delaines,[5] and calico nowhere else underwent such endowment with fashionable shapes', noted Margaret Carrington. (Carrington and Carrington 1890: 174)

The daily routine which Ellen Biddle followed at Fort Whipple, Arizona, in 1876 and 1877 was one which many of her fellow army wives knew. In the morning Biddle went for a horseback ride or a drive in a buggy. In the afternoons and evenings, she sewed – clothes, curtains, even upholstery. (Biddle 1907) An army woman made her own clothes, her children's garments, aprons and dresses for her servant and some of her husband's non-uniform items, such as the dressing-gown Elizabeth Custer 'laboriously cobbled out with very ignorant fingers'. (Custer 1889: 438) When stationed at Fort Leavenworth, Kansas, in 1868, she and her friend Jennie Barnitz also made their men flannel shirts; Elizabeth's original creations were red, but when she realized that the colour made her husband a vivid target, she switched to flannel of dark blue. (Custer 1885)

Mending and refurbishing helped the women economize by reusing old garments and by freshening them with new trims or silhouettes. Evy Alexander spent a pleasant evening in her parlour at Fort Union, New Mexico, 'busily engaged in sewing and mending, as my clothes are beginning to give out a little'. (Myres 1977: 123) If Elizabeth Custer was accompanying her husband's troops on the move to another post, she attacked the task during stopovers. She patched her riding habit and reinforced its seams with sturdy linen thread and inserted lead or small bags of shot in the hems to keep them down in high winds. (Custer 1885, 1889) Remaking clothes consisted of such tasks as taking seams in or out; picking items apart for cleaning or dyeing; transforming adult garments into children's; detaching skirts from bodices, turning them upside down or inside out and reattaching them; and other thrifty tactics. (Mills 1985) In 1866 a young house guest of the Custers' found it difficult to remodel her full silk dresses into what Elizabeth called 'tightly gored princess gowns' because she had snipped fabric from the seams in order to make more than one 'tiny neck-bow, called a butterfly tie' (Custer 1889: 502) as keepsakes for her friends.

Even though Custer's friend tried to keep abreast of current fashion by altering the silhouettes of her gowns, many army women claimed unconcern for the mode of the day. In 1874 Martha Summerhayes, en route to her post in Arizona, crossed paths with a group of army women on their way home. Summerhayes was startled: 'The women's clothes looked ridiculously old-fashioned, and I wondered if I should look that way when my time came to leave.' After four years in a desolate, remote place, she had her answer: 'I had become imbued with a profound indifference to dress.' (Summerhayes 1908: 39, 219) Frances Boyd agreed: 'Army women show the greatest unconcern regarding fashions, probably because their lives are so different from those of their city sisters.' (Boyd 1894: 219) When women visited their homes back in the East and Midwest, the reactions of passers-by and relatives to their dated appearances surprised and amused them. Elizabeth Burt and her sister Kate wore three-year-old dresses to visit their mother in Ohio, who teasingly called them 'an old fashioned looking group, showing unmistakable proofs of roughing it on the frontier'. (Mattes 1960: 178–9) When Katherine Gibson arrived at Fort Abraham Lincoln, North Dakota, in 1874, she noticed the old dresses of the two women on post, one of them Elizabeth Custer 'in a light-colored, out-of-date frock'. (Fougera 1940: 85) In fact, the women came to regard their unstylish clothing as proud badges of their status as officers' wives on the wild frontier. Army wives learned to enjoy their environment, where 'the requirements of social life did not demand that we should be clothed in fine linen and gay attire', wrote Elizabeth Burt. 'To be clean and comfortable was all that was expected.' (Mattes 1960: 142)

Nonetheless, even Elizabeth Burt welcomed the well-dressed wife of a new officer to Fort Smith, Montana, in 1868: 'What an unexpected pleasure to receive a lady just from the States, bringing [. . .] the new spring fashions.' (Mattes 1960: 164) Skill in sewing came in handy when remodelling rounded waistlines into pointed basques,[6] as Elizabeth Custer and her friends hastily did before dinner one night while on a visit to the East, (Custer 1890) or for drawing the fullness of the hoopskirted dresses of the 1860s into the bustles of the 1870s. Custer's husband helped with fashion updates, returning from his trips to the East bearing dresses, hats, yard goods, trims and news of the current styles which he had observed. (Custer 1889) Such presents gave the women 'immense pleasure', said Elizabeth Custer, and 'there was no one in that far country to prevent the screams of delight with which each gift was received'. (Custer 1889: 423–4) In the 1870s, Emily FitzGerald wrote home from Alaska: 'Please tell me what the women are wearing now. Are there any new ways of trimming that are used more than ruffles or folds? Are polonaise[7] worn as much as ever? Are they putting much trimming on polonaise and basques?' (Laufe 1962: 157) As for the length of black cashmere, she planned to send it back home, because she thought that, if an Alaskan seamstress made it into a dress, 'it won't look stylish and I will have to plan it all by myself anyway'. (Laufe 1962: 157) Apparently a woman of luxurious tastes but rudimentary sewing skills, FitzGerald bought readily available Alaskan furs and feathers, using grebe feathers to adorn her muff and cloak and swansdown to trim her children's coats. (Laufe 1962)

At least two army wives tried to reject a conventional standard of dress, but their officer husbands thwarted their practical and somewhat rebellious plans. Even if a frock brought to a military post from the East was a few years out of date, it was nonetheless a proper and appropriate garment for a Victorian woman and an officer's wife. However, in the 1870s Martha Summerhayes came to admire the cool, practical clothing of the 'scrupulously clean and modest' Mexican women in Arizona, where temperatures routinely exceeded 100° F: low-necked, short-sleeved blouses, calico skirts, muslin dresses, white stockings, and black shoes, and black shawls when they needed a wrap. 'I have always been sorry I did not adopt their fashion of house apparel', Summerhayes wrote. 'Instead of that, I yielded to the prejudices of my conservative partner, and sweltered during the day in high-necked and long-sleeved white dresses.' (Summerhayes 1908: 170) Eveline Alexander started her horseback journey to New Mexico in riding habits, smart dresses, and small hats, but she soon switched to a waterproof cloak and one of her husband's broad-brimmed hats. Toward the trip's end, 'in consideration of Andrew's supposed feelings and my proximity to civilization [. . .] I abandoned my usual bizarre costume for a proper riding habit and a small cap.' (Myres 1977: 78) As a result, Eveline suffered a severe sunburn on her face and ears.

Whether updating an old frock or making a new one, army women sewed together for company, to keep busy while their husbands were in the field and to help each other when needed. In 1872, Frances Roe and other officers' wives stitched together warm clothes for a recent widow and her children before they left Camp Supply, Oklahoma, for the East. (Roe 1909) In the 1870s Katherine Garrett joined Elizabeth Custer and other ladies in sewing bees to make clothes for children and husbands and to darn General Custer's socks. (Fougera 1940) On another occasion the women of Fort Lincoln helped a woman who had just lost a toddler son to pneumonia. For this project they instructed Elizabeth's brother-in-law, Tom Custer, in the operation of the sewing machine and he played his part when not on military duty. Elizabeth Custer described the scene: 'A roomful of busy women, cutting, basting, making button holes and joining together little garments, soon had a passable outfit for the brave mother's little ones, and even a gown for her own sweet self.' (Custer 1885: 101) In typical self-effacing style, Custer called the resulting garments 'cobbled-out woollen clothes our ignorant fingers had fashioned'. (Custer 1885: 101)

Another 1874 sewing bee at Fort Lincoln marked a happy occasion, the marriage of Katherine Garrett to Lieutenant Francis Gibson. Her mother had sent sufficient satin and a pattern, so a cheerful crew consisting of the bride-to-be; Elizabeth Custer; Mollie McIntosh, Katherine's sister and the wife of Lieutenant Donald McIntosh; and the wife of another lieutenant, Myles Moylan, of Custer's Seventh Cavalry, set to work. 'Mrs. Custer [did] the cutting and fitting,' wrote Garrett, 'I the straight sewing, and Mrs. Moylan and Mollie the fancy hemming and ruffling.' (Fougera 1940: 187) Apparently the bee took place before the arrival of the sewing machine on which Tom Custer apprenticed, for Garrett remembered that they lacked one, 'but with so many willing hands the work progressed rapidly'. (Fougera 1940: 187) Mollie McIntosh stitched faux orange blossoms (as real ones were hard to find on the windswept plains of North Dakota) out of satin and yellow embroidery silk and attached them to the gown. Elizabeth Custer gave Katherine a blue garter for the new and blue portions of her wedding ensemble and the other women presented her with handmade undergarments for her trousseau. (Fougera 1940) Clad in the lovingly made finery, Garrett marched down the aisle; two years later, in best army-wife fashion, she lined a small coffin with the satin dress after the death of a child of Captain and Mrs Frederick W. Benteen. (Fougera 1940)

Sewing bees and special occasions occasionally lightened the burden, but sewing was hard, never-ending work. As Ellen Biddle sewed trousers for her two determined young sons, who insisted on the addition of pockets, she found it 'a very difficult task [. . .] and I tried very hard to buy them off, but they were never willing to give them up; they would stand, one each side of me, helping to get them in right'. (Biddle 1907: 83) In 1871 Alice Kirk Grierson left Fort Sill, Oklahoma, for a much-needed rest with her family in Chicago. She wrote her husband, Benjamin Grierson, that 'the strain of having to cut, and make almost every article for the children, and the house at Ft. Sill, was greater on me, than you can estimate.' (Leckie 1989: 58) Elizabeth Custer wistfully thought that the soldiers of the Seventh Cavalry (her brother-in-law Tom Custer notwithstanding) as devoted to their womenfolk as they were, 'regretted that they could not sew, when they saw an overtaxed lady wearily moving her needle'. (Custer 1885: 162)

Frontier army life came to an end for the officers' wives when their husbands retired from the military or were reassigned to new posts. Some women left the West and military society because of the deaths of their husbands: Elizabeth Custer and Mollie McIntosh were widowed in June 1876 after the famous Battle of the Little Bighorn, while Katherine Garrett Gibson's husband survived. (Stallard 1991) Whatever their circumstances, the women always remembered their unusual experiences. Ellen Biddle, Frances Boyd,

Margaret Carrington, Lydia Lane, Martha Summerhayes and others wrote books about their army lives and Elizabeth Custer, the most famous of the group, published three volumes during her career as a tireless promoter of her late husband. Edited diaries and collections of letters also found their way into print.

From reading their accounts of sewing, one might suppose the army wives' experiences with making clothes were unique, but in fact they shared the same frustrations and solutions as their civilian sisters on the western frontier. (Brandt 1989; Helvenston 1990) Nonetheless, the army women took pride in how they had risen to the occasion, done what was necessary and set a standard for other officers' wives during their tenures in what Elizabeth Custer called 'a land where there were no seamstresses, no ready-made clothing.' (Custer 1885: 101)

Notes

1. In the nineteenth century, most of the military forts mentioned in this chapter were in United States territories, not states. For example, Fort Abraham Lincoln was in Dakota Territory, which encompassed the modern-day states of North Dakota and South Dakota. Today's visitor to the historic site at Fort Lincoln would go to North Dakota. For simplicity, I refer to the modern states.

2. In a popular nineteenth-century army fashion, many women tailored their husbands' uniform jackets from the men's cadet days at the US Military Academy at West Point, New York, and wore them as the top halves of their riding habits. (Roe 1909)

3. *Harper's Bazar*, first issued in the US in 1867, changed the spelling to *Bazaar* in 1929.

4. Calico is 'one of the earliest cotton fabrics known; perfect example of fine, plain weave; yarn-dyed, piece-dyed, or printed with patterns'. (Mills 1985: 181)

5. Linsey-woolsey is 'coarse, woollen linen or cotton warp' fabric; delaine is sheer wool and cotton. (Wilcox 1970: 196, 106)

6. A basque was a snug-fitting bodice seamed 'from shoulder to waist, with or without short skirt-like continuation'. (Mills 1985: 181)

7. Polonaise referred to a 'dress with bodice and looped-up tunic; named after Polish national costume'. (Mills 1985: 182)

References

Biddle, E. M. (1907), *Reminiscences of a Soldier's Wife*, Philadelphia: Press of J. B. Lippincott Company.

Boyd, F. (1894), *Cavalry Life in Tent and Field*, Lincoln: University of Nebraska Press, reprinted 1982.

Brandt, B. M. (1989), 'Arizona Clothing: A Frontier Perspective', *Dress*, 15: 65–78.

Campbell, J. A. and Brandt, B. (1994), ' "No Seamstresses, No Ready-Made Clothing": Clothing Consumption on the American Frontier, 1850–1890', *Clothing and Textiles Research Journal*, 12: 16–21.

Carriker, R. C. and Carriker, E. R., eds, (1975), *An Army Wife on the Frontier: The Memoirs of Alice Blackwood Baldwin, 1867–1877*, Salt Lake City: Tanner Trust Fund, University of Utah Library.

Carrington, H. B., and Carrington, M. (1890), *Ab-Sa-Ra-Ka; or Wyoming Opened: Being the Experience of an Officer's Wife on the Plains*, Philadelphia: Press of J.B. Lippincott Company.

Custer, E. B. (1885), *'Boots and Saddles' or, Life in Dakota with General Custer*, Norman: University of Oklahoma Press, reprinted 1987.

—— (1889), *Tenting on the Plains or General Custer in Kansas and Texas*, New York: Charles L. Webster & Company.

—— (1890), *Following the Guidon: Into the Indian Wars with General Custer and the Seventh Cavalry*, Norman: University of Oklahoma Press, reprinted 1966.

Demorest's Illustrated Monthly and Mme Demorest's Mirror of Fashions, (1865), July: 11.

Fougera, K. G. (1940), *With Custer's Cavalry*, Caldwell: The Caxton Printers, Ltd.

Helvenston, S. (1990), 'Fashion on the Frontier', *Dress*, 17: 141–55.

Lane, L. S. (1893), *I Married a Soldier: Old Days in the Old Army*, Albuquerque: University of New Mexico Press, reprinted 1988.

Laufe, A., ed., (1962), *An Army Doctor's Wife on the Frontier: Letters from Alaska and the Far West, 1874–1878*, Pittsburgh: University of Pittsburgh Press.

Leckie, S. A., ed., (1989), *The Colonel's Lady on the Western Frontier: The Correspondence of Alice Kirk Grierson*, Lincoln: University of Nebraska Press.

—— (1993), *Elizabeth Bacon Custer and the Making of a Myth*, Norman: University of Oklahoma Press.

Mattes, M. J. (1960), *Indians, Infants and Infantry: Andrew and Elizabeth Burt on the Frontier*, Lincoln: University of Nebraska Press, reprinted 1988.

Mills, B. (1985), *Calico Chronicle: Texas Women and Their Fashions, 1830–1910*, Lubbock: Texas Tech Press.

Myres, S. L., ed., (1977), *Cavalry Wife: The Diary of Eveline M. Alexander, 1866–1867*, College Station: Texas A&M University Press.

Roe, F. M. A. (1909), *Army Letters from an Officer's Wife, 1871–1888*, New York: D. Appleton and Company.

Schreier, J. (1988), ' "For This I Had Left Civilization": Julia Davis at Camp McDowell, 1869–1870', *Journal of Arizona History*, 29: 185–98.

Stallard, P. Y. (1991), *Glittering Misery: Dependents of the Indian-Fighting Army*, Norman: University of Oklahoma Press.

Summerhayes, M. (1908), *Vanished Arizona: Recollections of My Army Life*, Philadelphia: Press of J.B. Lippincott Company.

Wilcox, R. T. (1970). *The Dictionary of Costume*, London: B.T. Batsford Ltd.

8

Commodified Craft, Creative Community: Women's Vernacular Dress in Nineteenth-Century Philadelphia

Kathryn E. Wilson

In 1857, seventeen-year old Susan Trautwine noted in her diary: 'This morning my cloak came home. I did not like it as much as Clara's. So I expect to go with Clara to Mrs Mitchell's tomorrow and ask her if she will make me one like Clara's [. . .] Liny was here a good while since church; we had quite a talk about the cloak. I hope Mrs Mitchell will take it back.' Mrs Mitchell was willing to take the cloak back and make it 'more like Clara's' and when the cloak was finished, Trautwine declared with satisfaction: 'I like it much better now.' (Trautwine 1857: 18, 19 and 24 November) The genesis of this new cloak suggests much about the manner in which most women's clothing was produced in nineteenth-century Philadelphia. The cloak was custom-manufactured by a skilled craftswoman, its design shaped by a pattern drafted from prevailing modes. It was fitted to Trautwine's body and trimmed according to her specifications with materials she purchased at local shops. When she was not pleased with the initial results, Miss Trautwine looked around her, consulted her friend, and returned the cloak to the dressmaker to renegotiate its design, bringing her friend along to illustrate the desired style. Later, she retrimmed and mended the coat, eventually ripping it apart to be cleaned or remade. As she dealt with the uncomfortable situation of having to return work, Susan Trautwine was learning essential lessons and skills. She was gaining knowledge about design, negotiating both the authority of fashion and the aesthetic judgments of her local class peers. She was participating in local economic activity, cultivating expertise and engaging in productive work.

Her story suggests that women's clothing in nineteenth-century Philadelphia emerged from a discursive domain shaped only in part by national fashion culture and the mass-marketed technologies which moved women's work, bodies and minds toward greater degrees of commodification and object-ification during the second half of the nineteenth century. We might term this domain 'vernacular dress,' that is, personally-negotiated, socially-constituted knowledge about normative dress which emerges from and circulates within local contexts. The forms and meanings of vernacular dress are shaped by the various forces which intersect in any locality and impact on the emergence of specific clothing practices: what designs get disseminated, what women read and see and talk about, what goods get put into the stores by manufacturers, what technologies are available.[1] Although structured by larger social and cultural discourses, these forces are more fully understood when situated within their localized settings, the interactive sewing circles of middle-class consumers like Susan Trautwine who evaluated and laboured to produce, or not to produce, fashion in their everyday lives. Within this vernacular domain women in nineteenth-century Philadelphia had agency as disseminators of fashionable knowledge, producers of meaningful forms and active readers of fashion culture through everyday social practices (such as shopping, visiting, reading, and sewing) which shaped the form and meaning of clothing. They were not only fashionable objects, but creative subjects possessing important cultural knowledge and often aware of the tensions of their cultural positions.

By the 1830s, Philadelphia was a dynamic commercial environment in the throes of massive social and economic transformations. Work was increasingly industrialized and neighbourhoods increasingly segregated along class, race and ethnic lines as the city swelled with immigrants from Europe and migrants from the surrounding countryside. Transportation networks expanded, linking Philadelphia with major cities and rural hinterlands, at the centre of a distribution network for clothing goods and ideas. Market-places were increasingly stratified as specialized shopping districts for women's clothing and trimmings emerged in the 1840s and Philadelphia entrepreneurs such as John Wanamaker opened new department stores in the 1870s. Phil-adelphia was also a national centre for printing and publishing and played an important role in producing fashion culture, particularly through *Godey's Lady's Book*, published from an office on Chestnut Street, the centre of fashionable life in the city. Even as Philadelphia gave way to New York as the fashion capital of the nation by the turn of the century, its shops were stocked with the latest imported and domestic dry goods, trimmings and patterns, marketed to Philadelphia's ever-expanding middle class. (Wilson 1996)

Although men's clothing began to be mass produced after the Civil War, women's clothing remained in custom production throughout the end of the century, crafted by professional dressmakers and, after the introduction of new dressmaking technologies in the 1860s, by home sewers as well. Custom production established an interactive and highly localized social context for the production of women's dress. The production and meaning of dress was embedded in the structures of women's everyday social lives and clothing production was an important site of agency for women as producers and consumers. In custom production, women had creative input into their dress design within the constraints of traditional dressmaking techniques and patterns; garments were the result of interactive negotiations between clients and professionals. Since the skills to cut and fit a new dress accurately were the preserve of the professional dressmaker, many women relied on dressmakers to make new or special dresses, reserving the construction of undergarments and other plain sewing for their own efforts.[2] Because dressmaking practice was defined by a reliance on formulaic bodice, sleeve, and skirt patterns, modifications were inherent to the process as dressmakers catered to customers who made special requests for dress design elements and bought garments custom fitted to their bodies.[3]

As in Trautwine's cloak, design and taste were negotiated when clients ordered, as Wendy Gamber has observed, a 'product which had yet to be conceived.' (Gamber 1991: 187) The relationship between clients and fine dressmakers was shaped by race and class tensions, or marked by conflict when a maker's skill or economy was in question as clients complained of bad fit, high price or a perceived waste of material. As a result, these negotiations of taste, often between women of different class, racial and cultural backgrounds, could collapse in miscommunication, as in the case of one ill-fated gown ordered by Sarah Butler Wister in 1863: '[a] thing I have had before, square neck, gored skirt etc. but the French dressmaker did not take the idea, and made an incongruous sleeve, though it is still a pretty breakfast dress.' (Butler Wister 1863: Letter to Jeannie Field, 2 December) When ordering her new frock, Sarah Wister had in her mind something she would recognize as 'a breakfast dress' with all that entailed, including a particular sort of sleeve suitable to its overall style and associations. Women's praise and condemnation of their dressmakers' efforts illustrate the degree to which clients, like professionals, had aesthetic understandings, if not technical skills.

By mid century this interactive local context was increasingly shaped by larger commercial transformations in women's fashion such as the systematization of dressmaking, the development of home production technologies, and the expansion of fashion representation in periodicals, engravings, patterns, catalogues and store displays. After 1840, dressmaking began to take an increasingly codified and systematized form, as manuals and articles in ladies' magazines discussed the essentials of the craft. Often codifying traditional techniques, entrepreneurs invented and marketed new 'scientific' systems of garment design processes as well as fitting and sewing techniques. (*Graham's* 1856: 265; McCall 1882; Hecklinger, 1884; Fowler 1853; Kidwell 1979: 20–80) There is some evidence that Philadelphia women were interested in learning some of the new techniques. As early as 1839, a Mrs Field arrived in town and set up shop as a dressmaking instructor, advertising her expertise in *The Public Ledger*, a local penny paper. Charitable organizations such as the Magdalen Society Asylum and the Rosine Association for 'fallen' women also taught dressmaking as a potentially viable trade to those women under their care. (Public ledger: 7 April 1839)[4] It is difficult to ascertain the overall impact of these manuals and systems on dressmaking methods in Philadelphia.

Fashion plates circulated throughout the city, illustrating available styles and trimmings. These fashion plates were often anonymous, published as part of an engraving series or removed from periodicals for display or exchange.[5] In the ladies' magazines which developed after the 1830s, the representation of fashions changed over time, moving from an imitation of localized, interactive taste making to a more anonymous national trend setting. For example, throughout the 1830s, *Godey's* regularly reported on current styles under the rubric 'Philadelphia Fashions'. Throughout the early 1850s, *Godey's* included, in addition to its fashion plate descriptions and fancywork patterns, a regular fashion column entitled 'Chit Chat Upon Philadelphia Fashions'. This column stylistically mirrored the manner in which women themselves produced fashionable distinctions through exchanges and evaluative talk, appropriating notions of female community in an abstract manner. On another occasion, *Godey's* report on Paris fashions took the form of a fictional letter composed by an American tourist describing the fashions she saw in the French capital. Such 'chit-chats' disappeared for the most part by the 1860s, replaced by more generalized, authoritative discussions of styles and a profusion of fashion plates.

The fashion plate gained ascendancy in fashion reporting as the organizing icon of 'pictured femininity,' producing normative visions of objectified female bodies and female gender. These plates encouraged the reader not so much to understand the components of dress production, nor to see herself as a generator of fashion knowledge, but rather to project herself as an object into the setting and imagine herself as part of a community of fashionable bourgeoisie. As early as the late 1830s, the plates in *Godey's* no longer located styles specifically in Philadelphia. Rather, as 'Paris Fashions Americanized' or 'Godey's American Fashions,' they represented generic enactments of bourgeois life, situating fashions in domestic or pastoral settings like gardens or parlours. (Halttunen 1982) Representations of fashionable clothes and fashionable bodies circulated offering 'paradigms for women's production of appearances'. (Smith 1984) With the rise of fashion reporting in mass-marketed women's magazines, this authority shifted from an interpersonal relationship of dressmaker and client to an anonymous relationship between printed authority and reader. This shift had the effect of undermining the traditional skill of the dress professional and the conventional knowledge of her clientele. Women's specialized knowledge was now linked with leisure, a move which effaced women's work even as it codified and rendered it visible (but not visible as work), as the tools of women's labour were increasingly conflated with domesticity, beauty, and romance, a separate sphere of women's 'natural' concerns.

The sewing machine and proportional dress patterns, both heavily marketed to women after the Civil War, reinforced these trends in fashion culture. First Wheeler and Wilson, then Singer (after 1867), offered lighter, simpler, and more attractive machine models to the domestic market. The trick for Singer was to portray the sewing machine as a respectable object in middle-class homes by effacing its nature as a productive machine (and thus an instrument of industrialized labour) while downplaying the supposedly dangerous new leisure it would grant women. While making attractive machines effaced the labour that women performed in the home, the sewing machine probably fed an increase in labour devoted to clothing production. (Brandon 1977: 115–35; Cooper 1976; Forty 1986: 95; Strasser 1892: 138–9, 184) It also embedded this labour more deeply within the social relations of consumer culture, as women purchased commodities and imagined themselves in relation to commodities in order to produce the garments themselves. (Cowan 1983) This pattern of increased labour mirrors that of other 'labour-saving' devices marketed to middle-class housewives which increased the tasks women were expected to perform by themselves in the home. Patterns were available both through mail-order services and agents located in major metropolitan areas such as Philadelphia, Boston, Chicago and Cincinnati. (Ross 1963; Walsh 1979: 306–12) The major pattern producers Demorest and Butterick both exhibited at the Centennial Exhibition as did numerous sewing machine manufacturers. Susan McManus purchased Butterick and Demorest patterns from Wanamaker's in Philadelphia. (McManus: 12 February

1879)[6] She also mail-ordered patterns from ladies' magazines such as *Harper's*, which sold dress patterns to readers: 'I rec'd. a set of Princess patterns this morning from *Harper's Bazaar*, N.Y. They seem quite satisfactory.' (McManus: 1 February 1878) Almost all the pattern producers founded a woman's magazine, such as Butterick's *Delineator*, to illustrate and promote their products in the context of a broad range of specifically feminine domestic concerns, further conflating women's productive labour with consumption and the images of domesticity that characterized women's popular literature. (Tebbel and Zuckerman 1991)

Women's consumption of these technologies and representations encouraged them to identify with objectified female embodiments of domesticity. These texts naturalized gender constructions by effacing the fact that women's realization of fashionable images was work, 'a matter of conscious art and technique.' Yet these representations, Dorothy Smith suggests, implicitly indexed 'a work process performed by women,' involving the 'use of tools and materials and the acquired skills of its practitioners' completed only in the situation of their reading. (Smith 1984: 44) The situations of their reading were contexts of female community, cooperative work and creative expertise that worked against objectification to constitute women as subjects.

Much of the work women did in clothing production and design was cooperative, shared between female friends and relatives who helped one another with sewing labours and consulted one another about styles and dressmaking techniques. Resources were shared and work was done in an interactive fashion, often as part of these women's everyday sociality. This interactive context engendered the cultivation of aesthetic understandings and technical skills within groups of women and actively involved them in the generation of productive dress practices. As women corresponded with or visited relatives and acquaintances, they exchanged patterns and discussed fashions. Shopping was another means through which women tested fashion's waters and gained ideas. In the course of their daily lives, women talked about fashion and learned to judge the value and propriety of designs as well as the quality of materials. A mother's or friend's advice and aid could be invaluable, as Susan McManus noted in her diary:

Went to Lizzie Potts' helped her somewhat in fitting a dress & then she went with me to look at a dress at Wanamaker's & others at Sharpless' Strawbridge's [. . .] & to get my bonnet trimmed in 9th below Filbert. We did not like the way it was trimmed & had to wait for it to be altered. (McManus: 28 May 1874)

Met Lucy at Mrs Binder's – paid for my done up Leghorn hat, & bought trimmings for it. We decided that black and white look best. (16 April 1875)[7]

In local contexts, women selectively related to the fashions they discussed, evaluating designs on the basis of their needs, resources, and perceptions of what other women they knew were wearing. (Osaki 1988: 225–41) When weighing her need for a new overskirt, Margaret Stewardson considered her friends' dresses and then consulted her sister-in-law:

> I want to ask if you do not think I had better get a new Balmoral skirt or else make one out of my riding skirt which is wasting I suppose – cousin H.E.J. Smith made one out of merino, and sewed corded strips on it, and Margaret Robinson had one at their house too. I saw one last winter; it was very pretty – much nicer and prettier than any bought Balmoral skirt. It is quite a momentous subject to me whether I have a new one or not because my other having been washed hangs down in a most deplorable manner and the skirt gets soiled very easily. Please consider this subject I will take it as a great personal favour.[8]

In the end, she favoured making herself a skirt because others she had seen were so appealing.

Women clearly modelled their dress designs after what they saw each other wearing. In addition, women traded patterns for dresses and patterns circulated between the women of an extended family. Photographs of Gertrude and A. M. Zeigler, for example, clearly show the two sisters in a similar style of dress, a *zouave* bodice pattern made up with different fabric and trimmings. Ida Duval and her sister Rose Sarah Hechinger also seem to have shared patterns, and perhaps garments. In one 1864 photograph, Ida Duval wears a dark silk dress while in another portrait, her sister Rose wears a dress with bodice, sleeves, pockets, and skirt flounces of the same material and pattern as Ida's. These items were attached to a skirt of contrasting colour fabric, suggesting that the two dresses were made from the same pattern with different fabric, or that Ida's bodice, sleeves, pockets, and flounces were later attached to a new skirt, possibly after the first was damaged. At any rate, it is clear that the sisters collaborated on dress production or shared information. [Cartes-de-visite, Atwater Kent Museum, Philadelphia.]

Sharing designs was also encouraged before the development of proportional patterns when women circumvented the fitting and cutting problem by copying existing garments. Copying was accomplished by picking apart an item of clothing and laying a piece of muslin or paper over each piece, outlining the pattern piece with pin pricks or chalk marks. The pattern could then be used to cut the lining and dress fabric. For some women this method was a practical way to make new clothing and many early guides to dressmaking aimed at home sewers assumed women were copying dresses already made. (Byrde 1992: 137; Fernandez 1987: 103–4; Kidwell 1979: 13) In 1851, for example, *Godey's* recommended this method of drafting a new dress from an old one 'that sets nicely'. (*Godey's* 43, September 1852: 192) The colourful theft case of Lewina Miller, reported in the penny papers, illustrates the ingenuity some women exercised in a climate in which women often borrowed and remade each others' clothing:

> Lewina Miller, alias, Lowina Beck, is the name of a damsel young and fair, whose occupation was to get hold of clothing under false pretences, and dispose of it to the pawnbrokers. Lowina, it appeared, generally took board at different boarding houses, and passed herself off as a lady of independent fortune, and espying something worth carrying off, such as frocks, dresses, cloaks, &c, would exclaim, 'O dear! What a fit! How becoming! a tight sleeter in the bargain! Bless me, how I would like to have one just like that, won't you lend it to me? I'll get one cut out by it; it's such a pretty pattern!' Her wishes generally being acceded to she would possess herself of the praised article and carry it to keep company with some others, received in the same manner, to the office of 'Money Lent on Deposit.'[9]

Lewina Miller's ruse, although transgressive, relied on normative under-standings many women had about sharing clothing and fashion information. Thus women's garments referenced each other in production practice as well as interactive discussion.

This productive context was conducive to the development of locally shared styles and aesthetics between women of particular families, ethnicities, neighbourhoods, or social classes. Relations based on reciprocity between women in urban neighbourhoods has been noted elsewhere. (Stansell 1987: 56–7) Thus, dress was constituted by and within communities of women, and clothing worked to form and maintain bonds between women. (Young 1990: 182–7) These woman-centred contexts set the stage for the active renegotiation of fashion design and a consciousness about work process which fostered scepticism and resistance as well as the production of normative images. The realization of femininity was work and women knew that it was work. As Dorothy Smith points out, 'participation in the discourse of femininity is also a practical relation of a woman to herself as an object,' not necessarily as a sex object, but as an object of work or craft. (Smith 1984) Thus women are both objects in, and agents of, fashion. Even as women appeared to conform to dictates of gender ideology, their practice of femininity as agents allowed or opened a space for slippage from ideologically prescribed meanings and effects. (McRobbie 1978: 96–108; Peiss 1986: 56–87) In Janice Radway's terms, these moments of slippage constituted 'ideological seams' which, when rent, reveal women-centred subtexts and ways of reading patriarchal structures 'against the grain.' (Radway 1986: 93–112)

The experience of one Philadelphia woman in particular offers insights into the unevenly woven fabric of this production and resistance. Susan

McManus (née Trautwine) was in many ways typical of middle-class women of her generation. Born into a German-American family in Philadelphia, she regularly attended church, participated in charitable activities, sewed weekly with her Dorcas Society and read much of the popular literature of the period. In 1870 she married Charles McManus, a young partner in a brokerage firm. They raised three children (before her diary record ended) in Powelton Village, a streetcar suburb in West Philadelphia. Her diaries and accounts for the years 1857–80 record in detail her everyday purchases and sewing projects and illustrate well the changing dress practices of a young woman and later young middle-class matron.[10]

Growing up in her parents' household, Susan Trautwine learned to do plain and fancy sewing and make her own undergarments, generating fancy work for her chemises, drawers, and undersleeves. She also learned to be responsible for maintaining her garments by retrimming and repairing dresses. In the years shortly before her marriage, she began to experiment with altering old dresses and struggled with dressmaking in order to follow fashions more economically. Remarks in her diary suggest that the development of the sewing machine and proportional patterns may have been welcomed by an existing market of frustrated home-sewers already feeling the pressure of class-based expectations for appearance and economy. The necessity of using these new technologies, however, was constructed in part by an increase in fashion reporting and the newly elaborate clothing designs of the late 1860s. For Susan McManus, these new technologies expanded the range of options in her clothing practices. In the 1860s, before her marriage, she experimented with remaking things but found it 'hard to do.' Later, using proportional patterns, she cultivated dressmaking skills and collaborated on dressmaking projects with her friends. Like many middle-class women, she was very occupied in clothing production and maintenance. 'Do so much sewing every day,' she remarked on more than one occasion.

As a young married woman in the 1870s struggling to live within her husband's means, she became very involved with dressmaking, perhaps because she could no longer afford to have much of it done professionally. She commented in 1870, after completing her trousseau, that '[I] expect that this is the last of my dressmaking I shall have done out for some time.' (McManus: 25 November 1870) Using first borrowed sewing machines and later a Wheeler and Wilson her husband purchased for $55.00, she drew on a combination of strategies: sometimes making a new dress herself, sometimes hiring a dressmaker to help her salvage a failed project or make a new dress. She exchanged proportional paper patterns with her friends, remade dresses from her trousseau and made new dresses on her own. Her diary conveys a sense of the never-ending and extremely time-consuming nature of this sewing work. For instance, the black silk dress and sack she constructed in the spring of 1877 emerged from a lengthy and at times frustrating process. Initially, she purchased twenty-five yards of black silk at Zeigler's, consulting with a friend on the fabric. Using a princess pattern, she cut and fit the lining on 1 March, perhaps the most difficult step: 'By evening got it to fit pretty well with its innumerable seams. Quite tired.' By 19 March, she was ready to cut out the dress fabric; her friend Lizzie Potts came to call and helped her out. On 26 March she finished twenty-eight buttonholes, after labouring on them exclusively for three days, sewed up the seams and put bones in the bodice, generally finishing the dress bodice: 'Worked hard as long as I could see.' By 11 April she was still sewing on this dress and its elaborate knife-pleated trimming: 'Kept to my black silk. Spent nearly two days over the trimmings for the side,' remarking that 'It takes so long to do all one's self.' For the next two weeks, she sewed 'at odd times' on the dress when not obliged to mend or attend to other household tasks. 30 April and 1 May saw the final push to finish the dress as she worked hard on it all day with assistance from her mother. All in all, the dress, a basic princess suit and matching sack, took two months to make from start to finish. And when she finished the black silk, there was a green calico dress, begun when the black silk was still in process, waiting to be completed with help from her servant Mary. (McManus 27 February–1 May 1877)

In most cases, the development of new technologies did not wholly alter the manner in which women fashioned clothing and, in many cases, women used machines and patterns within already established cooperative sewing circles. McManus' sewing was almost invariably done with other women in her social circle. She collaborated regularly with her friends on dressmaking: they shopped together, showed each other their purchases, lent each other clothing, helped each other cut and fit, used each other's sewing machines, exchanged patterns, discussed current styles and generally helped out with the more tedious sewing tasks. Throughout the 1870s, for example, Susan McManus sewed regularly with her friend Lizzie Potts and her sister-in-law Lucy McManus. Together the three of them learned to dressmake, helped each other cut and understand pattern instructions and worked on each other's seams and buttonholes. Often they ran errands for one another, matching fabric and ribbon. For instance, Lucy brought McManus trimmings and notions after she moved out of the city centre. McManus likewise returned the favour when Lucy felt indisposed, matching and purchasing ribbon and flowers for a bonnet and then spending the afternoon with Lucy, helping her complete her bonnet trimming in time for church that Sunday. McManus also sewed frequently with her mother, remarking regularly in her diary that her mother had been there with her sewing that day.

In addition to the creation of new garments, women were also required to do a great deal of clothing maintenance work. The bulk of home sewing done during this period centred around renovating and remaking garments and bonnets, labour no new technologies aimed to save. Silk and wool dresses had to be ripped apart for cleaning and resewn after each process. Women renegotiated their garments style and design on a regular basis, retrimming, altering and remaking dresses over time. Susan McManus regularly retrimmed her clothing, replacing skirt braid, shortening hems, adding ruffles, resewing velvet trim, renewing collars and cuffs, and mending corsets and hoop skirts. For instance, one week in early November of 1869 she noted:

Household duties – worried over new poplin dress, bought last winter which is a perfect humby – looking as it if were rough dried. Pressed it.

Found brown poplin quite unfit to wear. Considerable disappointment. Must shorten grey very quickly.

Sewed – shortening my grey poplin.

I have been trimming my grey dress with a fold of velveteen. (2, 7, 11, 13 February)

Later, in February of 1870, she bought new trimming and fringe for this grey poplin dress. She sewed on this new trimming over the course of the next two days, in time to wear the renewed dress to a friend's reception that evening.[11] (McManus: 1–3 November)

Alterations were also made to improve the fit of garments or to follow fashionable changes in silhouette or style. Surviving dresses often show signs of having been let out, usually at the side seams and darts, as individuals' figures changed over time. Maternity required ongoing alterations to accommodate the changing form of the pregnant woman. During her first pregnancy Susan McManus had to alter her dresses at least three times. 'Dresses cannot be altered fast enough' she remarked, and marshalled the efforts of her mother and friends to keep up with the task: 'Lizzie Taylor came to help me sew. We altered three dresses – My blue satines, old maroon poplin & brown calico. We let them out to their full capacity. I trust they will be large enough to last me all winter, & I hope not to need having any more altered.' (12 December 1871, 22 October 1871) Alterations dramatically lengthened the life of valuable garments by renewing their novelty. Bodice fronts were changed and skirts were redone when fashionable silhouettes changed. On at least one occasion during the early 1870s, McManus altered her mother's skirts from gathered to the more fashionably gored pattern.

Susan McManus remade her dresses every season, adding new trimming or refashioning sleeves: 'Liny and I altered my brown flowing sleeves into gauntlet sleeves.' (29 January 1862) One surviving costume, a brown satin day dress in the Germantown Historical Society Costume Collection, embodies the alteration processes McManus described. Noting pin pricks and seam marks it is clear that the bodice front was changed, embellished with new trimming, while the sleeves were altered from bell into straight sleeves. The previously gathered skirt was remade into front gored skirt with back bustle gathers, an attempt to respond to the fashion change of the late 1860s. Alterations and remaking embody women's work process and yield a clear sense of women's agency and decision-making.

When women like McManus did adopt fashionable styles, they often adapted them to suit their tastes and the requirements of their daily lives, displaying a selective orientation toward fashion. A regular reader of *Harper's*, McManus kept abreast of changes in fashion and tried to follow them respectably. She purchased a bustle in 1873, about four years after the style was introduced and often remade the sleeves or trimming of her dresses to renew their currency. McManus seems to have relied heavily on her observations and the advice of friends: 'Before going out I altered my last winter's bonnet a little, and took special observations of others as I went along. Have concluded to wear mine with very slight changes.' (25 November 1871) At least one diary entry registers some of the dissatisfaction with her wardrobe produced by attention to fashion authorities: 'Read Harper yesterday and today. Looked over clothes &c. Want to make new things out of old ones and find it hard to do.' (15 October 1869) Looking at *Harper's* made her more keenly aware of the discrepancy between these images and her own garments. Modern fashion, like advertisements, organizes the desire that resides in this discrepancy (between the ideal image presented and the individual's imperfect attempts to realize it), structuring the everyday in relation to normative female gender. In part *Harper's* images perpetuated a sense of lack in McManus' appearance which organized, along with her observations of fashion change in her own community, an ongoing productive labour on her part.

Her reading of these representations also may have produced a sense of self that existed both in relation to women in her community as well as to a more abstract understanding of herself. According to Kathryn Shevelow, nineteenth-century women's periodicals constructed a community of women of and around the text by offering images in which women could locate themselves, images which were normative representations of feminine objectification. (Shevelow 1989) As Dorothy Smith points out, the reflection on one's conduct in the light of printed texts creates 'new social relations' as 'people scattered and unknown to one another are co-ordinated in an orientation to the same texts.' (Smith 1984: 420) These new forms of social relations were largely 'imagined communities' of gender, race and class. (Anderson 1983) In addition to more traditional means of observing, understanding and discussing fashion with her friends in critical ways, McManus' knowledge and selection gained a new and powerful referent in *Harper's* illustrations. *Harper's* became for Susan McManus an essential component in her dress strategies, providing guidance on styles, the patterns to realize them and the rationale for her labour in the form of a cultural discourse of need, reinforcing a larger ideology of middle-class domesticity at all points.

On the other hand, when fashion dictated major changes, she noted them, but was not always necessarily swayed by them: 'Worked at blk. silk dress. Have it ready to wear tomorrow [Sunday]. It is however quite out of fashion as all other things one has will be – according to *Harper's Bazaar* &c. but I expect to wear them nevertheless.' (10 October 1874) The ambiguity and scepticism of this last remark, articulated in the act of looking at and actively reading fashionable representations, reveals a sense of her own lack, but also suggests a conscious strategy of distancing herself from fashion's ideologically prescribed meanings and effects. She possessed a multivalent understanding of fashionable representation, grasping that in relation to fashion everyone's clothing is always out of date (the essence of fashion change). In the end, her final authority was still the local and the interpersonal, increasingly measured in relation to a non-localized and thoroughly commodified prescription.

Her practices reveal the sophisticated way in which middle-class women, limited in resources and inundated with cultural expectations, balanced and negotiated fashion's authority. When McManus consulted *Harper's* each month and ordered patterns from the journal, she effectively repositioned herself within an expanded sewing circle, a larger imagined community of white middle-class women consumers. This reading organized her labour and motivated her consumption of fashion. It encouraged her to identify with and measure herself in relation to representations of women's dressed bodies as beautiful objects and the gendered social relations these images organized. At the same time, her active reading with other women in her locality and her own practice of fashion indicate that the site of her production of fashion could also be the site of her resistance to it. By foregrounding work process and social relationship within her consciousness, she clearly constituted herself as both object and subject.

Notes

1. 'Vernacular' according to the *Oxford English Dictionary*, refers to the 'domestic, native, indigenous'. 'Vernacular' places culture in specific localities, such as a dialect 'naturally spoken by the people of a particular country or district [. . .] the native speech of a populace' or any arts 'native or peculiar to a particular country or locality'. While the vernacular often has been used to refer to 'low' or 'folk' culture, here it is used in a broader sense to refer to cultural forms which emerge in specific space and time, including all the various influences that engender and shape their emergence and specific formal contours.

2. Susan McManus (née Trautwine), for example, patronized her mother's dressmaker, Mrs Brown, for several years after she was married. (McManus: *passim*) Women's letters are filled with references to dressmakers and milliners: letter to Emily Duncan, (Duncan Irvine 1838: 31 August 1838); letter to Elizabeth Fisher, (Fisher Fox 1855: 14 November); Diary, (Armat Logan 1864).

3. Sarah Duncan for example, patronized two dressmakers residing in her Philadelphia neighbourhood, Miss Murphine and Susan Corly, dressmakers who kept patterns specifically for her, as an 1838 letter indicates: 'May I trouble you to have one [dress] made for me [. . .] Susan Corly might make it or Miss Murphine or any one in the neighbourhood – but they only have my pattern for dresses made as I would wish than one; high in the neck & with a cape to fit loosely.' Letter to Emily Duncan (Duncan Irvine 1838: 31 August).

4. Mrs Field remained in the city and built a clientele for her method. (*McElroy's Business Directory*, 1844) Her claim to avoid the 'usual trouble of trying on' suggests she was marketing a system involving proportional or direct measure techniques for pattern drafting. Other systems were published or sold in Philadelphia included Justin Clave's system, published in Philadelphia in 1859 by lithographer P.S. Duval. Marketed for $2.00, it was the equivalent of two days' wages for most dressmakers and well out of the financial reach of many women. (Kidwell 1979: 26) On charity dressmaking instruction, see Magdalen Society Papers, 1836–39. The Rosine Association kept on staff a woman versed in 'Fowler's System of Dress Cutting, by Measurement'. (Rosine Association 1855: 122–3)

5. One example: 'Morning and Evening Dresses for April 1825, Invented by Mrs Bell,' fashion plate, Germantown Historical Society.

6. Trade cards held by the Historical Society of Pennsylvania show that local agents for Demorest's patterns in Philadelphia included: dress- and cloak-maker Mrs M.A. Sawdon, 706 N. Eighth St.; Nichol's Millinery store at 1808 Market; E. W. Phillips Staple Trimmings, 805 Spring Garden; M.S. Truman, Dry Goods, at 839 Callowhill; and John Wanamaker's department store at 13th and Chestnut Streets.

7. McManus gained a lot of her ideas while shopping almost daily with other women: 'Spent the morning with Ma in Chestnut St. and only obtained ideas and ribbon for Mrs M's cap.' (20 April 1870) 'Went in town with Charlie [. . .] Went to look at fashions and pictures & bought some odds and ends for Lizzie and myself.' (14 March 1873)

8. Letter to Margaret Haines Stewardson. (Stewardson n.d.) For other mentions of fashion in women's correspondence, see: letter to Fanny Armat, (Brown: 7 December) Markoe Family papers; Maxcy/Markoe/Hughes Family papers; Stevens Hecksher (n.d.); Osaki 1988.

9. Police report, *Public Ledger*, 11 March 1838, Free Library of Philadelphia.

10. The McManus newlyweds set up housekeeping on $900–1,000 a year, Charles' 'assured' income, according to her diary, 17 January 1870. This figure is typical for the salary of a young business partner at this date. (Blumin 1989: 1, 112–19)

11. For an example of clothing renovated for seasonal changes, see the letter to Sarah Medford Clayton. (Hynson: 21 December)

References

Anderson, B. (1983), *Imagined Communities*, London: Verso.

Armat Logan, Anna (1864) Diary, Loudon papers, Historical Society of Pennsylvania, 5 May.

Blumin, S. (1989), *The Emergence of the Middle Class, Social Experience in the American City, 1760–1900*, Cambridge: Cambridge University Press.

Brandon, R. (1977), *A Capitalist Romance: Singer and the Sewing Machine*, Philadelphia: J.C. Lippincott.

Brown, Corinne (1844), Loudon Family papers, Historical Society of Pennsylvania.

Butler Wister, Sarah (1863), Wister Family papers, Historical Society of Pennsylvania.

Byrde, P. (1992), *Nineteenth Century Fashion*, London: Batsford.

Cooper, G. R. (1976), *The Sewing Machine, Its Invention and Development*, Washington, DC: Smithsonian Institution Press.

Cowan, R. S. (1983), *More Work for Mother: The Ironies of Household Technology from the Open Hearth to the Microwave*, New York: Basic Books.

Duncan Irvine, Sarah (1838), Newbold-Irvine papers, Historical Society of Pennsylvania.

Fernandez, N. P. (1987), "If a Woman Had Taste . . .' Home Sewing and the Making of Fashion, 1850–1910', Ph.D. thesis, University of California, Irvine.

Fisher Fox, Mary (1855), Fox Family papers, Historical Society of Pennsylvania.

Forty, A. (1986), *Objects of Desire*, London: Thames and Hudson.

Fowler, P. G. (1853), *Fowler's Improved Model; or, Dressmaking Made Easy; with Plain Instructions*, Chicago: Daily Tribune Steam Power Press Print.

Gamber, W. (1991), 'The Female Economy: The Millinery and Dressmaking Trades, 1860–1930', Ph.D. thesis, Brandeis University.

Graham's Illustrated Magazine of Literature, Romance, Art and Fashion, 49 (1856).

Halttunen, K. (1982), *Confidence Men and Painted Women, A Study of Middle Class Culture in America, 1830–70*, New Haven: Yale University Press.

Hecklinger, C. (1884), *Handbook on dress and cloak cutting*, New York: Peter de Baum.

Hynson, Anna N. (1846), John Clayton papers, Historical Society of Pennsylvania.

Kidwell, C. B. (1979), *Cutting a Fashionable Fit, Dressmakers' Drafting Systems in the United States*, Washington, DC: Smithsonian Institution Press.

Magdalen Society (1836–39), Minutes of the Annual Meetings of the Magdalen Society, Historical Society of Pennsylvania.

Markoe Family papers, Historical Society of Pennsylvania.

Maxcy Family papers, Historical Society of Pennsylvania.

McCall, J. (1882), *French and English systems of cutting, fitting and basting ladies' garments*, New York.

McManus, Susan (née Trautwine), Diaries and Letterbooks, Historical Society of Pennsylvania.

McRobbie, A. (1978), 'Working Class Girls and the Culture of Femininity' in *Women Take Issue*, Initiated by the Women's Studies Group, Centre for Contemporary Cultural Studies, University of Birmingham, London: Hutchinson.

Osaki, A.B. (1988), '"A Truly Feminine Employment": Sewing and the Early Nineteenth Century Woman,' *Winterthur Portfolio* 23: 225–41.

Peiss, K. (1986), *Cheap Amusements: Working Women and Leisure in New York City, 1880–1920*, Philadelphia: Temple University Press.

Radway, J. (1986) 'Identifying Ideological Seams: Mass Culture, Analytical Method, and Political Practice,' *Communication* 9: 93–112.

Rosine Association, (1855), *Reports and Realities from the Sketch-Book of a Manager of the Rosine Association*, Philadelphia: John Dross.

Ross, I. (1963), *Crusades and Crinolines, The Life and Times of Ellen Curtis Demorest and William Jennings Demorest*, New York: Harper and Row.

Shevelow, K. (1989), *Women and Print Culture: The Construction of Femininity in the Early Periodical*, London: Routledge.

Smith, D. (1984), 'Femininity as Discourse' in *Becoming Feminine: The Politics of Popular Culture*, ed., Leslie Roman and Linda K. Christian-Smith, London: The Falmer Press.

Stansell, C. (1987), *City of Women: Sex and Class in New York, 1789–1860*, Urbana: University of Illinois Press.

Stewardson, Margaret (n.d.), Stewardson Family papers, Historical Society of Pennsylvania.

Strasser, S. (1982), *Never Done: A History of American Housework*, New York: Pantheon.

Stevens Heksher, Lucretia (n.d.), correspondence, Balch Institute for Ethnic Studies.

Tebbel, J. and Zuckerman, M. E. (1991), *The Magazine in America, 1741–1990*, New York: Oxford University Press.

Trautwine, Susan (1957), Diaries and Letterbooks, Historical Society of Pennsylvania. See also McManus, Susan.

Walsh, M. (1979), 'The Democratization of Fashion: The Emergence of the Women's Dress Pattern Industry,' *Journal of American History* 66, September: 306–12.

Wilson, Kathryn (1996), 'Fashioning Difference: Women's Dress in Nineteenth-Century Philadelphia', Ph.D. thesis, University of Pennsylvania.

Young, I. M. (1990), 'Women Reclaiming Their Clothes' in *Throwing Like a Girl and Other Essays in Feminist Philosophy and Social Theory*, Bloomington: Indiana University Press.

9

Creating Consumers: Gender, Class and the Family Sewing Machine

Nancy Page Fernandez

Nineteenth-century promoters personified the family sewing machine in many different, and often contradictory, ways. Sara Josepha Hale, well-known editor of *Godey's Lady's Book*, praised the Wheeler and Wilson machine as the 'queen of inventions' (July 1860: 77–8), while the White Sewing Machine Company heralded their model as 'the King'. (White n.d.) These allusions to royalty contrast sharply with descriptions of the family sewing machine as 'the poor man's friend'. Still other promoters called machines a 'seamstress', 'woman's best friend', and 'mother's helper'. Grover and Baker simultaneously described their family sewing machine as the 'angel of the house' and an 'iron needle woman!' (Grover and Baker 1862) This essay analyses represent-ations in American trade literature of the second half of the nineteenth century to better understand the historical meaning of the family sewing machine[1] and contributes to the cultural history of advertising. (Garvey 1996; Lears 1994; Leach 1993)

Until recently scholarship generally argued that in the Victorian middle-class home the machine symbolized leisure and conspicuous consumption while for working-class women the sewing machine signified the exploitative conditions of the factory and homework. (Douglas 1982; Scott 1982) This dichotomy simplifies the sewing machine's significance in both the home and factory but more recent literature recognizes the need to move beyond it. (Stansell 1983; Connolly 1994; Coffin 1996) As one of the first modern appliances, the family sewing machine brought the Industrial Revolution into the home, heralding changes in women's economic roles and the meaning of consumer goods. Anxieties about the impact of industrialization on American life shaped cultural constructions of the family sewing machine.

Nineteenth-century sewing machine trade literature records a lively conversation about gender roles, family relations and class identities. The varied and conflicting narratives about the family sewing machine reveal how promoters, in their attempts to create a mass market, addressed anxieties about the social impact of industrial change. Appropriating familiar ideologies about gender and class to sell machines, advertisers mediated between conventional social roles and emerging modern ones. The multiple meanings they generated for the family sewing machine transported gender and class difference into new consumer identities, supporting mass consumption while simultaneously maintaining social hierarchies. By creatively constructing women and households as consumers, sewing machine advocates helped give meaning to changing economic roles.

Economic Roles and Family Relations

During the mid-nineteenth century, urban American women began to participate in new buying activities as the household shifted from a site of production to one of consumption. (Ulrich 1980; Cowan 1983; Jensen 1988; Clark 1990; Boydston 1990) Middle-class women's increasing consumer roles threatened the ideals of Victorian womanhood and challenged male economic privilege and household authority. (Leach 1984; Peiss 1986) In contrast to the antebellum feminine ideals of piety, purity, domesticity and submissiveness, mass consumption promised secular modernity, individual expression and personal pleasure. Popular novels and prescriptive literature warned of vain or gullible women whose spending led their husbands to financial ruin. Advertisers used a highly gendered discourse of social and personal relations to market the family sewing machine to American households. In narratives of rescue and romance, promoters employed familiar gender ideology to construct new consumer identities and ascribe meaning to women's shifting economic activities. (Loeb 1994: 72–99, 118–20, 32–9) The multiple narratives not only sold machines, but also defined and delimited notions about female buying power.

Joseph and Laura Lyman, authors of the popular household-economy manual *The Philosophy of Housekeeping*, hailed the debut of the sewing machine in starkly gendered terms: 'It is only within a few years that masculine invention has come to the aid of feminine patience and industry.' (Lyman 1867: 486–7) This narrative introduced the machine in the trope of hero, casting the machine as male agent coming to assist passive woman. The melodrama celebrated polarized masculine and feminine virtues: male progress contrasted with, and protected, female passivity. Constructing technological innovation as melodramatic rescue, the gendered narrative maintained male agency and female dependency.

Promoters also represented individual sewing machine purchase as rescue, playing out specific family tensions and relations. In a similar if less dramatic narrative, a Grover and Baker trade catalogue told the sad tale of a Mrs Aston who has become nervous and impatient, overwhelmed by the burden of endless household sewing. Her spouse, seeking a solution, purchased a Grover and Baker sewing machine. The story ended happily as a relaxed Mrs Aston now has leisure time to practice her music because the machine finished the sewing quickly and efficiently. (Grover and Baker 1863) Trivializing middle-class women's household labour, the story presented Mrs Aston's fragile physical and emotional state as the critical problem. The Grover and Baker narrative successfully introduced the sewing machine as an antidote for female distress. Its medicinal effect distanced the machine from connections with industrial power or economic change. Mr Aston's action demonstrated both husbandly virtue and sale of a sewing machine. As the machine did the work, Mrs Aston emerged as a symbol of middle-class female leisure. The narrative preserved male economic agency, maintained masculine and feminine family roles, and foreshadowed the middle-class servantless home.

Advertising narratives frequently encouraged men to purchase sewing machines to create harmonious households. A New Home sewing machine advertisement guaranteed: 'Happiness is what we all seek. Buy your wife a NEW HOME, and if it don't make her happy the New Home Company will refund the money and take back the machine.' The card's illustration depicted the story of Anthony and Cleopatra, suggesting the unhappy future of a sewing machineless home. (New Home 1890: 23) The Elliptic Sewing Machine Company, speaking again to husbands, outlined the benefits of adding a sewing machine to the home: '[S]ee how the money will come back in good dinners, in patience, kindness, and economy.' (Elliptic c. 1890) These advertisements cast men as agents – publicly and privately – purchasing the machine and securing household bliss. The machine's emotional work implicitly resolved notions that consumption changes women's household roles or economic power. A strong message underlay these ads, warning that a home without a sewing machine made for an unhappy family and that a husband who did not buy his wife a sewing machine would suffer as a result. Purchase of a sewing machine allowed men to fulfil their adult roles, exercise economic privilege and maintain family harmony. Representing women alternately as frustrated or happy housewives, the ads trivialized female work and roles, helping to construct twentieth century stereotypes of women's domestic identity.

Promoters exploited notions of romantic love by connecting successful relationships with buying a sewing machine. A trade card for the Domestic Sewing Machine Company showed a man proposing to his beloved, who replied: 'Yes on the condition that you buy me a "Domestic" with new wood work and attachments.' Cupid appeared in the top corner, phone in hand, calling: 'Hello. Send a Domestic quick.' In another example from the New Home Sewing Machine Company, a married couple faced 'a painful altern-ative' as the wife demanded: 'I will have a "New Home Machine!" A "New Home" or a divorce!' (New Home n.d.) Blurring emotional and economic power, the narratives granted agency to women because of their prerogative over personal relationships. Women acted as determined negotiators within romantic relations, bargaining their affections for a sewing machine. Empha-sizing the sewing machine's ability to produce successful relationships, not straight stitches or stronger seams, promoters disassociated the machine from work and economic or industrial change. Advertisers cleverly, and humorously, empowered female consumer choice while preserving male economic power.

Industrialization brought changes to the economic roles of women and the household, potentially undermining male power and privilege. One nineteenth-century commentator noted: 'A lady recently remarked that she believed a sewing machine was a more indispensable feature of a well-regulated household than a husband [. . .] there can be no doubt that the lady did not far overvalue the importance of having a sewing machine in the house.' (*The Fashion Courier* c.1896: 4) The male author of a testimonial for the Willcox and Gibbs machine wondered 'whether any thing stronger or longer is really needed in domestic life'. (Willcox and Gibbs 1863: 6) Tensions over the relationship between production and consumption, over male versus female household power, met in the cultural discourse over the family sewing machine.

Advertisers used a gendered discourse of family and personal relations to encourage greater female consumer influence, carefully distinguishing buying power from economic power. Narratives of rescue and romance maintained the centrality of men in household life. Defining female consumer identity within gendered roles and personal relationships, promoters relieved tensions over the social impact of industrial change and helped construct stereotypes about the modern housewife.

Class and Consumption

Consumer goods have long served as markers of social status. Historians of Britain and early-America demonstrate that this pre-dates industrialization.

(Carson et al. 1994; Brewer and Porter 1993; McKendrick et al. 1982) Both a tool for women's work and a modern consumer good, the sewing machine presented promoters with a complicated dilemma. The new household appliance might signify economic progress and modernity but, at the same time, for working-class families the machine connected women to homework and factory labour while for middle-class buyers machine ownership served as a reminder of the loss of servants. A mass market for family sewing machines also potentially levelled differences between social classes, further threatening its consumer appeal for the group most able to buy. To negotiate these dilemmas, promoters used a rhetoric of shared domestic values to popularize purchase while they granted the family sewing machine class-specific effects and identities which personalized ownership. Promoters employed domestic values to appeal to all families to purchase a sewing machine; simultaneously advertisements carefully delineated class-specific meanings for ownership. The varied and sometimes conflicting narratives about the family sewing machine reveal how promoters both bridged class boundaries and maintained social hierarchies as they created a mass market for the family sewing machine.

Promoters often appealed to working families to buy a sewing machine to preserve womanhood. An early New Home Sewing Machine trade card based on Thomas Hood's 'Song of the Shirt' depicted a woman in ragged clothing bent over her sewing. The card's reverse side pictured the same woman smiling and well dressed seated at a new sewing machine. (New Home c. 1860) The machine transformed the seamstress from a symbol of poverty to a symbol of respectability. An advertisement for the Elliptic Sewing Machine Company generalized the story: 'It [the sewing machine] has enabled whole families, in time of financial distress, or when the head of the family has been prostrated by sickness or removed by death, to maintain a comfortable independence.' The company further noted that 'charitable institutions and benevolent societies have in many cases, instead of supplying the needy with mere food and clothing, furnished them with the Elliptic Sewing Machine [. . .]' (Elliptic c. 1870: 2) Emphasizing domestic values to working-class buyers, promoters introduced the machine for women's work while disassociating mechanized sewing from waged homework and factory production. Machine sewing as a domestic virtue implicitly counteracted concerns that the machine might ruin women's health, exploit vulnerable workers, or encourage frivolous fashion expenditure. Sewing machine ownership signified a 'comfortable independence'. Almost touching on melodrama, promoters offered the family sewing machine as a prescription for working-class femininity and social respectability.

Advertisers also used the domestic value of preserving womanhood to attract middle-class purchasers. Similarly pleading that 'it is desirable to prevent the fairer portion of our race from wearing out the thread of life in weary hand sewing,' Singer described the machine as 'itself a "seamstress" – one which can be closeted in a cabinet case at pleasure – one which is never in the way, and never out of it'. (Singer c. 1860: 15) The family machine implicitly performed the work in both the working-class and middle-class home, distancing the appliance and women from associations with labour and economic status. Meanwhile the two narratives personalized ownership quite differently; the sewing machine appeared omnipresent in the seamstress's home, the means to, and symbol of, her 'comfortable independence', whereas in the middle-class home the machine obeyed as a servant, performing its work and then retreating. The advertisements constructed machine sewing as a domestic virtue, one which preserved both womanhood and social differences.

Advertisements often likened the sewing machine to a servant, appealing to desires for domestic help while replacing the human seamstress with the machine. In a testimonial supporting the Willcox and Gibbs sewing machine, S. Wier Roosevelt, described as an eminent lawyer, wrote:

> Your machine has certain moral and social advantages which make it peculiarly safe to introduce into the family circle. It is simple, swift, easily domesticated and very inoffensive. It is never obtrusive and noisy, overpowering domestic conversation, and has no violent or sudden fits, disturbing the family temper; it will not even chafe a lady's dress, and it will do a week's work in a single day with the least possible waste of patience and thread. (Willcox and Gibbs 1863: 6)

Roosevelt's testimonial represented the new technology as an ideal servant – a compliant, submissive addition to the household. Roosevelt clothed the machine's techno-economic identity with a feminized domestic one and conflated household economy with moral economy. Wasting neither patience nor thread, the machine performed moral rather than physical work as it emphasized the value of feminine frugality over masculine labour. Replacing servants with a new family sewing machine, the narrative constructed the modern household as a site of consumption rather than production.

Advertisers also used domestic values to make machine purchase a moral decision. A series of trade cards for the New Home Sewing Machine Company humorously empowered female moral authority for consumer choice. (Figures 9.1–9.4) In a tale of four acts, a couple considered the perplexing question of what to do about the household sewing: purchase a New Home sewing machine or contract a French sewing girl? Together they elected to hire a girl. In the next scene the wife (and the trade card reader) witnessed the husband kissing the hand of the young French assistant. The drama concluded

Figure 9.1. 'The Sewing Must Be Done. A Home Drama In Four Acts. Act 1st The Perplexing Question. A New Home Machine or A French Sewing Girl.' Trade card, New Home Sewing Machine Company, n.d. Courtesy of The Winterthur Library: Joseph Downs Collection of Manuscripts and Printed Ephemera.

Figure 9.2. 'The Sewing Must Be Done. A Home Drama In Four Acts. Act 2nd The French Sewing Girl Decided Upon – The Arrival.' Trade card, New Home Sewing Machine Company, n.d. Courtesy of The Winterthur Library: Joseph Downs Collection of Manuscripts and Printed Ephemera.

Figure 9.3. 'The Sewing Must Be Done. A Home Drama In Four Acts. Act 3rd The French Sewing Girl Duly Installed.' Trade card, New Home Sewing Machine Company, n.d. Courtesy of The Winterthur Library: Joseph Downs Collection of Manuscripts and Printed Ephemera.

Figure 9.4. 'The Sewing Must Be Done. A Home Drama In Four Acts. Act 4th The French Assistant Did Not Give Entire Satisfaction. A New Home Machine Has Been Purchased. All's Well That Ends Well.' Trade card, New Home Sewing Machine Company, n.d. Courtesy of The Winterthur Library: Joseph Downs Collection of Manuscripts and Printed Ephemera.

with mother at the sewing machine while her husband read the paper and happy children looked on, a home scene captioned: 'All's well that ends well.' (New Home, Lozier and Stokes, n.d.) This allegory suggested contemporary concerns about consumption, economic prerogative and class status. The French sewing girl and, by analogy, servants in general were represented as potentially dangerous to family harmony. Tellingly, the decision to hire the sewing girl appeared mutual; the decision to release her and purchase a machine was clearly the wife's. In this apparently middle-class companionate marriage, the woman's moral authority over her husband's behaviour empowered her to make an important economic decision – purchase of the family sewing machine. The drama conflated moral authority and economic agency, linking household consumption and gender ideology in the construction of the servantless, middle-class family. Representing sewing machine purchase as a solution to a servant problem, the narrative formulated both women and the household as consumers.

Promoters occasionally created scenes in which women of different social groups intermingled, showing that machine purchase blended harmoniously with existing work and class relations. A Wheeler and Wilson Trade Card for the New High Arm sewing machine depicted three women, possibly the lady with her dressmaker and the apprentice. One woman admired her new fashion in the mirror and a second fitted the skirt while the third gazed approvingly from her seat at the sewing machine. (Wheeler and Wilson n.d.) The scene appeared in perfect harmony, balancing class status through its complementary positioning of work and social roles. In another card, this one from the Domestic Sewing Machine Company, three women appeared together as a servant carried in a refreshment. The oldest, fairest and apparently most elite woman sat with a skirt panel draped over her lap; a Domestic sewing machine case and pattern envelope rested at her feet. Two quite similar looking women, perhaps her daughters or neighbouring sisters, contentedly cut and sewed. The entrance of the servant assuaged any implication that sewing with a Domestic machine and patterns compromised class privilege. (Domestic, Warshaw Collection) Again the scene is one of social harmony and complementarity. Blending the family sewing machine with existing work and social relations, promoters removed consumption from socio-economic change.

Sewing machine promoters represented the family sewing machine as a champion of domestic values – a supporter of womanhood, moral authority, family and social harmony. Their emphasis on values distanced the machine from work and production, creating women and households as consumers. Using representations of class to personalize ownership, sewing machine promoters constructed a mass market that maintained social difference.

Conclusion

What can we learn from sewing machine promoters' representations of gender, family relations and class identities? Located at the nexus of technology, women, work, and household life, the sewing machine became a lightning rod for tensions over the impact of industrialization on the economic roles of women and the household. The many varied and often conflicting narratives surrounding the family sewing machine defined multiple individual meanings for purchase within mass consumption. By grounding individual consumer identities within gender roles, personal relationships, and class difference, promoters disassociated consumption from economic change and relieved anxieties over the impact of industrialization on American life. Both scholarship and popular ideas recognize the many ways that industrialization transformed production and industrial work. The multiple narratives about the family sewing machine provide an entertaining and informative glimpse into a neglected part of industrialization, the social meaning of consumption and the creation of a mass market.

Notes

1. The author thanks the Henry Francis du Pont Winterthur Museum; the Hagley Center for the History of Business, Technology, and Society; Dr Mack Johnson; the Office of Graduate Studies, Research, and International Programs; Dean Ralph Vicero; the School of Social Sciences and the Department of History at California State University, Northridge, for their support of my research.

2. This chapter draws on chapter six of my book manuscript in progress, *Common Ingenuity: Home Dressmaking and the Industrialization of Women's Clothing Fashion, 1840–1910.*

References

Abelson, E. S. (1989), *When Ladies Go A'Thieving: Middle-Class Shoplifters in the Victorian Department Store* , New York and Oxford: Oxford University Press.

Benson, S. P. (1986), *Counter Cultures: Saleswomen, Managers, and Customers in American Department Stores, 1890–1940*, Urbana: University of Illinois Press.

Boydston, J. (1990), *Home and Work: Housework, Wages and the Ideology of Labor in the Early Republic*, New York and London: Oxford University Press.

Brewer, J. and Porter, R., eds., (1993), *Consumption and the World of Goods*, London and New York: Routledge.

Carson, C., Hoffman, R. and Albert, P.J., eds., (1994), *Of Consuming Interests: The*

Style of Life in the Eighteenth Century, Charlottesville: University Press of Virginia.

Clark, C. (1990), *The Roots of Rural Capitalism: Western Massachusetts, 1780–1869*, Ithaca, New York: Cornell University Press.

Coffin, J. (1996), *The Politics of Women's Work: The Paris Garment Trades, 1750–1915*, Princeton: Princeton University Press.

Connolly, M. A. (1994), *The Transformation of Home Sewing and the Sewing Machine in America. 1850–1929*, Ph.D. thesis, University of Delaware.

Cowan, R. S. (1983), *More Work for Mother*, New York: Basic Books.

Domestic Sewing Machine Company, (n.d.), Trade Card, H. J. Judd, Mt Holly, New Jersey, Sewing Machines, Household Furnishings and Equipment, Downs Collection of Manuscripts and Printed Ephemera, Henry Francis du Pont Winterthur Library.

—— (n.d.), Trade Card, Sewing Machines, Warshaw Collection of Business Americana, National Museum of American History, Smithsonian Institution, Washington, D.C.

Douglas, D. M. (1982), 'The Machine in the Parlor: A Dialectical Analysis of the Sewing Machine,' *Journal of American Culture*, 5: 20–9.

Dudden, F. E. (1983), *Serving Women: Domestic Service in Nineteenth-Century America*, Middletown, CT: Wesleyan University Press.

Elliptic Sewing Machine Company, (c.1870), *Elliptic lockstitch sewing machine*, Boston: A. Mudge & Son.

—— (c.1890), *Elliptic lock-stitch sewing machine*, Boston: Elliptic Sewing Machine Company.

Friedman, M. C. (1984), *Home, Home Sweet Home: the trade cards of the New Home Sewing Machine Company*, MA dissertation, University of Delaware.

Garvey, E. G. (1996), *The Adman in the Parlor: Magazines and the Gendering of Consumer Culture, 1880s to 1910s*, New York and Oxford: Oxford University Press.

Grover and Baker Sewing Machine Company (1863), *A Home Scene; or Mr. Aston's first evening with Grover and Baker's Celebrated Family Sewing Machine:* New York: Grover and Baker.

—— (1862), *The Seams of the Leading Machines, illustrated and compared*, New York: Grover and Baker.

—— (n.d.) Trade Catalogue, Sewing machines, Romaine Collection, University of California, Santa Barbara.

Jensen, J. M. (1988), 'Butter Making and Economic Development in Mid-Atlantic America from 1750 to 1850,' *Signs* 13: 813–29.

Katzman, D. M. (1978), *Seven Days a Week: Women and Domestic Service in Industrializing America*, New York: Oxford University Press.

Lasser, C. (1987), 'The Domestic Balance of Power: Relations between Mistress and Maid in Nineteenth Century New England,' *Labor History* 28: 5–22.

Leach, W. (1984), 'Transformations in a Culture of Consumption: Women and Department Stores, 1890–1925,' *Journal of American History* 71. 2: 319–42.

—— (1993), *Land of Desire: Merchants, Power and the Rise of a New American Culture*, New York: Pantheon.

Lears, J. (1994), *Fables of Abundance: A Cultural History of Advertising in America*, New York: Basic Books.

Loeb, L. A. (1994), *Consuming Angels: Advertising and Victorian Women*, New York: Oxford University Press.

Lyman, J. and L. (1867), *The Philosophy of Housekeeping*, Hartford: Goodwin & Betts.

McKendrick, N., Brewer, J., Plumb J. H. (1982), *The Birth of a Consumer Society: The Commercialization of Eighteenth Century England*, Bloomington: University of Indiana Press.

New Home Sewing Machine Company (c. 1860), Trade Card, Sewing Machines, Warshaw Collection of Business Americana, National Museum of American History, Smithsonian Institution, Washington, DC.

—— (1890), *Shakespeare Boiled Down*, Orange: New Home Sewing Machine Company.

—— (n.d.), Trade Card, Household Furnishings and Equipment, Downs Collection of Manuscripts and Printed Ephemera, Henry Francis du Pont Winterthur Library.

—— (n.d.) Trade Card, Lozier & Stokes, General Agents, Cleveland, Household Furnishings and Equipment, Downs Collection of Manuscripts and Printed Ephemera, Henry Francis du Pont Winterthur Library.

Peiss, K. L. (1986), *Cheap Amusements: Working Women and Leisure in New York City 1880–1920*, Philadelphia: Temple University Press.

Scott, J. W. (1982), 'The Mechanization of Women's Work,' *Scientific American*, September: 136–66.

Singer Manufacturing Company (c. 1860), *The Singer Sewing Machines*, New York: Singer.

Stansell, C. (1983), 'The Origins of the Sweatshop: Women and Early Industrialization in New York City' in Michael H. Frisch and Daniel Walkowitz, eds., *Working Class America: Essays on Labor, Community and American Society*, Urbana: University of Illinois Press.

The Fashion Courier (c.1896), New York: Domestic Sewing Machine Company.

Ulrich, L. T. (1980), 'Friendly Neighbor': Social Dimensions of Daily Work in Northern Colonial New England,' *Feminist Studies*, 6.2: 398–405.

Wheeler and Wilson Sewing Machine Company (n.d.), New High Arm Sewing Machine no. 9. Household Furnishings and Equipment, Downs Collection of Manuscripts and Printed Ephemera, Henry Francis du Pont Winterthur Library.

White Sewing Machine Trade Card (n.d.), Sewing Machines, Romaine Collection, University of California, Santa Barbara.

Willcox and Gibbs Sewing Machine Company (1863), *The Noiseless Family Sewing Machine*, New York: Willcox and Gibbs.

10

Patterns of Choice: Women's and Children's Clothing in the Wallis Archive, York Castle Museum

Mary M. Brooks

Changing choices of dress are increasingly of interest to dress, design, social and economic historians. However, it is rare to find a museum collection which enables such choices to be studied directly. The Wallis Archive in York Castle Museum, England, is a collection of one family's dress and related material which gives a unique insight into making and purchasing clothes at a time when consumer choice was expanding. It includes garments made at home as well as those commissioned from local costumiers and dressmakers or purchased from dress shops, department stores or chain stores. This chapter is a preliminary exploration of patterns of choice which also considers the problems of determining effective criteria for distinguishing between garments made at home, by dressmakers or mass production.

The Wallis Archive enables the study of unusually well-provenanced artefacts from both the curatorial and the conservation perspectives. Direct evidence presented by the garments and patterns as documents of twentieth-century clothing consumption together with the York documentation is at the centre of this chapter.[1] Such close study of the object provides both sensory and analytical information on appearance, touch, smell, materials, construction techniques, use and wear. The importance of research directly from the object was recognized by Buck (1998: 5): 'It is the evidence of the practice of costume that museums hold, and which is needed to give substance to evidence gathered from other sources.' The object is the basis for new knowledge and understanding and a means of informing and illuminating other historical sources. Curators and conservators can work together to tease out the literal and metaphorical meanings of such contextualized artefacts. Curatorial expertise can identify stylistic trends and propose dates for undated garments. The conservation perspective, based on detailed examination and identification, adds to this body of knowledge through analysis of fibres, dyes, construction methods and patterns of use and wear. In this instance, the object-based research focused on building up information as to which garments might be home-, dressmaker- or commercially made.

The Wallis Family

The Wallis family was a financially secure, middle-class Quaker family living in Darlington, County Durham, in northern England. Amy Mounsey married Anthony Wallis, a schools' inspector, in 1910 and moved to live in Penrith, Cumbria. She had three children: Edward, Henry and Rachel. (Figure 10.1) In the 1930s, Rachel studied music in London and Vienna, while there changing to studying architecture. (Clegg 1998) After her marriage, she moved to Cambridge and, as Rachel Rostas, combined architectural practice with motherhood.

Figure 10.1. Family photograph of Edward, Rachel and Henry Wallis c. 1914. By kind permission of City of York Museums Service.

The Wallis Archive – Chances and Choices in Preservation

The Wallis Archive consists of over 500 garments, accessories, textiles and printed material coming from four generations of the family spanning the eighteenth and twentieth centuries. This chapter concentrates on the twentieth-century dresses belonging to Amy Wallis (née Mounsey), Rachel Rostas (née Wallis) and Catherine (Cathy) Reeves (née Rostas) and children's clothes.[2] (Figure 10.2) The first decision to keep clothes was made by Amy; Rachel remembers her mother as 'keeping everything'. (Rostas 1989) On Amy's death, it was discovered that her children's clothes and the nursery contents had been preserved. (Clegg 1998) The family enjoyed a sufficient level of affluence to retain and store garments rather than using them to destruction, disposing of them or recycling them in different styles. Rachel herself kept clothes, but to a lesser degree, while far fewer of Cathy's clothes have entered the archive. It is likely that the adult garments which were saved were in some way special, either personal favourites or 'best' clothes associated with significant family or formal occasions as 'material memories' of important life events. (Kirschenblatt-Gimblett 1989) These may be the least worn and possibly more expensive garments. A twentieth-century garment made at home may also be kept on account of the individual's work in its creation and the pleasure derived from the experience of making something special. However, garments may also survive for precisely the opposite reasons. A dress which did not please or fit or was forgotten or was kept for sad occasions such as funerals may survive, whilst, paradoxically, favourite, flattering garments may not be preserved simply because they wore out.

The second significant decision point came when York Castle Museum acquired the first Wallis items in 1978 through John Reeves, Catherine Rostas' husband, then Education Officer at York Castle Museum. The Museum staff were making decisions about the acquisition of a range of items which survived the family's initial decision on their disposition. Inevitably, collecting decisions further modified the range of textiles which were retained. Pat Clegg, then Keeper of Costume and Textiles, recalls that 'both Rachel (Rostas) and I saw a rare opportunity to amass a collection which charted fashion and style in this century based on the taste of one family.' (Clegg 1998) Further material was collected in 1990 by Josie Sheppard, the current Curator. Crucially for the understanding of the collection, the museum acquired dressmaking patterns (Table 10.2), books on knitting, sewing and embroidery[3] and family photographs showing garments similar to those in the archive. The oral evidence collected is invaluable in understanding the meaning some of the garments had for the family and in distinguishing their origins. Even such a rich collection can only give a partial indication of the clothing owned and worn by the Wallis family and where and how it was acquired. The reasons behind their choices in selecting and retaining garments have to remain speculative, based on an interpretation of the impact of various social, financial, practical, geographical and emotional factors. Generalizations beyond this archive are difficult but it provides nevertheless a unique insight into the clothing choices of one family.

Costumiers, Dressmakers, Home Dressmaking

Table 10.1 presents a preliminary identification of the twentieth-century dresses by origin. Costumiers and local dressmakers provided an individual service of varying sophistication and quality. The individual consumer had a personal relationship with the 'manufacturer' and presumably was able to make choices based on understanding and interpretation of contemporary styles as well as financial and practical considerations. Modern home dressmaking is generally interpreted as garment-making carried out by a non-professional who receives no money for the labour and time involved. The garment pattern, fabric and sundries are usually purchased or recycled. Home dressmaking has a very strong association with women and is usually carried out by women for themselves and their children and worn by the maker or close family and friends.

Table 10.2 lists the eighteen patterns in the archive chronologically by envelope dates[4] and by garment style. Half appear to be used; most of these are for children's clothes which are discussed below. Dress pattern designers have always been responsive to fashion trends, making style available to many women. (Emery 1997; Walsh 1979) Margaret Trump (1988: 85) describes how, in 1948, she made herself 'working clothes' appropriate for her job in a ready-made dress department in Marshall and Snelgrove's, a fashionable London store where Rachel also shopped (York Castle Museum [hereafter YCM] 464.1 and 2): 'The exciting new silhouette filtered down quickly from the upper levels of Haute Couture to influence the cheapest mass-manufacturers and the dress-pattern producers [. . .] I bought a good pattern and [. . .] made myself a passably fashionable dress [. . .]'

The Wallis Archive highlights the difficulty of distinguishing between well-constructed, early twentieth-century dresses made at home from those made by a local dressmaker without a label or other provenance; both had access to the same patterns. Patterns can be sources of inspiration, modified or indeed made up for others beyond the family circle. None of the adult Wallis dresses is made directly from the surviving patterns but many relate closely in style. Pattern 0225 in the 1935 *Butterick* Fashion magazine (YCM 392.78),

Table 10.1. *The origins of dresses belonging to Amy Wallis, Rachel Rostas and Cathy Reeves.*

Date band	Costumier	Local dressmaker	Home-made	Guinea Gown shop	Commercially made
1910s	YCM 410.78 1910* silk satin wedding dress, train and veil Arthur Saunders Costumier, Darlington YCM 350.78 1910–12† silk evening dress, Eva Saunders Ltd, Costumier, Darlington				
1920s		YCM 351.78 1912† silk chiffon dress YCM 347.78 1920s† cotton voile day dress YCM 355.78 late 1920s or early 1930s† silk day dress	YCM 349.78 1920s† silk velvet evening dress YCM 449.78 1920s† regenerated cellulose day dress		

Table 10.1. *The origins of dresses belonging to Amy Wallis, Rachel Rostas and Cathy Reeves (continued).*

Date band	Costumier	Local dressmaker	Home-made	Guinea Gown shop	Commercially made
1930s			YCM 847.78 1934† cotton? velvet evening dress	YCM 846.78 1932† Rayon jersey evening dress	YCM 348.78 1930s† Man-made fibre day dress 'Marlbeck'
					YCM 352.78 1930s† ? fibre crepe evening dress hHeiressh
					YCM 352.78 1930s† cotton day dress 'Good Morning' USA
					YCM 354.78 1930s† cotton day dress 'June Arden frocks. Once tried, never denied'
			YCM 848.78 1938† Man-made moiré evening dress		YCM 453.78 1937‡ cotton tennis dress 'Made in London 1937'

Table 10.1. *The origins of dresses belonging to Amy Wallis, Rachel Rostas and Cathy Reeves (continued).*

Date band	Costumier	Local dressmaker	Home-made	Guinea Gown shop	Commercially made
1940s					YCM 450.78 1940s[†] Regenerated cellulose Utility day dress 'CC41' label
					YCM 845.78 1940s[†] cotton day dress 'John Lewis'
1950s					YCM 1.78 1950s[†] cotton day dress 'Horrockses'
					YCM 3.78 1950s[†] cotton day dress 'Marks & Spencer'
					YCM 392.79 late 1950s[†] cotton day dress 'St Michael' Marks & Spencer

Table 10.1. *The origins of dresses belonging to Amy Wallis, Rachel Rostas and Cathy Reeves (continued).*

Date band	Costumier	Local dressmaker	Home-made	Guinea Gown shop	Commercially made
1960s			YCM 406.79 1960s† cotton mini dress		YCM 464.1 & 2 1950s† cotton day dress 'Marshall & Snelgrove'
			YCM 408.79 1960s† cotton wrap-around dress		YCM 7.78 1966–68† cotton day dress (label cut out)
			YCM 404.79 1960s† cotton mini dress		YCM 4.78 1960s† silk evening/cocktail dress 'Cresta'
			YCM 405.79 1960s† cotton mini dress		YCM 390.79 1960s† dress, silk
					YCM 398.79 1960s† Evening dress (no label)
1970s			YCM 394.79 1970s† cotton dress		YCM 393.79 early 1970s† cotton day dress 95/3101 12.8

Table 10.1. *The origins of dresses belonging to Amy Wallis, Rachel Rostas and Cathy Reeves (continued).*

Date band	Costumier	Local dressmaker	Home-made	Guinea Gown shop	Commercially made
			YCM 395.79 mid 1970s† cotton dress		YCM 51.80 early 1970s† polyester evening dress
Unknown – Dressmaker/home-made					
1930s		YCM 53.78 1934† machine lace and silk evening dress			
		YCM 400.70 1935† machine net & lace bridesmaid dress			

Key: Amy Wallis
       Rachel Rostas
       Cathy Reeves

* = dated by oral evidence, † = dated by style, ‡ = unidentified dressmaker/home made

177

Table 10.2. *Patterns in the Wallis Archive.*

YCM No.	Date	Patternmaker number	Description	Size	Cost	Notes
391.78	GB Patent 12 November 1808 USA Patent 1899	Butterick 5248	Little boy's dress and separate knickerbockers		Not stated	Used
390.78	GB patent 12 November 1898	Butterick 7168	Little boy's suit		6d	Used for identical silk suits for Edward and Henry YCM 528.78
390.78	c.1914	Butterick 5248	Little boy's suit		6d	
387.78	Patented US and Mexico 1921, US 1923	Butterick 5248	Negligee	16	6d	
386.78	1929 copyright	McCalls 5908	Dress	16	45c	Used
374.78	1932 copyright	Vogue 5897	Woman's night dress	Small	50c	Unused
385.78	c. 1933	McCalls 7395	Woman's pyjamas and one-piece lounger pyjamas	18 36" bust 39" hip		Unused

Table 10.2. *Patterns in the Wallis Archive (continued).*

YCM No.	Date	Patternmaker number	Description	Size	Cost	Notes
381.78	1931 copyright	McCalls 6474	Dress	16 34" bust 37" hip		Appears used. Envelope information states: 'This garment is fitted closely at hip'
382.78	1930 copyright	McCalls 6459	Dress and Eton		50c	Possibly unused
376.78	1930s	Vogue 6551	Jacket-blouse	Small	1s or 55c	'Easy to Make'
377.78	1930s	Vogue S-3685	Woman's ensemble blouses skirt jacket	34" bust 37" hip	3s	Unused
381.78	1931	McCalls 6333	Dress		50c	Unused
378.78	1933 copyright	McCalls 7323	Set of Etons and scarf	16	35c	Used
384.78	1933 copyright	McCalls 7367	Dress	16	25c	
389.78	August 1932	Mabs Fashions	Dress and coatee	36" bust	free	Accompanied Mabs Fashion Magazine
379.78	1933 copyright	McCalls 7371	Blouse (three styles)	16	35c	Used by Rachel. Envelope bears pencil note: 'Rt front 101/2" + 3". Turnings Lt front 101/2" + 3" turnings"

Table 10.2. *Patterns in the Wallis Archive (continued).*

YCM No.	Date	Patternmaker number	Description	Size	Cost	Notes
376.78	?1937	Vogue 6551	Jacket-blouse	Small	40c	
388.78	1940s	Vogue 5364	Blouse	44" bust 47½" hips	2s 5d purchase tax	Unused. Envelope states 'Vogue patterns for coupons value. There are no restrictions on dress styles for the home dressmaker who can freely buy all Vogue Patterns in the shops*. But every Vogue Pattern is carefully planned to comply with the spirit of the regulations for saving materials. As a result all are economical in the use of fabrics. In many cases you actually save coupons by buying a Vogue Pattern. *Professional dressmakers are reminded that models made up by them must comply with Civilian Clothing (Restrictions) order.'

Source: The Wallis Archive.

although simpler, has features similar to Rachel's home-made velvet evening dress. (YCM 847.78)

The fabric type, techniques and quality of sewing and overall finish of the Wallis dresses were assessed for evidence of home dressmaking. Evidence from the dresses makes it clear that standards of acceptability varied in sewing and finish. However, generalizations are difficult here. Some women, such as ladies' maids, were often highly skilled dressmakers and could use their talents in a domestic as well as a professional context. Conversely, a 'poor' quality finish cannot be taken as conclusive evidence of a home-made garment. Mendes (1984: 84) notes that Poiret's 1924 dress 'Brique', in a colour similar to Amy's 1920s day dress (YCM 449.78), has poor-quality machine stitching and a crudely finished cotton taped hem.

More needs to be known about the availability of fabrics before it is possible to assess whether the home dressmaker and the dressmaker had access to different types and qualities. Fabric could be ordered by mail: Amy's 1914 issue of *Weldon's Bazaar of Children's Fashion* (YCM 396.78) contains advertisements for fabrics suitable for ladies' and children's clothing. One motive for home dressmaking could be the desire for a particular fabric, quality and style. Rachel recalls that both she and Amy disliked the early synthetics such as nylon and so home dressmaking using natural-fibre fabrics was a desirable alternative. (Brooks 1991: 377) The skill with which difficult fabrics such as lace or velvet are manipulated may also be an indicator.

The type of fastenings, the quality and method of making button holes or, indeed, their absence may provide another indicator of whether a garment is home- or professionally made. However, dressmaking sundries such as Barthelon's Sew So 'poppers' (snap fasteners) and Newey's Hooks and Eyes were widely advertised and available to home and professional dressmaker alike. The type and quality of stitching methods could be considered as a more reliable method of distinguishing home-made, dressmakers' and commercially made garments. However, both home and local dressmakers might have access to specialist machine finishes such as picot edging through Singer shops. (Burman 1996) Other machining techniques may be more informative, for example, until the increased availability of domestic overlocking (serging) machines from the late 1960s onwards, the presence of machined overlocking seam finishing was a fairly strong indication of a commercially made garment.[5]

The quality of a garment's fit was probably the most vital criterion in terms of the success of local and home dressmaking. The degree of success achieved is almost impossible to establish unless there is some supporting visual documentation or oral history testimony. Even then, differences of taste and changes in the acceptability of features such as wrinkles or visible hemlines need to be taken into consideration. The reminiscences of a Worthing dressmaker, Esther Rothstein, on changing perceptions of the quality of fit in the 1940s are illuminating here:

> [M]ore and more people were changing to buying 'ready-to-wear' as there was much improvement in fit by then. Indeed I was rather taken aback [. . .] when one of my clients, on seeing the dress I had just finished for her, remarked '[m]y goodness, it is just like a ready made!' I hardly knew whether to take it as a compliment or not. (Wise 1996: 83)

Purchasing Choices—'Madam' and 'Guinea Gown' Shops, Department Stores and Chain Stores

The shift from costumier or dressmaker to ready-to-wear involves a change in the relationship of consumer and producer. In the 1930s and 1940s, 'Madam' shops continued to offer individual customers a personal choice of model clothes, but for a price. They could also be rather forbidding. Tomlinson (1985: 3) recalls 'severe stands, the stark uncompromising display'. 'Guinea Gown' shops, where nothing cost more than a guinea, were less intimidating and, as their name suggests, were aimed at a less well-heeled market. (Rostas 1989)[6] At this time, shoppers had a range of purchasing options, including expensive or cheap manufactured garments and custom-made garments; for example, Marshall and Snelgrove still had a dressmaking department at this period. The improvement of mass produced garments and the growth of chain stores provided a wider choice, generally of acceptable quality at reasonable prices. However, fit could be less than exact and choice limited by the styles produced by manufacturers and selected by buyers as well as the practical issues of stock availability and price. Rachel recalls that, during the 1950s, she would go to the Cambridge branch of Marks and Spencers particularly early on a Friday morning when the stock arrived as later in the day the newest and best items had sold out. (Sheppard 1991: 375)

Amy Wallis's Dresses

Amy's twelve dresses demonstrate her personal style with a clear tendency towards 'aesthetic' design. Two of her earliest dresses were made by a local Darlington costumier, which seems to have been a family firm. Amy's white satin wedding dress (YCM 410.78) was made by Arthur Saunders whilst her 1910–12 sage green silk 'empire' style dress bears the label Eva Saunders

Ltd. (YCM 350.78) According to Rachel, her mother remained loyal to her home-town dressmakers, shoemakers and shops, even when living in Penrith. She bought custom-made dresses there, particularly from Arthur Saunders, as well as ready-to-wear. (Sheppard 1991) As a stylish young woman, Amy would also order dresses from London by mail. In later life, when she achieved her 'dowager' style, Amy bought most of her clothes from Binns, a Darlington department store. (Gill 1998)[7]

Rachel recalls that her mother had a strong interest in embroidery and dressmaking as a hobby for herself and her children rather than from economic need. (Sheppard 1991: 374) Her wedding dress (YCM 410.78) has been partially – and unsuccessfully – altered in an attempt to transform it into a dinner gown, possibly by Amy herself. As a girl, Rachel had several dresses which have embroidered motifs similar to those on some of Amy's clothes and in her embroidery books. Although no patterns for these dresses survive, the designs in the Weldon pattern book (YCM 396.78) are similar. At least three of Rachel's surviving girlhood dresses were made by Amy including the blue linen sun dress and matching hat decorated with white cross stitch. (YCM 478.78); (Sheppard 1991: 374) Rachel's 1920–23 drop-waisted, red wool crepe dress is trimmed with frills, decorative machine-stitching and geometric tree motifs in white pulled work. (YCM 474.78) Fastenings are minimal, consisting of metal 'poppers' at the neck. The seam edges are turned and machined. This dress, although having a definite artistic style, is relatively poorly made and compares in construction quality to known examples of Amy's dressmaking.

The surviving 1920s dresses made by Amy are significant evidence of her taste and sewing abilities, although no related patterns have survived.[8] These are simpler in style, cut and quality than her elaborately structured Saunders costumier dresses. It is clear Amy was prepared to accept a far lower quality of finishing in home dressmaking. The tubular line of her ochre plain-weave linen-look (regenerated cellulose) fabric day dress means there are few seams which are all handsewn. (YCM 449.78) The sleeves are cut in one with the dartless bodice; shaping is given through hip-gathering. There are decorative bands of simple running stitch at the hem and neck. Some seams are carefully turned and finished but others are raw and fraying. The dress is accompanied by fabric remnants, further evidence of its provenance. It is effective in terms of colour and line but simply made and decorated. The grey velvet evening dress, which once had a crudely constructed bow on the proper left hip, has a similar simplicity of cut and is constructed using poor-quality hand and machine sewing. (YCM 349.78) Significantly, neither of these dresses have any fastenings thus avoiding problems with button holes. The dropped waist seam is finished with the same lining fabric as the bodice and flying skirt panel. The sleeves are a puzzle: the brown silk georgette not only introduces a different colour but appears to have a commercially machined picot stitch hem. Singer shops offered such finishing services and local dressmakers used specialized hemstitchers to do such picot stitching. (Wise 1996) Several alternatives exist here: the sleeves could have been taken from an earlier dressmaker-made dress, made by Amy using a specialist commercial service for hemming or, indeed, made not by Amy but by another dressmaker working to a poor standard. These two dresses contrast strongly with another early 1920s handsewn blue and white cotton voile day dress which has complex construction and decoration, including embroidery, contrasting self-piping, faggoting and carefully worked side-waist button fastenings. (YCM 347.78) The exquisite hand stitching suggests, although there is no label, that it was commissioned from a highly skilled local dressmaker.

Three dresses of the late 1920s or early 1930s further highlight the problems of distinguishing home and professional dressmaking. Amy's 1928–31 blue embroidered dress is made from a heavy regenerated cellulose fabric with a slightly creped rib effect. (YCM 355.78) This has a more complex construction. The tubular bodice, with a deep 'V' neck, is gathered onto the piped shoulder yoke. The skirt is made from panels with curved heads which have been stitched together and then applied on top of the bodice to create a dropped scalloped waistline. The bodice itself extends under the skirt panels to hip level and is weighted with two lead weights encased in ribbons. The seams are machine-sewn and hand-finished. The only fastenings are 'poppers' at the wrists. The fabric is embroidered with stylized floral motifs in brightly coloured cross-stitch worked to follow the neckline. The embroidery is worked over the shoulder seam piping, indicating that it was carried out after the dress's construction. There are three back tucks which conceal some of the embroidery suggesting they were a later modification to achieve a better fit. This dress raises several questions. The construction combines some refined features, such as the piping, with an idiosyncratic skirt-construction and crudely-shaped, applied decorative bands at the wrists. The loop stitched in the back of the neck could suggest professional manufacture. It is conceivable that Amy did the embroidery after she or her local dressmaker made up the dress or it could have been worked by another hand altogether. Given the existing evidence it is not possible to be certain whether this dress was made by a home or local dressmaker or a combination of the two. Amy's 1933–36 evening dress of heavy, machine-made cream cotton lace with a black net ground presents a similar dilemma. (YCM 353.78) It has a draped bodice and full trained skirt over a grey-green underdress. Again, there are no fastenings, little shaping and no set-in sleeves, just flying cap sleeves. The seams are machine-sewn but there is also crude hand stitching on the sleeves.

The quality of the finish and the lack of fastening corresponds with that on dresses known to be made by Amy. On the other hand, the lace fabric needed careful handling to achieve the panelled effect on the skirt front suggesting a local dressmaker working to a lower standard than that seen on the costumier dresses.

The situation is not clarified by comparing the quality of these dresses with a dress known to be commercially manufactured. Amy's 1930s 'Marlbeck' day dress (YCM 348.78) in a man-made blue-and-white striped fabric has a complex structure with a deep revered neck opening, front waist seam and pleated skirt panel and back yoke. The machine-seaming is crude; some seams are neatly turned but others are untrimmed or roughly whipped. An edge-to-edge belt covers up the uneven waist seam. Once more, there are no fastenings except for 'poppers' at the cuffs. Clearly, quality of stitching and absence of fastenings cannot be used as definitive criteria for distinguishing between home-made, dressmaker garments or commercially made garments.

Rachel Rostas's Dresses

The earliest of Rachel's adult dresses in the archive is her 1935 bridesmaid dress. (YCM 400.79) This is in grey net with a fitted bodice, double-layered shoulder frill and full skirt over an unstructured pink rayon underdress. It is relatively crudely machine and handsewn but has a fairly complex structure. As was normal, even on high-quality dresses, the net is simply cut at the bottom without any hemming. There is a 'popper' and hook and eye side opening. In the absence of any corroborating evidence, it is impossible to say whether this dress is home-made or dressmaker-made.

In 1932, Rachel was studying in London with a living allowance of £250 per year, out of which she had to clothe herself. As well as making her own clothes, possibly for reasons of economy, Rachel remembers buying ready-made garments from department stores such as John Lewis, Whiteleys and Barkers. She considered Harrods too expensive and had been advised to avoid the costly 'Madam shops'. (Sheppard 1991: 375) Rachel described the 1932 salmon-pink, rayon jersey evening dress which she bought from a London 'Guinea gown' shop as 'vulgar'. (YCM 846.78); (Rostas 1989) Without this evidence, it would be hard to distinguish the dress, with its sleeveless bodice, net neck inset and intricately panelled skirt, from Rachel's home-made evening dresses on grounds of style, fabric, cut, construction or quality of finish. Her 1930s dress patterns are notable for their lack of instructions but complexity of structure, a marked contrast to the simple lines of Amy's 1920s dresses. Rachel's 1934 midnight-blue cotton velvet evening dress strives for glamour.

(YCM 847.78) The similarity to a pattern in the 1935 *Butterick* magazine has already been noted. The dress has a very fitted, bias-cut bodice. The skirt hugs the hips to the knees where it swirls out into full gores with scalloped headings. A single self-fabric rouleaux band decorates the hem while three bands finish the armholes. The dress is machine-sewn with pinked seams and demonstrates an ability to handle a difficult pile fabric in a complex structure, although paying relatively little attention to finish. The 1938 evening dress (YCM 847.78) shows a similar focus on impact rather than high-quality sewing. It is made from a highly-finished, red-brown moiré taffeta, which attempts to create the sinuous fashionable line despite the fabric's stiffness. The moiré effect is deliberately exploited; the trained skirt and bodice is cut with the design in a horizontal direction while the pleated hip band extending into a back bow uses the moiré in the vertical direction. This dress makes a feature of the fastenings – twelve self-covered centre back buttons and hand-made loops. The shoulder pads appear to be home-made, constructed out of a rubber or synthetic pad with a rayon fabric covering. The dress is machine-sewn with unfinished seams and must have required considerable skill and time to make. However, the unpicked seam lines on the bodice are evidence of the difficulty in achieving the correct fit despite the evident confidence in handling a difficult fabric.

None of the wartime day dresses which Rachel is known to have made survive; they presumably wore out or were remodelled. Contemporary evidence indicates the importance of home dressmaking during the war: 'The smaller the wardrobe, the better it must be and under clothes rationing, home-dressing pays!' (*Weldon Ladies Journal* 1941) By this time, Rachel was a working mother. Few dresses made at home between 1950 to 1970 exist; perhaps time was too precious to spend it on dressmaking for herself when attractive and well-made clothes were readily available and affordable. Like her mother before her, Rachel made dresses for her daughters. One button-front dress pattern, which has not survived, was made up, probably by Rachel, for both herself and Catherine between about 1968 and 1971. Rachel's version in a blue-black plain-weave cotton has self-covered buttons, patch pockets, belt latchets and top stitching. (YCM 395.79) Some seams have been finished with crude whipping over raw edges. Cathy's pocket and beltless version is in plain-weave striped-orange, pink and brown cotton with plastic buttons, now faded to pinkish-orange. (YCM 407.79)

Rachel made herself simple shift dresses in the late 1960s and early 1970s. One sleeveless blue and white cotton twill dress with long centre back and front darts has seams, neck and armholes accentuated with white top stitching. (YCM 394.79) The hem is turned, machined and then hand-whipped. This uncomplicated design and straightforward construction contrasts with Rachel's complex 1930s evening dresses. Again, it is not always easy to distinguish home-made from commercially made garments. At first glance, Rachel's late 1960s floral printed sleeveless day dress (YCM 393.79) has a very simple construction similar to her home-made dresses down to the vertical alignment of the crudely machine stitched buttonholes. However, the small label in one seam bearing the numbers '95/3101 12.8' and the commercial seam overlocking indicates its commercial origin.

Catherine Reeves' Dresses

Four of the five dresses belonging to Catherine were made at home by her mother or by Catherine herself. The simple styles of the 1960s lent themselves to unstructured home dressmaking. These dresses are mainly simply cut, tunic-style mini-dresses in bold colours and prints with obvious fastenings such as the Paisley print bell sleeved dress with a bold front ring-pull metal zip. (YCM 404.79) The popular Paisley recurs in the contrast yoke, cuffs and patch pockets of an early 1970s cerise twill cotton day dress. (YCM 405.79) This dress has a front opening with seven self-covered buttons and hand-worked buttonholes. It is machine-stitched with closely clipped raw seams although the front opening exploits the selvages at the self-facing. Another very short, home-made 1960s dress in a printed red/brown floral cotton with braid and ric-rac trim avoids the buttonhole problem through its simple wrap-around construction. (YCM 408.79) Cathy's taste for strong colours is vividly demonstrated by her pink and orange check, silk mini-dress with a centre front zip. (YCM 406.79) The flaring side seams and long, heavily interfaced cuffs are decorated with domed 'gold' buttons fastened with self-fabric loops. Close examination of the hand-stitching on the side seams reveals previous machine-stitching from an earlier construction; it seems a considerable degree of alteration has taken place. Was the dress made from another dress, possibly commercially made, or is this a modification of a home-made garment to improve the fit? Cathy's early 1970s polyester cotton evening dress with a Size 2 tab is definitely mass produced. (YCM 51.80)

Patterns and Clothes for Babies and Toddlers

The archive contains many of Edward's, Henry's and Rachel's baby clothes. Labels identify some as commercially made (YCM 541.78; 542.78; 543.78; 544.78), either purchased at local stores or through mail order. (Sheppard 1991: 374) Many are hand-made, possibly by the same dressmaker who made

Amy's clothes, including Edward's christening gown. (YCM 493.78) Amy owned a number of instruction books on the making of babies' and toddlers' clothes from which some paper patterns show signs of use. The high quality of the baby clothes manufacture contrasts strongly with the skills demonstrated by Amy in her own dressmaking so it seems likely that these baby patterns were used by her dressmaker.

Commercially made and expensive clothes for the children as toddlers were often bought by mail order, such as Rachel's cashmere coat from Wendy of North Audley Street, London. (YCM 487.78); (Sheppard 1991: 374) Edward and Henry, who were often dressed alike despite their age difference, had five blue linen romper suits from Harrods (YCM 519.78) and professionally made sailor suits. (YCM 525.78) However, many of the boys' clothes were made by a local dressmaker, possibly using patterns supplied by Amy. This seems to have been for practical or aesthetic reasons – soft greens and pastels predominate – rather than economy as many of the materials are relatively expensive. (Sheppard 1991: 374) There is some correlation between surviving patterns and garments. Amy's 1914 *Weldon's Bazaar of Children's Fashion* (YCM 396.78) contains patterns (No 48571) for a boy's tunic, knicker and coat suits which were clearly used. The brown paper pattern for the coat sleeve has been adjusted and the pin is still in place. There are eight pairs of suits in this style, varying in fabrics and colours. The turquoise and blue silk suits worn by Edward and Henry between 1918-1920 (YCM 528.78) were made from Butterick pattern 7168. (YCM 390.78) (Figure 10.2) The silk/ cotton mix tunic tops have falling collars, neck lacing cords and decorative self-covered cuff buttons. Butterick pattern 5248 (YCM 391.78) is a similar style which Amy clearly favoured for her small boys. Many such suits survive including ones in white linen (YCM 524.78), white cotton (YCM 530.78) and pale green silk. (YCM 532.78) Their contrasting dark green embroidery and self-covered buttons decorated with green silk threads are ample evidence of the care and expense lavished on the boys' clothes.

Three of Rachel's baby dresses survive. These are embellished with embroidery, lace insertions, feather-stitched seams, tucks and frills. (YCM 516.78; 517.78 and 518.78) Rachel's cotton piqué coat (YCM 489.78), worn when she was three or four, has lace collar and cuffs and is very finely made with exquisitely neat hand-stitching, suggesting professional manufacture. Her toddler's clothes include a printed sprigged muslin dress (YCM 475.78) which has fairly basic smocking decorated with French knots and is reminiscent of styles in the *Bestway* magazine. (YCM 393.78) It is possible this was worked by Amy. In contrast, Rachel's green linen dress (YCM 475.78) with smocked bodice and wrist panels and traditional spiral feather-stitched motifs is exquisitely hand-embroidered with machine-stitched seams. It is

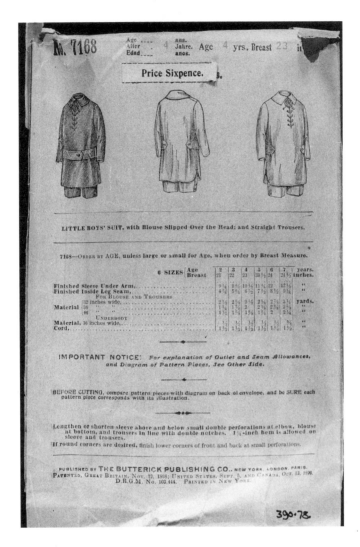

Figure 10.2. 'Little boys' suit, with Blouse Slipped Over the Head; and Straight Trousers.' 7168 paper pattern envelope by the Butterick Publishing Co. patented in Great Britain in 1898. This pattern was used for two suits surviving in the Wallis Archive. By kind permission of City of York Museums Service.

tempting to speculate that this dress originates from one of several schemes set up to provide poorer women with an income by practising traditional needlework skills. This type of home dressmaking has a very different impetus and economic status.

Persons whose garments are in the Wallis Collection are shown in **bold**.

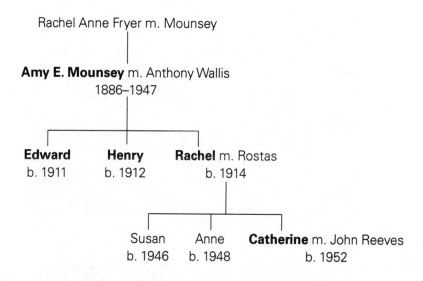

Figure 10.3. The Wallis Family Tree.

Conclusions

Home dressmakers could be motivated by a range of factors such as the desire to make garments which reflected personal taste in terms of design, fit, type of fibre and fabric as well as economic pressures. Financially secure women could choose to make clothes for themselves and their children for pleasure in the process and in the results, for economy and for freedom in creating their own style. Earlier in the century, the availability of local skilled dressmakers enabled women with sufficient money to make individual choices for clothing both themselves and their children without expending their own time and energy. Once mass produced and reasonably priced clothing was available, demand for the local dressmaker declined but home dressmaking continued. Motives of economy – ignoring the cost of time – could be combined with an active interest in fashion and enjoyment in skill. In doing this, the home dressmaker was closing the consumer/manufacturer circle; fit, cut and fabric choice were back, to some degree, in their hands. The Wallis Archive gives a valuable insight into these changing patterns of choice in women's and children's dress and the comparative values which may be placed on home-made and professionally made clothes.

Acknowledgements

The author would like to thank Josie Sheppard, Curator of Costume and Textiles, and Gill Greaves, Curator, York Castle Museum, for their generous support of this further research into the Wallis Archive. Discussions with Josie Sheppard on the dresses were particularly valuable. Thanks are due to Nell Hoare, Director, Textile Conservation Centre, for permission to publish and to Helen Colwell, Photographer. Special thanks are due to Dinah Eastop, Senior Lecturer, for her encouragement and constructive criticism of drafts. Without Pat Clegg, Keeper of Costume and Textiles, and John Reeves, Education Officer, York Castle Museum, this archive would not have been preserved and a great debt is owed to them for their foresight.

Notes

1. Further study of the Wallis material in Durham Record Office will enrich, it is hoped, the understanding of the family context.

2. Nineteenth-century clothes, accessories and other items are not discussed in this chapter. The whole archive has been reviewed in Sheppard (1991) and Brooks (1991).

3. Books in the archive include *Weldon's Bazaar of Children's Fashion* and E.M.'s *The Lady's Knitting Book*.

4. Issues involved in dating patterns by their printed copyright or patent dates have been comprehensively discussed by Williams (1996/97). I am indebted to Barbara Burman for this reference.

5. Overlock machines or sergers were first produced for domestic use by the Japanese in the late 1960s and have since become more generally available although they are still not common.

6. All prices are shown in the predecimal British currency of pounds, shillings and pence. One pound (twenty shillings) is equivalent to hundred new pence; one guinea (£1 1s 0d) is thus the equivalent of £1.05.

7. Binns Department Stores were taken over by the House of Fraser Group.

8. One unused wartime blouse pattern (Vogue 5364; YCM 388.78) was probably Amy's. The envelope notes are a particularly interesting reminder that, at a time of strict clothing restrictions, both home and professional dressmakers were using the same paper patterns.

References

Brooks, M. M. (1991), 'Man-made Fibres and Synthetics in the Wallis Archive, York Castle Museum' in *Per una storia della moda pronta. Problemi e ricerca. Atti del*

V Convegno Internazionale del CISST. Milano 26–28 feb 1990, Florence: Edifir Edizioni: 377–87.

Buck, A. (1998), 'Foreword' in *Museums & Galleries Commission Standards in the Museum Care of Costume & Textile Collections*, London: Museums and Galleries Commission.

Burman, Barbara (1996), Personal communication, June.

Clegg, Pat (1998), Personal communication, January.

Emery, J. P. (1997), 'Development of the American Commercial Pattern Industry: The First Generation, 1850–1880', *Costume*, 31: 78–91.

Gill, Jo (1998), Personal communication, January. Gill is County Archivist, Durham Record Office.

Kirschenblatt-Gimblett, B. (1989), 'Objects of Memory: Materials Culture as Life Review' in E. Oring, (ed.), *Folk Groups & Folklore Genres: A Reader*, Logan: Utah State University Press: 329–38.

Mendes, V. D. (1984), 'Women's Dress since in 1900' in N. Rothstein, (ed.), *Four Hundred Years of Fashion*, London: Victoria and Albert Museum/William Collins.

Rostas, Rachel (1989), Personal communication, November.

Sheppard, J. (1991), 'The Wallis Archive, York Castle Museum' in *Per una storia della moda pronta. Problemi e ricerca. Atti del V Convegno Internazionale del CISST. Milano 26–28 feb 1990*, Florence: Edifir Edizioni: 373–6.

Tomlinson, D. (1985), 'Introduction' in J. Tozer, *British Cotton Couture 1941–61*, Manchester: Manchester City Art Galleries.

Trump, M. M. (1988), 'When I was at Marshall and Snelgrove . . .' *Costume*, 22: 85–93.

Walsh, M. (1979), 'The Democratization of Fashion: The Emergence of the Women's Dress Pattern Industry', *The Journal of American History*, 66, 2: 299–313.

Weldon's Ladies Journal (1941), illustrated in Breward, C. (1995), *The Culture of Fashion*, Manchester: Manchester University Press.

Williams, B. (1996/97), 'On the Dating of Tissue Paper Patterns', *Cutters' Research Journal*, VIII, 3: 1–10. (Reprint of two 1990 articles.)

Wise, A. (1996), 'Dressmakers in Worthing, 1920–1950', *Costume*, 32: 82–6.

11

The Sewing Needle as Magic Wand: Selling Sewing Lessons to American Girls after the Second World War

Eileen Margerum

My life is involved in the events described below. I was born in 1939 and lived in a working-class family in New York City. In writing this essay, I have come to recognize that the chasm between my mother's strictly utilitarian attitude toward sewing and my teenage obsession with trying to make my own clothes comes from our being products of different decades. Back then, I thought her disapproval of my buying paper patterns and cutting fabric to sew into clothes was caused by my generally leaving the living room in disarray. Now I know it wasn't all caused by the sewing pins in the carpet.

In 1944, when Allied victory seemed certain, commentators on the United States economy began to propose ways of easing the transition to a civilian basis. Almost all agreed on one point: whereas the war economy prospered because of government spending, post-war prosperity would depend largely on civilians. American civilians had an estimated $100 billion in enforced savings, money earned during the Second World War when there was little to spend it on. When peace returned, commentators agreed, they had to be enticed to spend it. (Ware 1945: 13) It would be up to manufacturers to quickly retool their plants for peace-time production and to make their products as attractive to consumers as possible.

Manufacturers of domestic sewing machines aimed to match their best year ever, 1941, when 804,000 units had been shipped and sold in the United States. (The civilian economy had rapidly improved from 1939 through 1941 as the United States provided war supplies to European allies but was not directly involved in the fighting.) Their goal seemed quite distant in November 1945, when only 8,095 machines were produced. Sixteen months later, in March 1947, 54,452 units (worth $2.7 million) were shipped, an annualized rate still about 20 per cent short of the goal. (Facts for Industry 1947a) Sewing machines were far behind automobiles, adequate housing units and major home appliances on the American consumers' wish list.

To create a demand for sewing machines, manufacturers first had to develop a demand for sewing. The obvious target for such a campaign was American housewives, but they were not responsive. During the war, the role of sewing had changed drastically. Housewives had been dissuaded, directly or indirectly, from making clothes at home. Sewing became a 'make-do' activity: patching and remaking what one already had.[1] Once the United States entered the Second World War in December 1941, civilian life changed quickly; household appliances, including sewing machines, were out of production by February 1942. (Weatherford 1990: 202) Recent historians have described what happened to the basic necessities for home sewing: 'Sales of yard goods and sewing patterns soared [. . .] until these materials became scarce.' (Campbell 1984: 177)

> India's silk supply had ceased; any silk that happened to be available was needed instead for parachutes and gunpowder bags. Its substitutes, newly invented nylon and rayon, were needed for aircraft and military clothing. The same was true even of humble cotton, a stable now requisitioned for tents and other heavy military uses. Wool, normally imported from Australia and elsewhere, became very, very tight. (Weatherford 1990: 200)

Meanwhile, six million women joined the work force and almost 280,000 volunteered for military duty. (Campbell 1984: 20) Many of the twelve million women who had been working before the war moved from domestic and service jobs into heavy manufacturing, as men went off to war. For the first time in United States' history, the civilian workforce included over eighteen million women; more were married, older women than single, younger ones. (Thomas 1987: 118)

In farm households, the printed cloth sacks holding feed and grain became a treasured source of material for children's clothing. City housewives had no such resource. In 1944, economist Caroline Ware complained in print about the shoddy quality of material available for civilian clothing. (Ware 1945: 1, 3) My mother's war experiences permanently influenced her attitude toward sewing. She never used her Singer table model, bought in 1940, other than for repairs – turning frayed cuffs and collars on my father's work shirts or my brother's and my playclothes, adding fabric to lengthen my skirts, or sewing torn bed linen. Working outside the home to earn money for store-bought clothes was, to her, a better use of her time. By the end of the war, the habit of sewing their own clothes was no longer part of many housewives' daily lives.

The next most logical target was the 'war brides'. These newly married women, mostly in their twenties, had money to buy sewing machines but not the space. The explosive number of new post-war families created an extreme housing shortage that was not relieved until the early 1950s. Many couples, and their babies, shared space with in-laws. Others lived in makeshift housing on college campuses as husbands went to school under the 'GI Bill'. The pressures of raising babies in crowded conditions did not leave room for sewing machines or time for sewing. In the interim, the young families bought cars and saved for the down payment on their own house.

That left an unlikely market: teenage girls. Demographically, they were a small group, having been born during the great American birth slump that preceded and accompanied the Great Depression. In 1946, there were about four and a half million girls aged fourteen to eighteen, barely 3 per cent of the total population. By contrast, a decade later, girls between fourteen and eighteen represented 8.78 per cent of all Americans. (Historical Statistics 1975: 10)

Not only were teenage girls few in number, but they were also relatively poor. As the wartime economy subsided, so did their best opportunities for economic independence. Teenage girls were at the bottom of the employment chain. Returning servicemen took back jobs from women and teenage boys. The boys, in turn, reclaimed from the girls their 'right' to most part-time and after-school jobs as well as outdoor household chores done for pay. Even babysitting, the one job left to girls, was not a sure source of funds. The boom in post-war births did not mean a boom in babysitting jobs. The clusters of new mothers in campus housing shared their child-care efforts. Young families who were temporarily living with relatives relied on other females in the household as their babysitters.

Yet teenage girls, a small, economically dependent section of the American consuming public, proved an apt market for selling sewing machines. The teenage American girl in 1946 was highly vulnerable to suggestions about spending money. She had spent the last four years living under wartime conditions that everyone told her were unusual; but these conditions were most likely the only ones she remembered. She saw and heard adults (and the media) plan for 'when the war is over'. She knew that everyone looked forward to having things to buy with the money they'd been saving. Her world view was not coloured by the deprivation of the Depression when most people lacked money. She grew up in a time when they had money but lacked things to buy. She was, in effect, the child of consumer anticipation. Even if she lacked her own money, the American teenage girl belonged to a family which might have some wartime savings waiting to be spent. All that advertisers needed was a way to reach her so that she could help spend that money.

Selling to teenage girls had begun as soon as advertisers believed they had enough money to be worth targeting. The success of *Seventeen* magazine was the first indication of how profitable this market might be. *Seventeen* had been launched in 1944 by Walter Annenberg of Triangle Publications and was aimed directly at the female teenager as consumer. Annenberg had cannibalized two of Triangle's existing magazines to get enough government-rationed paper stock to print 500,000 copies of the 'outsized, thick, and slick' September 1944 issue, which sold out completely. Teenage response was so great that, by the December issue, the print run was up to 550,000 copies. Of its 120 pages, 66 were advertising ('Bobby-Sock Form' 1944) *Seventeen's* combination of self, fashion, and boys still works; in 1997, it outsold its nearest rival by over a million copies a month (McCloud 1997).

In January 1946, The Singer Sewing Company, America's largest domestic sewing machine maker, began selling directly to girls by offering the Singer Teen-Age Sewing Course, declaring that it was exclusively for girls aged twelve to seventeen. The ads appeared sporadically in four magazines aimed at middle-class teenage girls: *The American Girl, Modern Miss, Calling All Girls* and *Seventeen*. This study will concentrate on those that appeared in *American Girl*, the official magazine of the Girl Scouts of America, and in *Seventeen*. The campaign lasted until the mid-1960s, a two-decade period when Singer so dominated the home-sewing market in the United States that many American women would have been hard pressed to name another maker of sewing machines.

The first ad ran in *American Girl* in January 1946. Taking this ad as a starting point, it is possible to see how the Singer campaign fitted into the consumer role assigned to girls in the post-war society. Entitled 'The Prom Plotters', it is in the form of a three-scene play. Like later ads, its format is problem-solution-reward-evidence. The girl (in this case, twins) needs a dress for a social occasion (the prom), but Dad won't pay for it; she takes sewing lessons at Singer and makes the dress; she has fun at the dance; a picture of the dress appears in the lower right-hand corner of the page (below it is a caption specifying the pattern manufacturer, pattern number, and fabric yardage required). This ad, however, differs from later versions in some key elements: these girls are independent enough to have discovered the sewing lessons on their own, to make an unprompted decision to make their own dresses and to pay for the lessons from their earnings; the boys are almost an afterthought; and an adult, Dad, admires them for their initiative as much as for their dresses.

This ad reflects the time in which it was written and the magazine in which it appeared. In early 1946, *American Girl* still contained both articles and fiction that spoke to girls' self-reliance and citizenship in the larger community. For instance, the January issue contained both an article, signed by J. Edgar Hoover, praising women's roles in the FBI during the war and a reminder of the girls' duty to contribute to the Girl Scout-sponsored Victory Clothing Drive for Overseas Relief. In February, a short story reinforced a girl's independence: although the heroine of 'Betsy and the Youth Problem' must ask her father's permission before buying a lipstick, she buys it with her own savings. In 'The Purse', fiction in the April issue, a local girl who is popular in high school tells how she realized she must be more sensitive to the feelings of transient students and organized a student canteen for them.

These attitudes might be described as the after-glow of the war years, a time when teenage girls had been propagandized to fill boys' roles just as adult women had been propagandized to replace men. The contents of the magazine had no doubt been chosen months before the issues actually appeared.

By the fall of 1946, as the magazines caught up with the new post-war attitudes, message to girls in both magazine content and advertisements changed dramatically. When government rationing of paper ended in 1946 and other teenage magazines could buy the paper to add more advertising pages, they picked up *Seventeen*'s message. They narrowed the versions of self that they offered to girls to the one consistent with the message in advertising: the American girl is at her best when she is a consumer. The Girl Scouts even got into the act themselves. Effective with the September 1946 issue, *American Girl* began selling 'Hollywood Patterns' in teenage dress sizes; starting in November 1946, ads appeared for Girl Scouts Cosmetics (boxed sets of beauty cream, hand lotion, shampoo and scented soap). Both items were available by mail directly from the national headquarters in Washington.

The message that girls should pay more attention to their looks than their accomplishments was already present in February 1946 issue of *American Girl*. In the short story, 'Little Genius,' a female math whiz recounts how she became popular at college by willingly becoming the object of laughter and playing a dumb girl in a school play. For being such a good sport, she was invited to the Frosh Dance by the senior boy who convinced her to play the dumb role. That message could not be clearer: fit in, playdown your abilities, and you will get a boy.

These revised attitudes are articulated in the Singer ad that appeared in

Seventeen in September 1946. Like many short stories in teenage girl magazines, the ad is a first-person narrative. It contains all the key elements, both in content and design, that recur throughout the Singer campaign. The language is geared toward the teenage market; it is sprinkled with 'teenspeak'. Words like 'dreamboat', 'duds', 'marv' and 'hubba-hubba' signal that the writer and the reader are both of the same generation.

The situation in this ad takes the girl's story to a new level. She has been invited to a friend's home for a whirlwind weekend of social events. The friend's 'dreamboat' brother (presumably slightly older) also looks forward to her arrival. With this ad, the campaign adopted an underlying motif that lasted for more than two decades: the Cinderella story. (Figure 11.1) Like

Figure 11.1. Typical of Singer teen-age sewing course advertisements, this mini-drama ends with the girl having new clothes and a new boyfriend. Published in *Seventeen* and *Modern Miss*, September 1946. Young & Rubicam Agency Archives.

Cinderella, the girl can change her life if she can go to the important social event; however, she lacks the proper social accoutrements and faces an obstacle to get them. 'I thudded from my pink cloud [. . .] when I squinted into my closet. Despair! Such beat-up duds! And Dad still seething over my bills for last month's barest necessities!' Unlike the fairy-tale heroine, she is neither virtuous nor long-suffering and, certainly, there is no hint she serves anyone but herself.[2] She is Cinderella the spendthrift but, in 1946 America, having and spending money was itself the stuff of fairy tales. Most girls who read teenage magazines had far more limited social lives and much smaller clothes budgets than did the heroine of this ad. In 1947, 46.2 per cent of white American families had total incomes of under $3,000. [Historical Statistics 1975: 289. The events of this ad, like the events of many short stories in girls' magazines, are themselves a form of fantasy.

The ad heroine's deliverance comes indirectly, in the form of the message written on the back of her friend's picture. 'Sharp outfit, n'est-ce pas? I made it! Uh huh. Took those marv Singer Teen-Age Sewing Lessons. Fun! Sewing 'n styling 'n stuff. Made this while I was learning.' Her response: ' "Fate," I muttered, and zoomed out to the nearest Singer Sewing Centre.' In true fairy-tale fashion, she becomes a star instantly. 'Me in the hubba-hubba numbers Singer taught me to whip up-sensayshunal!' And the Prince Charming comes through, as well: 'Bud's got my week ends planned practically to 1950!'

Considering that the purpose of this ad campaign was to sell the idea of sewing, Singer sewing machines and sewing accessories, the act of sewing gets short shrift. There is no description of what she did for eight lessons at the Singer Sewing Centre. All she needed to do was 'zoom' to Singer, and her wardrobe magically appeared. In this campaign, the wish becomes the deed.

Typical of the design of these ads, three simple line drawings illustrate the story. The only 'real' element in the ad is the photograph of a young woman in a dress. This combination of drawings and photograph creates a tension in the ads. What is the purpose of the picture? Is it 'proof' that the fictive narrator of the ad really did make a dress and, therefore, may not be merely imaginary? Is it evidence that a girl-made dress can look as good as a commercially made one – the girls always strike poses like models in clothing ads? Is it an invitation for the teenage girl to look at another girl, in admiration or awe or envy?

In his ground-breaking study of cartoons, Scott McCloud argues that cartoons and line drawings allow, even invite, the viewer to participate in the events and, in effect, to become the central character. (McCloud 1993) Seen in this light, these ads become fantasies in which the teenage reader becomes (or becomes like) the heroine. The photograph at the bottom becomes a mirror in which the reader can see how she might look in this dress while, at the same time, it is a picture of the narrator as she looked when she impressed the boy of her dreams. It is feminine narcissism in the service of the consumer culture. As Hilary Radner described it,

> The grounding of the pleasurable image in product usage [. . .] positions feminine narcissism within a consumer economy. The possibility of the woman taking pleasure in herself, for herself, is circumscribed by the necessary contingency of the male gaze and the demand that she function as a consumer. (1995: 60)

The pattern for future Singer ads was set. The ads involved three elements: the desirable offer (social event involving a boy) along with the obstacle to accepting it (father's unwillingness to buy another dress); the magic answer to the impossible situation (hearing about the sewing lessons); acting on the answer and receiving her reward (making a dress during sewing lessons and getting the boy's attentions). The three line drawings and photograph of the girl in 'the dress' became a visual trope that allowed teenage girls comfortably to approach these commercial fairy tales and be sure of their conclusion.

A short story in the February 1948 issue of *Seventeen* illustrates how successfully this pattern of obstacle, choice, and reward could be developed. In 'Dance with the Devil', Norma (a college sophomore) can't get a date for the big dance: 'It was no ordinary sorority dance. It was the climax of the winter season. It was given off-campus, in a swank hotel [. . .] Last year as a freshman, Norma had not been eligible to go.' Exasperated, she declares she'd even go with the devil himself. Magically, a darkly handsome, slightly older, man appears in her room and offers to be her date. She accepts, though she assumes he is the devil. Together on the dance floor, they are the object of admiring attention but 'Norma remained a belle whomever she danced with!' Before the evening ends, she is asked for future dates by three men who accompanied other girls to the dance. It is the Cinderella story, with the devil (or, as he later reveals himself, an angel) as fairy godmother. Her reward is a busy future social life.

As other advertisers became aware of the power of fantasy, they played to the teenage girls' imagination by making the girl, not the advertised product, the star. A Tussy Lipstick ad, headlined 'Date Bait' and showing a line drawing of a teenage girl being ogled by two boys, appeared in *American Girl* early in 1947. Colour photographs of girls modelling the latest style dresses or coats, often in glamourous settings, accompanied ads by retail clothiers and fabric producers in *Seventeen*. Unlike earlier teenage models, whose faces were averted so that the viewer would pay attention to the clothing, these models look directly into the camera and invite the viewer to look at them as well as what they wear. In teenage-magazine advertisements, regardless of the product, there is one consistency: only one girl appears in each frame. The advertisers' message supported the image of the teenage girl as atomized; she relates to no one except a teenage boy.

While the fairy-tale pattern remained consistent throughout the campaign, the Singer heroine took on new attributes in 1950. Instead of being merely pleasing, the girl had a talent. This change may be connected with increasing self-confidence and wealth of the middle class. The daughter in a middle-class family was now privileged enough that she didn't need to find her consumption behaviour patterns in the actions of upper-class girls. In the April 1950 ad in *Seventeen*, she is a member of a successful debate team who needs a dress for the coming trip. When Dad's tax payments mean he won't buy her it, she overhears 'a fashion-plate-looking girl' tell a salesgirl that she makes all her own clothes, thanks to lessons at Singer. In typical magic-time formula, the heroine recounts:

I dash over to the Singer Sewing Centre. Sure enough, everything she said is true. I take their course, make a sensational dress in the process. I launch it on the trip and we win the debate! I win a date, too – with a wonderful-looking boy on the opposing team. 'Our Spring Formal's in two weeks – come back for it and I promise not to argue with you the whole evening!'

Lest the teenage reader mistake the point and believe the story is about the girl's accomplishments, its headline is quite specific: 'How to Win a Debate – and Make a Date!'

In a 1951 ad, the heroine wins the lead in the annual play. Inexplicably, costumes are not provided so she must make her own. As she passes the Singer Sewing Centre, she sees 'the other woman', her rival in the play (and in real life) for the male lead's attentions. True to the 'other woman' stereotype, this young woman leaves the shop when the heroine enters, but not before declaring, 'I make all my own clothes.' She does not give advice, but unwittingly provides the answer. Then, the heroine moves into magic-time.

Bunny-quick, I enroll! And, imagine, even while I'm learning to cut and stitch, I'm making my first-act dress [. . .] You ought to see the glamour-jobs I'm turning out for practically peanuts with my Singer know-how [. . .] The Play? It was heaven! Nothing like cute clothes to help poise. Incidentally, I 'got' the male lead, too!

Throughout the campaign, ease and speed are emphasized. The Sewing Course is never presented as a way to learn a new skill or to develop a competence that enhances the girl's self-reliance. Taking sewing lessons is just the girl's strategy to get the dress needed to catch the boy's attention.

Like the stories in teenage girls' magazines, these ads offer a life of social and personal success tantalizingly familiar but just beyond most girls' reach. Although the Singer Teen-Age Sewing Course was specifically for girls aged twelve to seventeen, and *Seventeen*'s declared target market was thirteen- to eighteen-year-old girls, both the advertisements and magazine fiction used stories that suggested older, more sophisticated participants: college freshmen rather than high-school freshmen. They were made of the stuff of dreams.

For most teenage girls in the 1940s and 1950s, taking sewing lessons had a more pedestrian goal. They did it to increase the number and variety of their clothes. But there was also an implicit hope that newer and fancier dresses might catch the eye of their Prince Charming: that they could live out the dream articulated in the Singer ads. (I couldn't wait to become part of that dream. In summer 1952, just shy of my thirteenth birthday, I eagerly enrolled in the Teen-Age Sewing Course at the nearby Singer Sewing Centre. Then I used my mother's sewing machine to make blouses, dresses and skirts throughout my high-school years.)

Even more important to the self-image of American girls is what these ads deliberately omitted. In true fairy-tale fashion, the mother is absent. Unlike the fairy tales, however, the ad heroine's motherless state is not a deprivation; it simply allows her to get advice from its most natural source: a non-authoritative commentator (usually another girl her own age) who speaks well of Singer. A mother in the ads would cause a problem: if she sewed, why wouldn't she herself teach the daughter to sew; if she didn't sew, why wasn't she taking lessons along with her daughter? In either case, her presence would complicate the neat arrangement between Singer and the girl.

Eliminating Mother from the ads solved another problem for Singer. The married woman was still a possible target for Singer's advertising pitches. A smart advertiser never alienates a possible customer; to have caricatured 'Mother' in the teen-directed ads as being an old-fashioned obstructionist or lacking a fashion sense (roles that a teenage girl might have given her mother), would be to risk losing the older woman as a customer.[3]

Singer's use of the Cinderella motif has been modified to meet its commercial needs. Unlike the original Cinderella story, the Singer ad heroine has no sisters and gets no help from a fairy godmother. Yet she does not escape the envy typical of Cinderella's sisters. In fact, she is envious herself. In virtually every version of the story used in this ad campaign, she sees and envies another girl's stylish clothes. Her envy is acute because she needs and lacks what the girl has. (Ulanov and Ulanov 1983) Rather than getting direct help from a fairy godmother or any authority figure, she gets the advice indirectly. In only one ad, (*'How a Fortune Teller turned Fairy Godmother'*, November 1948) is she told face-to-face that she should take sewing lessons; but even there the contact is not direct. 'A masked fortune teller in a fabulous costume,' tells her obliquely, 'Go to Singer's and you'll see the light!'

The fairy godmother's traditional magic wand is replaced by the Singer sewing machine, through which the girl transforms her fabric into a fabulous creation. As a result of this transformation (usually compressed into one sentence), the heroine then becomes the object of envy at the story's conclusion. The photograph of her in her fabulous (boy-getting) dress shifts the previous roles. As she was envious of an accomplished girl at the start, she now invites envy from the unaccomplished teenage girl who has just read her story. If that girl replicates the pattern of the story in the ad, she, too, will go to Singer and take sewing lessons.

To sell teenage girls on taking Singer Teen-Age Sewing Course, the advertising campaign presented them with a narrow and socially stultifying self-portrait. The female narrator has no reliable parental or adult advisors. She has no siblings. And, although she 'speaks' directly to the female reader/viewer, the absence of a community among teenage girls is implicit. She has few, very tenuous, links with other girls her age; at most, she has a single girlfriend. When she needs advice, there is no one to whom she can turn. She cares for no one but herself. Her sole goal in learning to sew is to serve her own need for 'glamour' dresses. Her only pleasure comes from a boy's admiration. (As a self-absorbed sewer, this teenage ad heroine stands in stark contrast to the tradition of women who sewed to make clothing and household goods for their families and their communities as well as themselves.)

The message throughout the campaign is clear: trust Singer to teach you to sew, trust yourself to make the glamourous clothes you need to catch a boy and trust him to make you happy. That a young woman's present and future happiness rested in male approval (implicitly, dating now, marriage later) was a comforting and uncomplicated message. Its very appeal was its contrast with the message that American women had heard ever since they had won the right to vote in 1920. That message had been that a young woman could be successful at anything she dreamed of; with ambition, work and courage she could be overcome physical obstacles, such as Helen Keller did, fly like Amelia Earhart, be a star athlete like Florence Chadwick and Babe Didrickson, hold her own in contests of wit like Dorothy Parker, flout conventional mores like Mae West and Sally Rand, dare to take physical risks like photographer Margaret Bourke-White.

As the Second World War wound down, these messages were overwhelmed by the single message, repeated loudly in every possible media outlet: once the war is over, women should return home; that is where they belong. After the Second World War, both the popular press and professional journals declared that women were happiest when marriage was their only life-option.[4]

In 1949, Simone de Beauvoir had written that 'the supreme necessity for a women is to charm a masculine heart; intrepid and adventurous though they may be, it is the recompense to which all heroines aspire; and most often no quality is asked of them other than their beauty'. (1960: 29)

The Singer campaign reinforced this message and helped American girls accept the only future open to them after the Second World War. It showed them that charming a masculine heart was their ultimate happiness and that making their own 'glamour' dresses as a result of taking Singer sewing lessons was the surest way to attract the Prince Charming on whom their whole future would depend.

Notes

1. In *How to Sew*, the only sewing book for beginners published in the United States during the Second World War, Nina R. Jordan extols the virtues of sewing with old cloth ('Used materials are much softer and therefore easier to stitch by hand') and includes instructions, with illustrations, on how to mend and patch clothing and to repair sheets.

2. The two best-known variants of the story, by Charles Perrault and the brothers Grimm, are among those contained in *Cinderella: A Folklore Casebook*. (Dundes 1982)

3. In 1951, Singer targeted older women. An annual contest offered regional prizes for the best outfit made at Singer Centres; regional winners got a trip to Washington, DC, where they modelled their outfits and competed for a cash prize which began at $5,000 but quickly increased to $25,000 by 1959. Teen-Age Sewing Course participants didn't qualify.

4. In *Just a Housewife*, Glenna Matthews recounts an April 1945 *Ladies' Home Journal* feature about the Ecks, a typical American family. Mrs Eck had abandoned a promising concert career because it conflicted with her marriage and was now educating her daughters 'for marriage, pure and simple'. (228) In the November 1946 issue of *The American Journal of Sociology*, Mira Komarovsky detailed female college undergraduates' self-reported conflicts between their personal career goals and their family's expectations, often leading to their acquiescence to marry.

References

'Bobby-Sock Form' (1944), in *Newsweek*, 30 October, 89–90.

de Beauvoir, S. (1960), *The Second Sex*. Translated by H.M. Parshley, London: Four Square.

Campbell, D. (1984), *Women at War with America; Private Lives in a Patriotic Era*, Cambridge, Mass., and London: Harvard University Press.

Dundes, A. ed. (1982), *Cinderella: A Folklore Casebook*, Madison: University of Wisconsin Press.

Emmons, B. (1948), 'Dance with the Devil', *Seventeen*, February, 78–9, 138.

Facts for Industry: see US Department of Commerce and the US Bureau of the Census (1946a; 1946b; 1947a; 1947b).

Historical Statistics, see: US Bureau of the Census (1975).

Jordan, N. R. (1941), *How to Sew*, New York: Harcourt, Brace.

Matthews, G. (1987) *'Just a Housewife': The Rise and Fall of Domesticity in America*, Oxford: Oxford University Press.

McCloud, S. (1993), *Understanding Comics: The Invisible Art*, Northampton: Kitchen Sink Press.

—— (1997), 'Teen Wanna-Bes: Mags Seek Girls.' *Crain's New York Business*, 27 October: p. 3.

Radner, H. (1995), *Shopping Around: Feminine Culture and the Pursuit of Pleasure*, London: Routledge.

Thomas, M. M. (1987), *Riveting and Rationing in Dixie: Alabama Women and The Second World War*, Tuscaloosa and London: The University of Alabama Press.

Ulanov, A and Ulanov, B. (1983), *Cinderella and Her Sisters: The Envied and the Envying*, Philadelphia: The Westminster Press.

Ware, C. M. (1945), *The Consumer in the Postwar Economy*, Washington, DC: American Association of University Women.

Weatherford, D. (1990), *American Women and World War II*, New York: Facts on File, Inc.

US Bureau of the Census (1975), Historical Statistics of the United States: Colonial Times to 1970, in two parts, Washington, DC: US Government Printing Office.

US Department of Commerce and the Bureau of the Census, (1946a), Facts for Industry, Series M39B–125, Report, November 1945–February 1946, Published 21 February, Washington, DC.

—— (1946b), Facts for Industry, Series M39B–125, Report, January–June 1946, Washington, DC. Published 16 October.

—— (1947a), Facts for Industry, Series M39B–125, Report December and Summary for 1946, Washington, DC. Published 7 February.

—— (1947b), Facts for Industry, Series M39B–125, Report January–March 1947, Washington DC. Published 19 May 1947. (This report is the last to include data on domestic sewing machine production and shipping.)

12

Virtual Home Dressmaking: Dressmakers and Seamstresses in Post-War Toronto

Alexandra Palmer

After the Second World War, the expanding Toronto social season was fuelled by the growing numbers of the upper middle-class. This social group required, and was able to afford high quality clothes, thus making it possible for Toronto to sustain an active local couture market. (Palmer 1994) Couture was available through department stores and speciality shops which imported European designs, as well as from local couturiers and designers. Integrated within this system of supply and demand, and at the bottom of the hierarchy, was the unacknowledged, yet traditional, role of lower profile dressmakers and seamstresses. This chapter examines these two levels of production that considerably broadened the choice of designs and prices available for building a society wardrobe, thereby permitting socialites to fulfil their roles as social leaders and professional volunteers within the community. By documenting and examining the home production and circumstances of dressmakers and seamstresses the subject of home dressmaking is set into a wider contextual arena where it is seen as an integral strategy for both patron and producer to sustain their family economies.

The significance of this trade is directly reflected in the 1961 census that records 4,953 dressmakers and seamstresses working outside factories in Ontario, marking an increase of nearly a thousand from 1951, and nearly two thousand more than in 1941. (*Canada Census* 1961: Table 8B-13) This statistic militates against the commonly held assumption that dressmaking skills were no longer needed at this time, due to a growing ready-to-wear market and increased mass production. However, these figures probably do not accurately document the real numbers of women who took in home sewing as a means of maintaining and furthering their family economy.

As the basis of this research is taken from oral histories with clients it presents a perspective from the satisfied consumer, as no one interviewed mentioned unsuccessful commissions. Clients were also the only source for material culture evidence and permitted garments still contained within their private wardrobes to be examined and analyzed during interviews. The importance of this is that the designs were linked to specific makers though few contained labels. Clients also provided information concerning the business and often were the only references for prices. There is only one perspective here documented from a seamstress, Mrs Jansons.

The most expensive custom-made clothing produced in Toronto during this time was from local couturiers who ran their own fashionable salons. They carried no stock as the businesses were based upon the Paris couture model. There were also designers who maintained a public profile with a shop front situated in or next to a fashionable shopping area. Some, such as Helmar, sold their own custom designs exclusively, while others combined their designs with retailing high-end ready-to-wear. Designers were less expensive than couturiers, and their direct competition came from dressmakers. Dressmakers did not set themselves up with a public façade but continued the nineteenth-century tradition of working with the client to create a garment. They usually ran their businesses out of their homes or a workroom and were patronized because of their creative design skills. Finally, there were local seamstresses who worked exclusively from their homes. They were employed to make 'unimportant' clothes that were considered functional and necessary to complete a good, working wardrobe. Some were also asked to copy existing designs from garments or pictures, or sew up garments from commercial patterns as well as undertake alterations.

Dressmakers

Toronto dressmakers were sought for their taste, originality and workmanship. Three, Mr Erle, Mrs Elisabeth Rasing and Carol Rash, demonstrate the similarities and differences of their clientele, production and business operations.

Mr Michael Erle was a private dressmaker who Mrs Rhind described as 'somebody of her (mother's) era [. . .] a nice crazy man' who had established a reputation in the old Toronto elite circle by the 1920s, when he made the trousseau and wardrobe for Mrs Rhind's mother, Mrs Green. She explained why her mother preferred to go to Mr Erle rather than to Toronto's chic retail shops:

My mother had an unusual figure with a very large bosom [. . .] she had very slim hips [. . .] she had a lot of her things made normally and he made a lot of them [. . .] he was probably in his 20s in 1920. He has died. (Rhind 1991)

Mr Erle worked out of his house in a district called Cabbagetown, which at that time was not considered a good part of the city by his clients. (*Toronto City Directory* 1950: 472; Rhind 1991) His background and training are unknown, though he may have attended the local Galasso School of Fashion Design. (Artibello 1993) However, he may have been self-trained as the 1937 *City Directory* (418) identifies him as a landscape gardener, and not until 1940 was he listed as a designer (*Toronto City Directory* 1940: 427). He was assisted by:

[. . .] a very nice English woman who was totally unfreakish in the sense that he was – and he was creative. She was very solid [. . .] very nice and she lived there, in the house [. . .] He and she did the fittings and she did the sewing and she probably had other people do some of it. (Rhind 1991)

It was implied that there was no sexual relationship between Mr Erle and his English assistant. Interestingly, Mr Erle is the only male dressmaker identified in this study of a normally female profession.

Another dressmaker whose clothing held a similar status within a society woman's wardrobe was Elizabeth Rasing, who developed a clientele of about one hundred Torontonians. (Bryce 1991; Boxer 1990; Bradshaw 1991) Contacts were made by word of mouth. Mrs Bradshaw was taken to Mrs Rasing by her mother who was introduced by a member of her reading club, Mrs Kenneth Kilburn. (Bradshaw 1991) Mrs Bradshaw introduced her neighbour, Mrs Bryce, who went to her from 1951 until May 1986, and then took her daughter. (Bryce 1991) Thus, Mrs Rasing's clientele spanned three generations of Toronto women over four decades.

She was a Dutch post-war immigrant, whose husband had died just after he was released from a prisoner-of-war camp in Indonesia, and then she came to Toronto with her daughter because she had a sister living in the city. She lived and worked out of her apartment where, in 1951, Mrs Bryce first went to her and remembers it being small with a curtain across part of a room to make a changing area. Later she opened a workroom on Yonge Street near Eglinton Avenue, above Maryann's, one of the best fabric stores in the city. (Bryce 1991)

Canadian-born designer Carol Rash, and her sister Val Poulos, ran a workroom, called 'Val-Carol' at 7 Adelaide Street West. (*Toronto City Directory* 1943: 59) The success of her designs were acknowledged by her client Mrs Hersenhoren who was nominated for *Liberty* magazine's 'Best Dressed List' in 1950. Mrs Hersenhoren went to Carol Rash from 1944, when she moved to Toronto, until the late 1950s. She first heard about her through the wife of a colleague of her fiancé, the first violinist with the Toronto Symphony Orchestra. Carol Rash made her 1947 wedding dress of silver-grey taffeta, and her trousseau including négligés, day suits and dresses, coats and evening dresses, averaging about six pieces a year, and eventually also her maternity clothes. (Hersenhoren 1991)

The process of acquiring a dress typically began with a discussion of the occasion, type of garment and the material. Mr Erle carried fabrics on the premises which he showed, though it is not known how he acquired them. He would drape and discuss various ideas and possibilities, developing an enjoyable relationship between himself and the client. (Rhind 1991) Mrs Rasing sometimes had fabric on hand that she had purchased at retail cost if she saw something that she thought would suit a particular person (Bryce 1991), but generally she went with her client to help with the selection, and the client would pay for it directly (Bradshaw 1991), then they would look at magazines together and she would sketch the ideas. (Bradshaw 1991; Bryce 1991; Boxer 1990) For instance, Mrs Bryce knew she wanted a dress of black velvet, but did not have any clear ideas beyond that. Mrs Rasing came up with a suitable design as 'She understood taste and my way of life.' (Bryce 1991) She never used existing patterns as she did her own cutting. (Boxer 1990; Bryce 1991; Bradshaw 1991) But, if the style was complex she would make up a muslin first, and there were always several fittings. (Bradshaw 1991)

In the case of Carol Rash, Mrs Hersenhoren purchased her fabric from Mr Ryan who was head of the fabric department at Simpson's department store. He knew her taste and would call her if he had a fabric he thought she would like; just as a saleswoman would call a client about new couture stock. It was also Mr Ryan who opened the fabric store Maryann's, and took with him a good clientele. Mrs Hersenhoren would take a picture of what she wanted and Carol Rash could copy it, or else she would sketch what she had in mind and then between them they would 'add or subtract,' making the design process a collaboration. (Hersenhoren 1991)

All three dressmakers were valued not only for their design skills, but also for their workmanship. Mrs Rasing was both a resourceful designer and needlewoman who was probably taught by her mother. (Bryce 1991) Her designs were very well finished, with details such as covered dome snaps, deep hems and always fully lined. She could design a garment around a distinctive fabric, such as an evening dress she made for Mrs Bradshaw from a 1940s Indian sari. (Bradshaw 1991) She would also embellish a textile with embroidery, beading, knitting or crochet. One ensemble was completed after the client was shown a sample of the floral decoration. It was a black wool twill skirt composed of gored panels trimmed with straw braid at the waistband and in diamond shapes around the lower half of the skirt. The diamonds were embroidered with wool flowers trimmed with coloured pastes, and each carried its own colour scheme. A black boat-neck, velveteen top trimmed with black straw braid at the neck and cuffs was made to complete the cocktail ensemble. It was such a success that two other similar ensembles were ordered. (Bryce 1991)

A notable aspect of Mr Erle's designs was his continuing dressmaking techniques that are more typically associated with the 1920s and 1930s. A 1947 garden party dress of Mrs Rhind's in cream silk jersey is appliquéd with cotton chintz flowers and has a scalloped hem and capelet collar that recalls 1930s styles. However, the full ankle length skirt and the padded trapunto detail on the hips very clearly reflect post-war fashions. Similarly, a 1948 black chiffon dress was part of her trousseau appears to be a post-war interpretation of a 1920s 'robe de style' popularized by Paris couturier Jeanne Lanvin, successfully fused with Christian Dior's 'New Look'. Thus his designs seem to reflect his age and the dressmaking he originally learned, though he successfully modified and updated these for post-war fashions. This probably unconsciously contributed to his success with two generations of clients, as he was obviously aware of the latest Paris look and design trends, yet interpreted them so that they were not extreme.

Custom embellishments were a characteristic of quality and couture techniques that were prized by consumers. This was an area of design in which Mrs Hersenhoren, though she did not sew up her garments, played an active role. She also continued the genteel tradition of needlework as a feminine accomplishment and wifely asset, and proudly said, 'A lot of my reputation was home-made.' For instance she beaded the hem of a pale peach evening dress, as well as the matching elbow length mitts. (Hersenhoren 1991)

Each of these dressmakers was highly valued by their clientele in several ways. Price was an important factor. Mrs Rhind was taken by her mother to Mr Erle for special clothes which were considered a 'treat', as his prices were not inexpensive. (Rhind 1991) Mrs Bryce commented that she never asked Mrs Rasing the price and would pay whatever was asked as her work was moderately priced for the quality. (Bryce 1991) Some of Mrs Rasing's clients went to her every season to plan out their wardrobes with her, taking into account special occasions. Mrs Bradshaw spent approximately a thousand dollars a season, and would buy a coat, a suit and a dress with matching coat or a dress with a jacket and an evening dress. Her clients valued the high standard of her workmanship and design skills, and her ability at 'spotting a trend and interpreting it'. (Bryce 1991) Thus it was the value of the design, being correct socially, and the economic value of dressmakers' production such which it ensured a long-term relationship with the client. Tied in with the initial economic value was the long-term value, or longevity of the clothes operating within a wardrobe. Mrs Bryce wore Mrs Rasing's designs on average for six years, though an early 1960s silk dress with an interesting bias cut was so successful she wore it for twenty years to cocktails and weddings. (Bryce 1991)

Furthermore, these dressmakers would also alter and update their garments when clients considered certain designs worth further investment. Mrs Rhind's 1948 wedding dress designed by Mr Erle (Figure 12.1) was purchased for five hundred dollars and remodelled by him into an evening dress which she wore to the Artillery Ball in the early 1950s. (Rhind 1991) Mrs Rasing also remodelled her designs, (Bryce 1991) while Mrs Hersenhoren recalled one dress Carol Rash had made in the mid 1950s which she wore for eight years.

Figure 12.1. 1948 wedding dress designed by Mr Erle for Mrs Rhind and later remade into an evening dress. Courtesy of Mrs Elizabeth Rhind.

It was originally white chiffon with long sleeves, and trimmed with pink roses. Later, it was dyed a pale violet and retrimmed with violets; then it was dyed black and worn with red poppies. (Hersenhoren 1991) These examples testify to the quality and success of the dressmakers' designs, and provide further evidence of the many meanings of value clothing held for consumers.

Thus, these three dressmakers, and there were certainly many, many more as listed in the census, were key in supplying clothing and creating a fashionable and appropriate presentation for Toronto's elite women. To a degree they operated as an underground alternative to both local and imported couture. However, a Toronto socialite's wardrobe was often further augmented by an even more inexpensive local seamstress.

Seamstresses

The traditional anonymous role of the seamstress who worked at home and sewed for families or individuals continued into the 1950s and 1960s. The majority of women interviewed remembered that they and their mothers had gone to one or more seamstresses, thus they inherited this tradition. Though information on individuals is skeletal and no examples of their work have been documented in this research, there are some patterns to be drawn.

The low status of seamstresses was reflected in their very inexpensive prices, and the fact that clients could recall little about them beyond their locations and names, and often these details were elusive. The importance of women working as seamstresses was a traditional means to supply or augment the family income, while still maintaining their role of homemaker. Further, working at home for women such as Mrs Boyd, who had worked as a seamstress at Eaton's department store, enabled her to continue to work and earn income after her marriage when store policy did not permit the employment of married women. Many of her Eaton clients continued to go to her privately. (Anonymous 1991)

Yet, a seamstress' nationality was more often remembered than her name, and the increased numbers of European-born seamstresses can be accounted for by Canada's embracing post-war immigration policy. Mrs Bryce's mother had an Irish seamstress, while Mrs Bradshaw's mother had a Finnish seamstress, Mrs Taskela, located on College Street, who also made clothes for Mrs Bradshaw. (Bryce 1991; Bradshaw 1991) It is significant that many had European roots as clients were well aware of the historical association of highly skilled dressmaking with European couture and sewing traditions, and in North America this tradition was available through skilled immigrant labour.

The type of clothes that seamstresses were asked to make depended upon their individual skills and the client's requirements. A high level of workmanship was not necessarily expected, but if they could alter and fit satisfactorily, they were called upon to assist in maintaining a wardrobe. However, cutting and sewing skills were prized, as in the case of Mrs Boyd who could copy designs beautifully, (Anonymous 1991) or a Finn, Mrs Swenson, who could copy a design from a picture. (Stohn 1991) Seamstresses became categorized by the type of their production. A German seamstress, Mrs Scherer, who lived on the third floor of a house during the war, was patronized by young girls and women wanting party dresses which she made for $2.50 each. (Weir 1991) Mrs Hass had a seamstress in the 1950s called Mrs Troop, who made party dresses and ball gowns for her and for her daughter, Mrs Susie Stohn, as well as Mrs Stohn's maternity dresses. However, they did not ask her to make suits which they felt should be made by a tailor. (Stohn 1991) This reiterates the historically gendered nature of the tailoring profession and the inherent belief held by some women that only a (male) tailor really knew how to make a suit.

Though the lives of home seamstresses are difficult to record, Mrs Velga Jansons' fifteen years of experience as a seamstress was probably fairly typical and can be read as a case study. In Latvia she had been taught to sew as a child, not by her mother but by a dressmaker, living across the road from her home. In 1947, while in a displaced persons camp in Germany, she upgraded her sewing skills by taking a two-month pattern-making course. She received a certificate from Zuschneidenschule owned by M. Muller and Son, founded in 1891. She also borrowed a machine from the school for the weekend to make a dress and would barter a thousand cigarettes for fabric on the black market and in return would get two kilogrammes of butter for her garment.

Clothing for those in the camp was supplied by second-hand donations from overseas. Those received from America were considered the best quality, and she used them as patterns to copy, as well as for the fabric. Two examples of her dressmaking include a suit she made in the camp from a American-sent man's brown houndstooth coat that she took apart and recut into a typical fitted suit jacket with shoulder pads and an A-line skirt. She also made a suit for herself that had twenty-six pieces in the back of the jacket and self-made buttons, and the blouse she made from a silk slip she dyed green to coordinate with the suit. (Figure 12.2) She had felt very smart in the ensemble and was obviously proud of her ability to be chic even then within the camp. Furthermore, these examples all proved her skill and ingenuity as a designer and pattern-maker as she was repeatedly called upon with limited resources available.

Figure 12.2. Velga Jansons in Germany in a suit she made in 1947 from a man's coat. The jacket has twenty-six pieces. The shirt is made from a silk slip which she dyed. Courtesy of Velga Jansons.

In 1948 she immigrated alone to Canada at the age of twenty-two, and lived in Winnipeg where she worked as a sewing machine operator for United Garments, a sportswear company, owned by Mr Bricker who signed her working papers on 8 December 1948 when she became a member of the Cloak, Dress and Knit Goods Union Local 216. After two months in Winnipeg she rented a sewing machine and altered and made clothes in the evening. By April she had saved enough money to buy her own sewing machine. She made a $45 down payment on a $135.00 Singer sewing machine, and ten monthly payments of $9.85. The purchase quickly paid for itself as she earned $16.67 a week at the factory and usually made an additional $5 a week by taking on extra sewing at night. She used this machine until 1983.

Mrs Jansons married a fellow Latvian, whom she met in Winnipeg, and they moved to Toronto in 1951, where she began to raise a family. She worked doing alterations in various mid-range womenswear stores, including Rose Winthrop, the May Company department store and Steins. All the while she continued to take in sewing work at home in the evenings. Her interest in fashion led her to keep up with the latest trends through magazines and by attendance at local fashion shows in the leading department stores. (Jansons 1993)

Her clients were wives of professional men, and many from the local Latvian community. Her modest prices served to ensure her of repeat and new business. During the 1950s she charged between $10 and $20 a dress, but if she made a dress from a pattern and there was no fitting, she charged as little as $5. Special occasions such as confirmations and weddings accounted for much of her work. She also attributed her success and large clientele to the fact that many middle-class Latvian-Canadians who had always gone to dressmakers in Latvia, did not know how to buy ready-to-wear as they felt that it was either of poor quality or too expensive. (Jansons 1993) This European tradition of custom ordering well-made clothes in the couture tradition, but without the couture price, was also commented on by other immigrant couturiers. (Fabbro 1988; Liska 1993; Hecht 1992; Berceller 1991) Thus, as previously suggested, Mrs Jansons' experience was fairly typical of a Toronto post-war seamstress and she shared many similarities with the dressmakers.

Conclusion

Although it has been virtually unrecognized, it has become clear that the patronage of dressmakers and seamstresses played an important role in equipping Toronto socialites with a complete working wardrobe. All the women interviewed sought well-made, and well-fitting, individual designs of high-quality fabrics that were intended to be worn over a period of several years. Dressmakers' and seamstresses' production served as this source for clothing which replaced or augmented couture purchases and permitted clients to acquire couture-like clothing without large capital outlay. Both made formal clothes for public occasions such as weddings, cocktails and volunteer meetings. They were also particularly valued for incidental and necessary clothes such as maternity wear, for alterations of garments already within a wardrobe and by women with 'problem' figures who would not readily fit standard sizes.

Interestingly, most of the clients who were interviewed continued their mothers' habits of frequenting a dressmaker and a seamstress, and Mrs Jansons' explanation of why she had so many clients from the Latvian community reiterates this point. Dressmakers and seamstresses appear to have inherited the tradition of home sewing from mothers or local producers. While Toronto's social leaders did not inherit home dressmaking skills they did learn how to skilfully negotiate and acquire designs which served to supplement their wardrobes. Consumers invested time in design decisions, purchasing fabrics and having fittings. Thus, for them, these garments were equivalent of home dressmaking.

Clients who patronized all these levels of couture-like sources uniformly considered themselves to be getting good value for money. Mrs Hersenhoren went to Carol Rash because she could have original designs custom-made for her at a very good price. This was important for her, as her husband was not yet well-off but held a prominent position in the arts and as such they were part of Toronto's elite society. As with her social contemporaries, her time was spent entertaining and volunteering.

Contacts between client and dressmaker or seamstress were commonly made by word of mouth, not via printed advertising. Dressmakers' and seamstresses' names were never mentioned by the local press in the society columns, even if a dress was singled out, as was the case with Mrs Rhind's 1957 blue cocktail dress designed by Mr Erle. (Rhind 1991) This is in contrast to the repeated naming of international couture designers when socialites appeared at events in their designs. For instance, Mrs B.B. Osler who was on the *Telegram* newspaper's 1957 best-dressed list ascribed her success to an unnamed 'New Canadian dressmaker'. (2 April 1957: 26, 31) By publicly acknowledging her source, yet retaining its secrecy, she created an exclusivity around her wardrobe which could not be easily imitated. Simultaneously, she presented herself as a woman who could achieve fame and recognition in dress – in fact couture status – without the capital outlay, and negated the image of well-dressed women as spend-thrifts and icons of conspicuous consumption. She could also have used this opportunity to name her anonymous dressmaker and perhaps assist her in attracting new business. But clients tended to guard the names of their dressmakers and seamstresses, perhaps in order to ensure their availability and to forestall possible inflation of their prices.

However, the anonymity of home dressmakers and seamstresses was also furthered by the producers themselves. Taking in home-sewing work often involved no startup expenses other than the initial cost of a sewing machine and so provided an easy and affordable means of furthering or creating income. This was despite the fact that none of the producers researched had any business training. They managed with self-taught skills of home economy and home sewing skills usually learned from mothers. Dressmakers, such as Mrs Rasing and Carol Rash, who took on the overhead of a workroom, had to sustain sufficient production to cover this cost. Most did not import or carry textiles but relied upon the client to supply them, thereby avoiding risking any capital outlay. Seamstresses in particular could set themselves up so that their labour was often not declared, though both dressmakers and seamstresses served to partially or totally support themselves and very often their families, as in the cases of Velga Jansons or Mrs Rasing.

The quiet and private trade of the professional home dressmaking trade leaves few records as its consumption and production system conspires to elude researchers and perpetuates its own anonymity. This research only hints at the historical post-war position of the role of the home dressmaker and seamstress in relation to their production for a select clientele, and serves to illuminate their importance in influencing taste and supplying an alternative source for the skilled consumption of couture-like wardrobes by Toronto's elite women.

References

Anonymous Interview (1991), with the author, Toronto, Canada, 21 May.

Artibello, J. (1993), Interview with the author, Toronto, Canada, 15 February.

Berceller, C. (1991), Interview with the author, Toronto, Canada, 14 March.

Boxer, N. J. (1990), Interview with the author, Toronto, Canada, 6 December.

Bradshaw, M. (1991), Interview with the author, Toronto, Canada, 25 July.

Bryce, E. (1991), Interview with the author, Toronto, Canada, 5 November 1961.

Canada Census (1961).

Crase, M. S. (1991), Interview with the author, Toronto, Canada, 5 June.

Fabbro, A. (1988), Interview with the author, Toronto, Canada, 13 October.

Hecht, F. (1992), Interview with the author, Huntsville, Canada, 13 June.

Hersenhoren, J. (1991), Interview with the author, Toronto, Canada, 4 March.

Jansons, V. (1993), Interview with the author, Toronto, Canada, 23 March.

Liska, R. (1993), Interview with the author, Toronto, Canada, 13 December.

Palmer, A. (1994), *The Myth and Reality of Haute Couture, Consumption, Social Function and Taste in Toronto, 1945–1963*, Ph.D dissertation, University of Brighton.

Rhind, Elizabeth (1991), Interview with the author, Toronto, Canada, 12 February.

Stohn, S. (1991), Interview with the author, Toronto, Canada, 18 February.

Toronto City Directory, (1937–1965).

Weir, F. M. (1991), Interview with the author, Toronto, Canada, 6 June.

Part 3

Home Dressmaking, Dissemination and Technology

13

The Lady's Economical Assistant' of 1808

Janet Arnold

Home dressmaking seems to have been confined to very simple garments, in particular those in the category of plain sewing, such as shirts, smocks, caps and baby clothes, until well into the nineteenth century. The reason for this is the lack of readily available patterns as a guide for cutting out. With the development of the commercial paper pattern, and the advent of the sewing machine, home dressmaking skills were developed, and made for considerable economies in families with a large number of daughters in the second half of the nineteenth century.

Home dressmaking in the eighteenth century included making garments for the poor, as well as the shirts and smocks. A forerunner of *The Lady's Economical Assistant*[1] was printed in 1789. *Instructions for Cutting out Apparel for the Poor; principally intended for the assistance of the Patronesses of Sunday Schools and other Charitable Institutions*[2] was also 'Useful in all Families,' as the author pointed out. This book was published for the benefit of Sunday school children at Hertingfordbury in the County of Hertford, and its main purpose was to calculate the quantities and how cheaply the garments could be made by buying each commodity wholesale. This reduced the price for sale to poor people.

Thirteen plates with full-size printed patterns were mentioned in the text. In Figure V there is the body of a gown, with shoulder straps, 'for a girl of the smallest size'. The author had some difficulty in calculating the cost as 'there are such a variety of widths and prices, 'that it is not easy to ascertain the value, or quantity, for the different size of gowns; or to give any directions about the larger sizes, as they are generally made, (even amongst poor people) by some whose particular employment it is'.

Francois Garsault's description of the professional dressmaker's work in 1769[3] has illustrations which shows the relatively simple pattern shapes. He explains the method of measuring and assembling straight lengths of a sack gown without cutting out from a pattern. By the end of the eighteenth century the professional dressmaker, or mantua maker, as she was known, made gowns with fitted bodices, and more complicated cut, as well as other garments. *The Book of Trades*, printed in 1804, illustrates a mantua maker taking the pattern off from a lady by means of a piece of paper, or of cloth. The text explained that 'the business of a mantua maker [. . .] now includes almost every article of dress made use of by ladies, except, perhaps those which belong to the head and the feet.' (Arnold 1972: 9) Most women, even those who were not very well off, would have their gowns made by a woman with some experience in handling cloth, even if they carried out alterations at home. *The Workwoman's Guide* of 1838, written by a Lady who was clearly interested in a charity school and for which her collection of patterns was begun, commented:

> No one who has not been a frequent visitor in the homes of the poor, is aware of the extravagance and waste usual among women of a humble dress, arising from their total ignorance in matters of cutting out and needlework, nor how much instruction they want on these points even to the making of a petticoat and a pinafore. The same ignorance and unskilfulness, and the same consequent waste of laborious and scanty earnings is common among our female household servants; who by putting out their clothes to dressmakers pay nearly half as much for the making up as for the materials.[4]

The author does not mention the fact that women of a humble class, and servants, would probably not be able to afford scissors or shears to cut out, let alone have the table space to spread the material, nor that the dressmakers would be out of work. Even some poor dressmakers could not afford all the equipment they needed. When pinked trimmings were fashionable in the nineteenth century, dressmakers would go to a funeral parlour for the undertaker to punch out strips of material with scalloped edges for dresses, when he had finished the coffin linings.[5]

There are many contemporary diaries and letters upon which to draw for information, but perhaps the most relevant in this case are the novels and correspondence of Jane Austen. It is clear from the letters that Jane and her sister Cassandra bought lengths of muslin, cambric, gauze and silk, from linen-drapers such as Grafton House in London, The materials were made up by the mantua-maker to their instructions. In 1798 Jane wrote: 'I cannot determine what to do about my new gown; I wish such things were to be bought ready made.' (Chapman 1932: 24 December 1798) It seems, however, that alterations were within their capabilities. Jane wrote to Cassandra in

1809: 'I can easily suppose that your six weeks here will be fully occupied, were it only in lengthening the waist of your gowns.' (Chapman 1932: January 1809) There was a slight fluctuation in the level of the waist at this time. Jane, herself, in 1814 mentioned that she had 'lowered the bosom, especially at the corners, and plaited [pleated] black satin ribbon round the top' (Chapman 1932: 9 March 1814) of one gown. She could also make caps, from the evidence of her earlier letters. (Chapman 1932: 1 December 1798) Other simple garments, such as her own smocks, or shifts, shirts and cravats for male relatives, baby clothes and simple garments for the poor were certainly made at home by Jane and other members of the Austen family. The custom of making clothes for the poor was quite general. In *Mansfield Park* Mrs Norris told Fanny: 'If you have no work of your own, I can supply you from the poor basket.' (Austen, 1923a: Volume 1, Chapter 7) Mrs Norris also managed to make a blue and pink satin cloak for Mr Rushworth in his role of Count Cassel in *Lover's Vows*. It seems to have been fairly simple, however, as she said to Fanny: 'you may give me your help in putting it together. There are but three seams, you may do them in a trice.' (Volume 1, Chapter 18) Presumably the cloak was made of four lengths of material joined together and gathered up to the neck. Perhaps it was one like this that Jane wrote about to Cassandra in 1801: 'When you have made Martha's bonnet you must make her a cloak of the same sort of materials.' (Chapman 1932: 21 January 1801)

Although paper patterns were not in common use at this date, old and new garments were copied, or taken apart to use as patterns. In 1801 Jane wrote to Cassandra that: 'Mary [. . .] will be much obliged to you if you can bring her the pattern of the Jacket and Trowsers, or whatever it is, that Eliz'th's boys wear when they are first put into breeches: or if you can bring her an old suit itself she would be very glad.' (Chapman 1932: 21 January 1801) In *Sense and Sensibility* the Misses Steele took patterns from some of Lady Middleton's elegant new dresses. (Austen, 1923b: Volume 1, Chapter 21) One new or particularly fashionable garment made by a professional mantua maker might serve as the pattern for several others. In 1813 Jane Austen's niece Fanny was disappointed when she bought a new cap. Jane wrote that: 'She finds she has been buying a new cap without having a new pattern, which is true enough.' (Chapman 1932: 23 September 1813) Since it took some time and trouble to obtain patterns they were highly valued and carefully guarded. Jane wrote to Cassandra in June 1799: 'I am quite pleased with Martha and Mrs Lefroy for wanting the pattern of our caps, but I am not so well pleased with your giving it to them.' (Chapman 1932: 2 June 1799)

It was for people such as Jane and Cassandra Austen that *The Lady's Economical Assistant, or The Art of Cutting out and making the most useful articles of Wearing Apparel, without waste: Explained by the clearest directions and numerous engravings of appropriate and tasteful patterns* was written by A Lady. Both the copy in the British Library[6] and that at the Yale Center for British Art[7] were published in 1808, but they differ in the typesetting. The twenty-seven folded paper patterns are the same size in both copies. The Yale copy has the instructions set on smaller pages, so is bound in two parts. The British Library copy has the instructions printed on a larger size of page, to match the shape of the folded patterns.

In her introduction, the author explains how to calculate quantities of material, how to enlarge or reduce the patterns and gives directions for cutting out each type of garment. For men there are only shirts and night caps and, although there is a far greater range of garments for women, including shifts and night shifts, caps and night caps, night jackets, night gowns and bed gowns, the greatest number of patterns is for children of about two and about five and for babies. On page forty-two she notes that

The following pages contain directions for cutting out the clothes generally considered necessary for poor lying-in women.

For the Infant
Four little shirts
Four little caps
Two frocks
Two little bed gowns
Two flannel blankets
Two rollers
Two pairs of stays and flannel coats
Two upper petticoats
Twenty four napkins

For the Woman
One large bed gown
Two calico night gowns
Two skirts
One pair of sheets

The British Library catalogue offered no clue to the identity of the anonymous author. However, a few letters were preserved in the archive of the publisher, John Murray,[8] from Anne Streatfield. The first she wrote is dated 22 February 1808, and written at her home 'The Rocks', but no further details of the address are given. Later research showed that it was on the outskirts of Uckfield in Sussex.[9] The letter begins by acknowledging receipt 'By this day's Coach' of proofs 'of four plates etc', and was pleased to find few errors, and the plates accurately engraved. However, she was worried that she did not have all the plates to check the numbers in the text, and decided to keep the proofs until all the plates mentioned in them had arrived. She continues

> I am also at a loss to know how we are to continue about the references which in some instances are forward; for instance in page 10 of the *printed* sheets there is a reference to page 65 in my *MS*. This article will undoubtedly be in a different page in the printed sheets and I am fearful we shall have some difficulty in the matter as I conclude the proofs cannot be set for so many pages together; I am unwilling to make the change if it could be avoided but if not, we must I suppose refer to the article instead of the page as for instance See infant stays for the poor – instead of – See Page 65.

Advances in printing technology over the last thirty years may make it difficult for the younger generation, used to word processors, to understand the complications of printing a book with illustrations and diagrams in the days when each word was set with metal type and clamped into a wooden frame, or forme, which took up quite a lot of space. It was essential to return proofs quickly so that the book could be printed, the type broken up, and the next lot of setting put in hand. Anne Streatfield was quite obviously aware that the corrected proofs should be returned quickly. Anne continues her letter:

> I have made some additions to the introduction and trust you will approve them: you may rely on my being equally anxious to improve the work to the utmost of my ability as if it were published on my own account. I do not send it to you just yet as I am desirous of meeting your wishes on the subject; and I think it possible in the course of correcting proofs some new ideas may strike me.

This is a condition well known to both publishers and authors, and must have struck terror into the heart of John Murray. In fact, he did take on all the additions and alterations, which are printed, and kept the first draft of the introduction in his files, where it has remained until today. All the rest of the manuscript would probably have been discarded at the printers, unless Anne had requested its return. In the days before the typewriter and carbon copies, there would have been a first draft manuscript which she kept, and then a carefully written copy for the printer. Anne signed her letter 'with Mr Streatfield's compliments, I am, Dear Sir, your obliged Anne Streatfield'. I have not yet been able to discover if Mr Streatfield was Anne's father, brother or husband. His initials, recorded in Paterson's *Roads* of 1803 were R.T. She ended – 'N.B. I have just remarked that in the form you have sent me the price of the Book is five Shillings and in the last General Evening post it is advertised at 7s 6d.' In the second volume of the Yale copy, containing the twenty-seven folded plates, is printed 'Price 12s.' It would seem that the additions and alterations to proofs had forced John Murray to raise the price, or perhaps he had become convinced that there were enough ladies needing this kind of information, prepared to pay a high price. No price is printed in the reset copy in the British Library. It would seem that the first printing sold out quickly, as the date of the reprint is also 1808.

The second letter from The Rocks, on 8 March 1808, notes some correct-ions and commends the engravings in the body of the work. These are

> sufficiently exact except that which refers to Men's shirts page 79, in which I confess myself rather disappointed; it ought to represent a square and is incorrect, as well as out of proportion, as the division for the wristbands which is 6 inches wide appears narrower than the divisions for the shoulder straps, which are only three inches wide. I enclose my original drawing that you may compare it with the engraving.

A new plate was engraved.[10] (Figure 13.1) Anne continued: 'I also send the Introduction for your approbation.' This, I think, must be what is now printed, and has not survived in manuscript. She also wrote: 'I have likewise made out a table of contents and an index, but as this is a part of book-making I do not much understand, I submit it to any corrections or alterations you may think proper.'

The next letter is dated Wednesday night, 12 March 1808. Anne acknow-ledges receipt of further plates and is still waiting for the last five:

> It is very unlucky the plates could not be finished in time to be corrected with the letter press as I find two references wrong. The first is in page 46 and in the 16th line [. . .] The other error is in page 100 – where it refers to plate XXII figure 3. That plate (which I now send you) contains only patterns for a woman's night Jacket; and for want of the rest of the plates I cannot ascertain what plate page 100 really refers to. These are both very material to the clearness of the work, and I cannot imagine how the latter mistake can have arisen, except that after making the reference I was forced to put that little pattern of the hollowing of a shift bosom for children from one to two years old, into some other plate for want of room in plate 22. I fear you are hardly *workwoman* enough to discover the pattern so as to set this matter right without me. My only hope is that it is possible the letterpress may not yet be printed off and perhaps, in that case, you can delay it till I have rectified the error by seeing the rest of the Plates – if the printing is already compleated what must we do? Put in a horrid errata I am fearful!

This seems to be Fig. 3 on plate XXVII in the printed book. (Figure 13.2)

namely, two collars, two pair of sleeve gussets, two pair of shoulder-straps, two pair of sleeve binders, two pair of wristbands, two pair of side gussets, and two pair of neck gussets. Cut them by the following example— supposed yard square:

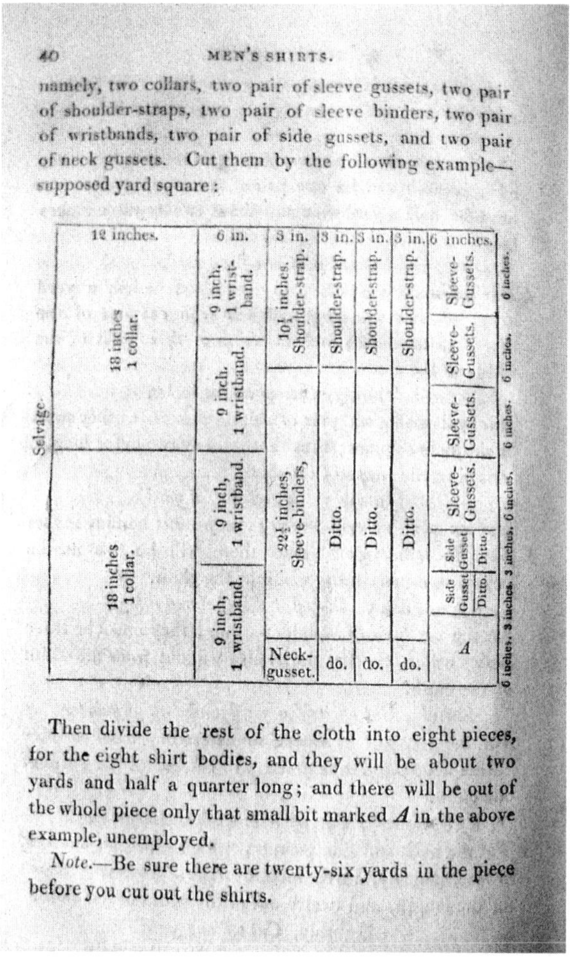

12 inches.	6 in.	3 in.	3 in.	3 in.	3 in.	6 inches.
18 inches 1 collar.	9 inch, 1 wristband.	10½ inches. Shoulder-strap.	Shoulder-strap.	Shoulder-strap.	Shoulder-strap.	Sleeve-Gussets.
	9 inch. 1 wristband.					Sleeve-Gussets.
18 inches 1 collar.	9 inch, 1 wristband.	22½ inches, Sleeve-binders,	Ditto.	Ditto.	Ditto.	Sleeve-Gussets.
	9 inch, 1 wristband.	Neck-gusset.	do.	do.	do.	Side Gusset / Ditto. — Ditto. / *A*

(left margin: Selvage. Right margin columns: 6 inches. 6 inches. 6 inches. 6 inches. 3 inches. 3 inches. 6 inches.)

Then divide the rest of the cloth into eight pieces, for the eight shirt bodies, and they will be about two yards and half a quarter long; and there will be out of the whole piece only that small bit marked *A* in the above example, unemployed.

Note.—Be sure there are twenty-six yards in the piece before you cut out the shirts.

Figure 13.1. Pattern pieces for a man's shirt, as described in Anne Streatfield's letter, 8 March 1808. Photograph by Janet Arnold from the book in the Yale Center for British Art.

On March 18 Anne wrote again, about confusions in the title page and an advertisement:

I [. . .] cannot help thinking that the printer has made a mistake in blending the two subjects of cutting out Linen and Cookery – as it appears on opening the book in the first page 'The Lady's economical assistant,' in the second 'Domestic Cookery,' and in the third returns to the economical assistant. It is true on examination the 2nd page proves to be only the advertisement of another work, but surely that advertisement should be put at the end of my book.

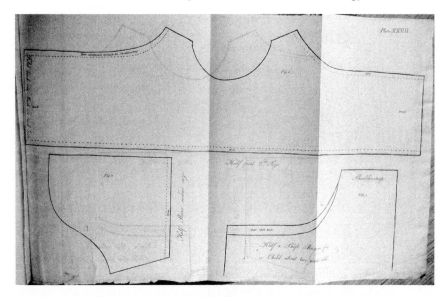

Figure 13.2. Plate XXVII showing Fig. 3: '[T]hat little pattern of the hollowing of a shift bosom for children from one to two years old.' Photograph by Janet Arnold from the book in the Yale Centre for British Art.

A compromise was reached, and the advertisement was placed after the contents page, before the Introduction, certainly in the copy in the British Library.

In the next letter, dated 20 March, Anne has managed to 'correct the mistakes in the corrected sheets that you have just sent me', as well as those in page forty-six and page 100. The plate on page seventy-nine had been altered and 'appears quite as it should do'. Anne concludes with the news that 'On Wednesday morning we leave home for a short time: you will therefore be so good as to direct your next parcel to me at the Honble. G. Nevill's, Flower Place, near Godstone, Surrey.'

The last letter to John Murray in the file is dated 28 March, written from Flower Place. Anne thinks it 'best to trouble you with a few lines to inform you I shall return home tomorrow morning: therefore I must beg you will have the goodness to direct to me at the Rocks as usual. I was in hopes of receiving a parcel from you while at this place but conclude the engraver has disappointed you.' In the end, all the proofs were corrected and the book was printed for John Murray, Fleet Street; J. Harding, St James's Street; and A. Constable and Co., Edinburgh; at the Union Printing Office, St John's Square by W. Wilson. Presumably the book had quite a wide circulation, and there may be other copies in the libraries of country houses all over

England, if the original readers took the author's advice: 'To avoid damaging the patterns in the plates, the best way is to trace them on thin paper, then to cut out the pattern, thus traced, accurately; and by marking each paper with the number of the plate, there cannot be any mistake.' (Note 1, *The Lady's Economical Assistant* 1808: xi) However, many readers may have ignored this advice, and once the patterns were detached and used repeatedly, they would have been easily mislaid, and the instructions eventually thrown away. Anne had obviously used all these patterns many times; for Plate V of infants' caps she writes: 'I shall give patterns of four sizes of caps; the smallest I seldom use as it is so very soon outgrown: however, I insert it here, because for children who are born small, it will be found sufficiently large: as indeed it is for a christening cap, when made solely for that purpose.'

In the Introduction Anne points out that 'she has taken some pains to calculate the different widths and lengths of various materials – so as to cut out wearing apparel to the greatest advantage, not only for my own family, but also for the poor.' She continues 'In consequence of the solicitations of some friends who have used and approved of my patterns and calculations, I have determined to publish this little work for the benefit of those who will take the trouble of attending to this very material part of female economy.' (Note 1, *Lady's Economical Assistant* 1808: vii)

Dedication

Janet Arnold died in 1998 during the preparation of this book. She had hoped to expand this chapter slightly but it proved impossible. It is printed here with amendments she approved. I am grateful to Santina Levey, Miss Arnold's literary executor, for her co-operation and assistance in seeing this work to press. *B.B.*

Notes

1. A LADY. *THE LADY'S ECONOMICAL ASSISTANT or THE ART OF CUTTING OUT, AND MAKING The most useful Articles of Wearing Apparel, WITHOUT WASTE; EXPLAINED BY THE CLEAREST DIRECTIONS AND NUMEROUS ENGRAVINGS OF APPROPRIATE AND TASTEFUL PATTERNS BY A LADY. DESIGNED FOR DOMESTIC USE. LONDON. PRINTED FOR JOHN MURRAY, FLEET STREET; J. HARDING, ST. JAMES'S STREET; and A. CONSTABLE AND CO. EDINBURGH,* At the Union Printing Office, St John's Square, by W. Wilson. 1808

2. Facsimile edition produced by the Costume and Textile Association for Norfolk Museums. Another copy is in the collection of Parks, Canada and is stored in the regional warehouse in Cornwall, Ontario. Both copies are dated 1789 and were sold in London. The printed words 'Sold by J. Walter, Charing Cross' are crossed out and 'Sold at the Parliament Office Old Palace Yard Westminster' written in by hand in both copies.

3. François Alexandre Garsault, *L'Art de la Couturière et la Marchande des Modes*, Paris (1769), in Arnold (1972): 5–6. A limited number of copies of the stitches shown in François Alexandre Garsault, *Art du Tailleur*, Paris (1769), and *L'Art de la lingere*, Paris (1771), with samples, are available in a loose leaf volume entitled *The Williamsbury Fashioner: being a compendious view of the Art and Mystery of those Tradesmen who furnish us with Apparel calculated for the instruction of the Garment-worker containing many useful particulars relative to the foregoing* by the Practitioners of Apparel at the Costume Design Centre, the Colonial Williamsburg Foundation, Virginia (1996).

4. A Lady, *The Workwoman's Guide containing Instructions to the inexperienced in cutting and completing those articles of Wearing apparel etc, which are normally made at home* . . . 1838, second edition 1840, facsimile reprint, 1975.

5. Hesba Stretton (1873), *Lost Gip*. 'On the ground floor there was a large shop window, with a very dingy hatchment in the centre, and above it a bunch of funeral plumes, brown with age. On one side of the hatchment hung a card, framed in black, with "Funerals performed!" on it, whilst in the opposite pane was another card, displaying the words, "Pinking done here."' I am indebted to Mrs Helen Wood for this extract.

6. British Library, 7742 cc 23. Microfiche published by Chadwyck-Healey, 1994. Another copy is preserved at the Gallery of English Costume, Manchester.

7. Yale Center for British Art, L425-485 (40).

8. I am indebted to Virginia Murray for finding the letters in the archive, and for photocopying them for me.

9. I am very grateful to Rosemary Hawthorne of the Vicarage, Tetbury, Gloucestershire, for her letter of 16 April 1998 with an extract from Daniel Paterson, *A NEW AND ACCURATE DESCRIPTION OF ALL THE DIRECT AND PRINCIPAL CROSS ROADS IN ENGLAND AND WALES AND PART OF THE ROADS OF SCOTLAND. With correct Routes of the MAIL COACHES; And a great Variety of NEW ADMEASUREMENTS. Also, A Table of the Heights of Mountains and other Eminences, from the Grand Trigonometrical Survey of the Kingdom, under the direction of MAJOR MUDGE: An Account of NOBLEMEN'S and GENTLEMEN'S SEATS: And other remarkable Objects near the Roads: A GENERAL INDEX of the ROADS to the different TOWNS, denoting the COUNTIES in which they are situated, their MARKET DAYS, and the INNS which supply POST-HORSES: An INDEX to the COUNTRY SEATS: A List of the RATES of the POSTAGE OF LETTERS, &c, &c, &c. The Whole greatly augmented and improved by the Assistance of Francis Freeling, Esq., Secretary to the Post-Office, and of the several Surveyors of the Provincial Districts, under the Authority of The Post-Master General,*

by LIEUTENANT-COLONEL PATERSON, *Assistant Quarter-Master-General of His Majesty's Forces. THE THIRTEENTH EDITION: London: Printed for the PROPRIETOR, and sold by Messrs. LONGMAN and REES, Paternoster-Row, and Mr FADEN Charing Cross, 1803.* This is a guide for stage coach travel, which she found in a junk shop in Tetbury in February 1998. One of the landmarks on the London to Brighton road was The Rocks, given on p. 54: 'At Uckfield, on ɪ the Rocks, R.T. Streatfield,' in Chapter IV, 'Great and Direct Roads measured from the Surrey side of Westminster Bridge with the roads branching from them to Market and Sea-Port Towns.' The Ordnance Survey map of 1.c.1974 still shows The Rocks.

10. The diagram appeared on page 24 with instructions on pages 23–24.

References

Arnold, J. (1972), *Patterns of Fashion c. 1660–1860*, London: Macmillan.

Austen, J. (1923a), *Mansfield Park*, Oxford: Oxford University Press.

—— (1923b) *Sense and Sensibility*, Oxford: Oxford University Press.

Buck, A. (1970), 'The Costume of Jane Austen and her Characters,' *The So-called Age of Elegance*, Proceedings of the Fourth Annual Conference of the Costume Society: 36–45.

Byrde, P. (1979), *A Frivolous Distinction*, Bath: Bath City Council.

Chapman, R.W., ed., (1932), *Jane Austen's Letters to her sister Cassandra and others*, Oxford: Oxford University Press.

14

Dreams on Paper: A Story of the Commercial Pattern Industry[1]

Joy Spanabel Emery

The birth of the dressmaker pattern industry was an event waiting to happen. Many factors contributed to the gestation of the tissue paper pattern. Until the advent and acceptance of ready-made clothing, all clothing production was one of a kind made by individuals for individuals by professional tailors, dressmakers and skilled amateurs.

Methods of cutting fabric to make up garments were devised and published from the sixteenth century. These were pattern drafting systems based upon tailors' personal observations of human proportions. The published patterns were unscaled and unsized. For the made-to-measure garment, tailors used individual narrow strips marked with key body points. From this evolved the inch tape measure. This simple device would ultimately revolutionize made-to-measure garments from patterns.

For the home dressmaker, 'How-To' books were published as early as the late-eighteenth century. Essentially these described three methods for cutting out a garment to achieve proper fit: drafting garments using set instructions, picking apart a favourite garment to use as a flat pattern piece, or fitting thin paper over the body to pin in fitting darts and scribe arm and neck holes. This latter method is arguably the inspiration for the tissue patterns of the dressmaking industry.

By the 1840s, the basic elements for mass production of garment patterns were in place. Diagrams of pattern shapes had been refined and were printed in various professional journals and women's magazines. Applications of various proportional systems for arriving at a correct body shape were established with many patents for new systems throughout the nineteenth century. (Kidwell 1979) Explanations on how to cut and make garments became more common.

This essay offers a brief summary of the commercial pattern industry in the United States. It is a complex story of entrepreneurship, mass-marketing and the promotion of fashionable wear for everyone. Capitalizing on self-reliance, patterns provided inexpensive access to the latest fashions thus accelerating the democratization of fashion. From the variety of approaches, I have chosen to concentrate on the formation of major companies and the primary periodicals that promoted their products. Unlike contemporaries in continental Europe and Great Britain (Adburgham 1964), United States pattern manufacturers produced mass-market patterns for the retail and mail-order market-place from the outset, thereby establishing the commercial pattern industry.

Antecedents: Prior to 1860

The earliest tailor's patterns appeared in Juan de Alcega's works dating from 1580. Diderot's *L'Encyclopédie Diderot et D'Alembert: Arts de l'habillement* played a crucial role during the Enlightenment to disseminate practical knowledge. Published in 1776, the pattern drafts were the first which were generally available to the public. Manuals with full-size patterns and pattern drafts written for charitable ladies sewing for the poor included *Instructions for Cutting out Apparel for the Poor*,[2] *The Lady's Economical Assistant*,[3] and *The Workwoman's Guide*.[4] The first two works contain full-size patterns for caps, baby linen, women's and children's undergarments and men's shirts. *The Workwoman's Guide* consists of pattern drafts, drawings of finished pieces and instructions for drafting garment pieces. A number of other publications, such as *The Tailors' Instructor* by Queen and Lapsley[5], as well as journals specifically for the professional tailor, were published primarily for tailored garments during the first half of the century.

Pattern drafts or small diagrams of pattern pieces were a popular method of promoting the latest styles. Early experiments with scaled pattern drafts in periodicals appear to have begun in France. *Journal des Demoiselles* began publishing drafts in 1833. In that year, Mme Gaubert, a dressmaker in Philadelphia, issued trade cards advertising the acquisition of 'patterns of the latest French fashions' but their source is not identified.[6] Perhaps she was using the diagrams from *Journal des Demoiselles*. At any rate, evidence suggests that Mme Gaubert used these patterns in her dressmaking establishment and they were not for sale to the public. What is clear is the rapid exchange of fashion news and the popularity of such pattern diagrams.

The next step was the use of full-scale, fold-out patterns in periodicals, again apparently introduced in *Journal des Demoiselles* as early as 1841. *Petite Courrier des Dames* introduced fold-out patterns in 1842. Full-scale patterns appeared in England as early as August 1850 when *The World of Fashions* announced the 'First collection of patterns for fashionable Dresses and Millinery in order that Ladies of Distinction and their Milliners and Dressmakers, may possess the utmost facilities for constructing their costumes'.

Early US History

In the United States, *Frank Leslie's Gazette of Fashions* offered full-scale, fold-out patterns in 1854. In this instance, unlike those in other publications, the pattern designer is identified. Her name was Mme Demorest.

Demorest patterns were the first commercial patterns in the United States. Mme Demorest promoted 'the Mme Demorest's System of Dress-Cutting' as being easily understood and 'as certain as the art of Daguerreotype'. (Demorest 1862: 8) The system was used to cut patterns which were exhibited as paper dresses, fully trimmed and available to professional dressmakers and private families all over the country.

The Demorest approach offered single patterns, either plain or trimmed, of bodices, sleeves, children's clothing, ladies' wrappers, undergarments, cloaks, mantillas and others. Full sets of patterns were offered to the professional dressmaker at reduced rates. Patterns were available at selected retail shops, dressmaker's establishments or by mail-order. (Emery 1997).

Clothing the family was a primary function of every homemaker in the nineteenth century. For those who could afford to do so, families were advised in the September 1851 *Godey's Lady's Book* to hire a dressmaker: 'A dressmaker's charge is seventy-five cents a day, and, including mantillas and capes, no family can well dispense with less than a week's service every season.' However, women were strongly encouraged to develop their own dressmaking skills. *Godey's* continues to admonish young ladies not to consider dressmaking 'vulgar': 'You may consent to share the fortune of some noble minded adventurer in the new country – California or Minesota [sic] [. . .] As an American woman, in this era, you may be placed in many positions quite as remote. And then what becomes of the helpless?' [1851: 192] As United States frontiers expanded so did the need to supply information and methods for making fashionable garments. Mail-order patterns were an ideal solution to that problem.

At first, Demorest patterns were advertised in existing periodicals such as *Frank Leslie's Gazette of Fashions* and *Godey's Lady's Book*. In 1860, Demorest introduced its own publication, *The Mirror of Fashion*. It was first offered as a quarterly and later was incorporated in *Demorest's Monthly Magazine*[7] Creating their own publication to promote patterns and numerous other Demorest products established a practice that was to be followed by pattern companies in the future.

The history of United States fashion magazines is inextricably linked to the history of the United States pattern companies. The advantage of owning and publishing their own periodical was economical in many respects. Income from subscriptions off-set the publication costs. Extensive portions of the magazines provided ample, well-illustrated coverage of the patterns while extolling their stylishness. Further, in-house production of give-away flyers and catalogues of the patterns was cost-efficient.

Publication of promotional periodicals combined with the offer of mail-order patterns to establish the commercial pattern industry, a United States phenomenon. It could be argued that the pattern companies established the concept of mail-order catalogues. A significant factor that contributed to the success of mail-order was the expansion of the US Postal Service. In 1845, the service accepted lithograph circulars, handbills and every other kind of printed material. Prior to this the postal service was essentially limited to personal letters. The service also introduced Post Office money orders. Sending money through the mail was also acceptable. *Demorest's Monthly Magazine*, noted: 'We find, however, no difficulty or want of security in sending money through the mails.' (May 1866: 127)

An equally significant factor was the introduction of the sewing machine. Elias Howe patented a machine in 1846 which would be the prototype for most later models. Although originally intended for manufacture of simple ready-to-wear, the machine quickly became a much desired addition to the home. The advantages offered by the sewing machine were quickly recognized by the pioneers of the pattern industry.

For the Demorests and subsequent pattern companies, the foundation for the United States pattern industry was firmly established by the close of 1860. Patterns were sold to retailers such as dry-goods stores and dressmaker shops around the country. Patterns were readily available through mail-order and the consumer could select the desired items from fashion periodicals. However, the patterns were available in one size only. To acquire a pattern to match individual dimensions, the client had to rely on a professional dressmaker, be clever enough to adapt the pattern to the appropriate size, or order a special pattern by sending measurements to Mme Demorest. That deficiency was resolved by Ebenezer Butterick.

The Early Pattern Companies 1860–74

A none too successful tailor in Sterling, Massachusetts, Ebenezer Butterick was familiar with patterns in graded sizes. His revolutionary idea was to make children's patterns available in sizes according to age, such as three to five years. The idea is said to have come from his wife, Ellen. The story is that Butterick decided to design a pattern for her after watching her struggle to cut fabric for her child's dress on the dining room table. He began his business selling sized men's and boys' patterns in late 1863. His first advertising was a Currier print of 'Juvenile Fashions' published in 1864. A plate in the Butterick Archives in New York inscribed 'This is my first printing – E. Butterick' illustrates fashions for young men and boys. (Figures 14.1 and 14.2) Butterick expanded his line with women's fashions in 1866. The women's patterns were available in sizes using a proportional system based upon the bust measurement.

Butterick built a substantial business and quickly added a publishing division beginning with *Semi-Annual Report of Gent's Fashions* in 1865

JUVENILE FASHIONS,
PUBLISHED BY E. BUTTERICK, 192 BROADWAY, N.Y.

Figure 14.1. 'Juvenile Fashions', c. 1864, published by Ebenezer Butterick. The lithograph is by Currier with a notation on the back: 'This is my first printing,' signed E. Butterick. Courtesy of Butterick Pattern Company Archives.

Figure 14.2. Exhibit from 'Dreams on Paper: Home Sewing in America' held at the Fashion Institute of Technology in 1997. The two boys' garments on the right were made up from Butterick patterns c. 1864 and match the figures third and fourth from the left in the 'Juvenile Fashions' print, reproduced here as Figure 14.1. The garment on the left is an example of a Garibaldi suit for which Butterick was well known. Butterick suits made by the University of Rhode Island Theatre Department, Garibaldi suit courtesy of The Children's Museum of Indianapolis. Photograph by Irving Solero.

followed by *Ladies Report of New York Fashions* in 1867 and *The Metropolitan,* a literary and fashion magazine, in 1868. This magazine ultimately evolved into *The Delineator* which continued publication until 1937.

The competition for business between Mme Demorest and Butterick expanded in 1870 when James McCall founded McCall's Pattern Company. McCall brought his background as a tailor to his enterprise. As the copyright holder of a pattern drafting system, 'The Royal Chart', he had experience with grading garments to size. (Kidwell 1979: 85)

In addition, McCall worked as a sewing machine representative in Scotland and then in the US. McCall emigrated from Scotland as a full journeyman tailor in 1868/9. He set himself up in business through the income from certain improvements he had made in the sewing machine. In 1871 he began advertising 'Bazar Cut Paper Patterns' in *Harper's Bazar.* Ladies' patterns were available in sizes 'ranging from 30 to 46 inches bust measure; also for misses from 10 to 16 years of age, and for children of both sexes under 10'. (*Harper's* 1871: 687)

McCall renamed his patterns 'Bazar Glove-Fitting Patterns', undoubtedly to take advantage of name recognition associated with two popular fashion periodicals: *Der Bazar* of Berlin and its imitator *Harper's Bazar* of New York. The Harper brothers introduced the New York periodical in November 1867. It was a small sixteen-page folio, published weekly until 1901 when it changed to a monthly. Each issue contained a pull-out pattern supplement sheet typically thirty-one by twenty-two and one-half inches, printed on both sides. Known as overlay patterns, these supplements consisted of a number of patterns, often twenty-four or more on a single sheet. The pattern pieces were defined by different line codes for each piece superimposed on each other. The result is a maze of intricate lines. The patterns ranged from accessories such as collars and caps, to household items such as pen wipers and foot stool covers, to women's and children's garments, cloaks and undergarments. None of the patterns on the sheets were sized, gowns generally consisted of bodices and sleeves. Skirt patterns were rarely included, small skirt diagrams were used instead. By 1871, *Harper's* was offering cut paper patterns 'graded to fit any figure and are fitted with the greatest accuracy', (*Harper's* 1871: 687) although they continued the overlay pattern sheets well into the 1890s. (Figure 14.3)

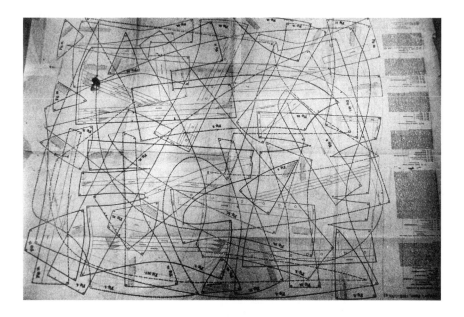

Figure 14.3. One side of an overlay pattern sheet from *Harper's Bazar*, 1883.

The patterns in *Harper's* were essentially imports, so too were the patterns in *Le Bon Ton* published by S.T. Taylor Company of New York. Full-scale tissue patterns were included in each issue of *Le Bon Ton*, beginning in 1868. Taylor also had a dressmaking system: 'Taylor's Dress Cutting Simplified and Reduced to Science', (Trautman 1987: 3) so he, too, was familiar with pattern grading. Following the Demorest example, he offered both trimmed and plain patterns.

Taylor was very conscious of the competition. In the January 1868 edition of *Le Bon Ton* he was 'compelled to notice a new-comer called *Harper's Bazar*'. Acknowledging the reputation of *Der Bazar*, he noted that Harper's did not 'come up to the mark by a great deal'. He continues:

> Why is it that the old and respectable *Bazar* should be so mutilated at this time? Leslie, Godey and others have lived on it for years and the Harper's propose to republish it in this country, but for some reason give only about one-third of that given by the publishers on the other side [. . .] Can it be possible that these wealthy gentlemen are unwilling to pay out the necessary amount of gold to get the paper completely from Europe? [. . .] Or do they intend to fall into the very common error of other home journals of stealing fashion plates? (*Le Bon Ton* January 1868: 4)

Thus by 1871, five pattern companies were actively competing for the market: Demorest, Butterick, McCall's, Harper's and S.T. Taylor. All, except Mme Demorest, were offering patterns graded to size although *Harper's* and *Le Bon Ton* also continued with unsized patterns. Demorest and Butterick offered trimmed and untrimmed patterns and all were publishing their latest styles in their own periodicals. McCall began publishing *The Queen* in 1873 possibly taking advantage of the cachet of the very popular English fashion magazine of the same name. The title was changed to *The Queen of Fashion* in 1891 then to *McCall's Magazine* in 1897.

Two more companies joined the competition in 1873, Domestic and A. Burdette Smith. Domestic patterns were a subsidiary of the Domestic Sewing Machine Company and were promoted in *The Domestic Monthly*. These patterns were available in a range of sizes, also based upon the bust measure. Smith's patterns differed from the others. The pattern came with a cloth model to facilitate the fitting process. (*Smith's* 1874: Vol. 3 No. 4: 9)

The Sewing Machine

Each of the pattern companies had strong affiliations with promoting the sale of sewing machines. Since its inception, the machine impacted upon the clothing industry but not without some anxiety. There was concern of displacing professional tailors and dressmakers as well as seamstresses. There was resistance to the quality of machine-made versus hand-made and the machine was expensive and not readily affordable for many families. However, in September 1856, a mere ten years after Howe's patent, *Leslie's* reported that 'Women are not yet wholly superseded, being extremely useful in their appropriate place – in fact, absolutely indispensable; yet the improvement attempted by the sewing machine has exerted an important influence on her social state.' The article concludes:

> Full one-half of the machines now made are sold to the laborious class of people known as needle-women, sewing-girls and employees in manufacturing concerns; though very many are made for family sewing, several families often passing it around as needed. As some instruction is desirable, there are places on Broadway where ladies gather each day to receive lessons, and among them are those of affluence and highest respectability [. . .] The sewing machine promises permanent relief to wearisome bondage to the needle-woman. (Leslie 1856: 120)

The article also notes 'the great improvement which has taken place in the quality of sewing silk, twist, thread, etc. made necessary by the rapid and accurate movement of the sewing machine'.

Demorest's sold machines under their name and offered them as premiums to individuals who sold substantial numbers of subscriptions to *Demorest's* magazine. McCall had experience with sewing machines and promoted their use from the beginning. Domestic began the pattern business as a sideline to the manufacture of sewing machines. Butterick was not directly associated with a machine company but diligently promoted its necessity in every home. The copy that accompanied the 'Sewing Machine Costume' in Butterick's 1869/70 Catalogue advised every young lady with $1.00 to invest $0.50 in a Bible and $0.50 towards a good sewing machine. There is further advice to

> [Y]oung men and ladies who are just sipping the sweets of connubial felicity, before you get a bed-stead, purchase a sewing machine. If you can't have both, sleep on the floor until you can earn enough with your sewing machine to pay for a bed-stead. Saw off half a dozen pieces of maple boards for dinner plates [. . .] [use] logs for seats.

The Pattern-Making Process

Patterns were made of thin tissue paper with a series of circles, squares and notches cut into each piece. Notches indicate points where pattern pieces are joined. Partially derived from tailor's markings, a typical code for the punched out holes is:

1. Small eyelets or circles indicate take-ups such as tucks, pleats, darts, hems and the like.
2. Large single eyelets indicate pockets, centre front, centre back, and the like.
3. Large double eyelets, often in a triangle, indicate no seam; place the edge on the fold of the fabric.
4. Large triple eyelets in a row indicated the lengthwise grain of the fabric.
5. Triangles indicate fullness as for gathers or shirring.
6. Squares indicated attachments such as buttons, trimmings and yokes.
7. Numbers punched in the tissue identify the pattern piece.

Typically, pattern companies produced thirty to forty pattern styles each month, averaging 350 to 450 each year, although Butterick produced an average of 1,000 per year in the 1890s. Butterick, McCall and Vogue produced 600 or more per year during the 1930s and early 1940s. *Tide* Magazine reported pattern sales of 45,000,000 in 1939 and 97,216,000 in 1949.[8] The number of styles produced dropped to around 500 by the late 1940s and remains at this number, although more craft styles than garment styles are now produced in response to the current market.[9]

Expansion, Attrition and Mergers: 1886–1926

Perhaps the depression that followed the Panic of 1873 is the reason no new major pattern companies were formed until 1887. In that year, Frank Keowing, a former Butterick employee, formed Standard Fashion Company. To establish his business, he agreed to exchange all unsold patterns at cost, rather than for credit or at a percentage as was the typical practice of the existing companies. This tactic allowed him to place patterns in a number of leading department stores.[10] Standard Fashion began publishing *The Designer* in 1888 but changed the title to *Standard Delineator* in 1894 in the true imitative tradition of the nineteenth century. After Butterick brought litigation against the company, the magazine was retitled *Standard Designer* in 1896. The company also published *Ladies Standard Magazine,* a less expensive black and white duplicate of *Standard Designer.*

Three more important new pattern companies were formed before the turn of the century, New Idea, Pictorial, and Vogue. New Idea was formed in 1894 by J.W. Pearsal, a former manager of the pattern division of Domestic

Sewing Machine Company. Pearsal's 'new idea' was the $0.10 pattern. The other companies' pattern prices ranged from $0.20 to $0.50 depending upon the garment and style. Early New Idea advertisements in farm journals and almanacs appealed to middle-class and farming community clients. The company began publishing *New Idea's Woman's Magazine* in 1896, the title changed to *Woman's Magazine* in 1901 and continued until the company was purchased by Standard Fashions and became *Designer/Woman's Magazine* in 1920.

Pictorial Review patterns were an extension of the Albert McDowell System of Dressmaking and Tailoring. McDowell held several patents for his system and published pattern drafts in *Pictorial Review*. (Kidwell 1979: 54) The first issue, published in 1899, included one paper pattern for a 'Paris flounce skirt'. By 1903, the company was offering pinned paper and cut-to-measure patterns. This practice ceased by 1910.

Vogue's history is different from the other companies in that the periodical existed before the pattern division was formed in 1899. The periodical began in 1892 as a society weekly. On 13 February 1899 *Vogue* presented its first pattern, a 'Louis XV jacket'. Patterns were issued weekly and gradually increased in number over the course of the year. When Condé Nast assumed the leadership of *Vogue* in 1909, the Vogue dressmaker pattern division was an established business.

A fourth company joined the ranks after the turn of the century: Curtis Publishing Company added a pattern division to its successful publication, *Ladies' Home Journal*. The periodical, first published in December 1883, added patterns in 1905 when Condé Nast organized the Home Pattern Company. The company ceased producing patterns in 1932 although *Ladies' Home Journal* continued to carry patterns from other firms such as New York, Vogue and Hollywood until the 1950s.

Several other less important pattern companies were formed between 1895 and 1925. Three specific companies: May Manton (1894 – c.1926), Royal (1896–1925) and Excella (1922–1936) had important roles in the changes in marketing practices and in the mergers that took place during the first quarter of the twentieth century.

The May Manton pattern company is another example of a company established by former employees. It was organized by Mr and Mrs George Bladworth who originally worked for McCall's. Mr Bladworth became president of McCall's in 1890 and Mrs Bladworth was editor of *The Queen of Fashion* writing under the name of May Manton. The couple left McCall's in 1892/3. In 1894 'Hints by May Manton' appeared in the periodical *Modes and Fabrics* which offered patterns from The Columbia Manufacturing Company. There is no indication as to whether the patterns were May Manton patterns but the March 1897 issue of *Modes* offers 'dress designs originated and adapted by May Manton'.[11] May Manton patterns appeared in a number of publications including *Mothers' Magazine* and *Today's Magazine*. The company used advertising in other periodicals rather than publishing their own.

Royal and Excella typify new companies that were ultimately absorbed by their larger competitors. Royal Pattern Company published *Le Costume Royal* offering patterns in a range of sizes as well as scaled diagrams. The periodical was acquired by Condé Nast publications in May 1923. In April of the following year, Royal patterns merged with Vogue patterns and for a brief period of time Royal was added to the Vogue logo and then dropped.

Excella Corporation published Excella patterns beginning in 1922. The company became a subdivision of Pictorial Review in 1930 but kept its own identity until 1936. The company history is an excellent example of the expansion and acquisition that was prevalent in the early twentieth century.

Butterick made the most dramatic acquisitions. First, Butterick purchased Standard Fashion Company in 1900 and then New Idea Pattern Company in 1902. The magazines *Delineator, Designer* and *Woman's Magazine* became known as 'the Butterick trio'. Each of the new acquisitions maintained its own sales forces and periodicals until they were completely merged under the *Delineator* title in 1926.

Of the original pattern companies, Butterick and McCall grew and expanded their businesses. Demorest's ceased producing patterns when Ellen Curtis Demorest, Mme Demorest, retired in 1887, although the periodical continued until 1899. Domestic Pattern Company ended pattern production in 1895. *Harper's Bazar* stopped including patterns around 1913 and *Le Bon Ton* ceased publication in 1907.

Innovations between 1916–26

The early patterns had scant information on how to cut the garment and little or no instruction on how to make the garment up. Pattern envelopes were introduced by Mme Demorest in 1872, but they did not become standard until the 1890s. The envelope provided more space for information than the typical small sheet pasted directly on the folded pattern. In 1916 Butterick began experimenting with a separate, detailed instruction sheet called the 'Deltor', which was patented in 1919. A contraction of the periodical title *Delineator*, the Deltor was promoted on the pattern envelope with the logo: 'Pattern and Deltor Butterick Design'. Other companies such as Pictorial Review, Excella, and Home, quickly followed this lead and included instruction sheets with their patterns.

McCall's took out a patent for printed patterns in 1919. Printed patterns were gradually introduced to the marketplace beginning in 1921. The new printed pattern eliminated the need for cut-and-punched markings since all information such as construction marks, pattern piece identification and seam allowances were printed on each piece. In 1923, McCall's added the 'Printo Gravure', a detailed instruction sheet, to the package. Promotional materials for printed patterns stressed the accuracy of the process because 'it is the only pattern printed, one by one, from a metal plate, which, because it is metal, cannot vary a hair's breadth'. (McCall's *Quarterly*, Spring 1924: 2) The advantage of the printed pattern was its accuracy, no worry about variations of the hand-cut patterns. The economic disadvantage was the cost of setting up the presses if a short run was wanted.

Other companies, such as Ladies' Home Journal, extolled the value of hand-crafted rather than machine-made patterns: 'Ladies' Home Journal patterns are NOT Printed. Every Pattern is hand made, cut by hand from the latest exclusive styles.'[12]

The patent for printing patterns did not expire until 1938 when the method for printing patterns became public domain. Of the major companies, only Vogue did not immediately begin using the printed pattern process. However, a variation on the printed pattern was introduced in 1924 by Exella and Pictorial, now under the same umbrella. They printed the name of the pattern piece and grainline on their cut-and-punched patterns. They also printed instruction sheets called 'Excellagraf' and 'Pictograf'.

In August 1925 McCall's introduced patterns for designs by the top French couturiers. These patterns were not inspired by, or taken from, photographs but were licensed designs. They were exact patterns from the original designers. From 1925 to 1929 the pattern styles included a large number of designs from major couturiers in Paris including Chanel, Vionnet, Drecoll, Poiret, Worth and others. To enhance the appeal of the couturier and regular pattern styles, McCall's introduced colour images on envelopes in 1926.

The innovations introduced became standards of the future. Instruction sheets became *de rigueur*. Printed patterns ultimately dominated the market although Vogue patterns continued to be hand-cut until 1956. The use of colour on the envelopes created a more appealing package for the consumer. While copies of couturier designs had been common place from the outset, McCall's practice of licensed designs paved the way for future attributed designer patterns that each of the major companies practiced to some degree. Vogue ultimately became the leader with the *Paris Original* patterns.[13]

This period of the history is marked by keen competition, mergers and consolidation. Of the ten major new companies which were incorporated between 1886 and 1926, only four companies emerge as primary companies: Butterick, McCall's, Home and Vogue.

For Smartness and Thrift 1927–47

Depending on the type of garment and the pattern manufacturer, patterns were selling for $0.25, $0.50 or for as much as $1.00 in 1927. As with the formation of New Idea in 1894, once again the impetus to produce a less expensive pattern led to the development of a new company.

As Joseph M. Shapiro told the story, he was working for a New York fashion magazine (possibly *Pictorial Review*) as an advertising salesman when he happened to see a dress pattern priced at $2.00. (The price must have grown in the telling. At that time the highest priced dress patterns were Vogue Special Design at $1.00.) Shapiro couldn't understand why a few pieces of paper should cost that much. He determined that he could produce a dress pattern for $0.15. In partnership with his son James, Shapiro started Simplicity Pattern Company in 1927. (Simplicity Company History n.d.) The phrase 'For Smartness and Thrift' became the company motto.

The company developed quickly and at the height of the great Depression secured a manufacturing plant in Niles, Michigan in 1931. This acquisition proved to be a major cost-saving move and garnered a great deal of support from the community during the Depression.[14] The following year they introduced 'Three-in-One' patterns. The thrift-minded consumer could get three pattern styles in one for $0.15. They also formed a partnership with the Woolworth Company to produce a special line of patterns initially selling for $0.10. Woolworth's, dubbed 'five and dime' stores, specialized in low-cost items and became a multinational firm. The subsidiary company was called DuBarry. This line of patterns remained popular well into the 1940s. They were ultimately phased out of production by 1947. The Simplicity Company was so successful they purchased *Pictorial Review* and *Excella* from the Hearst Publishing Company in 1936. *Excella* was phased out immediately and *Pictorial Review* ceased publication in 1939.

Not wanting to reduce the price and thereby cheapen the image of Vogue patterns, Condé Nast introduced Hollywood patterns in 1932. The idea is attributed to Mary Reinhardt (later Lasker) who suggested that Nast bring out a cheaper line of patterns. (Seebohm 1982: 331) Vogue patterns were selling for as much a $2.00 by this time. Appealing to the national fascination with the movies, many of the envelopes featured a picture of a Hollywood star. Selling at $0.15, they were an immediate success, affordably priced and gave women an opportunity to dress like a movie star.

Another $0.15 pattern, 'a jump ahead of fashion' was produced by Advance Pattern Company. Established in 1932, evidence suggests the company was formed in affiliation with J.C. Penney Company, a large chain store featuring moderately priced goods and a mail-order catalogue. The March 1933 flyer, *Advance Fashions*, prompts consumers to 'Buy Advance Patterns Now and Save!' J.C. Penney Company Inc'.[15] The patterns were promoted through the Penney's catalogue, *Fashion and Fabrics*, into the 1950s.

All four new pattern companies advertised in a variety of existing periodicals rather than establishing their own major fashion magazine as their predecessors had done, though each produced their own catalogues and flyers promoting the latest pattern styles. The Hollywood catalogue was so popular it evolved into *Glamour of Hollywood* in 1939.

Syndicated pattern services were also flourishing. Begun as early as the 1920s, these companies produced inexpensive patterns for sale primarily through newspapers as editorial features. The companies sold patterns outright to the newspaper. Before television evening news, newspapers were the staple for information in every household. Sold as a loss leader, mail-order patterns were a popular editorial feature, drawing the homemaker's attention to the paper's advertising pages. Designs were targeted specifically for the homemaker and the family in the middle- and lower-income brackets. (Flint 1996) The patterns were inexpensive, available only through mail-order from newspapers. Sold in a full range of sizes, these patterns especially filled the need for large sizes. Generally, these companies sold patterns under their house name such Anne Adams, Sue Brunett and Marion Martin. As with previous company employees, when *Ladies Home Journal* stopped producing Home Patterns in 1932, the employees formed New York Pattern Co. with subsidiaries called Our Own and Own Name. Their new company was essentially a syndicated company which also advertised in leading women's magazines, such as *Ladies Home Journal*.

Pattern companies responded to the depressed economy of the 1930s and subsequently to the restrictions created by the Second World War. New companies producing less expensive patterns impacted on the marketplace. Two of the four new companies, Simplicity and Advance, survived the difficult times to join Butterick, McCall's and Vogue as the major pattern producing companies after the war.

These new companies helped define different marketing strategies, combining forces with major retail companies such as Woolworth's, Penney's and outlets other than traditional department stores. They shifted the emphasis from in-house monthly fashion periodicals to well organized, indexed counter catalogues displayed in the retail stores and paid advertising in other periodicals rather than the company-produced fashion magazine. Recognizing the need to promote home sewing during the war years and after, Simplicity established an educational service department hiring a home economist to develop promotions for teaching sewing skills. The intent to build future markets was recognized by the other companies as they established educational departments aimed at school-age girls to expand and perpetuate market potential.

Postscript: 1950s to the Present

The story is on-going. Four major companies are actively producing patterns. Butterick acquired Vogue in 1961 but continues to produce patterns under both signatures. Simplicity and McCall's are active, energetic companies. Advance ceased operation in 1964.

Diversity was a major incentive after the mid 1950s. The companies began developing global markets, producing patterns in numerous languages including Spanish and Japanese. African-American models were included in promotional materials. Expanding beyond the popular Paris designers, Vogue began to feature European, English and American designers. Patterns were designed to accommodate the new synthetic materials and knits. Building upon the do-it-yourself incentive, companies expanded their educational services and the less structured 1960s styles promoted high sales volume. By the mid-1970s many patterns were identified as 'Quick-and-Easy' and 'Jiffy' to promote sales. In addition, the rising interest in making hand-crafted objects began to supplant the interest in garment-making. The pattern companies expanded their craft lines to constitute a major portion of the business.

During the 1980s the pattern business was subjected to many shifts. No longer family-owned, companies became subsidiaries of large conglomerates. Simplicity changed hands four times, McCall's twice and Butterick/Vogue became a division of American Can Company. By the early 1990s the three companies emerged as relatively equal in the market. However, the state of the pattern business was relatively stagnant and new initiatives were needed. Butterick, for example, expanded to include greeting cards. (Sherman Chatzky 1992: 156)

Tissue of Dreams

Although innovations such as printed patterns and new marketing strategies were formulated during the first half of the twentieth century, the basic premises and promotional techniques developed in the nineteenth century remain firm. Mme Demorest established the foundation and Butterick instituted the use of sized patterns. The entrance of James McCall formed the three-way competition that delineated a marketing formula which persists throughout the industry. Periodic introduction of lower-priced patterns from companies such as Standard Fashions, New Idea, DuBarry and Hollywood stimulated competition, but these companies were ultimately absorbed by their larger competitors.

The companies' maxim can be summarized by a *Standard Designer* advertisement from 1917: 'There is nothing so cheap and yet so valuable; so common and yet so little realized; so unappreciated and yet so beneficial as the paper dress pattern. Truly one of the great elemental inventions in the world's history – Tissue of Dreams.'

Notes

1. The title is taken from the exhibition 'Dreams on Paper: Home Sewing In America' at the Fashion Institute of Technology in New York, February through April 1997. The exhibit was dedicated to the memory of co-curator, Betty Williams as is this essay. Betty pioneered the research in the United States pattern industry and is the inspiration for my work on the subject.

2. Full title: *Instructions for Cutting out Apparel for the Poor; Principally Intended for the Assistance of the Patronesses of Sunday Schools and Other Charitable Institutions, but Useful in all Families. Containing Patterns, Directions, and Calculations, Whereby the Most Inexperienced May Readily Buy Materials, Cut Out and Value Each Article of Clothing of Every Size, Without the Least Difficulty, and With the Greatest Exactness: With a Preface, containing a Plan for Assisting the Parents of Poor Children Belonging to Sunday Schools, to clothe Them, and Other Official Observations.* (London: J. Walters, 1789)

3. Full title: *Lady's Economical Assistant; or the Art of Cutting Out, and Making, the Most Useful Articles of Wearing Apparel Without Waste; Explained by the Clearest Directions, and Numerous Engravings, of Appropriate and Tasteful Patterns.* (London: John Murray, 1808)

4. Full title: *The Workwoman's Guide Containing Instructions to the Inexperienced in Cutting Out and Completing Those Articles of Wearing Apparel, &C. Which are Usually Made at Home; Also Explanations on Upholstery, Straw-Plaiting, Bonnet-Making, Knitting & C.* (London: Simpkin, Marshal & Company, 1838)

5. Full title: *The Tailors' Instructor, or, a Comprehensive Analysis of the Elements of Cutting Garments of Every Kind. To Which Are Added, Directions for Cutting Various Articles of Dress for Both Sexes, Without the Usual Seams, and Regimentals of All Descriptions, With Instructions for Making Up Work with Accuracy and Precision.* (Philadelphia: The Authors, 1809) Considered to be the first publication on pattern making in America. This work imitates of the 1796 English publication *The Taylor's Complete Guide.*

6. Smithsonian Institution Archives, Warshaw Collection, Washington: Tailors, Box 3.

7. There are several title changes for the Demorest fashion magazine. *Demorest's Monthly Magazine* is the half title. *Mme Demorest's Mirror of Fashions* is a segment of the periodical.

8. 'Simplicity Patterns', *Tide*, 12 August 1949: 13; 'From Pattern Book to Fashion Magazine', *Tide*, 23 February 1951: 50.

9. Information on the number of patterns produced is taken from the style numbers issued each year. Vogue began with one pattern in each issue of *Vogue*, the number increased in 1907 when a separate pattern division was formed. By the early 'teens, *Vogue* was producing as many styles as the other companies.

10. For more information on the economics of the pattern business, see: Carol Anne Dickson, 'Patterns for Garments: A History Of The Paper Garment Pattern Industry in America to 1976', Ph.D. thesis, The Ohio State University, 1979.

11. *Modes and Fabrics*, March 1897, 30. Following the McCall tradition, May Manton patterns were identified as 'Bazar-Glove-Fitting Patterns'.

12. Ladies' Home Journal Pattern Instruction Sheet, Style Number 5090, 1926.

13. For more details on designer patterns, see Emery (1997/98: 78–91).

14. In 1934 Simplicity employed 'about 350 men and women' in the Niles factory. 'Third Anniversary in Niles', *Simplicity Impressions*, December 1934: 1.

15. Pattern flyer, *Advance Fashions*, 1933: 8.

References

Adburgham, A. (1964), *Shops and Shopping*, London: George Allen & Unwin Ltd.

Demorest, Mme (1862), 'Mme Demorest's Emporium of Fashions, 473 Broadway, New York' *Mme Demorest's Mirror of Fashions*, Winter.

Emery, J. S. (1997), 'Development of the American Commercial Pattern Industry, 1850–1880', *Costume* 31: 78–91.

—— (1997/98), 'Dating Vogue Designer Patterns: 1958–1988' in *Cutters Research Journal*, Winter, Vol. IX No. 3.

Flint, Daniel (1996), Interview.

Godey, L. and Hale, S. J. eds, (1851) *Godey's Lady's Book*, Vol. 42, September.

Harper's Bazar, 28 October 1871.

Kidwell, C. B. (1979), *Cutting a Fashionable Fit, Dressmakers' Drafting Systems in the United States*, Washington: Smithsonian Institution Press.

Le Bon Ton, (1868), January.

Leslie, F. (1856), *Frank Leslie's Gazette of Fashion*.

Seebohm, Caroline (1982), *The Man Who was Vogue*, New York: Viking Press.

Seligman, K. (1996), *Cutting for All!*, Carbondale: Southern University Press.

Sherman Chatzky, Jean (1992), 'Reaping from Sewing' in *Forbes*, 25 May.

'Simplicity Company History' (n.d.), unpublished manuscript, Simplicity Archives, Niles, Michigan.

Smith's Illustrated Pattern Bazaar, (1874), Summer, Vol 3, No. 4.

Smithsonian Institution Archives, Warshaw Collection, Washington: Tailors, Box 3.

Trautman, P. A. (1987), *Clothing America,* Costume Society of America Region II.

15

Homeworking and the Sewing Machine in the British Clothing Industry 1850–1905

Andrew Godley

The clothing industry in Britain has attracted little of the fascination historians have displayed for the textiles industry despite the close links between the two. No doubt this is partly a result of the difference in the perceived significance of the two sectors in the history of British industrialization. Whereas the technological developments in textiles manufacturing often appear as proxies for British economic health in standard economic histories, the industrialization of clothing is conventionally seen as the by-product of a single invention: the sewing machine. (Clapham 1930: 92; Lazonick and Mass 1990) The impact of this invention was undoubtedly profound on the industry, but the workers who felt this impact most directly were not only those working in the relatively small number of clothing factories, but rather the vast army of clothing industry homeworkers who benefited enormously from the increased productivity that the sewing machine gave them and it is with this group of sewing machine consumers that this chapter is primarily concerned.

Homeworkers (sometimes called outworkers, contemporaries used the terms interchangeably) were overwhelmingly women who took bundles of unstitched garments from a clothing wholesaler or merchant and made them up at home. They received little pay and conditions were often harsh. In the 1840s and 1850s Victorian public opinion was inflamed at what was thought to be the exploitation of the homeworking handstitchers by clothing wholesalers. Nonetheless, hundreds of thousands of British women took in clothing for homework during the nineteenth century, their numbers diminishing only towards the century's end. (Godley 1995)

This chapter first considers the developments in sewing machine technology. In particular, the adoption of incremental innovations from the 1850s to the 1880s is charted and linked to the developing homeworker demand. The growth in demand for sewing machines was especially dramatic in Britain in the 1870s and 1880s and one sewing machine manufacturer, Singer, rapidly gained a stranglehold in the British market. It was this dominance by a single company of the British sewing machine market which allows the possibility of using that company's sales figures as a proxy for sales of all sewing machines in Britain and, therefore, as an index of the dispersion of the new technology through the British clothing industry and further analysis of whether it was to factories, workshops, homeworkers, or families.

Developments in Sewing Machine Technology and the Rise of Singer

A series of patents granted in the United States in the late 1840s and early 1850s formed the key components of the early sewing machine. The patent owners combined to form a patent-pool from 1856 to 1877, which determined the early structure of the sewing machine manufacturing industry. (Hounshell 1984: 67; Davies 1976: 5–12)[1] The principal manufacturers – Wheeler and Wilson, Willcox and Gibbs, Grover and Baker, and Singer – quickly established themselves in the American and then foreign markets. The initial reception of these machines was one of amazement and astonishment at their technical virtuosity, engineers everywhere admired them. (Hounshell 1984: 67–123) Moreover, there was no doubt that these early machines quickly led to efficiency gains in the assembly of garments. British clothing-manufacturers, most famously John Barran's of Leeds, expanded their operations, employing more machines and more workers. (Davies 1976: 21–2; Kershen 1995: 26, 32; Ryott 1951) But these early machines were limited. They could only sew in straight lines. The fastest machines used the inferior chain-stitch not the more reliable lock-stitch, and, at least initially, only a limited number of textiles could be stitched together. (Munby 1951: 39, 54–6; Kershen 1995: 13–15; Thomson 1989: 49–62, 73–9, 83–90, and especially 93–117)

The leading four sewing machine manufacturers continued to improve their products after the pioneering years of the 1850s, with incremental innovations focusing on the speed and quality of stitch. 'Stitch-forming patents and improvements of needles, presser-foots, take-ups, [and] tension devices' continued the refining process. (Thomson 1989: 114) With gains in reliability, speed and wider applicability demand grew. As sewing machine manufacturers were able to invest in ever more efficient methods of production so unit costs and prices fell, further stimulating demand. (Davies 1976: Chapter 1; Hounshell 1984: 67–123; Thomson 1989: 101–4)[2] Moreover, the introduction of the hire-purchase system brought the sewing machine down to the market of ordinary American families. (Thomson 1989: 102–3; Davies 1976: 20–1) In 1856 Singer introduced its first machine aimed at the family market. An improved version – the Letter A – followed in 1859 and six years later the New Family machine was unveiled. (Davies 1976: 18; Hounshell 1984: 89–90, 93) The success of this latter model was so dramatic that by 1867 Singer had become the leading producer of sewing machines in the world, outstripping the sales of its American rivals both at home and, especially, abroad. (Carstensen 1984: 18)[3] Foreign markets were more competitive for the American producers because they fell outside the protective confines of the patent pool. Prices in America were up to twice as high as in the United Kingdom and Europe. Singer, with its extensive investments in its foreign marketing organizations and in its British factories in the 1860s and 1870s, became increasingly dominant outside the US market. (Carstenen 1984: 17–24; Wilkins 1970: 37–47; Davies 1976: 56–7)[4] Within three years of the end of the patent-pool arrangement Singer claimed that its sales represented three quarters of the world market. (Singer c. 1881: Box 108, Folder 3) By 1890 the company's market share had further increased to a remarkable 80 per cent. (Carstensen 1984: 23)

Historians of the Singer Manufacturing Company all agree that its success was squarely based on developing markets for its products rather than concentrating on product development. (Chandler 1977: 302–5, 402–14; Davies 1976; Jack 1957) Singer, through its two key innovations – the introduction of a company-controlled sales force and purchase by instalments – revolutionized the marketing of sewing machines. Nonetheless, Singer was also assiduous in trying to improve the standard model and, in 1881, introduced the Improved Family machine, which incorporated a number of attractive features: an oscillating shuttle; a much faster lockstitching mechanism and an increasing number of 'automatic' features such as automatic winders, self-threading shuttles and stitch-regulators. The result was a faster, quieter operation with a smoother cloth-feed and better quality stitching.[5] Initial problems in the production of the Improved Family Machine notwithstanding, sales of this new model soared. (Hounshell 1984: 109–20) With the Improved Family model sewing machine, technology had matured and there were few changes thereafter. Singer had become the largest producer in the US home market, but, more importantly, it had created a stranglehold in the rest of the world.

Sales of Sewing Machines in the United Kingdom

With these incremental improvements in sewing machine marketing and technology demand grew. And demand grew most quickly in the world's richest consumer market of the 1870s and 1880s: Britain. (See Figure 15.1)

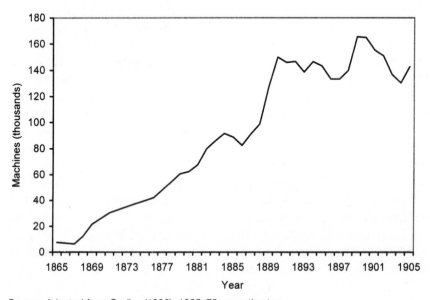

Source: Adapted from Godley (1996); 1865–79 are estimates.

Figure 15.1. Sales of Singer Sewing Machines in the United Kingdom 1865–1905

Figure 15.1 shows the phenomenal rate of growth of sales of machines enjoyed by Singer in the United Kingdom. The size of the UK market in the early 1860s was relatively modest, with all imports from the American producers totalling perhaps 5,000 machines, when their combined output was around 75,000 machines per annum. (Jack 1957: 136 note 2)[6] Despite this Singer decided to commit themselves to the UK market when Edward Clark, Singer's leading light, sent the company's first agents in 1861 to London and Glasgow. A senior executive permanently based in London followed in 1864. The first small finishing plant was established in Glasgow in 1867, then a further factory there in 1869, culminating in 1871 in the establishment of a genuinely significant production centre. (Hounshell 1984: 93–6; Wilkins 1970: 40–5; Godley 1999) UK sales of Singers more than doubled in the

258

1870s, from 26,000 to over 60,000. In 1890 over 150,000 Singer sewing machines were sold in the UK, two-and-a-half times the figure of 1879. This represents a compound annual growth rate of 8.3 per cent, sustained for twenty years, a remarkable performance. Thereafter sales stabilized slightly below the 1890 level, apart from the few years at the turn of the century and the growth rate was negligible.

This extraordinary rate of growth obviously reflected an enormous increase in the demand for sewing machines and especially for the Improved Family model. However, Figure 15.1 might well stand as a perfectly respectable proxy for total sewing machine sales in the UK, so completely did Singer dominate the British market. Singer's American competitors were too concerned with their domestic sales to fight for uncertain overseas markets in the formative period of the 1860s and 1870s and so had a negligible share of the British market. German competitors were also insignificant before the 1900s and the only real alternative in Britain at this time was a machine produced by Bradbury's of Oldham. Bradbury's produced around 25,000 machines per annum in the early 1890s, which, if all were sold domestically, was only one eighth of Singer's 1890 sales.[7] Singer, it is safe to assume, had therefore cornered at least three quarters of the British market. This had been achieved by a sustained reinvestment of profits into a wider and more efficient branch network of sales offices and, in particular, into the apotheosis of nineteenth-century inward investment into Britain, the Clydebank factory – the largest sewing machine factory in the world and the largest single factory in Britain. (Carstensen 1984: 25; Hounshell 1984: 95; Davies 1976: 197; Godley 1999)

Figure 15.1, then, shows much more than the results of a firm's successful marketing of new technology. Rather, given the sheer magnitude of Singer's dominance of the UK market, Figure 15.1 comes very close to showing the total sales of sewing machines in the UK. This, in turn, then comes very close to giving some sort of index of the diffusion of sewing machine technology in the UK clothing industry, whether it was factory, workshop, homeworker or family demand.

The Market for Singer Sewing Machines

Singer had identified the potential of the family market in the United States already by the mid-1850s. Early advertising emphasized the suitability of their machines for both working tailors and domestic consumers.[8] The changes to the retail network in the United States pioneered by Clark and his deputy, George McKenzie, in the 1870s were, in part, aimed to maximize the company's exposure to the family market. (Carstensen 1984: 17–24)

However, there is good reason to assume that the British market for sewing machines was different to that in the United States.

The demand for sewing machines was derived from the demand for machine-stitched clothing. In the United States, with a much lower population density, much less urbanization and a less developed retail sector, the ready-made clothing industry was relatively backward compared to Britain. Britain was 'by far the leader in production of ready-made clothing' before the 1880s. (Jack 1957: 136 note 2; Godley 1997) A far greater proportion of total clothing consumed in the United States was assembled in the family home than in Britain. In Britain the ready-made clothing industry had developed early in the nineteenth century and had become the most sophisticated clothing sector in the world. (Chapman 1993; Kershen 1995: chapters 1 and 2; Godley 1997)

With a working class already relatively well-off by mid-century, purchasing ready-made clothing had already become normal in England. The largest clothing retailer in London, E. Moses & Son, claimed that 80 per cent of the English public bought their garments ready-made by the early 1850s. (Lemire 1997)[9] The result was that when garment assembly became mechanized, those in Britain principally concerned with this technology were labourers in an industry rather than mothers in a home. For Singer in Britain, while the company's advertising stressed the benefits of family use, senior management clearly recognized that the majority of its customers were using the machines to manufacture clothing for resale not for personal consumption. By 1898 the Improved Family model was being advertised as 'the most perfect sewing machine for family use'. (Singer 1898: Box 108, folder 3) But it would be incorrect to assume that sales of the Improved Family model were exclusively for the family market, or, conversely, that sales of the closely related Improved Manufacturing model were exclusively for the industrial market. In fact, the company made no attempt to discriminate between the different models sold in its monthly internal accounts. Calculating the mean unit price of Singer's retail sales between 1880 and 1905 doesn't help much either, because the Improved Family and Manufacturing models were so closely priced. (Godley 1996) Singer did sell non-standard machines to what they called the 'wholesale trade'. This was composed of the large clothing factories, which required power-driven and often customized machinery. In this sector Singer was less dominant, with British machine-tool manufacturers threatening the company's leading position, but sales of belt-machines and buttonhole machines as well as the standard sewing machines were clearly an important part of the overall business.[10] The retail trade remained the priority though, even in areas with a high concentration of clothing factories.[11] But this did not mean that the majority of the company's retail customers were purchasing their machines exclusively for family use: they were not. The majority of customers until the mid-1870s were related to the clothing industry, either as working tailors or homeworkers. Company advertising from the early 1880s makes this clear:

> We have seen the sewing machine revolutionise the old manual sewing in the cottage; we have seen it completely change the refrain of the 'Song of the Shirt' into something less plaintive and agonising: and now, to crown it all, we have seen it, in its trimmest guise, take a conspicuous place in the drawing room as an article of the highest ornamentation and beauty. It is, however, for the purposes of wholesale manufacture that the sewing machine commands the greatest admiration [. . .] One sewing machine will accomplish the work of a score of women with the hand, and do it as well, too.[12]

The apparent division between the Family and Manufacturing models was not significant either. They were as often as not simply referred to together as Oscillating Shuttle machines in the company's internal accounts.[13] This explains why there was no attempt within the company to present disaggregated sales data. The principal retail market was the enormous ranks of overwhelmingly female, working-class homeworkers. One of the company's British auditors claimed to McKenzie after examining the accounts of the South London office that 'the district is one of the most important for the Co(mpan)y in this country, containing as it does a vast population of the working classes, who are the back-bone of our business.'[14] Singer's dependence on this most vulnerable of all customer bases led to flexibility in pricing:

> [T]he Company have decided that these (oscillating shuttle) Machines may be put out against a first payment of not less than 10/- when supplied to families, and [. . .] when Machines are hired by outside workers for factories or other poor persons earning a living by their use – a less sum may be taken.[15]

Even so a depression in demand for clothing could have devastating consequences for sales. In the Manchester region in 1892 the knock-on effects of American tariff barriers against imported cotton textiles were that local 'trade and employment have to a certain extent been paralysed'. Consequently,

> In Manchester perhaps 5 out of 12 of the m(achine)s are put out to outworkers and if they cannot get employment they cannot earn money to pay us. At this moment some of the leading trades employing outworkers are practically stagnant (the Mantle, Handkerchief-hemming, Pinafore etc.) and we are receiving daily constant applications from customers verbally and by letter to repossess their old m(achine)s as they have no means with which to continue payments.[16]

This reluctance to differentiate between those customers purchasing for domestic and those for homeworking or workshop uses reflects the organization of the British clothing industry. It was highly fragmented, with a small average size of workshop, dependent on a vast army of self-exploiting homeworkers who were themselves very often wives and mothers. (Godley 1995) It was this group, not the relatively small number of clothing workers in factories, nor the middle-class families, which benefited most from the mature sewing machine technology. It was, therefore, this group which represented many of Singer's customers.[17] Thus, the demand for sewing machines in the UK up until the mid-1870s was predominantly made up neither of those who bought the machines exclusively for manufacturing use nor those who wanted the machines exclusively for domestic family use. Rather the most significant component of demand was from homeworkers, who used the machines both for waged work, to supplement family income, and non-waged work, to subsidize family expenditure.

Regional Sales of Singer Sewing Machines

The nature of sewing machine demand becomes more apparent when the pattern of regional sales is considered. (Table 15.1) Table 15.1 indicates that sales in the London region were consistently greater than any other office, and especially so in the 1880s and early 1890s. Leeds was clearly second to London with its share of sales especially important in the 1890s. The next most important regions varied from period to period, with Liverpool and Newcastle initially important sales centres before fading and, conversely, areas such as Nottingham, Plymouth and the Western region becoming more important. The picture of the geographical dispersal of sewing machine technology implied in Table 15.1 is somewhat obscured by the reorganizations and redefinitions of regions, however. The Liverpool office, for example, had a diminishing share of sales over the period partly as a result of sub-offices being relocated out of the Liverpool, and into contiguous regions.[18] There were at least two important reorganizations of the branch network in the early 1880s and the mid-1890s, about which surviving records give little information, especially for the latter period. Thus, a more precise analysis of relationships between the regional distribution of sewing machines and the regional distribution of clothing industry employment cannot be anything other than informed speculation. Singer's regional divisions did not follow the Registrar General's and the hinterlands of some of Singer's district offices was often very different from those accorded to the cities and county towns in successive censuses. Singer's Manchester office, for example, had a

Table 15.1. *Distribution of Sales of Singer Sewing Machines in the United Kingdom, 1880–1904 per cent.*

England and Wales	1880–84	1885–89	1890–4	1895–9	1900–4
Birmingham	3.9	4.6	4.9	5.3	5.0
Bristol	4.8	4.9	4.2	6.0	3.7
Cardiff	4.6	3.7	4.2	4.2	5.2
Leeds	6.2	6.8	8.4	8.3	8.1
Leicester	3.2	3.8	3.3	3.8	3.4
Liverpool	8.7	7.5	6.6	5.5	5.3
London	13.2	14.2	17.6	11.3	10.5
Manchester	6.7	6.6	5.3	7.0	7.1
Newcastle	7.9	5.7	6.5	4.8	4.4
Norwich	3.2	3.3	2.8	3.0	3.3
Nottingham	2.8	3.0	2.7	4.2	5.1
Portsmouth	2.9	2.9	2.3	4.5	4.0
Plymouth	2.0	2.4	2.2	–	4.4
Southern region	7.9	7.5	6.0	6.4	5.6
Western region	3.1	3.0	2.9	5.8	6.6
Scotland					
Edinburgh	5.6	6.5	6.3	5.7	5.4
Glasgow	7.4	7.8	7.2	7.5	6.9
Ireland					
Belfast	1.9	2.4	2.1	3.3	2.6
Dublin	3.8	3.7	4.7	4.0	2.9
Total (machines sold 000s)	386.8	487.9	727.6	715.5	715.9

Source: Adapted from Godley (1996).

hinterland which spread across the Pennines, with sub-offices in Halifax and Huddersfield reporting to the main Lancashire, not the Yorkshire, district office.[19]

These caveats notwithstanding, Table 15.1 gives one very important result which goes some way to confirming the relationship between Singer sewing machine sales and the adoption of sewing machine technology in the British clothing industry. This is the trend of sales in London and Leeds during the key period of growth in overall sales to the early 1890s. In Figure 15.1 it was seen that UK sales overall increased during the 1880s to a peak in 1890. Table 15.1 shows that the regions which were leading this surge in demand for sewing machines were London and Leeds – the two great centres of the clothing industry. In 1881 London and Leeds sales accounted for 15 per cent of total UK sales. By 1892 London sales were 20 per cent alone, with sales in the Leeds region accounting for another 9.1 per cent of total UK sales. (Godley 1996) London was, of course, the greatest centre of homeworking in the clothing industry.

Conclusion

Locating the clothing industry centres of London and Leeds as the driving forces of the rapid growth in demand for, and sales of, sewing machines in the UK during the 1880s and early 1890s suggests demand was derived from the rapidly growing need for machine-stitched clothing made-up in factory, workshop and, especially, in an outworker's home.

Demand for sewing machines in Britain must, therefore, be seen as clothing industry-led, continuing in importance up until the 1890s. Thus, the data presented here represents an index of technological dispersion within the British clothing industry during the second half of the nineteenth century. Moreover, the leading centres of sewing machine sales were those where homeworking was very closely identified with the organization of the clothing industry. In conclusion then, this chapter links the chronology of technological dispersion in the clothing industry to the technological innovations in the sewing machines and shows how the principal regional centres of the UK clothing industry pioneered the demand for sewing machines in the 1880s. Moreover, it would appear that the homeworker-dominated London industry was the pioneer in the fast growth of sewing machine sales in the 1880s, perhaps to be followed by the factory-dominated demand from the Leeds industry. There are important questions which remain to be answered, for example, concerning the relationship between sewing machine technology and industry organization – whether mechanization subsequently led to a demise of homeworking – but these require further research. However, the conclusion of this chapter is that the sewing machine introduced a new technology into Britain's garment trades from the 1850s and 1860s, moreover that the people who really benefited from this new technology, especially after the later incremental innovations led to the improved machines of the 1870s and 1880s, were the hundreds of thousands of homeworkers. These women used the machines both to supplement family income from waged work and also to subsidise family expenditure through making family garments.

Notes

1. The following section is drawn from Godley (1996).

2. Carstensen (1984: 5) claims the later machines led to 70-90 per cent saving in labour.

3. Davies (1976: 5) cites a Singer Company agent remarking in 1882 that 'until 1865 there was scarcely a man of recognized sound business judgement who ever believed that the sewing machine would arrive at a commercial success'. Hounshell (1984: 5) shows that Singer became the leading producer in 1867, overtaking Wheeler and Wilson.

4. On Singer's UK factories see Godley (1999).

5. Examples from Singer archives include advertising: Box 108, folder 3, c. 1898 lists the following features: 'new vibrating shuttle', 'bobbin winder', 'self-threading shuttle', and 'stitch-regulator'. US advertising material dated 1889 lists: 'oscillating shuttle', and 'vibrating shuttle'. Box 94, folder 1 includes a cutting of an undated Singer Company advert from *Oldham Chronicle* (c. 1880–81) which gives comparisons of stitch speeds of Willcox and Gibbs chainstitch machine (2,600 stitches per minute), Bradbury's lockstitch machine (1,200 per minute), and Singer's 'New lockstitch sewing machine' (2,100 per minute). See also Hounshell (1984: 109).

6. Estimates of US producers' output vary quite considerably but Hounshell (1984: Tables 2.1 and 2.2) suggests that Wheeler and Wilson sold over 30,000 per annum between 1862–64 (70), Singer sold less than 24,000 per annum (89), and Willcox and Gibbs around 8,000 per annum (353 note 30). Grover and Baker, despite being technological pioneers and initiating the patent pool, were falling behind. By 1872 they had sales of 72,000 which was comparable to Willcox and Gibbs. They probably sold 10,000–15,000 in the early 1860s. There were other, lesser manufacturers as well, of course.

7. American competitors' muted taste for foreign competition is picked up in Davies (1976: 158–63). By the early 1880s only Wheeler and Wilson provided any competition for Singer, even in the domestic US market. German firms' insignificance is referred to in Singer records. (Box 94, folder 1, letter from G. McKenzie to E. Clark, 31 May 1881) Their later international presence is confirmed by Carstensen. (1984: Chapter 2; Davies 1976: Chapter 9) Bradbury's output is cited by Saul (1967) where he claims they employed 600 people and produced 500 machines a week in the early 1890s at their Oldham base. (124) By the late 1890s they were diversifying into bicycles. (129 note 2) Bradbury's are also occasionally referred to in Singer internal correspondence. See, for example, Box 98, folder 3, 'Audit of Manchester region'. Both Bradbury's and Willcox and Gibb's received (unflattering) comparisons in Singer Company advertising, for example in 1881: Box 94, folder 1. Bradbury's

were the only other sewing machine referred to by name by tailoresses and outworkers in London's East End when interviewed by George Arkell in the late 1880s under the auspices of Charles Booth's investigation into the London labour market, see Godley (1993: Chapter 5).

8. See, for example, the reproduction in Hounshell (1984: 87 Figure 2.11).

9. On Moses, see Chapman (1993).

10. Singer (Box 95, folder 8) 'Sales of Improved Button hole Machines, 1885', shows that these more expensive machines (£15–20) went to the rapidly growing number of clothing factories, especially in Manchester, London and Leeds. Box 93, folder 2, 'Belt Machines, 16th January 1900', shows that the prices of these machines to manufacturers went up to £125 12s. Box 96, folder 3, Whitie to Bourne, 22 February 1888: 4, on the competition of 'English makers' in heavy machines. The vast majority of machines even in factories were the standard sewing machines though.

11. Box 94, folder 1, McKenzie to Clark, 10 May 1881, where McKenzie is critical of the Leeds office agent for having 'occupied most of his time in the wholesale trade to the detriment of the retail business'.

12. Box 94, Folder 1, Advertisement cutting from *Oldham Chronicle* (n.d. c. 1880–81).

13. Box 94, folder 4, 'Memo to all sub-offices in the UK, 25.9.1882', 'with respect to Improved Family and Improved Manufacturing machines [. . .] These machines are peculiarly adapted for Stay work, Shirt and Collar work and other manufacturers [. . .]' Box 95, folder 5, 'Memo from McKenzie to all UK agents, 21.9.1885', 'with special reference to the (new) Oscillating Shuttle Machines [. . .]' Also Box 96, folder 3, Whitie to Bourne 22 February 1888: 'Prospects would be much improved 'if we can have the improved shuttles in IF & IM m/-s [. . .] and such other novelties to meet the demands of certain manufacturing centres'.

14. Box 93, folder 10, 'Robertson to McKenzie, 13.11.1880'. The literature on the sweated outworkers is immense but see Schmiechen (1984) and Morris (1986).

15. Box 95, folder 5, 'McKenzie memo to all UK agents', 21 September 1885.

16. Box 98, folder 3, 'Audit of Manchester office, by G.B. Dobson, May 1892'. He goes on to say, 'The trade is very varied using S(ewing) machines for many purposes e.g. Stays, Corsets, Pinafores, Handkerchiefs, (linen and silk), Underclothing & Other White Work, Clothing and Belting, etc., etc.'

17. The aggregate output of clothing factories was a small fraction of industry output, even by 1907. See Godley (1995). After 1892 surviving Singer Company records for UK activities become sparse, thus, it becomes increasingly difficult to make any judgements concerning the composition of the UK market from company records from that date.

18. Liverpool was a very big region in the early 1880s, with sub-offices as far away as Barrow, Wolverhampton and Shrewsbury reporting to it. (Box 103, folder 5, list of offices 1885; and Box 93, folder 10, 'Audit of Liverpool district office by Henry Raper', 20 January 1880: Also see sources in Table 15.1.)

19. Box 103, folder 5, list of offices for 1885. Also Box 98, folder 3, Audited Manchester office, by G.B. Dobson, May 1892.

References

Carstensen, F. V. (1984), *American Enterprise in Foreign Markets,* Chapel Hill: University of North Carolina Press.

Chandler, A. (1977), *The Visible Hand,* Cambridge: Harvard University Press.

Chapman, S. (1993), The Innovating Entrepreneurs in the British Ready-Made Clothing Industry', *Textile History,* 24.

Clapham, J. H. (1930), *The Economic History of Modern Britain,* Cambridge: Cambridge University Press.

Davies, R. B. (1976), *Peacefully Working to Conquer the World: Singer Sewing Machines in Foreign Markets, 1854–1920,* New York: Arno Press.

Godley, A. (1993), 'Enterprise and Culture: Jewish Immigrants in London and New York 1880–1904', Ph.D thesis, University of London, London School of Economics.

—— (1995), 'The Development of the UK Clothing Industry, 1850–1950: Output and Productivity Growth', *Business History,* 37 (4).

—— (1996), 'Singer in Britain: The Diffusion of Sewing Machine Technology and its impact on the Clothing Industry in the UK, 1860–1905', *Textile History* 27 (1).

—— (1997), 'Comparative Labour Productivity in the British and American Clothing Industries, 1850–1950' *Textile History* 28 (1).

—— (1999) 'Pioneering Foreign Direct Investment in British Manufacturing', *Business History Review* 73 (3).

Hounshell, D. (1984), *From the American System to Mass Production, 1800–1932,* Baltimore: The Johns Hopkins University Press.

Jack, A. (1957), 'The Channels of Distribution for an Innovation: The Sewing Machine Industry in America, 1860–1865', *Explorations in Entrepreneurial History,* Series A, Vol. 9.

Kershen, A. (1995), *Uniting the Tailors: Trade Unionism Amongst the Tailors of London and Leeds.* Ilford: Frank Cass.

Lazonick, W. and Mass, W. (1990), 'The British Cotton Industry and International Competitive Advantage: The State of the Debates', *Business History* 32.

Lemire, B. (1997), *Dress, Culture and Commerce: the English clothing trade before the factory, 1660–1800* Basingstoke: Macmillan.

Morris, J. (1986), 'The Characteristics of Sweating: The Late Nineteenth Century London and Leeds Tailoring Trade' in Angela John (ed.) *Unequal Opportunities: Women's Employment in England, 1800–1918,* Oxford: Blackwell.

Munby, D. (1951), *Industry and Planning in Stepney,* Oxford: Oxford University Press.

Ryott, D. (1951), *John Barran's of Leeds 1851–1951,* Leeds: John Barran and Co.

Saul, S. (1967), 'The Market and the Development of the Mechanical Engineering Industries in Britain, 1860–1914', *Economic History Review* 2nd Ser., Vol. XX.

Singer Manufacturing Company Archives, State Historical Society, Madison, Wisconsin.

Schmiechen, J. (1984), *Sweated Industries and Sweated Labour, the London Clothing Trades, 1860–1914,* London: Croom Helm.

Thomson, R. (1989), *The Path to Mechanized Shoe Production in the United States*, Chapel Hill: University of North Carolina Press.

Wilkins, M. (1970), *The Emergence of Multinational Enterprise: American Business Abroad from the Colonial Era to 1914*, Cambridge: Harvard University Press.

The Singer Archives are held in the State Historical Society of Wisconsin, Madison, Wisconsin. References are to Box and folder numbers there. My thanks to the archivists at Madison for their help.

16

The Sewing Machine Comes Home

Tim Putnam

This chapter examines the mechanization of sewing in the middle years of the last century and its articulation of relations between design, production, distribution and consumption. It will be argued here that it was the emergence of sewing machines as consumer durables which set the paradigm of mass production and consumption and had far-reaching effects. This development was premised on a regendering of the machine from its initial contexts of use and it raises a number of questions about sewing which require further examination.

The emergence of the sewing machine as a consumer durable in the 1850s is a founding episode in the history of mass production and consumption. While timepieces and small arms had already entered the household, the sewing machine was to be the first labour-replacing domestic appliance of any complexity, opening the way for legions to follow. (Cowan 1983) This revolutionary potential only gradually became apparent; sewing machines had been designed for the workshop and only became home appliances when claimed by women as their own. Through its influence on the evolution of the sewing machine as a product, the complex inter-relation between home and commercial sewing had an extensive influence on modern life.

The idea of the sewing machine as a harbinger of a new order is a familiar one. Ruth Brandon's (1977) *A Capitalist Romance: Singer and the Sewing Machine* touches on several aspects of this paradigm-setting role. To paraphrase, the development of the sewing machine and its establishment as a product played a critical role in the enlargement of the imaginative scope of invention, in the consolidation of several inventions in product innovation, in the deployment of precision volume-manufacturing technology, in elaborating vertically integrated production and distribution, in the creation of a constructive address to the consumer and in the extension of divisions of managerial responsibilities.

These same elements figure large in the macro-structures of modern mass production and consumption found in Alfred Chandler's classic account *The Visible Hand,* published in the same year. The pivotal position of the sewing machine in what was to become a global order is underlined by the status of I.M. Singer & Co. as the first manufacturing multinational. (Davies 1976) Thus Brandon sets her story of Singer in an extraordinary context, a conjuncture in which key relations of production and consumption are redefined as the basis for a new phase of capitalist development. This chapter re-examines how these developments in different spheres came together to establish the sewing machine as the first consumer durable.

Discussion of 'the sewing machine' as an innovation conventionally acknowledges three phases: seventy-five years of unsuccessful inventions in France, Britain and the USA, culminating in Howe's desperate near miss of the mid-1840s, followed by a breakthrough in the American northeast in 1850, with parallel entrepreneurial ventures converging on a viable type-form and then a period of expansion, refinement, and diffusion after 1857 when such makers as Grover and Baker, Wheeler and Wilson, Willcox and Gibbs, and Singer began to sell machines on a substantial scale. (Brandon 1977; Cooper 1976; Godfrey 1982; Hounshell 1984) This phasing focuses attention on the key moments of transition. The length of the initial gestation period has been attributed to both the impossibility of directly replicating hand-sewing and a polarization in the labour market for sewing between entrenched elites on the one hand and a swelling pool of sweated seamstresses on the other. But what changed to enable rival makers to launch similar designs and enjoy a measure of success? And, given the convergence on a basic technological configuration of the new product at the beginning of the 1850s, why was it that the industry only began to grow steadily towards the end of the decade?

Assembling the Elements of a New Paradigm: Willcox and Gibbs

Patent disputes among early makers and inventors were a factor inhibiting the expansion of the industry. The agreement known as the 'Sewing Machine Combination' concluded this 'war' at the end of 1856 and established a common technological platform. The Combination's decision to license rather than restrict rights represented a belief in the very wide potential dissemination of machines for sewing and an acceptance that design, production and marketing innovation could not be controlled by, or limited to, its members. This decision was timely because, encouraged by the rights confusion, jobbing machine shops were beginning to make generic sewing machines.[1] (Brandon

1977: 89–104; Godfrey 1982: 79–83) Licensing worked to control entry to the trade and, along with economies of scale and innovations in production and distribution, ensured that the ensuing 'sewing machine boom' was dominated by a handful of firms. These lessons, which were taken to heart by subsequent innovators of complex products who wished to see speedy rewards, confirm one of the ways in which the sewing machine served to establish essential preconditions of mass production and consumption.

During the 'sewing machine war' of 1852–56, the pioneering manufacturers encountered other obstacles to development. They struggled to achieve economies of scale in manufacturing and with ways to organize channels of distribution, and they experienced difficulties in organizing an adequate division of managerial responsibility within the established culture of entrepreneurial partnership. Further, their efforts at marketing were hampered by inadequate knowledge of their potential customers and their requirements. (Brandon 1977: 67–89; Godfrey 1982: 45–79) The expansion which took place after 1856 was premised on the resolution of these 'teething problems' and centred on the production of sewing machines for the home market in a way which had not been anticipated in 1850. Both the product and the mode of its production and consumption had quietly changed in fundamental ways.

The problems encountered by the pioneering firms during this period were significant enough to enable new competitors who could resolve them to enter the market. The case of Willcox and Gibbs, which became one of the 'big four' soon after entering the industry in 1857, bears this out. Thanks in part to the licensing policy of the Combination, the new entrant was able to access the technological results of the formative period at little cost. But the new competitor's success also stemmed from integrating embryonic channels of mass distribution and techniques of mass production. Hardware wholesaler Willcox's desire to have an 'own-brand' sewing machine ensured a committed, knowledgeable source of investment. Though his firm carried a great many lines for the rural and urban homestead, the most elaborate machine it had distributed was for peeling apples. From this experience, however, Willcox was convinced that many American women would take risks with newfangled labour-saving machinery. In a pioneering example of vertical integration, Willcox set about engaging an inventor and a manufacturer. Across temperamental differences, Gibbs the inventor and Willcox the entrepreneur were able to focus clearly on what their market wanted: a quality robust product for home use, capable of being distributed widely and working effectively with minimal maintenance or service, lighter and cheaper than the Singer and competitive with Wheeler and Wilson. In the end two models were designed, one slightly smaller than the other, licensed under the Combination and with Gibbs' original features patented in June 1857.[2]

The requirements of the design and the intention to achieve considerable economies of scale pointed the partners towards the style of highly standardized manufacturing practised by Colt the small-arms manufacturer, but such firms were not jobbing machine shops but highly capitalized and specialized manufacturers who, should they be prepared to invest in the necessary tooling, were potential competitors. Willcox did not see himself as helping rivals into the industry, but this left him facing the risk of setting up his own factory and staffing it with appropriate expertise. Then, in early 1857 he learned, through a mutual friend, of the small Brown and Sharpe toolmaking business in Providence, Rhode Island. J.R. Brown was an exceptionally talented inventor-engineer who devised and made precision measuring instruments and understood armoury practice, whilst Sharpe was a classic financial controller who exuded confidence in logistics. The firm was short of work because of the economic crisis of 1857. Although he held no particular desire to enter Colt-style volume manufacture, Brown was attracted by the challenge of making all the tooling in advance so that all would be 'near perfect' from the start and economies could be made in assembly by designing the tooling for interchangeable parts. Willcox agreed to fund this development work by paying for the first dozen on an hourly cost basis and trial production runs of fifty of each model, before agreeing terms for repeat orders. Gibbs would supply a design suitable for interchangeable manufacture. An historic alliance between the embryonic technologies of mass distribution and mass production appeared to have been forged.[3]

The new partnership was to enjoy lasting success, but only after its capacities and confidence was stretched to the limit. Initially, things seemed set to go well, with castings, dies and tools being made from drawings of the machine, using Brown & Sharpe's own vernier caliper, the most accurate means of translating flat measurement in three dimensions then available. However, eighteen weeks later $600 had been expended and the tooling remained unfinished. It had been a mistake to design tools for two models at the same time, when there were many mechanical refinements to be made the design of working parts and in the manufacturing process. Additional armoury experience was drafted in, but in trial manufacture it was difficult to usefully occupy the men 'who are not capable of doing the nicer parts'. Brown & Sharpe, finances exhausted, requested an advance, but they could not yet estimate a unit production cost as the first hundred machines were not yet finished. In the middle of a major economic crisis, this was a severe challenge to the vision and commitment of the two partnerships. Willcox would agree an advance only if the manufacture of sewing machines went ahead whether the tooling was ready or not. But reverting to normal manufacturing practice produced chaos at Brown & Sharpe and 'from the disadvantage of making the machines before the tools are completed', they saw prospective profit evaporating.[4]

Willcox then offered to order a further thousand machines, if only Brown & Sharpe could produce some. A tense meeting in New York saw the contract extended rather than curtailed, and two weeks later the first completed machines were entering testing. Sharpe was disappointed that 'it takes our best men to put them up. Being the first that have been made they go together with more difficulty than the others will hereafter.' While this remark indicates that some fitting was still necessary, Sharpe's confidence was soon borne out. A comparison of the Brown & Sharpe's shop with that of Singer offers a classic example of the difference between engineering for assembly and filing to fit. (Hounshell 1984) The difference in manufacturing methods was also evident in the machines. (Figure 16.1) The Willcox and Gibbs Sewing Machine was soon being offered for sale at $30, with table and treadle, where Singer's normal price was $100 ($50 for wives of ministers or with a trade-in). Brown & Sharpe boasted in an advertisement from painful experience:

> It will be observed that no pains or expense has been spared by the Manufacturer in the making of these machines, as the workmanship will compare with the highest priced Sewing machines. Further, as they have been made with all parts *interchangeable,* they are readily replaced.

Figure 16.1. Assembly of sewing-machines in 1867 at Brown and Sharpe, Providence, Rhode Island. Browne and Sharpe Historical Collection.

The judges of the Fair of the Franklin Institute in Philadelphia also welcomed the new competitor 'as nearer to the requirements of a Family Machine, than any other'.[5]

Willcox had realized his aim of establishing an own-brand sewing machine which could compete successfully with those of the pioneering firms, in little more than a year. This was achieved by harnessing the new volume precision manufacturing technology to a product designed to be delivered to domestic consumers through extensive channels of distribution, in ways which were to be widely imitated. But Willcox and Gibbs's route was not the only one by which the sewing machine industry evolved towards mass production and consumption. Although Willcox's hardware business provided an excellent platform from which to enter the industry at this time, firms such as Singer which laboriously built their own distribution network could emerge in a stronger position to associate their machine with the distribution of dress-maker's paper patterns and other support for the culture of home. (Brandon 1977: 111–37; Godfrey 1982: 83–110) Although in the late 1850s the adoption of assembly with interchangeable parts offered significant advantages for those who took the plunge, these were not overwhelming and tended to diminish as the techniques of precision manufacture became more widely diffused. If Singer was unable to produce a competitive lower-cost home machine, they devised marketing techniques which admirably exploited their prestige, size and price. Singer & Co.'s eventual domination of the industry, as much as Willcox & Gibb's successful sudden entry into it, support Chandler's argument that the effective exploitation of mass production technology depended on the organisation of mass distribution and consumption.

From Technical Possibility to Market Opportunity

Throughout the sewing machine story, there is a need to pay greater attention to how market opportunities were perceived and approached. Brandon follows the explanatory pattern found in conventional histories of technology, in which invention, understood as the exploration of technological possibility, is followed by production and distribution. Within the sort of history of technology produced a century ago by the first generation of professional engineers, the sewing machine was a by-product of the elaboration of an 'American System of Manufacture', as it was the first civil product made with armoury methods and a number of the early gun-makers turned to sewing machines to replace small-arms orders after the Civil War. We now recognize that this idea of an 'American System' conflates the elaboration of a system for gauge-based and substantially mechanized manufacture of sets of components for assembly (as pursued in the US armouries) with a looser form of standardization which employed jigs, templates and semi-automatic mechanisms to relieve bottlenecks, e.g. in watch and clock making. (Hounshell 1984; Putnam 1986) The sewing machine did not emerge from the diffusion of interchangeable parts technology from the armouries. The early inventors and manufacturers did not come from within the armoury culture. (Godfrey 1982: 17–45) However, the socialization of contractors' innovation pursued by US Ordnance helped establish a technical culture favourable to the use of jigs and fixtures in the US northeast and accelerated the development and diffusion of machine tools, such as the milling machine. The contribution of the armouries to standardized manufacturing technique may still be over-estimated. *Pace* Hounshell, Brown & Sharpe's records indicate that its capacity for interchangeable manufacture developed quite independently of the armouries.

Thus, it could be said that the evolution of manufacturing technique removed a constraint on the ability to produce marketable sewing machines. As refinements in tooling and machine-shop practice became more widespread in the 1840s, small batch production costs for small mechanisms could have fallen by as much as half between the period of Howe's attempts in the mid-1840s and those of Singer and his contemporaries five years later. While this difference was significant enough to open new potential markets, it does not appear that those who made the breakthrough circa 1850 were motivated by a desire to realize a new manufacturing potential. Once competing machines were in production, product simplifications and techniques to realize economies of scale received due attention and unit costs were halved again during the decade. Aspects of gauge-based or interchangeable parts technology were adopted by certain makers during the 1850s as part of this process and for what they offered in smooth running and ease of repair. However, the spread of full standard parts for assembly systems throughout the industry depended on the demonstration of its potential and confirmation of the existence of a mass market for sewing machines and the means of reaching it. Only gradually did sewing machine making provide a field for the elaboration of a technical culture of mass production. (Godfrey 1982: 46–68; Brandon 1977: 41–52, 61–6; Cooper 1976)

If the mechanization of sewing was neither occasioned by, nor the occasion for, major innovations in mechanical engineering or manufacturing strategies, the history of technology can contribute little to explaining why viable machines for sewing appeared suddenly in 1850, or why the growth of the industry was not assured until near the end of the decade. More light can be thrown on these questions by examining how the potential market for sewing machines was perceived and actualized, focusing on the particular qualities of work which they were designed to carry out or replace. Although the early inventors had focused on specialized applications in tailoring or corsetry, sewing was predominantly women's work and work which, despite commercialization, continued to be embedded in the culture transmitted in the home between generations of women; consequently, the mechanization of sewing led ineluctably from workshop niche to a universal appliance. In a further transformation crucial for the new regime of mass production and consumption, the gendering of the sewing machine led to the idea of producing and distributing for home use versions of what had been initially conceived of as a capital good. It was around the notion of the sewing machine as a consumer durable that the industry 'took off' in the US and, with the associated trade in dressmakers' paper patterns, established a new culture of home sewing, linking precision mass production and the channelling of desires, efforts and purchases.

How Sewing Machines Became Peculiarly Suited to Women

What later became known as the sewing machine was only one of many machines for sewing. The difficulties of the early inventors in breaking away from the replication of motions in hand-sewing were compounded by the fact that, in common with most contemporary efforts at process mechanization, their attention was focused on particular niche applications, either in the tailoring trade or in cap- or corset-making. A crucial stage in which it begins to become possible to talk of innovation was the development of a flexible replacement for a range of human sewing actions. This breakthrough depended on recognizing the rapidly growing and changing nature of commercial sewing, for which women's sweated skill was the predominant source of labour. The result was immediately acclaimed as peculiarly suitable to women, although none of the inventors had explicitly set out to design a machine especially for female operatives. Thus, in an unforeseen way, the sewing machine became gendered, claimed by women as their own.

To understand how this came about we are led to examine the distinctive character of the market for sewing and the perceptions of it which influenced inventors and investors in the early projects. Machines for sewing were introduced precisely in a context where household sewing (usually by women) was virtually ubiquitous, but challenged in the urban USA and UK by the expansion of commercial tailoring and dressmaking, both bespoke and ready-to-wear, involving employed or more usually subcontracted, sweated labour. Behind the growth of employment in sewing was the entry of a larger proportion of the population into the wearing of newly made costumes according to current fashion – a development which although abundantly evidenced, has yet to be properly measured or analyzed. Enabling this were changes in per capita income and the distribution of income affecting the middle strata and the cheapening of the costs of textiles, which made possible a wider access to new costume and other sewn goods. Along with a gradual easing of economic constraint there was also an intensified interest on the part of certain social groups in relating themselves to fashion and thus changing their patterns of expenditure. Such dynamic and fashion-oriented consumption may be seen as a response to the insecurity and polarization which accompanied profound and rapid socio-economic change and as an investment in establishing new interpersonal relations through the creation of status. (Sennett 1977; Wilson 1985; Davidoff and Hall 1987; Halttunen 1982; Stansell 1983; Brandon 1977: 67–9; John 1986; Godley 1996; Tilley and Scott 1989)

Thus the growth in commercialized sewing work inextricably linked qualitative changes in the design of what was sewn with the dominant processes of design innovation and transmission. This extension of the social reach of fashion tended to draw sewing out of the home. Most forms of sewing (women's sewing in particular) had been historically taught and practised in the home or domestic workshops. The intergenerational trans-mission of techniques was bound up with the making of culturally recognized model goods. The design for these, while it might incorporate fashionable or extraneous motifs, worked within a family – and community – centred tradition. Fashion and its associated social change interacted with these vernacular processes, affecting the parameters of such sewn objects as trousseau goods, those connected to coming-of-age ceremonies, or items whereby proficiency was demonstrated and relationships commemorated. There was a spread of comments revealing increased awareness of fashionable currency or sensitivity to correct detail. These mark the moving of certain design processes outside the home, and where design went, work might be expected to follow. At the same time, sewing skill continued to be reproduced within families as part of learning how to be a woman. Cost continued to limit the purchase of commercial sewing, if to a lessening extent, and both copying and the use of dressmakers' paper patterns helped bridge this gap between taste and tradition.

It was into this stream that the various attempts at mechanizing sewing were launched. The inventors of early machines for sewing typically thought of particular workshop sewing operations, but because of the growing pool of highly flexible skilled seamstresses and the rapidly changing design content of sewn work, they realized that sewing work was not going to follow the usual pattern of incremental specialized mechanization. A machine capable of being worked by anyone, and turned to any kind of work, was required. The relatively small number of improvements made over Howe's machine by the innovators of 1850 – a table, fabric-feed mechanism and presser foot – focused on this flexibility of use. The universality of vision behind the new machines is also evident in their modes of distribution. So long as the would-be innovators saw themselves as selling a new kind of machine to employers, they faced huge problems in finding potential clients. The segmented organization of the trade and the lack of knowledge of it by machine agents didn't help. But the pioneering makers of the early 1850s envisaged a universal market. They addressed this through general advertisement and publicity, by public demonstration (in a variety of contexts and using both female and male operatives) and competition, followed by the opening of offices which were akin to shops. This wider public address not only opened wider channels of communication, it also underpinned the credibility of the invention as well as the maker and by inviting clients to be self-selecting it obviated much of the cost of trying to find the appropriate clients in a dispersed trade. The new prototype was thus inextricably linked with new modes of distribution for invention. (Brandon 1977: 34–64; Godfrey 1982: 22–60)

Through this wider address makers rapidly gained important feedback about their invention. Published comment, overwhelmingly male, both from those engaged in the trade and more generally, was ambivalent about the usefulness of the new machine in the given division of sewing labour, though respectful about its potential as a labour-saving device. Elite labour (predominantly male) need not be cheapened and non-elite sewing (over-whelmingly female) was cheap enough already. Compared to Howe's lack of success in the 1840s, this was progress, but hardly an impressive breakthrough, given the generally favourable climate for mechanization in the American northeast, and the relatively lower degree of specialization among firms making sewn products there as compared to the UK. But the machine was warmly welcomed by women. As the least organized labour force, earning by piecework, sweated seamstresses could readily recognize its labour-saving potential. The desire of women to have the machine quickly became a factor to be reckoned with, even if relatively few women had themselves the means to acquire it. The practice of hire purchase of machines by outworkers was revived to address this contradiction and extended along with other new marketing techniques to address the home market in ways which were to prove of far reaching significance. Throughout this critical conjuncture, it was women's interest which ensured that the sewing machine did not, once more, pass into eclipse. (Brandon 1977: 51, 57, 61–7)

This allows a different way of reading the statements that the sewing machine was peculiarly suited to female use. Rather than a capitalist calculation these may be seen as women welcoming something which they never thought would be made for them. The skill-base of sewing (outside men's tailoring) had its fount in the making of sewn things for family use. Thus the non-acquisition of the new machine was perceived as a disadvantage not only in a commercial context and in a labour-saving sense but as a disqualification. In claiming the sewing machine as their own, women brought it into the home environment which was their school for intergenerational transmission of technique. These were not only women who first experienced the machine in a workshop and adopted it for domestic sewing but also those who wanted to teach their daughters to sew well, not only because it was a possible way to earn, but because it was essential to the care of the family and part of a complex of creative skill. In so doing, they confounded the usual pattern of mechanization at the time where it was associated with a regendering of work from female to male.

A Machine in the Home

Through their emporia, the embryonic sewing machine makers began to notice machines bought for home use. The possibility of making sewing machines for domestic use had always existed because they could be hand-powered and be produced in small and inexpensive forms. Type-forms for the home market had however not been pursued in the earlier phases of development. As the sewing machine became more affordable, it became an item of aspiration for those women who made a living by taking in sewing at home. Machines bought principally for family use (e.g. by men for use by female relatives) introduced new relations of consumption. It was in the home that the sewing machine's labour-saving potential could be best and most directly recognized unobscured by craft opposition or the cheapening effects of sweating. But the focus on family-oriented sewing made the sewing machine as important for conspicuous productive consumption as for its economic productivity. This is not to deny its labour-saving role, which was perhaps more evident in the home than in the commercial sphere, but to say that it also became involved in an exchange of gifts as well as an exchange of labour. (Brandon 1977: 124–39; Cooper 1976; Godfrey 1982: 83–110; Godley 1996; McMurry 1988: 96–7)

Possession of a sewing machine could help maintain a culture of sewing in the home, with all that implied for the transmission of gendered identity and skill. The sewing machine was introduced precisely at a point where the culture of home sewing was being eroded by commercialization and the ideology of separating home from work. The early inventors assumed that their machines would complete a process by which sewing would be industrialized like other aspects of work and skills taken out of homes and into the industry. But they failed to reckon with the forces which produced the intergenerational transmission of gendered and classed positions, not only those roles and performances sanctioned by tradition but new forces produced by their encounter with the combined effects of commercial and industrial change. These tended to increase the cultural separation between social groups and mapped this onto signs of culture as distinct from industry, marking out the higher-status home as something distinct from a place of work and from the public realm generally. (Davidoff and Hall 1987; McMurry 1988) This polarization rendered the tensions between the control of design and the location of sewing work more antagonistic and posed a new dilemma – if sewing was to remain a respectable woman's accomplishment, means had to be found to secure its exercise in the home in these new conditions.

Thus, when sewing machine makers perceived that their machines might be used in a domestic context they attempted to respond by producing machines specially suited to home use. This was not simply a matter of producing simpler, lighter or cheaper variants, although there was experiment on a broad front, ranging from very light, palm-sized chain-stitch machines through to cut-down versions of industrial lock-stitch prototypes employing two threads at a range of weights and costs. In part these designs diversified the universal model to accommodate different kinds of sewing work and different roles in producing sewn goods. But the 'home' or, as the Franklin Institute would have it, 'family machine' was also designed and presented to be culturally acceptable in an environment which had been redefined to exclude 'work'. Thus, to competition between makers on grounds of price, mechanical refinement, features or durability, was added the decoration and disguise necessary to accord with contemporary norms of comfort and convenience, with well-known results.

With hindsight we can see that, at the point where the home became less of a place of industry, it began to be populated with machines. This does not necessarily imply a diminution of household work. (Cowan 1983; McMurry 1988) In so 'cross-dressing' the sewing machine, its makers were pioneering techniques for design and marketing which were to be elaborated in conjunction with future generations of consumer durables. But what they were trying to achieve through these forms and terms, the making of a domestic or family machine, was not a simple and straightforward matter. The cultural position of home sewing had become more complex and in some ways contradictory. The very success of women in maintaining their pervasive presence in sewing, wherever and however it was conducted, ensured that the sewing machine entered the home like a little Trojan horse loaded with wider contradictions which had to be disarmed. The most sensitive of these, on the face of it, was the way the machine's presence connected the priceless labour of family sewing with the cheap and degraded labour of the sweat shop. Hence the rewards for those, like Singer, which paid particular attention to status in marketing and pricing, as well as those who invested in elaborating the software of the culture of home sewing such as dressmakers' paper patterns. At the same time, given the stratification of incomes and tastes, there was room for those, like Willcox & Gibbs (and later, Henry Ford), who designed a quality volume product to a price.

In entering a phase of expansion centred on the home market, these were factors the industry had to take into account. To put their creative achievement in a less teleological perspective, we need to discover more about how their efforts interacted with those of contemporary consumers. To discover, for example, the different routes by which differently constructed and presented models of sewing machine actually entered homes of the period, in different places, would place the promotional efforts of manufacturers in a different perspective. To discover the reasons why sewing particular kinds of fashionable goods was taken up (and when they were to be made up at home rather than made up by a paid seamstress) would help us understand the interaction between cosmopolitanism and the domestic, between taste and observed tradition. We know from more recent history that activity of this kind is associated with particular complexes of cultural change, economic constraint and social ambition. Simple rationales, such as saving money, cannot be taken at face value for practices which regulate such complex cultural material: a consumption which is also a making, not only of artefacts, but of lives.

Acknowledgements

I am very grateful to the Brown and Sharpe Manufacturing Company and the American Precision Museum, Vermont, who have assisted this project by allowing access to their archival materials, to the UK Department of Education and Science and the School of History and Politics of Middlesex University, which have supported the research, and to the graduate students and colleagues at Middlesex and colleagues at the Ironbridge Institute, Winchester School of Art (University of Southampton), and University of Portsmouth whose comments have helped articulate the argument.

Notes

1. For evidence of the emergence of an illegitimate generic machine, see Sewing-Machine Collection and Lamson, Goodnow and Co. order book, American Precision Museum, Vermont.

2. This account of the development of the Willcox and Gibbs machine is based on Putnam (1986: 110–18), which draws on Brown and Sharpe's correspondence with James Willcox and Brown & Sharpe Historical Collection, Brown and Sharpe Manufacturing Company, North Kingsdown, Rhode Island.

3. Letter to from Brown and Sharpe to William Angell, 11 March 1858 and from James Willcox to Brown and Sharpe, 16 February 1858, (Brown and Sharpe Sewing Machine,) Brown and Sharpe Historical Collection.

4. Letters from Brown and Sharpe to James Willcox, 21 July, 24 August, 21 September and 6 November 1858, (Brown and Sharpe Sewing Machine,) Brown and Sharpe Historical Collection.

5. These comments were quoted in an advertisement which appeared in *The American Machinist*, Vol. 1, No. 1, following competitive evaluation of machines exhibited at the Centennial Exposition held in Philadelphia in 1876.

References

Brandon, R. (1977), *A Capitalist Romance: Singer and the Sewing-Machine*, Philadelphia: J.C. Lippincott.

Chandler, A. (1977), *The Visible Hand: The Managerial Revolution in American Business*, Cambridge: Harvard University Press.

Cooper, G. R. (1976), *The Sewing-Machine, Its Invention and Development*, Washington, DC: Smithsonian Institute Press.

Cowan, R. S. (1983), *More Work for Mother: The Ironies of Household Technology, from the Open Hearth to the Microwave*, New York: Basic Books Inc.

Davidoff, L. and Hall, C. (1987), *Family Fortunes: Men and Women of the English Middle Class, 1780–1850*, London: Routledge.

Davies, R. B. (1976), *Peacefully Working to Conquer the World: Singer Sewing Machines in Foreign Markets 1854–1920*, New York: Arno Press.

Godfrey, F. P. (1982), *An International History of the Sewing Machine*, London: Robert Hale.

Godley, A. (1996), 'Singer in Britain: the diffusion of sewing machine technology and its impact on the clothing industry in the UK 1860–1905' in *Textile History*, 27, 1.

Halttunen, K. (1982), *Confidence Men and Painted Women: a Study of Middle Class Culture in America, 1830–70*, New Haven: Yale University Press.

Hounshell, D. (1984), *From the American System to Mass Production*, Baltimore: The Johns Hopkins University Press.

Jewell, F. B. (1975), *Veteran Sewing Machines: a collector's guide,* Newton Abbot: David and Charles.

John, A., ed. (1986), *Unequal Opportunities: Women's Employment in England 1800–1918*, Oxford: Oxford University Press.

McMurry, S. (1988), *Families and Farmhouses in Nineteenth Century America: Vernacular Design and Social Change*, New York: Oxford University Press.

Putnam, T. J. (1986), 'American Toolmakers and the Origins of Standardised Manufacture', M.A. dissertation, Industrial Archaeology, University of Birmingham.

Sennett, R. (1977), *The Fall of Public Man,* New York: Alfred A. Knopf Inc.

Stansell, C. (1983), 'The Origins of the Sweatshop: Women and Early Industrialization in New York City' in M.H. Frisch and D. Walkowitz, ed. *Working Class America: Essays on Labour, Community and American Society*, Illinois: Urbana.

Tilly, L. A. and Scott, J. W. (1989), *Women, Work and Family,* London: Routledge.

Wilson, E. (1985), *Adorned in Dreams: Fashion and Modernity*, London: Virago.

17

A Beautiful Ornament in the Parlour or Boudoir: The Domestication of the Sewing Machine

Nicholas Oddy

This chapter sets out to explore the visual appearance of the domestic sewing machine from its introduction in the 1850s until the present, with a special focus on the second half of the nineteenth century. During that time the type of machine characterized by the Singer 'New Family' was established as the dominant pattern. This chapter centres on the development of type-forms and on the machine in a context, not only its place in the home, but also in relation to other consumer goods which share common features. Its object of study, the sewing machine, is approached from a non-technological stance in order to provide a somewhat different overview from that which has characterized much of the literature to date. Histories of sewing machine makes or technology have already been written. (Cooper 1968; Duncan 1977)

The sewing machine industry, though rooted in the United States, was quick to become international with the great American makers exporting to Britain and other European nations, often from the start of business. This soon encouraged the setting up of sewing machine factories in Europe, particularly once the market was firmly established in the late 1850s. To reflect this characteristic of the industry, this chapter is not specific to the US, Britain, or other industrially-developed nations. It makes the point that the problems which beset designers and manufacturers were ones which were met on an international basis.

A consideration of published sources available to the researcher in the topic shows that sewing machines have attracted considerable commentary at various times. In the early stages of the machines' development, their novelty, cleverness and potential usefulness provided copy for comments on exhibits at expositions. Sewing machines were exhibited at the Great Exhibition of 1851 in London and at almost every major exhibition of manufactures thereafter. The many manufacturers of sewing machines have left a huge repertoire of trade literature, from advertisements in magazines and newspapers to the in-house journals of companies such as Singer in the twentieth century.[1] A further primary source for research are the numerous user manuals, many put out by the large manufacturers, but increasingly through the twentieth century also written by specialist authors discussing particular applications for machines such as embroidery or patchwork. (Picken 1954; Clucas 1973; Hall 1980; Osler 1980)

Since the 1960s the machine has enjoyed a steadily expanding output of secondary literature. The bulk of this is aimed at collectors and generally provides detailed listings of the output of manufacturers, often prefaced by a general history of the development of the machine itself – almost invariably from a technological standpoint. (Bays 1993: Jewell 1985; Landgraff c. 1990; Thomas 1995) The manufacturers themselves have also attracted the attention of biographers and economic historians. Ruth Brandon's *Singer and the Sewing Machine: A Capitalist Romance* (1977) is perhaps the best known of these.

We can see that the aesthetic of the machine is more or less disregarded by this literature. The sewing machine is seen as part of the world of technology. Even the collectors, who are evidently willing to pay highly for the extremely decorative machines, seem to be approaching their subject from the point of view of classification in terms of maker and model number, then the technology and, finally, the appearance. In Britain (at least) the sewing machine is to be found in the Science Museum and not the Victoria and Albert Museum.[2]

In the publications on the history of design is to be found the exception to this. Adrian Forty's *Objects of Desire* (1986) provides an important, if brief, study of the aesthetic development of the sewing machine in the context of the middle-class home. In this, Forty considers the problems besetting manufacturers' attempts to popularize the sewing machine beyond the sphere of industrial applications and it is here that I intend to focus my own discussion. Forty points out that the sewing machine had been successfully sold to industrial concerns since the early 1850s. In this he is referring to a machine which we would recognize as a modern sewing machine; there had been many pre-1850 attempts at producing machines, some of which seem to have been mechanically successful but for various reasons had not been widely adopted. The obstacles facing early inventors seem to have been the usual ones of lack of capital and enthusiasm from potential markets coupled with more specific problems. One of the most successful designers, Barthelemy Thimonier, had his machine smashed by Luddite actions of hand-sewers and later fell foul of the French Revolution of 1848. (Jewell 1985: 15–168) Most of these early inventors worked in Europe where industrial working practices were well developed and possibly offered more opposition than the USA. It was eventually in the United States that the modern sewing machine was successfully developed and sold.

As with the European designers, the Americans at first aimed their products at the industrial market, but it was soon realized that this was not extensive enough to provide a firm future for the industry. Isaac Singer, who had produced his first commercial machines in 1850, was particularly aware of the potential of the domestic market and was aided in his attempts to exploit it by his partner the lawyer Edward Clark. (Brandon 1977: 81) Singer and Clark's first response was to address the problem of cost.

Machines in the early to mid 1850s were expensive. Commenting on 'The Sewing Machine' on 5 November 1854 the British *Illustrated Magazine of Art* said:

> Immense numbers of the sewing machines are disposed of every week to tailors, clothiers, hosiers, sail-makers etc., and some to private families. The price, £30, will, of course, for the present, place it out of the reach of most of the latter; but that it will one day be an essential article of furniture in every well regulated household we have no doubt.

How 'immense' such sales were is a matter of judgement. The number of machines produced by all the major American manufacturers put together in 1853 was little greater than 2,500. However, even here the message is clear, the machine could be an essential article in every 'well regulated household' so long as it was made less costly.[3] Clark's response was to devise a hire purchase scheme – the first ever – introduced for 1856. A $5 deposit was followed by $3.50 per month 'rent'. Sales from 1853–55 had been somewhere about 850 machines a year; in 1856, after the scheme was introduced, this figure increased to over 2,500. Clark's next innovation was a part-exchange scheme by which old machines could be traded in for $50 against the price of a new one – this increased sales by an extra 40 per cent. (Brandon 1977: 115–120) Singer and Clark's manoeuvrings, although successful sales ploys, still seem to have not been enough. This was in spite of their being further supported by the Sewing machine Combination agreement of 1856 in which the major patent holders pooled their patents and agreed a table of royalties payable for each machine sold either by any of the patent holders, or those under licence. (Jewell 1985: 29–30) The fact that sales were still unsatisfactory is suggested by the reaction of makers such as Singer to Willcox and Gibbs entry into the market in 1857. Gibbs had set out to design a machine which was not only simpler and cheaper than those of his rivals, but, importantly, would be visibly more of a domestic machine by being petite by comparison. (Jewell 1985: 30–2; Forty 1986: 96)

Is it coincidence that Singer introduced their 'Family' machine in 1858, which was small with an exaggeratedly light head? Forty cites Singer's own brochure for the machine:

> A few months since, we came to the conclusion that the public taste demanded a sewing machine for family purposes more exclusively; a machine of smaller size, and of lighter and more elegant form; a machine decorated in the best style of art; so as to make a beautiful ornament in the parlour or boudoir [. . .] (Forty 1986: 98–9)

Forty argues that in some way it had to look non-industrial to sell and this was the key element to the development of the aesthetic of the domestic sewing machine. Yet is this actually the case? Singer's 'Family' machine was not a success; it was only made until 1861. It was superseded by the 'Transverse Shuttle Letter A' introduced in 1859 which sold far better, and yet this is a much heavier and more substantial machine.[4] It is perhaps a mistake, too, to focus on Singer alone – something which their later domination of the market leads us to do. Forty mentions that Wheeler and Wilson, another major manufacturer, had deliberately designed their machines to be 'domestic' in the early 1850s. However, their sales were not to any great degree better than Singer's until, paradoxically, 1858, when they outstripped them by 100 per cent and contrived a substantial lead well into the 1860s.[5] Willcox and Gibbs' much cheaper small and simple chain-stitch machine seems to sell evenly from its introduction through the 1850s, but never outstripped either Singer or Wheeler and Wilson even in 1857 and 1858 and lagged well behind thereafter. Its price of $50 at the time of its introduction, half that of its rivals, might well account for its success as much as its other attributes.[6]

It would seem to be a mistake, therefore, to overestimate the importance of the 'style' of the machine to its success in the domestic sphere. Whilst it is clear that most manufacturers realized the limitations of the industrial market in the early 1850s and set out to exploit the potential domestic market, their most successful means of so doing were probably more to be found in pricing, reliability and particularly market awareness than any major redesign of the machine around some idea of aesthetic acceptability in the home. Interestingly,

Forty concludes by looking at what collectors now call 'figural' machines. Generally designed in the late 1850s, these machines were clearly aimed to be at least as ornamental as they were useful, being cast in the form of animals or figures. They strongly support the idea that the aesthetic of the machine was of crucial importance at this time. Yet this has to be balanced by the fact that all these machines are extremely rare. There are only a handful of designs and some of these, including the 'Squirrel' machine illustrated by Forty, may have never got beyond the patent office. (Forty 1996: 98)[7] To collectors the sculpted qualities and the rarity of these machines invest them with the aura of a holy grail and they are therefore given prominence in many publications, with the result that their importance in design terms tends to be exaggerated; they were, and are, no more than amusing novelties.[8]

While the aesthetic appearance of the domestic sewing machine in its early years might not be reacting as vigorously to its industrial counterparts as Forty suggests, there is no doubt of the machine's awkwardness in the context of the affluent middle-class home. Both as a machine and as an object it was without precedent and it had no obvious applications. In terms of design there had been machines produced for the drawing room, but of a very different nature. The brass and mahogany of equipment for demonstrations of scientific principles was generally demountable and only brought out for an evening's entertainment; automata did not reveal their mechanisms and were purely ornamental; the clock or timepiece carried with it social status and while its 'function' was clear, its meaning was ambiguous. Of course, there was no shortage of domestic machinery intended for the kitchen quarters and one might at first think that the sewing machine should be destined there; but, as manufacturers realized, this was not actually the case. The sewing machine was essentially a hemming and seaming machine, and few households employed a servant to carry out these tasks. Seamstresses were generally freelance who had work 'put out' to them, or were employed on an *ad-hoc* day-to-day basis. What needlework which was required of household servants was probably perceived as not significant enough to merit the purchase of such a costly tool and therefore the sewing machine had to be aimed at 'above stairs' users, who perhaps might employ it to finish panels of hand embroidery, for example, But there were obvious problems. The chief of these was to break into an established system. It was not so much the appearance of the machine which was against its adoption, it was its uselessness to the person who had £30 or $125 to spend. It was essential for manufacturers to bring the machine within the reach of those people who either, for one reason or another, would find it very advantageous not to have to employ a seamstress, or who did large amounts of hemming and seaming themselves, while the machine itself had to be proven to be reliable.

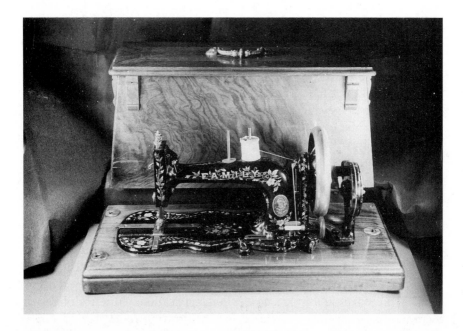

Figure 17.1. Kimball and Morton 'Family' portable sewing machine No. 75806.

This places cost and mechanism as the key elements in the 1850s domestic adoption of the machine. Once in the home, the machine's usefulness would compensate for any perceived ugliness or inappropriateness. Luckily for sewing machine makers, the crucial moment came in 1858 with the combination of by then established sales practices of hire purchase and part-exchange, far cheaper machines and clearly established and presumably reliable marques. Between 1858 and 1859 production of both Singer and Wheeler and Wilson machines trebled.[9] In fact one could argue that the buoyancy in the market allowed Singer to carry their less than successful 'Family' machine, which had been designed with more of an eye to lightness and 'the best style of art' than to reliability and price.

This is not to say that sewing machine manufacturers had ignored the aesthetic appearance of their products until Singer's 'Family' machine came on to the market, but rather it illustrates that the significance of such detail was subsidiary to price and mechanism. Even the earliest machines had been given a considerable amount of decorative attention. For instance, the earliest surviving Singer machine similar to the patent model is elaborately lined with the head relieved by painted leaf and scroll work, while the No. 1 machine at Clydebank Museum has the spokes of its flywheel formed of neo-rococo scrollwork.[10] At this period it was common practice for delicate and precision industrial equipment to be ornamented, so such detail is unsurprising, but it does suggest that the appearance of the domestic machine has a direct lineage to the industrial versions, rather than adopting any radically different approach.

In fact, the sewing machine's general appearance, particularly in terms of finish, was to remain fairly constant until the mid twentieth century. From the early 1850s by far the majority of machines were finished in black 'Japan' enamel, more or less ornamented with gold and sometimes colour, with bright

RECENT SCIENTIFIC IMPROVEMENTS.

Mistress. " You needn't be so frightened, Maria. It's only the Phonograph."
Maria. " Lor', Mum! I thought it was a Sewing-Machine. And I only just touched the Handle, and it spoke just like the very Moral of Master ! "

Figure 17.2. *Punch* cartoon of 6 April 1878. Although satirical, this cartoon draws attention to the sewing machine's importance in setting the pattern for the look of subsequent 'machines for the drawing room.'

metal working surfaces. Black Japan was a stove enamel, which could be applied by brush, spray or most commonly dipping, in a number of thin coats. The earlier finishes tend to be more paint-like and softer than those of the late nineteenth-century when the process had been brought to a perfection which has never been bettered; but even in its earliest guise it was resilient and lustrous, it took hand-finishing with gold and coloured enamels and also transfer applications very well and could be finished with clear lacquers which were also stoved. The effectiveness of this mode of finishing is reflected in the fact that very few makers ever attempted to deviate from it into coloured enamels, for example. It remained the standard until the introduction of plastic housings in the 1950s. In the domestic context of the late 1850s there is a clear precedent in lacquered papier mâché which was then fashionable for light furniture, trays, writing boxes and other occasional objects found in middle-class drawing rooms, parlours and boudoirs. This too was usually finished in black relieved with gold and colour, indeed many of the ornamental details are almost identical, even to the eventual use of mother-of-pearl inlay, often used in lacquer work, on some late nineteenth-century machines. (Figure 17.1)

It is important to observe here that collectors and historians have focused on the machine itself, but this is very limiting as the machine generally came in two guises. The first was the portable, hand-operated model. Here the machine was stored in a case and brought out for use as necessary. The second was the treadle-operated model which came complete with its own table. Here the machine was part of a permanently-sited piece of furniture. In each case the machine would be similar, but clearly its general prominence would be very different. In the first instance the machine's aesthetic was ostensibly less important, as the machine would only be brought out when actually in use; in the second the machine was only a component in an overall ensemble. If Forty's reasoning is to be followed then one might expect to see treadle machines dominated by 'cabinet' types which, when not in use, are entirely contained within a piece of furniture which could be fashioned to look identical to any other piece of domestic furniture. Yet even in the 1850s and early 1860s most machines seem to have been supplied on a cast-iron stand with a plain polished wood tabletop on which the machine was mounted. In many cases the machine would have a case to protect it when not in use, but this would hardly compensate for the stand which generally had no attempt made to hide its treadle mechanism, while its use of cast iron was more akin to hall or conservatory furniture than parlour or boudoir. This is further evidence, if any be needed, that as a rule there was rarely any need to disguise or conceal a sewing machine to make it an acceptable feature in the home.

The treadle stands offered real opportunities for elaborate decoration: they were generally in the form of two finely cast-iron pilasters separated by an X stretcher and/or rods. Slung between the two pilasters would also be the foot treadle plate, or slippers – also finely cast – and the flywheel, which offered further scope for cast decorative detail. Through the nineteenth century variations on neo-rococo formed the favoured treatment for the ironwork, which lent itself to the C and S scrolling of the style. Earlier stands were anonymous, but such was the popularity of the machines that from the 1870s it became common for the ironwork to incorporate prominent makers' names and trademarks, seemingly without much market resistance. The stands, though not nearly as highly finished as the machines, were normally also black-enamelled with gold highlighting.

In comparison to the stands, the forms of many of the machines by the larger manufacturers were relatively simple. Singer's machines, which came to dominate the market after the 1860s, had never been elaborately sculpted, and the 'New Family' of 1865 was of the same basic shape and form which became the standard pattern of the sewing machine of the early twentieth century. What these machines lacked in cast decoration was made up in the painted or transferred ornament applied.

The machines which did indulge in cast ornament again favoured the neo-rococo. A whole genre of machines, particularly miniature versions, had their arms formed of open scrollwork; bases of portable machines also offered opportunities for elaborate skirting and feet. Another popular decorative form in the 1860s and 1870s, again particularly for miniatures, was that of the 'pillar'. American 'paw foot' machines (those with lion paw feet) are commonly of this type where a rococo arm is supported by an architectonic column, often in the form similar to that we now associate with American fire hydrants. This type of arrangement is particularly associated with Shaw and Clark whose early 'pillar' machines exhibit a rare instance of 'Gothick' detailing – the pillar being a four-sided 'Gothick' arched pavilion crowned by an over-sized neo-classical urn, more reminiscent of the 1800s than the 1860s.[11] While rococo was undoubtedly the dominant decorative form, it was, of course, not the only one in a period of widespread eclecticism in decoration.

An observation which can be made here is that the smaller the machine, the more cast ornament it was likely to receive. It is notable that most of the 'figural' machines are miniatures and not full size. Carter Bays suggests this might be because such machines were often less than reliable and made up for the deficiency in their mechanisms with attention to their appearance. (Bays 1993) I would suggest that miniature machines were only designed for the very lightest of use and that their function was that of being little more than a toy and their ornamental qualities were proportionately more important. Their success was possibly built on the fact that nicely-finished, working miniature objects are attractive to many purchasers who might not consider the full-size equivalent. In empirical terms even today they tend to appeal to a broader audience than their full-size brethren.[12]

While the machines of the 1850s to 1880s might have displayed extensive variations in terms of both cast decoration and mechanical arrangement, they were of course very similar in finish. As the century progressed increasing stabilization of form was also to be found, with the number of machines displaying cast ornamentation diminishing in favour of the simpler forms carrying elaborate painted or transferred decoration favoured by the big makers, such as Singer, although treadle stands remained elaborately cast. 'By 1890 the overall features of [American] sewing machines for home use had pretty much stabilized – with few exceptions all machines looked just about alike, save for their cabinets.' (Bays 1993: 29) Meanwhile, in the European market, 'the configuration of sewing machine mechanisms had been set by the early years of this century and everyone knew what a sewing machine should look like. Any Edwardian child asked to draw a sewing machine would have produced a shape resembling a Singer or a Frister & Rossmann'. (Jewell 1985: 37)[13]

This stabilization of design was due largely to consolidation within the sewing machine industry which favoured the large-scale makers. Although sales were generally sound through the late nineteenth century, many of the smaller makers found that they were uncompetitive, possibly by just being too small, or by producing less than effective machines. The larger makers all employed developed production line manufacture using standardized parts and had extensive dealer and maintenance networks which only heavy capitalization could provide. It has been noted that America had 124 makers in 1880 and that in spite of sales increasing during the following twenty years, in 1890 the number of makers had dropped to sixty-six and to only about twelve in the early years of the twentieth century. (Bays 1993: 21; Jewell 1985: 32)

I have focused on the early period of sewing machine design in order to question whether the machine's aesthetic was in any way compromised by its intended market in the way that Forty suggests. My own conclusion is that in fact the opposite was true: even in the late 1850s sewing machines had established their own particular design form, a sewing machine aesthetic which was unique, although linked to other domestic and industrial design forms. Indeed the machine became the pattern on which other products would be based.

Most obvious of these were bicycles and tricycles and typewriters, but the list could be expanded to cover a large number of other mechanical items which made their way into the domestic environment such as phonographs and telephones. (Figure 17.2) An obvious reason here was that sewing machine manufacturers were often involved in the manufacture of new products such as these.[14] (Jewell 1985: 65, 66, 110; Post 1981) Many sewing machine makers met with little or short-lived success and were often taken over by entrepreneurs in the new industries, for example Colonel Albert A. Pope whose great Columbia bicycle enterprise began manufacture in the Weed Sewing Machine Company of Hartford, Connecticut, in 1878. The Peugeot company also made sewing machines, and, crucially, James Starley, often perceived as 'the father' of the modern cycle industry,[15] had been involved in sewing machine manufacture before turning his attention to cycles in the late 1860s. (Jewell 1985: 35, 36, 61, 67, 73, 126, 127) It should come as no surprise then to find that after 1870 cycles were generally turned out in black Japan, sometimes relieved by gold lining and with working surfaces bright finished, an aesthetic treatment which had become almost universal by 1880. Interestingly, a difference in market perception here was that commentators on the cycle industry of the 1880s managed to convince the market that machines not finished in plain black with a minimum of brightwork and other decoration were likely to be of substandard quality, hiding beneath a finish which might 'best please the untrained eye'. (Erskine 1885) So persuasive was this argument that even when ladies' bicycles were introduced in the years after 1885 they generally followed suit and few, if any, appeared with the complex gilt transfers and mother-of-pearl inlays of the equivalent sewing machines, in which heavy elaboration generally denoted a deluxe model.

What the sewing machine established was an aesthetic formula for any iron or steel machine which would be seen above stairs in the domestic sphere, and also in the office, such as phonographs, telephones, sealing/embossing/stamping tools, typewriters and rotary duplicators. Black Japan, nickel plating, gold lining and ornament became unquestioningly accepted until well into the inter-war period. It could be argued that the wooden cases which contained many such machines also owed their appearance to those which commonly contained sewing machines. I contend that this period of the late nineteenth and early twentieth century should be considered as the high point of the sewing machine, not merely because of its popularity and reliability as a piece of domestic equipment, but for its far reaching influence on other products. In more recent years it has become more of a follower rather than a leader.

The very success of the machine in its turn-of-the-century guise and its aesthetic longevity doubtless did not encourage makers to seriously experiment with drastic remodelling. From the early twentieth century electric motors were applied for a long time as a kind of bolt-on accessory rather than being fully incorporated into the machine.[16] Treadle-stands (or stands for electrically powered machines) moved with prevailing tastes; drop-head machines (in which the machine can be folded under the table surface when not in use) became standard and therefore the stands carried more woodwork, which became increasingly 'moderne', while ironwork lost its neo-rococo detailing in favour of more classical or 'moderne' styles. On the machines themselves the heads became fatter and heavier-looking, but followed the same form as established by Singer's 'New Family' in 1865. Transfers moved through a number of styles such as art nouveau, and in Singer's case, Egyptianesque (complete with sphinx). Some machines appeared with geometric art deco transfers. The influence of modernism tended only to dissuade manufacturers from applying any ornamental transfers at all and in the early post Second World War years standard models were reflecting the bicycle aesthetic of the 1890s in being plain black Japan with bright parts plated.[17]

Admittedly not all machines merely 'tweaked' the tried and tested formula. Some more modern case designs appeared in the 1920s and 30s and in colours other than black, but until the post-war period these were exceptions. However, during the 1950s major redesigns became more frequent and plastics began to replace what would have been metal body parts. Since then sewing machine design has become just another exercise in bland-coloured plastic and metal casing, following in the wake of food mixers and other kitchen equipment, or more recently, personal computers. In developed countries the use of domestic sewing machines has begun to diminish while, in any case, the machine is only one of numerous complex mechanical, electro-mechanical or electronic appliances to be found in 'every well regulated household'.

To a great extent then, the aesthetic history of the domestic sewing machine follows its relative status within the domestic environment. As an unprecedented piece of equipment-cum-furniture not easily related to anything else in the home, the earliest machines develop their own look; this in turn becomes a style for future domestic technologies as they develop, given the often close manufacturing links coupled with the tendency for appliance designers to look for established aesthetic forms to ease the acceptability of a new product. Finally as the number of domestic appliances steadily expands, the domestic sewing machine loses its preeminent position and itself becomes a follower of stylistic changes in other domestic technologies.

This still leaves the question of why the sewing machine aesthetic developed in the first place. Why were so-called 'cabinet' models not the norm and why was there largely no need for manufacturers to resort to the sort of stylistic manipulation which Forty suggests? Logically, taking the Forty argument to its conclusion, makers of 'family' machines of the 1850s and early 1860s would surely have begun to address their market in terms of gender and the machine's aesthetic would have been systematically feminized, using, say, white enamel set off with gold and colours, appropriate to rococo decoration. Yet this did not happen. Why not? Indeed, the machine is remarkable in being ungendered in spite of the fact that manufacturers and commentators assumed (and were quite right in assuming) that the domestic machine's market was almost entirely female. Perhaps it was this very certainty of the market which allowed manufacturers not to design especially for it? A key factor here is the fact that the domestic machine developed directly from those for industrial use. In the industrial context there was certainly no need to disguise the machine, many would have looked upon it as something to be shown off as an icon of modernity and cutting-edge manufacturing process. Black Japan was probably the most hard-wearing and serviceable finish for ferrous metal components of sewing machine size and was an obvious choice for an industrial machine, and, like many other mid-nineteenth-century machines, their status was enhanced by applied painted decoration.

At first glance the pattern set by the industrial machine seems so wildly at odds with mid-nineteenth-century middle-class femininity, it is not a surprise to find commentators such as Forty looking for obvious accommodations in the design of early domestic machines thus targeted. However, I would argue that when the machine was sold and/or designed for domestic use its very function determined the gender of its user and there was no need to 'feminize' it in any way. Even if the size of newly-designed domestic machines tended to diminish so as to be more in scale with their surroundings, manufacturers continued to turn the machines out in the ubiquitous black. This colour, no matter how 'relieved' it was by gold or colours, made sure that the aesthetic of the machine never became 'feminine'. Indeed, exactly the same aesthetic, black with hand-enamelled leaf and flower decoration copiously applied, could be found on a contemporaneous metal object, the user of which would almost certainly be assumed to be male, namely the company seal embossing tool. Also, it should be remembered that the industrial sewing machines themselves, which were not so obviously gendered in user terms, were often fairly elaborate in terms of applied ornament, even if not so much as their domestic counterparts. Even the most flimsy and whimsical rococo castings do not read as 'feminine' when finished in black.

It is more difficult to see the reason for machines not to have more often been 'cabinet' models which looked like normal pieces of drawing-room furniture when not in use, but probably cost is a key factor here. Earlier I suggested that the major market for the domestic machine seems to have been the lower middle classes rather than the affluent. Clark and Singer's part-payment scheme is evidence of the realization of this even before the launch of their 'domestic' models. This market would benefit most from what savings the machine could offer in not 'putting out' work to seamstresses and/or in saving time and labour and therefore had a real reason for investing in it in spite of limited resources. Cabinet machines were considerably dearer than their iron treadle-stand counterparts and it might be this factor alone which established the cast-iron treadle-stand as an acceptable piece of furniture. However, one is tempted to argue that the machine itself, once purchased, was an expensive status symbol and more likely to be shown off rather than hidden away, making a cabinet positively disadvantageous.

In conclusion it would seem that the industrial origins of the domestic sewing machine coupled with the certainty of the gender of the domestic user and the systematic targeting of the lower-middle-class market allowed the black Japan relieved by gold aesthetic to develop and pass unchallenged from industrial to domestic machine and for it to genuinely become a 'beautiful ornament in the parlour or boudoir'. Without intention, the sewing machine manufacturers had created a design style which had little or no precedent, had no gender implications and was to become the standard for almost all iron- or steel-framed or cased above-stairs domestic and office appliances for almost a century. This alone would be impressive enough in the history of design, but the sewing machine did more than this, it was the first ever domestic appliance (in the modern sense of the term) to climb out of the kitchen and by having its own peculiar aesthetic it set the precedent for all others. It became accepted that the domestic appliance in the living room should look like what it is, rather than being disguised as something else.

Notes

1. An example being the *Red S Review*, published by Singer in London from 1919.

2. Admittedly there *is* a sewing machine in the Victoria and Albert Costume Court, but serious collections are to be more typically found in venues such as the Science Museum, London; the Smithsonian Institute, Washington, DC; the Museum of Science and Industry, Birmingham, England; Clydebank District Museum, Scotland. Notably, at the polymath Royal Museum of Scotland, Edinburgh, sewing machines are the preserve of the technology department in spite of the museum's substantial holdings of textiles and costume, furniture, and decorative art and design in their art department.

3. Machines cost approximately $125. The US dollar was roughly equivalent to a British crown (5s or 25p).

4. The 'Family' machine is commonly called the 'turtleback' after the shape of its head. According to Bays (1993: 166) only about 1,500 were manufactured in the three years of its production, despite the encouragement made to potential purchasers by the 'new for old' scheme. In comparison, Bays (169) goes on to state that approximately 75,000 Letter A machines were made between 1858 and 1865. Bays illustrates both types and the turtleback is illustrated in Forty. (1986: 96)

5. On the Wheeler and Wilson machines of the early and mid 1850s, 'Wilson formed a partnership with Nathaniel Wheeler who financed the production of Wheeler and Wilson machines, whose compact size and smooth works were a tribute to the inventive genius of the latter. Wheeler and Wilson machines were smaller, more decorative, and suited to the home rather than manufacturing use. In this respect they differ greatly from the clunky early creations of Singer.' (Bays 1993: 12) Bays gives a comparative illustration of a mid-1850s Singer No.1 and a contemporaneous Wheeler and Wilson photographed side by side. (1993: 13)

6. Production figures are available for Singer, Wheeler and Wilson, and Willcox and Gibbs respectively. (Jewell 1985: 120–1, 139, 141) These have been worked out from serial numbers and therefore could be subject to inaccuracy, although the big makers seem to have been fairly conscientious in their use of serial numbers. A Willcox and Gibbs machine is illustrated in Forty. (1986: 96)

7. The engraving used by Forty of this machine first appeared in *Sewing Machine News*, November 1885. It was subsequently reprinted in Cooper (1976) and Jewell. (1985) The comment: 'no examples are known to survive' (Jewell 1975) was amended to 'it is thought that the machine was never put into production' in Jewell (1985). The machine was the subject of a US patent granted to S.B. Ellithorpe in 1857, a patent model which seems to be for this machine survives and is illustrated by Bays (1993) who also thinks the machine was not made. The patent model bears little resemblance to the *Sewing Machine News* illustration which was probably not drawn from an actual machine.

8. The 'Cherub' machine illustrated by Forty (1986: 98) is typical. Designed by T.J.W. Robertson and probably manufactured by D.W. Clark of Bridgeport, which specialized in such 'figural' machines, it measures only five inches across. Although extremely rare, an example survives in the Smithsonian Institute, Washington, DC, making it easily accessible. Production figures are unknown, but Bays (1993) comments that 'Foliage', one of the more common of these machines, probably had a production run of about 1,500.

9. Using the serial numbers listed in Jewell (1985) in 1858 Singer produced 3,593 machines compared with Wheeler and Wilson's 7,977; in 1859 the figures were 10,952 and 21,305 respectively. It should be noted that these figures cover all model types and that the Singer Letter A was already in production in 1859, side by side with the 'Family' or turtleback model.

10. The former of these machines is illustrated in Bays. (1993: 10) The Clydebank Museum's machine (No.1988-10(1)) is a somewhat later example; it is finished in green enamel lined out in red and in this respect is considerably less elaborate than the earlier version. The flywheel might be a slightly later addition, it is in black

Japan with complex interlacing gold lining on its rim. The Clydebank machine is illustrated in Jewell. (1985: opposite 65)

11. Illustrations of this and other 'pillar' machines can be found in Bays. (1993: 163) I use the term 'Gothick' deliberately as the detailing is more that of the Regency than of the mediaeval.

12. This is an observation made at numerous museums, exhibitions and fairs. Visitors will be more likely to enthuse over miniature machines and pass over full-size versions. I have yet to meet a dealer or collector in any area of domestic technology whose views or prices contradict this.

13. Frister and Rossmann were a major Berlin-based manufacturer. Their early machines were copied from Wheeler and Wilson and Willcox and Gibbs, but from the late nineteenth century the bulk of their domestic models were similar to the Singer 'New Family'.

14. For example, Remington diversified from gunsmithing into sewing machines and then to typewriters in 1873. The early Remington typewriter 'resembled a sewing machine, with its stand and foot treadle for return of the carriage, the Remingtons having been engaged in the manufacture of sewing machines on a large scale.' (Post 1981)

15. Starley was a designer of both sewing machines and cycles, the most famous of the latter being the Ariel bicycle (1871) and the Coventry Lever tricycle (1876).

16. The awkwardness of such fittings was not unnoticed even prior to the First World War. The best were typified by that promoted by Lancaster: 'I also illustrate a system supplied by the Bissell Company of Toledo. The driving motor is the same size as, and takes the place of the hand wheel [. . .] this type of attachment has the advantage that it does not interfere with the workings of a drop-head machine, but closes with it out of sight.' (1914: 267) This was being compared with other attachments which mostly ran the machine by means of a gripped wheel rolling on the hand-wheel rim.

17. In as much as modernism was ever considered by sewing machine manu-facturers. In terms of form, the standard sewing machine had, since the late nineteenth century, little unnecessary or inappropriate decoration. Manufacturers probably dropped using complex ornamental gold transfers when such decoration was becoming old-fashioned and doubtless were aware that it was cheaper to produce machines without it. To what extent such actions were a conscious design statement in a theoretical sense is open to question.

References

Bays, C. (1993), *The Encyclopaedia of Early American Sewing Machines*, Columbia: BOOK Box 6782.

Brandon, R. (1977), *Singer and the Sewing Machine: A Capitalist Romance*, Philadelphia: Lippincott.

Clucas, J. (1973), *Your Machine for Embroidery*, London: Bell.

Cooper, G. R. (1976), *The Sewing Machine, Its Invention and Development,* Washington, DC: Smithsonian Institution Press.

Duncan, J. B. (1977), *The Development, Construction, and Characteristics of the Sewing Machine,* United Kingdom: Singer.

Erskine, F. J. (1885), *Tricycling For Ladies,* London: Iliffe.

Forty, A. (1986), *Objects of Desire: Design and Society 1750–1980,* London: Thames and Hudson.

Hall, C. V. (1980), *The Sewing Machine Craft Book,* New York: Van Nostrand Reinhold.

Head, C. (1982), *Old Sewing Machines,* Aylesbury: Shire.

Jewell, B. (1975), *Veteran Sewing Machines – A Collectors Guide,* Newton Abbot: David and Charles.

—— (1985), *Antique Sewing Machines,* Tunbridge Wells: D.J. Costello.

Lancaster, M. (1914), *Electric Cooking, Heating, Cleaning &c. Being a Manual of Electricity in the Service of the Home,* London: Constable.

Landgraff, O. (n.d. c. 1990), *Oldtimer Nähmaschinen,* Schweinfurt: Weppert.

Osler, D. (1980), *Machine Patchwork, Technique and Design,* London: Batsford.

Picken, M. B. (1954), *Singer Sewing Machine Book,* London: McGraw-Hill.

—— (1981) 'A Condensed History Of The Writing Machine' in *Typewriter Topics,* October 1923, reprinted with extra material in Post.

Post, D. R. ed, (1981), *Collectors' Guide to Antique Typewriters,* Arcadia: Post-era.

Thomas, G. (1995), *Toy and Miniature Sewing Machines,* Paducha: Collector Books.

18

Home Economics and Home Sewing in the United States 1870–1940

Sally I. Helvenston and Margaret M. Bubolz

Sewing is an art as old as mankind. Transmitted by women from century to century, it has never lost its utility or its charm. Mother taught daughter; neighbor taught neighbor. As an attainment, it constitutes, for women and men alike, a lore all its own.

(Fleck 1952)

In the late eighteenth century sewing instruction in the United States began to be formalized and by the late nineteenth century was taught in schools around the country. Home economics was founded in that period and became a major avenue for teaching home sewing. This chapter presents a social-historical perspective on how and why home economics became a major transmitter of, and contributor, to the culture of home sewing, teaching skills and knowledge, passing on patterns of social relationships, and reinforcing cultural values.

The chapter summarizes social, educational and ideological developments which influenced the founding and development of the field. Early instruction in home sewing which provided a foundation for formal education is described. It concludes by describing education for, and research in, home sewing from the time of the founding of home economics to the 1940s. During this period home sewing was a necessity for many families and was considered an essential art and skill for women.

Home economics grew out of, and helped support, American values and a democratic vision of equal economic, social and educational opportunities for all Americans. This involved an ideology of progress, self-reliance, social acceptance and mobility and a better life. The American philosophy of pragmatism with emphasis on the testing of knowledge by usefulness and practicality was another factor in the development of home economics. (James 1907) It was also influenced by nineteenth century ideals of domesticity, the significance of home and family in maintaining social order and forming human character and the important role of women in this regard. Home sewing, as a gendered activity, was an integral part of this ideal.

The latter part of the 1800s was a time of social and technological change. Following the Civil War came industrial expansion, settling of westward frontiers with extensive internal migration and great waves of immigration from Europe. While the majority of the population was rural, urbanization was increasing, with concerns about corruption, sanitation and health, poverty, and poor living and working conditions. It was a time of social reform and optimism. Many believed that life would be better if science were applied to improve technology, health, social institutions and the environment. A growing middle class was emerging with enough money to purchase the new material goods being produced. The women's movement had begun and some women were seeking education beyond primary or elementary schools.

Belief in education as the means to a better society and self-improvement is an integral part of the American ethos. By the mid-nineteenth century a system of free public education for all children replaced or supplemented private systems based on social class, economic, national or religious distinctions. Years of schooling increased and programmes expanded beyond reading, writing, spelling and arithmetic to education for citizenship, work and personal development. An important advance was emergence of secondary (high) schools open to all. By the time of the Civil War these had grown to several hundred and included not only college preparatory courses but terminal education for those not going to college. These developments reflected growing industrialization and urbanization, needs of children of immigrants to learn English and become Americans and belief that the family could not provide training for the new vocations emerging. Education for homemaking became part of this new vision and role of education.

In *The Young Lady's Friend*, Eliza Farrar wrote, 'A woman who does not know how to sew is as deficient in her education as a man who cannot write.' (1837) To acquire this skill, a young woman's instruction in sewing in the early nineteenth century was conducted by her mother or older family members and friends. Girls and young women were assigned projects by older members of the household which included needlework and the construction of garments. They took pride in their needlework and kept workbaskets which they carried into the parlour when visiting to complete their sewing. These projects also could be completed as a group project among family members or with the assistance of professional seamstresses. This made sewing a social network and not merely a production process. (Osaki 1988)

Examination of extant garments from this era shows that even though individual techniques might differ somewhat, there was a consistency of technique within regions of the country. For example, Kidwell (1978) describes the similarity of cut and construction techniques in the making of short gowns in the late eighteenth and early nineteenth centuries. Though not stated explicitly, an explanation for the similarities is that women passed down sewing techniques or created community networks to teach and learn sewing skills.

The seeds of what was to become domestic science or domestic arts, later home economics, started with classes on needlework and sewing at the end of the eighteenth and beginning of the nineteenth century in schools in Boston and Philadelphia. When families could afford it, they sent their daughters to young ladies academies, where needlework was an important part of the curriculum. (Ring 1993) Even though sewing skills could be obtained from family members, formal schooling ensured a systematic approach with continuity of technique and design. The first basic stitches a girl learned were referred to as 'plain sewing', 'common sewing', or 'useful work'. This included seaming, hemming, making buttonholes, mending, or knitting. The types of clothing a woman made for herself included underclothing, caps, bags, pockets and aprons. For her husband she might sew shirts, handkerchiefs and underdrawers. For her children, she sewed the basic layette for infants and most of the clothing of young children. More elaborate clothing in the family who could afford it was made by professional dressmakers or tailors.

After the basic stitches were mastered, a girl moved on to more decorative 'ornamental work'. The girls were taken through various exercises in alphabet embroidery which would prove useful for marking laundry. Samplers hung on the walls as decoration where they provided evidence of a girl's skills in this arena. Ornamental pictures in silk embroidery were the next step. A variety of embroidery stitches also were used to apply white cotton thread to a white cotton or linen ground. This 'muslin work' could be used to decorate various types of household linens as well as caps, infant's clothing and undergarments.

Girls attending the Mary Anna Longstreth school in Philadelphia were taught to make sewing models. The model system consisted of constructing samples of various construction processes such as seams and seam finishes, darning and mending techniques, methods of applying laces, insertion of plackets, application of cuffs and many other techniques designed to perfect the student's clothing construction skills. Miniature garments (especially undergarments) also were made and mounted on pages which were bound together into sampler books which students could keep and use for future reference.

At this time household instruction books were beginning to be published with many of the early volumes copying English publications. One of the earliest examples was Eliza Leslie's *The House Book: A Manual of Domestic Economy*, published in 1840. This included useful instructions on sewing. Mid-nineteenth century women's periodicals, in addition to fashion information, also included information on sewing techniques. *Godey's Lady's Book* which began publication in 1830, *Peterson's Magazine* (begun in 1855), and *Harper's Bazar* (1867) were the major women's periodicals to include sewing information, yet this appeared only as a means to achieve a fashionable look rather than offering organized lessons designed to teach the full spectrum of sewing techniques. Instructions on topics such as 'Making and Mending Men's Clothing', 'Women's Apparel, Its Making and Mending', and 'Children's Clothing', intended for the 'inexperienced' were published in the *New England Farmer* in the late 1860s.

The early instruction in home sewing provided a basis for domestic science or arts courses which were introduced in public schools around the country in the 1880s and 1890s. (Andrews 1915) Specialized schools in sewing also were established. (Craig 1945) Home sewing was an indispensable activity for most families because they lacked the resources for, or access to, dressmakers or servants and 'store bought' clothing was largely unavailable, especially in rural areas. Home sewing machines had become widely available and simplified home sewing as well as making it more complex by providing new creative possibilities.

Expansion of elementary and secondary education provided more opportunities for both boys and girls, but most colleges and professions were closed to women.[1] However, Oberlin College admitted women as early as 1837 and by 1850 some female seminaries and colleges had been founded, some of which required training in 'housewifery' or participation in domestic work of the college. Normal (teacher training) schools and some state universities admitted women but it was in the land grant colleges where women's participation in higher education began to increase appreciably. These colleges played a critical role in education of women and growth of home economics.

The Morrill Land Grant Act of 1862 donated lands to each state to support colleges to teach agriculture and mechanic arts to promote education of the industrial classes. This Act opened doors to many who previously had no opportunity to enter higher education and contributed to the development of agriculture, engineering and home economics. During the last quarter of the nineteenth century some land grant colleges offered courses in domestic economy or domestic science or art, with Kansas State College one of the earliest, in 1873, where the first courses were in sewing. (Lang 1975) By the turn of the century, to meet the need for domestic science teachers, teacher training began in land grant colleges, normal schools and some private institutions.[2]

East (1980) has identified four models which influenced home economics during its founding period. The inductive reasoning model proposed that students through 'hands on experience' with actual materials and real things would learn principles underlying the activity and how to apply them in other situations, stimulating intellectual training and a scientific approach to problems. John Dewey (1916), philosopher and educational reformer, was a leading progenitor of this model. In 1899 in Dewey's laboratory school at the University of Chicago one of the departments was Domestic Sciences and Industry. Dewey believed that children should learn to 'get some practical hold of the activities which centre in the family [. . .] as well as to deepen and widen the ethical spirit of mutual service'. (East 1980: 14)

The household management model can be traced to Aristotle who proposed that wise management was needed in order for people to live together in households. Good households were basic to good societies and both were necessary for a good life. Women were of signal importance in household management. The application of science model had its genesis in the work of Francis Bacon (1561–1626), the English philosopher and writer, who promoted a redefinition and new methods of science to 'endow the condition and life of man with new powers or works'. (Bacon 1965: 995) Bacon's ideas were promoted by Benjamin Thompson, 'Count Rumford', a British-American scientist of the late eighteenth century, who championed application of science to everyday life. Ellen Swallow Richards, first woman to receive a degree from the Massachusetts Institute of Technology and first female faculty member of any science school in the United States, was a primary proponent of this position.[3]

The education for womanhood model assumed that woman's primary role was in the home and family. The writings of Catherine Beecher[4] were especially influential in developing this stream of thought. Beecher urged education for matrimony, based on the Victorian ideal of a well-managed family, to be part of school work for females. She believed that families alone could no longer prepare girls for the responsibilities of a changing family and home life. Traditional knowledge no longer passed intact from parents to children nor met needs of the coming generation. Beecher's reformist philosophy is expressed in her exhortations concerning clothing in which she quotes the *Young Ladies Friend*:[5]

All styles of dress which impede the motions of the wearer; which do not sufficiently protect the person; which add unnecessarily to the heat of the Summer, or to the Cold of Winter; which do not suit the age and occupation of the wearer; or which indicate an expenditure unsuited to her means; are *inappropriate*, and therefore destitute of one of the main essentials of beauty. (Beecher 1841: 99)

Beecher's advice influenced the content of home sewing education in home economics from its beginning. It did not focus narrowly on technical skills but emphasized principles and encouraged critical thinking.

The philosophical stances and social changes and concerns of the era generated reformist organizations concerned with family and household, health, living conditions and women's education. Home and family was the primary sphere for most women, but some were assuming or desiring a wider range of roles in public life. All these developments came together in the founding of home economics.

In 1892 Ellen Swallow Richards proposed a science of living to be called 'oekology' (ecology) to teach 'principles on which to found [. . .] healthy [. . .] and happy life'. (Clarke 1973: 117–120). Her scientific studies helped her see the connection between behaviour, the health of people and the quality of the environment. She saw ecology as a means for applying science to improve people's lives and environments. This application must be done in home and family; women should be the focus of education in the field.

In 1899 Richards brought together, at the Lake Placid Club in New York State, a small group involved in domestic science/home economics to expand the growing field to deal with emerging environmental, economic and sociological problems of the home and to improve women's education. Ten conferences were held, growing to over 700 attendees at the last one in 1908. Agreement was reached in 1902 on a definition for home economics, the name by which the field was then known. Richards' proposal for the name of ecology was not adopted, but a human-environment perspective was implicit in the definition which stated that the field was concerned with the physical environment, humans as social beings, and 'specially of the relation between these two factors'. (American Home Economics Association 1902: 70) The relationship between objects and features of the environment and human needs and activities is a unique element of home economics (Eicher 1972) and especially important for study of clothing and sewing.

Home economics was considered a unified field centred on home and family, but separate subjects were identified, with clothing and textiles a major component. A paper on college work in sewing illustrates the issues surrounding the goals and content of education at various levels:

Sewing is taught in all kinds of schools from the grade to the university and means in its strictest sense a form of manual training; as exprest by some of its teachers, its objects are 'to train the hand, mind and eye to work in unison'; 'to develop manual dexterity and mental training;' 'a thoro preparation for the practical life of the home'; added to these 'the eye is trained to color, the sense of proportion cultivated and better taste in dress developt' [. . .] In the college or university course, study of materials is often combined with sewing, design and color are emphasized, but still there is the manual training and in most cases the emphasis is there. Study of materials involves economic and hygienic principles as well as utilitarian ends [. . .] Applied art means many things, but in this special connection, usually weaving, embroidery or stenciling. It will not be questioned, I think that each of these subjects taught singly or combined helps fit woman for life whether it be thru the practical side in sewing, the economic side in study of materials or the artistic side in applied art. The questions then of most importance are, which is of university standard, and on what shall we spend most of our time? (Gibbs 1907)

Syllabi outlined courses for various levels. The American Home Economics Association,[6] organized in 1908–09, furthered curriculum development, terminology and standards. Elements of the four philosophical models were incorporated, with the addition of an aesthetics perspective focused on art and design with emphasis on simplicity, utility and beauty. (Dohr and Forbess 1984) The models coalesced in teaching students how to carry out their responsibilities as women.

Several legislative acts during the founding and early years of home economics provided support which made substantial contributions to its growth and direction. The nineteenth century legislation was enacted when the country was primarily rural and was directed toward improving agriculture and rural life. When the other bills were enacted over half of the American population was still rural and legislators from the farm states were powerful. Hence, federal support linked home economics closely to farming and rural life and illustrates the political forces at play in development of home economics as well as the value placed on home and family and the traditional role of women.

The Land Grant Act discussed earlier and the second Morrill Act of 1890, which authorized black land-grant colleges, legitimized home economics (and clothing as a component of the field) as part of higher education for women, provided career opportunities, and a foothold in academia for college-educated women. They were also important in developing graduate study and research and in bringing education to a wide audience through extension programmes.[7]

The Hatch Bill of 1887 funded experiment stations at the land grant colleges. This, and subsequent bills, provided funds for research related to agriculture and related subjects and opened the door for funding clothing research. The Smith-Lever Act of 1914 provided support for extension education in agriculture and home economics at the land grant colleges. Clothing and home sewing became important emphases in extension.

Historically, American education has been the responsibility of each state. States began to support education for home-making in the late nineteenth century and by 1915 it was authorized in about three-fourths of the states. (Andrews 1915) The federal government entered home economics education through the Smith-Hughes Act of 1917, which supported home economics education as vocational training for girls and tied it still more closely to agriculture.[8] The Act had far-reaching effects on home economics through its influence on college programmes by stressing practical home-making skills.

The Office of Home Economics was created in 1915 in the US Department of Agriculture for research on more effective use of agricultural products. Work expanded beyond food and nutrition to include fibres and textiles. The First World War created need for large supplies of wool and cotton and stimulated research on care and conservation of fibres and textiles. Introduction of rayon and acetate created a need for standardization and labelling of textile goods. (Joseph 1984) Landmark studies were conducted on standardization and test methods for textile fibres and fabrics. At first, university researchers were limited, because of the expense of equipment needed to conduct physical tests on textiles.

In 1924 the Division of Clothing and Textiles was established in the Office of Home Economics. (Craig 1945) The Purnell Bill of 1925 expanded funding and clothing research, as distinct from textiles research, began in a significant way at that time. In 1930, a committee on research in the textile and clothing division of the American Home Economics Association was formed and held annual conferences to present research reports. Research methodology and appropriate directions for clothing and textiles research in universities were debated at these conferences. Research on physical and chemical properties and care and use of textile fibres and fabrics expanded, although much of the research in the early years was of the survey type.

Anspach (1959) reports that from 1925–29 design and home sewing were the major areas of clothing research with emphasis on health, comfort, durability, fitting and construction techniques. Some studies involved sizing, economics and management. Controversy over the value of home-mades versus ready-mades stimulated some research and indicated a transition from training women as skilled producers of clothing to skilled consumers. In the Depression years when new clothing was out of the question for many, emphasis was on management, durability, care and repair. In 1937 the Bureau of Home Economics led the first scientific study on the sizing of children's clothing, which led to work on standardization of pattern sizes. (Craig 1945)

Physical science and practical issues dominated much of the early study in clothing and textiles but by the 1920s home economists were concerned with aesthetics and psychological and other social science themes. (Rosencranz 1984) Research and theoretical work by social scientists provided the basis for instruction and stimulated research which home economists conducted in subsequent periods.

For many years experiment station funds were a primary source for university clothing research. Research problems were influenced because of ties to agriculture, but the support was essential in establishing the knowledge base of the field as well as in fostering scientific attitudes to problems. Home sewing education also incorporated innovations in equipment, fabrics, construction methods, simplified design and durability developed by the military, other government programmes, industry, labour unions and retailers. The role of the home economist has been to adapt and bring knowledge to the consumer as chooser, user and as a source of market demand. (Anspach 1959)

Not all content and methods of home sewing education were based on research. What and how sewing was taught was also based on creativity, experience, problem solving, tradition and trial and error. But research influenced home sewing, although it was not always recognized.

The highest percentage of students in the years before the First World War were preparing for home-making (63 per cent); however, a substantial percentage (about one-third) were preparing for teaching careers which further spread home economics into the public schools. Less than 5 per cent were preparing for administrative positions. After passage of the Smith Hughes Act in 1917, college home economics programmes increased rapidly and by 1939–40 had grown to 348 with 36,521 majors, over 95 per cent of them women. (East 1980) College programmes greatly influenced the spread of home economics concepts throughout society.

Most programmes offered work in clothing construction. Typically, to meet requirements for vocational funding, two or three construction courses were required for education majors, the largest programme in the majority of colleges. In the decades up to 1940 construction courses were required also by many colleges for all home economics students.[9] Specialization was increasing and new professional roles were emerging, but home economics was seen as an integrated field centred on women's traditional role in home and family. Learning something about clothing and sewing was considered necessary for all home economists.

Early teaching of sewing at the college level incorporated the methods described earlier, such as making samplers and models of various techniques.

The role of sewing in the curriculum changed from the 1890s through the first decades of the twentieth century.[10] Almost from the founding of the American Home Economics Association, educators expressed opinions on the teaching of sewing in its journal. By the time the first volume was published in 1909 a revolt against teaching sewing only as a skill was underway. Teaching by the sampler or model method was criticized as not encouraging thinking. As one educator wrote, 'If our courses were spoken of as courses in clothing rather than sewing it might give opportunity and inspiration for a broader treatment of the subject'. (French 1917: 61) Numerous articles appeared promoting the 'problem method' of teaching. This focused on providing an example of a real-life situation for the students to solve. A particular garment might be chosen as a problem for the class (a petticoat or bloomers, for example), and the students would be responsible not only for the construction of the garment, but also for skillful selection of the fabrics according to durability and economy, choice of appropriate sewing techniques and making appropriate aesthetic decisions. This approach coexisted with sampler making into the 1920s.

By the 1930s a new approach referred to as the 'individual assignment' method was ushered in. With this concept in teaching, educators were focused on individual differences in student performance. Allowing the student to work at her own speed yet reach the maximum of her potential was important. Students worked independently completing various assignments including written answers to questions about construction, reports on various aspects of the project, examination of sewing samples placed in the classroom, completion of tests, and construction of a completed garment. Admittedly this took a great deal of coordination on the instructor's part and to what degree this method was embraced is unknown.

An examination of textbooks used in sewing classes provides a picture of the development of the subject to 1940. Few textbooks were published before 1900. However, with the publication of Mary Woolman's *A Sewing Course for Teachers* in 1893, we see one of the first books published on sewing processes and their teaching. By the second decade of the twentieth century, sewing texts were moving away from the sampler method of teaching to focus on construction of garments. With time a greater inclusion of additional topics of pattern drafting and draping, applied design, garment construction, textiles and the economics of consumption occurred. By the 1930s preparing young women for careers in the fashion industry became important. Courses in the clothing and textiles curriculum could prepare women for positions as stylists, department store buyers, fashion analysts, fashion illustrators, or dress designers. Clothing construction courses as well as a course in the history of costume were deemed necessary for the designer's job.

Up to and including 1895 only eleven states gave instruction in household arts (including sewing) in the public schools; by 1917 instruction was offered in every state in the union. By 1938–39 more than 90 per cent of schools in cities and towns with populations of 2,500 or more had programmes. Ninety per cent required it for seventh and eighth grade girls. Over half required it for those in high school. (Craig 1945)[11] Enrollment was almost all female with barely 1 per cent of boys enrolled. During the four decades after its founding, millions of American girls had instruction in sewing through home economics, helping to maintain the perception of home sewing as a necessary gender-based activity. Many women also had instruction through adult classes.

Initially, the content of sewing education was similar to that described earlier, but as training of teachers changed, programmes in the schools changed. In early grades attention was paid to 'plain sewing' and basic stitches, including decorative stitches, mending and making samplers. Use of the machine and other equipment was also taught. Typically, a simple garment was the first project, with some attention to design, comfort and durability.

In higher grades, more complex garments, using fabrics requiring more technical skill were made. Greater emphasis was placed on fit, design, appearance and wardrobe planning. Clothing was an important vehicle for social acceptability and success; learning how to sew made it possible for many girls, regardless of economic or social class, to conform to a middle-class ideal. Attention was given to avoiding a 'home-made look':

> Peggy has a vivid memory of her ninth grade home economics teacher showing the class a beautiful pink spun rayon dress made by a senior in which the hem was invisible. Being able to execute such a perfect hem became an important goal. To reinforce the idea that one should aim for high standards of construction and appearance, she remembers what the teacher wrote on the blackboard: 'As you sew so shall you rip.' (Personal Communication)

During the 1920s when ready-made clothing became more available or affordable, knowing how to make clothes as a basis for better selection of purchased clothing was given attention. Many more women had entered the workforce at this time (as a result of the First World War) and thus increased their buying power. During the Depression years of the 1930s, attention was given to patching, mending, and other money-saving practices. Attention was paid to social responsibility in clothing classes and students often constructed garments in school which were given to the less fortunate. Making over garments, a time-honoured tradition since pioneer days when clothing and fabrics were hard to come by, became a part of sewing classes.[12] Teachers faced many challenges in providing fabrics, patterns and other sewing supplies.[13]

In keeping with the aim of early leaders to challenge creativity, rational thought and a scientific attitude attempts were made to emphasize planning, decision-making and evaluation of outcomes. However, the field was criticized for being mainly 'cooking and sewing' – published recipes and commercial patterns. (Apple 1997) There was probably some truth to this, but in sewing, as in other courses, what was learned was influenced not only by how it was taught but by the aptitudes and interests of the students. The practice of putting 'slow' pupils and those not planning to go to college into home economics classes came into play. Prejudicial attitudes toward these students affected perceptions of home economics as non-academic.

In talking with women it is interesting how many have vivid memories of the garments they made and of their experiences in sewing classes. While many have positive memories, this was not the case for everyone. The following illustrates this but also depicts another dimension of home sewing:

> Elsie felt her teacher didn't know very much and she recalls how tired she became of the dress she made – and how tired looking and grimy the dress became before it was finished. She didn't wear it very often. But she was fortunate in being in a family where sewing was a valued activity and tradition; she learned much at home and through 4H club work. She sewed for her family for many years, as did her sisters, and as their mother and grandmother had done before them. (Personal Communication)

Other women also spoke of sewing as a family tradition:

> Sue, a clothing and textiles professor, says that one of her most cherished memories is that of sewing with her mother and grandmother. She remembers that after her grandmother died her mother was unable to sew for two years. Sewing brought memories of the times they had spent together that were too painful. Sue sees home sewing as playing an important role in family bonding. (Personal Communication)

Sewing classes, along with the family and out-of-school programmes, contributed to sewing as a shared family activity, important to building intergenerational continuity and transmitting traditions.

Home economics in the schools changed to incorporate new technology, fabrics, fashions and consumer goods as well as adapt to changing lifestyles and social and economic conditions. Throughout the period it centred on preparing girls for a dominant role of home-making in which tending to the family's clothing and knowing how to sew were important responsibilities. A study of adult women following the Second World War (Ostapovich 1961) reported that high-school and adult classes had been important sources of training in home sewing. Wives of white-collar and higher-income males sewed mainly because of its creative appeal and enjoyment and because they could have more clothes for the same amount of money. Lower-income and blue-collar wives sewed mainly to save money.

Not everyone who took sewing in school continued to sew in their adult years, but sewing classes made a significant contribution to a meaningful and satisfying activity for many women. They transmitted skills; reinforced values of economy, practicality, careful workmanship, creativity and social acceptability and helped strengthen family bonds.

After passage of the Smith-Lever Act in 1914, funds increased for extension work. State specialists in clothing were added; counties began to employ home economists, called home demonstration agents. Staff for youth programmes increased. With participation in the First World War interest and growth in extension increased greatly. Emergency programmes were directed to improving production of food and fibre, preservation and economical use of food, and care and conservation of textiles and clothing. (Abraham 1986)

Much of extension home economics work was conducted through training of volunteer leaders who taught members of neighbourhood groups and 4H clubs, the name adopted in the early 1920s for the boys and girls clubs established earlier. This practice fostered personal and leadership development. The word demonstration in the name of the programme and the agents carrying it out was not simply semantic, it had important implications. It meant teaching and learning how to do something through 'hands on experience'. John Dewey's inductive reasoning model was translated into the dictum of 'learning by doing', which became a popular slogan to describe extension education. Stress on practical experience emphasized skills, management and problem-solving on the farm and in the home.

4H members pledged their 'head to clearer thinking, heart to greater loyalty, hands to larger service, and health to better living' for their home, club, community and country. (Abraham 1986: 110) To achieve this aim, members carried out projects related to farming and home-making. The pledge and projects exemplified Dewey's vision of learning principles, developing reasoning and other skills and deepening the spirit of service through engagement in work in the family. Clothing and sewing projects fit this model well and were popular in both youth and adult programmes. During this period much home production took place and sewing was carried out in the majority of farm families.

An important element of 4H work was competition in which members exhibited their projects at fairs or achievement days and were judged and received white, red, or blue ribbons, reflecting the level of skill in meeting standards. Champions received purple ribbons and went to the state fair. Competition was intended to motivate learning in order, as the 4H motto said, 'to make the best better'. Initially, judging was on the garment but expanded to include demonstrations and the dress revue in which a queen and attendants were selected.

The dress revue reveals not only America's fascination with royalty and what they wore, it reinforces the importance given to personal appearance based on fashion, fit, suitability, and attractiveness. Brumberg (1997) discusses *Teen Togs*, a film produced by the Georgia Extension Service which conveys the message that there are right and wrong clothes for different places and occasions; the right clothes contribute to social success and self-esteem. By learning to sew, a smart wardrobe can be within any girl's reach and she can be appropriately dressed for any occasion. Thus, in addition to a major emphasis on construction, economy and other practical matters, personal appearance was important in extension clothing work.

Programmes changed to meet changing social and economic conditions, fashions, fabrics and equipment. During the Depression, a popular slogan said: 'Use it up; wear it out; make it do or do without.' Much attention was given to conserving clothing and textiles – 'making do'.[14] When electricity came to farms in the 1930s and 40s, learning to use electric sewing machines and irons became important.

An important factor associated with sewing was the challenge which came with more difficult projects and the feeling of achievement which accompanied completion and evidence of success. In many communities and cultural groups being known as 'a good sewer' was a source of prestige. Another contribution of home economics in 4H as well as in school was motivating hundreds of girls, inspired by their leaders, extension agents or teachers to study home economics in college. The history of home economics is replete with examples of home economists who got their start in 4H work or home economics classes. Many became leaders in the field.[15]

The network and bonding aspects of home sewing discussed earlier were important parts of extension. Extension groups provided a means of friendship and support for women to come together to carry out necessary work for the home or community. Priscilla, a New Hampshire homemaker, said: 'I feel that the sociability of your own locality is another binding point. You have such a good time, you make so many new friends. In time of need, they're there. This builds up from your working and learning together.' (Arnold 1985: 249)

Extension work in home economics, like that of the entire field, had critics, some of whom saw it as unnecessary or frivolous.[16] When home economics was shown to have economic value because of its practicality and contribution to management and work on the farm and in the home, positive assessment increased. Julia, a Tennessee home-maker, summarizes the feelings of many about the value of extension programmes:

It [the extension club] has taught me how to save and economize; it has taught me how to sew; how to can and preserve food. Without the Home Demonstration Club, I don't think I could have made it. There isn't too much of anything that I can't do for my self. (Arnold 1985: 248)

Like programmes in public schools, extension classes and projects reinforced and transmitted practical skills, social patterns and societal values and contributed to personal growth and self reliance.

As discussed earlier, magazines have been sources of information for home sewing since the nineteenth century; after delivery of mail to rural America began in 1896 they became more widely circulated. Many home economists became editors or wrote articles for magazines.[17] In addition to women's magazines, farm magazines had sections edited by home economists.[18] Magazines also offered printed matter for sale and sold patterns, a boon to rural women who frequently had little access for purchasing patterns. In addition to text books, home economists wrote books for the public, as well as material for extension and other programmes. When radio came in home economists provided information on topics related to sewing.

The Home Economists in Business section of the American Home Economics Association (AHEA) was formed in the early 1920s, but work with commercial enterprises started earlier. As early as 1880 Sarah Tyson Rorer, a domestic scientist, provided consulting work for business and in the 1850s the Singer Sewing Machine Company hired women, forerunners of the home economists it employed later, to demonstrate sewing machines. (Goldstein 1997) These women provided home sewing education and stimulated sales of the new mechanical marvel. Another early connection between home economics and business came in the early 1900s when Boston stores employed students to train them for salesmanship. Demands grew for teachers for such courses and led to development of college merchandising programmes in clothing and textiles. This emphasis provided new career opportunities for home economists.

Growth of consumer products companies after the First World War stimulated employment of home economists. By 1927 the business section of AHEA had over 169 members and by 1940 over 600. (Goldstein 1997) Department stores, mail-order companies, sewing machine manufacturers and companies supplying fabrics, patterns and other supplies employed home economists. An important function of home economists was to educate women in the use and care of the company's products. They conducted classes for consumers and home economists, prepared teaching materials and provided consultation with customers. The Singer Sewing Machine Company continued the work it had started earlier by offering classes with the purchase of sewing machines. This company and others also assisted education by providing discounts to home economists and purchase plans for schools and colleges whereby machines and equipment were periodically replaced. Business and industry sponsored 4H awards, scholarships and events and programmes at professional meetings. Exhibits with the latest equipment, educational materials and discounts were major attractions for many at the annual conventions of AHEA.

Several companies hired home economists for research and product development and testing, contributing to product design, use and care. A notable example is Elizabeth Weirick, a chemist, hired in 1919 by Sears, Roebuck and Company, a major source of consumer goods through its catalogue and chain stores, to head the textiles division of the testing laboratory. (Goldstein 1997) Her work as director of the Sears technological laboratories and that of others influenced textiles, equipment and other supplies available for home sewing, providing a basis for educational materials and programmes. Business and industry also supported university research.

Home economists in business and industry had the dual task of educating companies to consumer needs, improve product quality and take a more consumer oriented approach to service and that of educating consumers with information on use of the products. Bridging the two constituencies was often difficult and provided dilemmas for home economists and the profession. (Goldstein 1997) Debate over conflicts between ideals of the profession to serve families and consumers and demands of business to get people to consume more began in the 1920s and continued thereafter.

The J. C. Penney stores were an important source of fabrics and other sewing supplies for many generations, especially in rural America and have a long history of consumer education. While not employed in business until after the period covered in this analysis, Satenig St. Marie, first woman vice president in the J. C. Penney Company provides an example of a home economist who provided exceptional services for both consumers and the company. She was responsible for educational programmes and publications, including J. C. Penney *Forum* and developed programmes to bring the voice of the consumer into the company. (St. Marie 1997)

We cannot evaluate the education provided to consumers *vis-à-vis* serving the company but business and industry provided necessary and useful products for home sewing and helpful materials for teachers and extension workers. Relationships between home economics education and consumer capitalism illustrates the interdependence between public institutions and private business which characterizes American society.

In addition to agencies previously discussed, home economists worked in offices of education where they were influential in funding and curriculum development. In the US Bureau of Standards they contributed to standardization of pattern and clothing sizes. They also supplied product labelling information such as fabric use and care. During the Depression and two world wars home economists served in emergency programmes concerned with conservation, economics, and use of textiles and clothing.

To conclude, this chapter has described philosophical and educational ideologies and social, economic and other changes during the later years of the nineteenth century and early decades of the twentieth century in which home economics developed as a field focused on women's primary role in the home and family. Learning to sew through home economics was a significant component of education for countless girls and women in schools, colleges and other programmes. Home economics opened doors to professional careers and academic positions for many women. Clothing and textiles became a well-established field of study and research through home economics. Early ties to agriculture were important but as the country grew and urbanized, the field expanded and home economics became a participant in the consumer society.

In years since the period covered in this chapter major changes have occurred. Feminism has challenged gender stereotyping of women's roles. More educational and occupational opportunities are open to women and, while the majority marry and have children, large numbers are employed away from home for a major part of their lives. Internationalization of industry and the economy have transformed production and distribution of consumer goods with easy availability of low-to-moderately priced clothing. Social norms, fashions and life styles have influenced what people wear. Incomes have risen for many citizens. Some women have less time for sewing but have money to buy the kind of clothes needed – clothing for the job or 'dress-up' and jeans, pants, tops and T-shirts for everyone for all occasions.

Despite these changes, millions of women continue to sew. A study reported in 1997 (Owens) indicates that nearly one-third of the country's adult female population – more than 30 million, mostly between age twenty-four and fifty-four and college educated – sew at home. This is an increase from the 1960s, when home sewing had begun to decline. Today people sew for many reasons: desire for originality, creativity and challenge or for enjoyment and satisfaction. Economic need is not a primary reason but some women and girls sew because they can make garments of higher quality or desired fashion or fit at lesser cost than they can purchase ready-made. Technological advances in machines, fabrics and other supplies also stimulate renewed interest in sewing.

These changes have influenced home economics and its role in home sewing.[19] By the 1970s and 1980s various names were used for home economics and in 1993 the name 'Family and Consumer Sciences' was proposed and subsequently adopted by major professional groups in the field.[20] (American Home Economics Association 1994) The change reflects a wider remit and shift from skill-oriented activities and home production. (Vincenti 1997) Students prepare for specialized occupations serving families, consumers, individuals and communities rather than for their own home and family life.

Clothing or apparel, as the field is now commonly called, is still important with emphasis in college programmes on design, historic and cultural studies and greater links to business and industry but sewing receives less attention and where it is a part of clothing programmes, intellectual components and processes are emphasized. Attention is given to design (including computer-assisted design), structural features of a garment for desired fit and appearance and to principles of sequencing in construction. Research is undertaken on social-psychological and cultural factors and functional design and inter-national aspects are emphasized.

In schools, sewing is generally taught in the sixth, seventh or eighth grades with the accent on using the machine, basic seams and hems and care and repair of clothing, as it was in the early days. In many places the emphasis in upper grades is on clothing selection and consumer education while in others construction receives more attention. Emphases also vary in extension programmes. Clothing is still popular in 4H programmes.[21] In adult pro-grammes major attention in some places is given to responding to consumer problems but in others construction workshops and seminars are offered.[22] Boys now enroll in public school classes and 4H sewing projects but home sewing remains almost exclusively a female activity.

Sewing is taught in classes offered by stores, sewing machine companies, home sewing organizations and via television. Videotapes, computer pro-grammes and Web sites are available and print media provide information. Home economics is no longer the principal source for sewing education, but it contributed teaching methodologies, experimental construction techniques, textile standards and labelling, standardization of pattern sizes and a body of academic knowledge which continue to provide foundations for current activity in home sewing. Home economics reinforced cultural values and social patterns and contributed to personal development. In this regard, home economics played a unique role in the transmission of culture.

Notes

1. Many believed that women did not need advanced education since they would most likely marry and have a family; women were also thought to lack the intellectual ability required for a rigorous education.

2. The College for the Training of Teachers (later Teachers College, Columbia University) founded in 1887 in New York City, grew out of work to help children learn home-making skills and organizations for older girls and boys to provide training related to the house and home. (East 1980) One of Columbia's five professors was in domestic economy. Other private colleges with courses in home economics before the twentieth century included the University of Chicago and Stanford University.

3. Ellen Swallow was not admitted as a regular student at MIT because she was a woman; to gain acceptance by other students and faculty she made herself useful in traditional womanly ways such as sewing on buttons. She eventually received her degree but her doctoral studies were discouraged because MIT did not want to grant its first Ph.D. in chemistry to a woman. (Stage 1977)

4. Beecher's sister, Harriet Beecher Stowe, was the author of *Uncle Tom's Cabin*, the famous anti-slavery novel. They were sisters of Henry Ward Beecher, a religious reformer.

5. This was the original name for the magazine *Godey's Lady's Book*.

6. Publication of the *Journal of Home Economics* by the American Home Economics Association began in 1909. This organization is now called the American Association for Consumer and Family Sciences.

7. During the first decades of the twentieth century land-grant colleges were fewer than 20 per cent of the total of those offering degrees in home economics, but they enrolled a majority of the students.

8. The discussions which led up to the bill did not include home economics because home-making was not considered a wage-earning occupation. Some home economists did not support the bill because they did not want home economics to be considered vocational training versus a liberal education. A senator from a rural state pressed for including the field and reflected the prevailing ideology when he insisted that 'the Almighty [. . .] has ordained that woman do the housework and man do the work which he does'. (Apple 1997: 82) Other rural senators supported this position; home-making was defined as a vocation, and while not wage-earning, had economic value since production went on in the home. At the last minute home economics got into the bill with agriculture, trades and industrial education.

9. The programme at Michigan State was typical of many programmes in requiring a set of core courses for all majors. In 1929–30 two courses in clothing construction and one in selection were part of the core; by 1940–41, one of each was still required. By 1950 this requirement was dropped. (Lee, Hart and Mentzer 1972)

10. Every issue of the *Journal of Home Economics* from 1909 to 1940 was reviewed for this research.

11. Apple (1997) reports that the decision in some places to require home economics at the junior high school level was made because many girls did not attend high school.

12. Peggy, a farm-girl in a large family, made over a suit of her father's in home economics. Much of her high-school wardrobe came from making over garments

given by her city aunts; when she started college she made a winter coat for herself out of her brother's – he was then in military service in the Second World War. For college she made a suit out of her father's wedding suit of navy blue woollen serge, hardly ever worn. She passed it on to a sister who later made it over into a vest and pants for her son; later it was passed on to another sister for her son. The suit took on a life of its own through three generations. (Personal Communication)

13. During the Depression many of Betty's students could not afford to buy material. She spent part of her small salary to buy material for them or had them make garments for her nieces out of cloth she furnished. Clare taught home economics in a small community in Arizona, a sparsely settled western state. Clerks at a department store in Phoenix, 70 miles away, put aside bolts of fabric they thought would be suitable for schoolgirls and let Clare take the fabrics and pattern books to her classes for a week. After the students made their choices, Clare returned to Phoenix and made the purchases. Getting sewing supplies was considered so important that during the Second World War the Ration Board gave Clare extra gasoline stamps for the trip. (Personal Communication)

14. Margaret took the 4H thrift project during the 1930s in which she made underwear and a dress of cotton flour sacks. At that time unbleached muslin was not the fashionable fabric for clothing it became in the 1970s. She did not wear the dress away from home very often but she learned that acceptability and fashion sometimes conflicted with economy. When patterned flour sacks were introduced, they were widely used in home sewing. (Personal Communication)

15. Bea and her sisters attended a small rural high school where home economics was not offered. 4H was one of the few activities available for girls. Their club, The Steuben Sewing Songsters, was an important part of their life during childhood and adolescent years. Bea studied home economics in college and became one of the most influential and honoured leaders in the profession, nationally and internationally. Her theoretical work in management and decision-making influenced home sewing at all levels. (Personal Communication)

16. Some critics with a sexist bias saw education for women as unnecessary or threatening.

17. Mary Brooks Picken, well-known home economist, served for many years as the dressmaking editor of the *Pictorial Review*. She also served as the Director of Instruction for the Women's Institute of Domestic Arts and Sciences in Scranton, Pennsylvania, which taught sewing as a correspondence course. She also authored *The Language of Fashion* (1939), one of the earliest attempts to standardize fashion terminology.

18. *The Farmer* was an eagerly awaited magazine in the Minnesota farm home of the elder author. The series 'Betty's Scrapbook of Little Stitches for Little Folks' stimulated her early experiences in making doll clothes and in sewing her first dress for herself. In the 1920s, 'The Christmas Present Page' in *The American Girl* provided practical and clear instructions for sewing projects for young girls.

19. Degree programmes increased in the post-war period, reaching 473 in 1949–50, but declined as small programmes were discontinued. But enrollment grew,

reaching more than 100,000 in the late 1970s. (East 1980) Enrolment declined from 1970–90 (Vincenti 1997) but some institutions have had increases during the 1990s.

20. Human Ecology, a name that goes back to the founding of the field, has been adopted by several universities. Life Management Skills or some variant thereof and Family and Consumer Sciences are names used in public schools.

21. A Michigan extension specialist reports that combining sewing with community-service projects has been successful. (Schultink 1998) Club members learn to sew on easy-to-use fabrics such as polar fleece while making garments for the homeless or others in need. Programmes for young children combine sewing and reading in a 'Sew-Read' project.

22. A Minnesota specialist reports a series of successful clothing expositions in which extension has worked with businesses to provide sewing education in a rural area. (Gahring 1998)

References

Abraham, R. H. (1986), *Helping People Help Themselves: Agricultural Extension in Minnesota, 1879–1979*, St Paul: Minnesota Extension Service, University of Minnesota.

American Home Economics Association (1902), *Lake Placid Conference on Home Economics: Proceedings of the Fourth Annual Conference*, Washington DC: American Home Economics Association.

—— (1994) *The Scottsdale Meeting: Positioning the Profession for the 21st Century*, Alexandria, VA: American Home Economics Association.

Andrews, B. R. (1915), *Education for the Home*, US Bureau of Education Bulletin, 1914, No. 37, Washington DC: US Government Printing Office.

Anspach, K. (1959), 'Clothing Research in Home Economics, 1925–58' in *Journal of Home Economics*, 51: 767–70.

Apple, R. D. (1997), 'Liberal Arts or Vocational Training? Home Economics Education for Girls' in S. Stage and V.B. Vincenti, eds, *Rethinking Home Economics*, Ithaca, New York: Cornell University Press.

Arnold, E. (1985), *Voices of American Homemakers*, Bloomington and Indianapolis: Indiana University Press.

Bacon, F. (1965), 'Francis Bacon' in *Encyclopaedia Britannica*, Vol 2, Chicago: Encyclopaedia Britannica Inc.

Beecher, C. (1841), *A Treatise on Domestic Economy*, New York: Schocken Books. References are to the 1970 and 1977 editions.

Brumberg, J. J. (1997), 'Defining the Profession and the Good Life: Home Economics on Film' in S. Stage and V.B. Vincenti, eds, *Rethinking Home Economics*, Ithaca, New York: Cornell University Press.

Clarke, R. (1973), *Ellen Swallow: The Woman who Founded Ecology*, Chicago: Follett Press.

Craig, H. T. (1945), *The History of Home Economics*, New York: Practical Home Economics.

Dewey, J. (1916), *Democracy and Education*, New York: Macmillan.

Dohr, J. and Forbess, L. (1984), 'Art and Design: Impact in Home Economics and on Families' in M. East and J. Thomson, eds, *Definitive Themes in Home Economics and their Impact on Families 1909–1984* Washington: American Home Economics Association.

East, M. (1980), *Home Economics Past, Present, and Future*, Boston: Allyn and Bacon.

Eicher, J. B. (1972), 'The Tenth Decade' in J.A. Lee, K.M. Hart, and R.B. Mentzer, *From Home Economics to Human Ecology*, East Lansing: Michigan State University, College of Human Ecology.

Farrar, E. W. R. (1837), *The Young Lady's Friend*, Boston: American Stationer's Co.

Fleck, J. (1952), 'Introduction' in S.K. Mager, *A Complete Guide to Home Sewing*, New York: Pocket Books.

French, M. (1917), 'Courses in Sewing for Elementary and High School and Their Correlation with Drawing' in *Journal of Home Economics*, 9 (2): 61–4.

Gahring, S. (1998), Personal communication.

Gibbs, C. M. (1907), 'Problems in University Work in Textiles' in *Lake Placid Conference on Home Economics, Proceedings of the Ninth Annual Conference*, Washington: American Home Economics Association.

Goldstein, C. M. (1997), 'Part of the Package: Home Economists in the Consumer Product Industries, 1920–1940' in S. Stage and V.B. Vincenti, eds, *Rethinking Home Economics*, Ithaca, New York: Cornell University Press.

James, W. (1907), *Pragmatism*, New York: Meridian Books. References are to the 1955 edition.

Joseph, M. (1984), 'Natural Science Themes in Clothing and Textiles' in M. East and J. Thomson, eds, *Definitive Themes in Home Economics and their Impact on Families 1909–1984*. Washington: American Home Economics Association.

Kidwell, C. (1978), 'Short Gowns', *Dress*, 4: 30–63.

Lang, C. L. (1975), 'A Historical Review of the Forces that Contributed to the Formation of the Cooperative Extension Service', Ph.D dissertation, Michigan State University, East Lansing.

Lee. J. A., Hart, K. M. and Mentzer, R. B. (1972), *From Home Economics to Human Ecology*, East Lansing: Michigan State University, College of Human Ecology.

Leslie, E. (1840), *The House Book: A Manual of Domestic Economy*, Philadelphia: Corey and Hart.

Osaki, A. B. (1988), '"A Truly Feminine Employment", Sewing and the Early Nineteenth Century Woman', *Winterthur Portfolio*, 23 (41): 225–41.

Ostapovich, A. D. (1961), 'A Study of the Motives for and Satisfactions of Home Sewing as Expressed by a Selected Group of Michigan Women Who Do Home Sewing', M.A. dissertation, Michigan State University, East Lansing.

Owens, M. (1997), 'Sewing: 30 Million Women Can't Be Wrong', *New York Times*, March 4, B1, B2.

Ring, B. (1993), *Girlhood Embroidery: American Sampler and Pictorial Needlework, 1650–1850*, New York: Alfred Knopf.

Rosencranz, M. L. (1984), 'Social Science Themes in Home Economics, in Clothing and Textiles', in M. East and J. Thomson, eds, *Definitive Themes in Home Economics and their Impact on Families 1909–1984*, Washington: American Home Economics Association.

Schultink, J. (1998), Personal communication.

Stage, S. (1997), 'What's in a Name?' in S. Stage and V. Vincenti, eds, *Rethinking Home Economics*, Ithaca, New York: Cornell University Press.

St. Marie, S. (1997), 'Reminiscences' in S. Stage and V.B. Vincenti, eds, *Rethinking Home Economics*, Ithaca, New York: Cornell University Press.

Vincenti, V. (1997), 'Home Economics Moves into the Twenty-First Century' in S. Stage and V.B. Vincenti, eds, *Rethinking Home Economics*, Ithaca, New York: Cornell University Press.

19

'Your Clothes Are Materials of War': The British Government Promotion of Home Sewing during the Second World War

Helen Reynolds

In 1942, in the fourth year of the Second World War in Britain, Hugh Dalton, President of the British Board of Trade (BoT) wrote in an open letter to the women's voluntary organizations.

> If every single garment now in the homes of Britain, every pot and pan, every sheet, every towel is used and kept usable until not even a magician could hold it together any longer, the war will won be more surely and more quickly.[1]

This letter came at the end of a year of active campaigning by the BoT to persuade the nation's women to make, remodel and renovate their families household linen and clothing.[2] The BoT was the British government organization set up to promote trade and industry.[3] During the Second World War Britain's trade was disrupted and all possible manufacturing industry was turned over to war-related production. As a result the BoT found itself promoting self-reliance. One of the key ways the BoT saw of doing this was to encourage all women in the traditional task of sewing. This chapter examines the initiatives taken by the British government through the BoT during the Second World War to encourage women to make and recycle their family's clothing and household textiles. It uses official BoT papers and correspondence which are housed in the UK Public Record Office.

The fact that there was increased activity in home sewing during this period has already been highlighted by fashion historians. (Woods 1989) This is hardly surprising as high-class women's magazines, such as *Vogue, Harper's*

Bazaar and *Tatler*, unable to report on the abundance of new fashions followed the examples of the cheaper women's weeklies and wrote articles which encouraged readers to sew. These articles, together with BoT information advertisements on home sewing, which in the later years featured Mrs Sew-and-Sew, a capable cartoon figure, resulted in women's needle skills becoming a high profile subject. Whilst censored magazine material in the public domain has been subjected to scrutiny, little is known about why the campaign was started, the needlework classes it promoted and what legacies it bequeathed. By examining the BoT records this chapter proposes to offer a different perspective to home sewing in Britain during the war.

Although Britain declared war on Germany in September 1939 the British government clothing programme of price control, rationing and the resultant campaign to persuade women to sew with renewed vigour was not started until Winston Churchill formed his government on 10 May 1940. The Prime Minister who reluctantly declared war on Germany was Neville Chamberlain. Unlike his father, 'Radical Joe',[4] Neville, was a traditional conservative with a *laissez-faire* approach to governing. In the first years of the war clothes remained plentiful due to the increasing numbers being clothed by the armed forces, the introduction of purchase tax on clothes and high prices, the result of profiteering. While his government was forced to introduce food rationing on 8 January 1940, Chamberlain saw no reason intervene into the domestic clothing markets.

When Winston Churchill formed his all-party Coalition Government it contained a number of prominent socialists.[5] The result was social and economic change. Equality of resources, 'fair shares for all', was regarded as a vital tool in gaining total support for the war.[6] 'Fair shares' was quickly extended to clothes when it was revealed that the clothing retail price index was 66 per cent higher than it was in 1938. (Economist 1989: Table 4.) The first measure taken to evenly distribute clothing was the introduction of clothes rationing. This was announced with immediate effect on 1 June 1941. All adults and children over four were given coupons which were handed over to retailers with the relevant money when an item of clothing was being purchased. In the first years of the war the yearly allowance was sixty-six coupons. Almost every clothing item had a coupon value, for example, regardless of quality or price an overcoat was valued at eighteen coupons, a lady's cardigan at six coupons and a man's jacket at fourteen coupons. Unlike food coupons which allowed each person a set ration of butter, sugar and meat, clothing coupons could be spent as the person chose. Once spent, however, no more clothing could be purchased until the next set of coupons were issued.

Although Purchase Tax and rationing had reduced the consumption of clothes the measures did not ensure supplies were evenly distributed. After a government-sponsored survey in August 1941 revealed that the average working-class family lived on a budget of less than £5 a week, there was a general feeling, chronicled in the British press and by consumer groups, that only those on a high income could afford new clothing. (Advertising Services Guild 1941; *Times* 4 December 1941) Aware of the deep unrest shortages had caused in the First World War the new government actively ensured the 'fair shares' policy was being carried out by devising the Utility Clothing Scheme. The Utility Clothing Scheme was a direct government intervention into the British clothing markets, to control quality and limit prices charged on the majority of all ready-made clothing and cloth. Purchase Tax was then removed on most Utility cloth and clothing and increased on the small proportion of non-utility goods.[7] This stabilized prices aligning them to the majority of people's personal income. The result of these measures was that clothing became more affordable to the majority of British families. Interestingly the scheme was examined by Dexter M. Keeser and members of the United States Office of Price Administration who pronounced Utility the 'silver lining of the BoT programme of price control and rationing' and subsequently used some of the ideas in American wartime clothing regulations.[8]

These measures, whilst they ensured the majority of the population had access to necessary items of new clothing, unwittingly had enormous impact on upper-class British women. These women were used to consuming vast quantities of clothing. Many undertook only recreational sewing. Unable to make or mend clothes they employed ladies' maids and seamstresses to undertake routine maintenance and simple dressmaking. However women working in this capacity were being called up or volunteering for essential and better-paid war work. This left many households in the top-income bracket bereft of women skilled in plain dressmaking and routine mending.

It was at this juncture, in late 1941, immediately after the Utility Clothing Scheme had been announced and six months after rationing had been introduced, that the 'lady' volunteers on the executive committees of the Women's Group on Public Welfare and the National Council for Social Services approached the new President of the BoT, Hugh Dalton.[9] They wanted him to sponsor a campaign extolling the benefits of home sewing. They suggested a campaign similar to the one organized by the Ministry of Food which focused on cooking nutritious food using garden produce. Their idea was for the government to provide dressmaking and mending classes to women so they could use unwanted cloth for making new clothes and learn how to extend the life of their existing clothes by mending and remodelling. This idea was not new. Most families in the lower-income brackets already made use of 'left-overs' and remodelled old garments into new ones to clothe their families. Many used these skills 'below stairs' in domestic service. Womens' magazines at the cheaper end of the market had an established tradition of offering free dress patterns which encouraged these skills. Moreover the National Federation of Women's Institutes (WI) were already offering their members advice on this same subject. However to both the 'lady' volunteers on these executive committees and to the BoT these were both novel concepts.

The BoT was keen to the curb consumption of new clothing still further than the 'fair shares' policy allowed. The war in Europe had been running two years and the government was finding it difficult to meet the demands for the clothes for which it had issued coupons. Stockpiles of pre-war clothing held by retailers were now virtually sold out. The position had became particularly acute after the fall of France in June 1940 when vast amounts of equipment were abandoned by British forces retreating from the beaches of Dunkirk. It was unsurprising therefore that they readily took on the women's groups suggestions and quickly produced a consultative paper.[10] This paper viewed home sewing initiatives by women to save manufacturing civilian clothing as a very attractive and inexpensive suggestion. Out of this paper came Dalton's open letter to the women's voluntary associations which finished 'we must do all in our power to make the whole nation conscious of the need to mend and make do.'

'Make-do and Mend' was based on the idea that a nation's wardrobe was one of its most important assets. It encompassed the executive committee's views that vast amounts of material available in the nation's homes and could be used in their present or another form. At the beginning of 1942 the suggestions outlined in the consultative paper were put into place and a small 'Make do and Mend Department' was set up within the BoT Civilian Clothing Directorate's Public Relation's Department. Make- do and Mend was now widely promoted as an important part of the war effort and a duty to be carried out by every woman.

Throughout the war, although the Make-do and Mend Department assumed responsibility for a great many activities, it remained small. This was because Dalton considered much of the work could be done by the Board of Education and women's voluntary groups. Mr C.C. Simmonds, a BoT civil servant, was given overall responsibility, whilst the day to day running of the campaign was left to three women civil servants, Miss Gemmell, with the part-time assistance from Miss Stucley and clerical help from a Miss Shepherd. The BoT also established two voluntary groups which were based in London. They were the 'Advisory Panel on Make-do and Mend' and the 'Advisory Committee on Make-do and Mend'. The two groups were given different functions. The Advisory Panel was made up of four people working in the textile and related industries. They rarely met but individual members gave written technical advice to the BoT. This advice was used by the BoT when it compiled the literature which was to promote Make-do and Mend. The committee was the most active. It was made up of a collection of professional and upper-class women and the three women civil servants. It was appointed to co-ordinate the national campaign and help set up regional committees to promote the teaching of Make-do and Mend. The volunteers on the advisory committee, consisted of Miss Hinks from the Association of Teachers of Domestic Subjects, Lady Smith Dorrien, Principal of the Royal College of Needlework, Miss Haslett, of the Women's Group of Public Welfare, Miss Harford, of the National Council of Social Service, the Dowager Countess of Listowel, of the WI, Lady Hillingdon, representing Woman's Voluntary Services, Miss Cowper, His Majesty's Inspector (HMI) Board of Education and Miss Kennedy, Board of Education in Scotland. Both groups were chaired by Mr Simmonds.[11]

The BoT, having set up its department of three women and its advisory committee and panel, devised a two-pronged nation-wide campaign. First it was decided to increase adult evening and sewing classes with immediate effort. Secondly, a national press, radio and cinema campaign was planned to persuade women to attend these classes and make them aware of the need to preserve and remake their clothes. Working with the BoT, the Board of Education instructed existing HMI Technical Inspectors to Local Education Authorities (LEAs) to recruit trained teachers and run training and refresher courses in needlework particularly those concentrating on basic dressmaking and renovation skills. Full-time teachers of needle skills in technical colleges and polytechnics and needlework teachers in secondary, central and elementary schools were encouraged to run evening classes, as well as those not in full-time employment. In addition a number of courses were run for potential instructors from industry and the voluntary sector. This was done though 'Circular 1616', popularly known as the 'Domestic Front Circular'. This circular also instructed the LEAs to work with women's organizations through the 'Domestic Front Committees' and run joint demonstrations and advice centres.[12]

Demand for these wartime Make-do and Mend classes was enormous. Many were viewed as social events. Not only did women who genuinely needed the skills enrol but classes also included those receptive to the BoT campaign which stated that 'no material must lie idle' and all women should 'turn out and renovate'. (Board of Trade 1943: 19) By early 1943 the Board of Education was running 12,000 Make-do and Mend and dressmaking classes in their evening and technical schools. A similar number were also run by women's voluntary groups.[13] The BoT intended these classes to teach basic garment-making and traditional making-over techniques; turning of collars and cuffs, the darning of socks and stockings and the patching of trousers. Whilst the majority of the LEA classes did teach these skills, others, mainly in the volunteer sector, did not. This led to some complaints. BoT field reports detail a small proportion of volunteers teaching 'handicrafts', including the making and dressing of papier mâché dolls and the embroidering of evening slippers.[14]

One reason some of these classes offered 'fancy needlework' instead dressmaking and genuine Make-do and Mend could be attributed to the differing British school needlework curricula in the first half of the twentieth century. As already shown, many women working voluntarily in senior positions within the voluntary associations came from the upper-middle and upper classes. Most would have been educated privately or at home. Needlework was taught to these women as an 'accomplishment'. Emphasis was placed on fine hand embroidery rather than on dressmaking, mending and renovation techniques. (Parker 1984) This situation was further compounded by some of the more academic private schools replacing needlework with extra science lessons and the classics. This evidence would suggest that not all volunteer instructors possessed basic renovation and modelling skills. However in the publicly-funded elementary schools where the majority of girls received their education, needlework was a core curriculum subject with lessons centred around simple garment-making, mending and renovation techniques. Needlework had been compulsory in these schools since the mid nineteenth century, formalizing a long tradition of teaching working-class girls needle skills in charity schools. (Aldrich 1996) Indeed, Board of Education inspection reports for the end of the nineteenth century and early twentieth century suggest an over-emphasis on renovation techniques to the detriment of more artistic handicrafts. This trend continued in publicly-funded schools, exemplified by Dorothy Howlett's widely used teaching manual. (Howlett 1934) The Young Women's Christian Association, The Girls Friendly Society and the LEAs all ran needlework and dressmaking classes for working women. These classes built on the skills learnt in the elementary school. The London County Council had a great many listed in *Floodlight*, 'an illustrated guide to evening classes'. These skills were then routinely used by working-class women mending their families clothing or working in service or as professional seamstresses.

By May 1943, the haste in which the scheme had been started and the lack of appropriate needle skills of some of the senior volunteers was causing further problems. Mr Bailey, a full time BoT civil servant petitioned for extra funds to provide extra staff for the BoT Make-do and Mend Department. This was to assist the Domestic Front Committees which needed help in co-ordinating the voluntary sector and the LEAs, as they were both 'hamstrung by inappropriate classes and absurd jealousies'.[15] The BoT had only allowed limited funds to cover Make-do and Mend. These funds were used for the salaries of the three civil servants, advertising costs, coupon floats for classes, occasional use of the 'volunteer car pool' and 'first-class' train travel for those serving on national committees.[16] The LEAs paid teachers running their Make-do and Mend classes and some women's voluntary organizations offered instructors expenses.[17] This approach relied on the women volunteers who were able to give of their time freely. Traditionally these women had not 'made-do and mended' but were now helping to organize a campaign for the majority of women who had often 'made-do and mended'. It could be argued that trained teachers and those who had traditionally practised the skills were not receptive to having their skills re-invented by these 'lady volunteers'.

By 1944 supplies of new material were becoming scarcer and the BoT was working on plans to cut the civilian clothing ration.[18] Make-do and Mend took on further importance. The BoT regularly collected data on how many classes were being set up. They regularly issued circulars urging local authorities to continue to expand classes 'both for the experienced and the beginner'.[19] The BoT also encouraged women's organizations in the setting-up of community mending clubs. These took place in a number of locations including factories where women workers were encouraged to make repairs on such things as overalls.[20] In addition both the LEAs and various women's groups ran demonstration classes and advice centres in most parts of the country. Attendance at these events was promoted as a duty, regardless of whether women already possessed and practised Make-do and Mend skills.

In addition to encouraging Make-do and Mend classes the BoT saw its second function as advertising. Although the BoT discouraged clothing companies from advertising their new lines, the promotion of Make-do and Mending was now considered a necessity. The first BoT advertisements appeared in Sunday newspapers. These were followed by regular adverts in women's magazines, *The Radio Times* and the London and provincial evening newspapers. Titles included *Unpicking, the first steps to save coupons*. As the campaign progressed advertisements took a lighter turn and featured a smiling 'Mrs Sew-and-Sew' giving sewing tips and the 'how to save coupons' examples include *Which Stitch says Mrs Sew-and-Sew, I'm cut out to save 18 coupons, Look what mummy's done with my old overcoat-8 coupons saved* and *Those old white Flannels saved 7 Coupons*. All advertisements carried information about sewing classes with encouraging slogans such as 'Needles Fly At Make-do and Mend Classes'.[21]

Although BoT advertisements were carried in all women's magazines, editors were encouraged to give editorial space to home sewing. Regular meetings with editors were conducted by the BoT to encourage this and with the suppressed demand for ready-to-wear clothing, magazines were only too eager to comply. (*Woman*, 11 December 1942) Using Pathé News, the Ministry of Information put together a number of jauntily slanted reports on the exciting outfits which could be made out of left-overs. Always included in these reports was information about sewing classes and mending clubs which were portrayed as places to meet and make friends as well as to learn skills. These items were interwoven with Pathé morale-boosting news stories. Sewing tips were also given in women's programmes on the radio. Shop window displays were another target for the Make-do and Mend. Many gas and electricity showrooms carried Make-do and Mend displays and exhibitions for which a special poster was produced. (Figure 19.1) One exhibition, opened by Hugh Dalton, was mounted in Charing Cross underground station. Writing of the event in his autobiography, he stated that when opening the exhibition he declared he would buy no new suits until the war was over, a promise he states he kept. (Dalton 1957: 410) During the campaign other high profile visits were arranged. In 1942 the Queen visited a number of Make-do and Mend exhibitions arranged by the WI and in the same year the Princess Royal opened an exhibition in Bradford.

Leaflets on Make-do and Mend were first published in August 1942 and new ones appeared at various times throughout the rest of the war. Compiled by the Good Housekeeping Institute, they included titles such as *Getting ready for Baby* and *Household Linen has got to last*. Each leaflet had a first print run of 200,000 with popular titles going into second and third runs. Instructional posters on the same themes were made to be placed in welfare, health and advice centres, church rooms and doctors' surgeries. Posters were also printed on Make-do and Mend for teenagers. These were placed in girls' and boys' clubs and handed out to the Scout and Guide movements. The BoT also compiled charts as backdrops to classes and demonstrations and commissioned a Make-do and Mend booklet.

Always keen to promote Make-do and Mend, the BoT Public Relations Office worked very closely with a number of firms which were willing to include information in their advertising campaigns about prolonging the life of their product as a goodwill wartime gesture. One such firm, Wolsey, the producers of underwear, had a number of meetings with the BoT during the course of 1943 and devised a campaign which met the requirements of the Board.[22] In addition, many churches had their own Make-do and Mend and clothing campaigns.

The BoT Make-do and Mend campaign was highly successful in so far as it conveyed a great deal of information on sewing to the female population

Figure 19.1. Poster designed by Donia Nachsen for the 'Make-do and Mend' campaign. n.d. By permission of the Imperial War Museum.

using an unprecedented variety of high profile sources. This renewed interest in home sewing was responsible for the BoT receiving, on average, 150 letters a day from women offering their advice.[23] During the period of the Make-do and Mend campaign (1942–5) there was no assumption that women possessed needle skills. All women, regardless of social class were actively encouraged to attend classes and demonstrations. The campaign was undoubtedly responsible for furthering the needle skills of many women, who not only made-do and mended but took the skill further, remodelled and added extra creative decoration. Not only was Make-do and Mend encouraged but so in turn was home dressmaking using remnants and unwanted household textiles.

Whilst undoubtedly the poorer sections of society had always renovated old clothes it was a new skill for many members of the upper classes. For example, three privately educated members of the present Horsham WI had only sewn as a leisure pastime before the war. Previously all household mending was left to a visiting seamstress. These women took on the advice of the Make-do and Mend campaign very seriously. They had all attended a Make-do and Mend Advice Centre run by the Women's Voluntary Services in the Causeway, Horsham (now the local museum). They also used the Clothing Exchange, set up in the same building and which they considered quite a novelty. Although some men were involved in the Make-do and Mend campaign and one instructional poster was aimed at the Boys' Brigade and the Boy Scout movement, the majority of the campaign was run by women for women in spite of the fact there was a tradition of men being employed as bespoke tailors and sailors and fishermen carrying out their own textile repairs. Although some Make-do and Mend volunteers and their literature were seen as patronizing, it was generally regarded as a war- time success. However there was disquiet about the campaign which was echoed by one of the advisory committee members. In a letter to the BoT, she stated she was seriously 'alarmed at the number of appeals addressed to the housewife, each of them making fresh demands on her time'.[24]

The war period also saw full employment and many more women undertook paid work. Utility clothes had actually meant a higher proportion of these women could buy good quality ready-to-wear clothing. Far from having their clothing expenditure cut, they were now in a position to buy new clothes. Not used to a high expenditure on clothing they were able to 'manage' quite comfortably on the new rationed clothing. Make-do and Mend was for them not a novelty but a 'drudge'. Whilst Pathé News, the BBC and women's magazines actively encouraged sewing, this minority did not Make-do and Mend. Silenced by the press propaganda these women were served by the many department stores and small dressmakers which still offered a reduced mending, alterations and remodelling service. These, however, were the silent minority. Much was written instead of the benefits of the campaign. Lady Smith Dorrien, the widow of General Sir Horace Smith Dorrien, a member of the Make-do and Mend Advisory Committee and Principal of the Royal College of Needlework, wrote in the foreword to *Needlework in Wartime* of the aim of 'helping those whose thoughts are constantly with their men on active service, whose vivid imagination pictures tragedy whenever their minds are not fully occupied. Needlework is the best possible remedy for over-strained nerves'. (Smith Dorrien n.d.)

In conclusion, during the war home sewing was promoted by the government as never before. The numbers of teachers employed by local authorities to teach the subject dramatically increased. In 1945 LEAs faced shortages of teachers in many subjects. One-year emergency training programmes were introduced. However, due to Make-do and Mend, women needlework teachers were never in short supply and continued to teach in the new secondary schools. When the 1944 Education Act came into force, great importance was attached to girls learning practical dressmaking skills. All girls in state schools were required to do some needlework. The new Secondary Modern Schools were equipped with the latest sewingmachines and commercial pattern books. Many post-war private and finishing schools introduced the subject realizing their students had to be less reliant on domestic labour. In the 1950s the General Certificate of Education was introduced and, in 1964, the Certificate of Secondary Education. Both included needlework exams with syllabuses which not only included dressmaking but incorporated Make-do and Mend techniques. Many more women's magazines of the 1950s and 1960s promoted home dressmaking as a way of obtaining fashionable clothes. These magazines relied heavily on women being very experienced needle women with skills which were perfected during the war.

Notes

1. UK Public Record Office (PRO). B.T 64/3024. Letter from the Right Honourable Hugh Dalton M.P.

2. See, for example, Pathé News (1942), *Sabotage* the first of a series of propaganda films shown in British cinemas designed to encourage the general public to mend their clothing to save new materials for the armed forces.

3. The BoT was first set up in the reign of Charles II (1660–85) to promote Britain's import and export trade. By 1939 it was a large government department whose President was automatically a key member of the British cabinet. In 1939 the BoT was expanded even further and given far-reaching powers, enforceable by statutory order, which enabled it to exercise complete control over all British industry other than food and munitions. This was to ensure firms produced only the minimum of civilian goods and concentrated their production on the needs of the armed forces and the export market. The later was vital as foreign currency was needed for the purchase of munitions.

4. Joseph Chamberlain (1836–1914) was a Liberal who rose to became President of the BoT Neville (1869–1940) was his second son.

5. For example, Clement Attlee, Deputy Prime Minster, Ernest Bevin, Minister of Labour, Herbert Morrrison, Home Secretary and Minister of Home Security, and Hugh Dalton, President of the Board of Trade.

6. Policy term used by the Churchill Coalition Government.

7. The exception being Utility Fur Coats which attracted a Purchase Tax charge in 1945.

8. PRO BoT 64/994. Report given to the BoT on 12 March 1943 by the United States Foreign Service.

9. PRO BoT 64/3023.

10. The Extension of the Life of Clothing; The Need For a National Campaign to Stimulate the Public to Remake Mend And Renovate. PRO BoT 64/3024.

11. PRO BoT 64/3023.

12. PRO BoT 64/3023.

13. PRO BoT 64/3023.

14. PRO BoT 64/3024, August 1943. Letter to Miss Harford from the Secretary of the National Union of Townswomen's Guilds.

15. PRO BoT 64/3023.

16. PRO BoT 64/3023.

17. PRO BoT 64/3024.

18. PRO BoT 64/1440.

19. PRO BoT 64/3023.

20. PRO BoT 64/3024.

21. PRO BoT 64/3024.

22. PRO BoT 64/3024.

23. PRO BoT 64/3024.

24. PRO BoT 64/3023.

References

Advertising Services Guild (1941), 'Clothes Rationing Survey' in *Change 1, Bulletin of the Advertising Services Guild*, August, London.

Aldrich, R. (1996), *Education for the Nation*, London: Cassell.

Board of Trade (1943), *Make-do and Mend*, London.

Dalton, H. (1957), *The Fateful Years, 1931–45*, London: Muller.

Economist, The (1989), *One Hundred Years of Economic Statistics*, London: The Economist.

Howlett, D. M. (1934), *The Teaching of Needlework*, London: University Tutorial Press.

Needlework in Wartime n.d. (c.1942), forward by Lady Smith Dorrien, London.

Parker, R. (1984), *The Subversive Stitch*, London: The Woman's Press.

Woods, M. (1989), *We Wore What We Got. Women's Clothes in the Second World War*, Devon: Warwickshire Books.

General Reading

McDowell, C. (1997), *Forties Fashion*, London: Bloomsbury.

Minns, R. (1988), *Bombers and Mash: The Domestic Front 1939–1945*, London: Virago.

Index

NOTE: Publications – all titles of women's and girls' magazines are listed under 'women's magazines'; all other titles are listed alphabetically

Index